MR. JUSTICE
AND
MRS. BLACK

MR. JUSTICE AND MRS. BLACK

The Memoirs of

HUGO L. BLACK

and

ELIZABETH BLACK

Foreword by
Justice William J. Brennan, Jr.

Random House New York

 Published in the United States by Random House, Inc., New York, and simultaneously in Canada by Random House of Canada Limited, Toronto.

Grateful acknowledgment is made to the following for permission to reprint previously published material:

Alfred A. Knopf, Inc.: excerpt from *A Constitutional Faith,* by Hugo L. Black. Copyright © 1968 by The Trustees of Columbia University. Reprinted by permission of Alfred A. Knopf, Inc.

Kraus International Publications, Inc.: (Opinions of) Hugo Lafayette Black, from *Supreme Court of the United States, 1798–1982: An Index to Opinions Arranged by Justice,* edited by Linda A. Blandford and Patricia Russell Evans. Millwood, New York: Kraus International Publications, 1983. Reproduced with permission.

Library of Congress Cataloging in Publication Data

Black, Hugo LaFayette, 1886–1971.
Mr. Justice and Mrs. Black.

Includes index.
1. Black, Hugo LaFayette, 1886–1971. 2. Black, Elizabeth (Elizabeth Seay) 3. Judges—United States—Biography. 4. Judges' wives—United States—Biography.
I. Black, Elizabeth (Elizabeth Seay) II. Title.
KF8745.B55A35 1986 347.73'2634 [B] 85-11960
ISBN 0-394-54432-3 347.3073534 [B]

Manufactured in the United States of America

Designed by Jo Anne Metsch

24689753

First Edition

The following passage is an excerpt from *A Constitutional Faith* by Hugo L. Black, published in 1968.

I . . . [wish to say] a few words to express my deep respect and boundless admiration and love for our Constitution and the men who drafted it. These men met in convention at Philadelphia with instructions to do no more than amend the original Articles of Confederation. They disobeyed those intructions and came out of their convention with a document designed to unite the thirteen jealous, independent colonies into one powerful nation. By this remarkable achievement they transformed that which had been the dream of a few into a living reality. They created a government strong enough and with power enough to protect itself against its enemies, both foreign and domestic, while leaving its control to the selected representatives of free citizens themselves. I am a typical example of this highly successful experiment in government. I was born in a frontier farm home in the hills of Alabama in the troublesome times of Reconstruction, after the Civil War, and my early life was spent in plain, country surroundings. There I became acquainted with the "short and simple annals of the poor," among plain folks who learned most of their law and sound philosophies from the country schools and churches. In due course the people of Alabama chose me to be their United States senator. I served in the Senate until appointed Associate Justice of the United States Supreme Court in which position I have now served for more than thirty years. It is a long journey from a frontier farmhouse in the hills of Clay County, Alabama, to the United States Supreme Court, a fact which no one knows better than I. But this nation, created by our Constitution, offers countless examples just like mine. My experiences with and for our government have filled my heart with gratitude and devotion to the Constitution which made my public life possible. That Constitution is my legal bible; its plan of our government is my plan and its destiny my destiny. I cherish every word of it, from the first to the last, and I personally deplore even the slightest deviation from its least important commands. I have thoroughly enjoyed my small part in trying to preserve our Constitution with the earnest desire that it may meet the fondest hope of its creators, which was to keep this nation strong and great through countless ages.

Foreword by William J. Brennan, Jr., Associate Justice, United States Supreme Court

The place of Hugo Lafayette Black in the pantheon of great Justices of the Supreme Court grows more and more secure with each passing year. His contributions to contitutional jurisprudence, particularly in the construction and application of the Bill of Rights, probably were as influential in shaping our freedoms as any. His fiercely asserted constitutional views, always expressed with complete respect for the differing views of colleagues, reflected his awe for the scheme of government devised by the Framers, and the intense patriotism and unbounded faith in his country that highlighted his every performance in public office. He was emotional, as all who hold deeply felt convictions are emotional, but in his relations with people he was also extraordinarily compassionate, kind to a fault, and immeasurably tolerant of human frailties, keenly aware that he had some of his own.

We now have the great good fortune to have Hugo Black's partial memoirs as well as the diaries of his widow, Elizabeth Seay Black. Justice Black's account of his own early life in Alabama is illuminated by his integrity and his great spirit. Mrs. Black opens the window into the life she lived with Justice Black for fourteen years, until his death. It is at once a love story, tender and touching, and a picture of a great man that helps us know Justice Black as unfortunately, for want of like material, we cannot know Justices who preceded and followed him. It is much more than a daily diary, although it is some of that. It tells us much of the agony of decision known by every Justice, of the uncertainty one feels as one treads one's way to the judgment that cannot be escaped. It tells us too, however, of the friendships on and off the Court that become precious—and why—of the social demands that too often one feels have to be honored. But best of all, there emerges in living color the portrait of a great American all of us would want to know. Hugo Black's memoir and Elizabeth Seay Black's diary are beautifully written, fascinating reading. Without question, in preserving Hugo Black's memory, Mrs. Black has made a contribution of the first rank to the story of a vibrant if sometimes turbulent period of the Court's history.

Acknowledgments

MANY THANKS TO:

My son, Fred DeMeritte, and his wife, Janice, for their enthusiasm for the book and for their confidence that I could do it.

My extended family, Hugo, Jr., and Graham Black; Sterling and Nancy Black; and Josephine Black Pesaresi; who allowed me to use their father's personal memoir.

Paul R. Baier, Professor of Law at Louisiana State University, who was my editor for four years, and who by his enthusiasm and help is responsible for the book's completion to the point it could be submitted for publication; for the countless hours of his busy life as a law teacher that he unselfishly devoted to researching, editing, and annotating the book; and to his wife, Helgard, whose helpful advice and cheerful cooperation made for a better book and a happier editor.

Charlotte Mayerson, my editor at Random House, for whose great assistance I am at a loss to express my appreciation; who edited this book with intelligence and competence and with complete sympathy and understanding of my feelings. She has eliminated the extraneous matter and compacted it so that it is what I have always wanted it to be: of interest to lawyer and layman alike, and a tribute to my husband, Hugo Lafayette Black.

William J. Brennan, Jr., Associate Justice of the United States Supreme Court, for his beautiful foreword.

Sidney M. Davis, Hugo's seventh law clerk and steadfast friend through the years, and my good friend, who introduced and recommended the book to Random House.

Chief Justice Warren Burger and the Associate Justices of the Supreme Court, who have been unfailingly cooperative when called upon; and to their wives, especially, for their friendship and interest.

My friends who work at the Court for their cheerful assistance and patience.

The friends who have helped me in various ways with the manuscript in the early days of its creation; especially to Carolyn Betts of Miami, Florida; Berniece and Harry Neal of Culpeper, Virginia; and Anne Freeman, wife of former law clerk George Freeman, of Richmond, Virginia; all of whom are published writers.

Margaret Izzard and Mary McGihon for their hours of emergency typing when I was on my own.

Marx Leva, John Frank, and Louis Oberdorfer of Hugo's family of law clerks, all of whom read the manuscript at an early stage and made suggestions for its improvement; and other law clerks for their enthusiasm and for the inspiration they have given me because they, too, loved the Judge.

—Elizabeth S. Black

Contents

Introduction

Hugo Lafayette Black, who was my husband, began to write his memoirs in 1968, when he was 82 years old. He had only got up to the year 1921 by the time he died. Perhaps because of his age, he did not directly mention in the memoirs certain issues that had been troublesome when he was a young man. Still, what he did record is so interesting both personally and historically, and the writing is so alive with his fine character, his intelligence, and his compassion that it seemed to me and to his children very important to share his book, partial though it may be, with the general public.

Hugo Black's memoir constitutes the beginning of this volume. The middle section aims to "catch the reader up" both by way of further explanation of certain gaps in Hugo's writing and with a brief chronology of his subsequent life and career. I also have written here of the beginnings of my relationship with him, and of those parts of my own life that seemed relevant to our life together.

The last—and I'm afraid the longest—section of the book is made up of excerpts from the handwritten diaries I kept from 1964 until my husband's death in 1971. These diaries cover what we did during our days together, what we said and how we felt. They also treat of the public events of that period, including the important cases that were then before the Supreme Court and how they were reflected in our daily life.

Sometimes the book seems to me like one of the collages I've made and have hung on the wall at home; for example, one is devoted to my family, and there, displayed behind the glass, is my father's gold pen, an elocution medal my mother won at school, an old picture of our house, and a snapshot of my father's 1907 car. Yet that is, I suppose, what one's life is like, a bit of this and a bit of that. I hope that the assemblage herein presented results in a written portrait of our life together, Hugo Black's and mine.

PART ONE

The Memoirs of Hugo L. Black

Preface

This is May 27, 1968. Born February 27, 1886, in the middle of Grover Cleveland's first term as President of the United States, I am today eighty-two years and three months old. I have now been an Associate Justice of the Supreme Court of the United States for thirty years and nine months. Unless something unexpected happens, the Court has finished its argued cases for this term and is awaiting the writing of all opinions that have been assigned for the term or dissents to opinions already written. Personally all opinions assigned to me have already been written, together with all dissents I now expect to write. I have two Court opinions awaiting dissents of some of my Brethren, and what I hope are my three last dissents have already been circulated. In this situation I have decided to begin to write my memoirs. While, doubtless, very many of the detailed events of my life have been forgotten, I must say that memories of my past seem very vivid to me. For this reason I now intend to spend most of the next few months jotting down those memories from their beginnings. If interesting to no one else, they should be significant to my family.

My birthplace was a small wooden farmhouse in Clay County, Alabama, which lies along the Appalachian foothills. That explains the reference to the County's people as "Clay County hillbillies." I was the eighth of a family of eight. The post office was named "Harlan," for my cousin Dr. John Harlan, who attended upon my mother when I was born. Dr. Harlan regularly went to the Harlan family reunions at the time when they were also attended by Associate Justice John Marshall Harlan of the Supreme Court. His name and family history are recorded in the Harlan family biography.

My mother was Martha Ardellah Toland, born in Laurens County, South Carolina. The Tolands, so family tradition says, were cousins of the eloquent Irishman, Robert Emmet, and my Toland ancestors were said to have fled their home in Tyrone County, Ireland, to South Carolina to escape their distinguished cousin's fate. It was in South Carolina (Laurens County) that the Harlan and Toland families intermarried, many of both families later moving to the section of Tallapoosa County, Alabama, that was later partially incorporated into Clay County. In my office is a file in which can be found much about my ancestry. Hesekiah Street later became one of the wealthiest merchants, plantation owners, and slave owners in East Alabama. My mother's mother, Mildred, was his daughter. His father, David Street, born in Pittsylvania County, Virginia, was an early Baptist preacher, or Elder, as they were then called. My father, William Lafayette Black, was the son of George Walker Black, a merchant and farmer, son of Lemuel Black, all of Elbert or Oglethorpe Counties, Georgia. George Walker Black married Jane Vernon, born in South Carolina. Many of the most prominent Georgia families are said to have originated in Oglethorpe County. President Lyndon Johnson's great-grandfather was once Sheriff of that County. Thus, I am what might be called an unadulterated product of the South, a fact that I recall with pride.

I can remember little about the small frame house in which I was born. I do know, from what I have been told, that the days around that time were troublesome ones for my mother. February in Alabama is a windstorm and hurricane period and just five days before my birth a storm swept our area, lifting and moving houses from their insecure moorings; a part of our roof was blown off and carried a short distance, I have been told. This frightful memory so greatly impressed my brother Robert Lee, fifteen years old at the time, that he continued, up to the time of his death, to be afraid of the slightest windstorm. At one period of his life he had a storm cellar just outside his house, which he kept fully equipped with chairs, lamps, and improvised places to sleep; he frequently rushed to this cellar at practically the first sign of a wind. Another circumstance that must have greatly distressed my mother before my birth was the death of my little two-year-old sister, "Little Della," named for my mother. The week before I was born she was laid to rest in Old Mount Ararat Cemetery at Bluff Springs, a cemetery which can almost be called the Street-Toland burying grounds. The time within which the little headstone was bought that marks the spot where she lies is still within my memory. Usually when I return to Alabama, if I have any time, I go back to Old Mount Ararat to drop a tear at this little grave that, while in the midst of the remains of my relatives, somehow seems so lonely away from her immediate family. My little sister, whose departure from this world so nearly coincided with my entrance, was undoubtedly a victim of the inadequacies of the frontier days, the cold, damp, murky houses, and the absence of those miracle drugs which are perhaps just beginning to make people live longer with more ways to combat the deadly microscopic enemies of mankind.

It is a long span of time between February 27, 1886, and May 27, 1968. Most people in my Clay County surroundings when I was born cut and chopped the wood for their own fires, cooked on wood stoves and coals on the fireplace, spun their own wool, wove their own clothes, repaired, if they did not actually make, their own shoes, grew and ground their own wheat, got water out of country springs unless affluent enough to dig a well, and in fact lived as frontier people always have, largely on their own resources. Most of our neighbors were transported on the backs of mules or in wagons pulled by mules. The roads were narrow, muddy, and frequently impassable. These were the conditions that prevailed when I first came screaming, I suppose, on what I have been told was a blustery, rainy February night more than eighty-two years ago. I shall now pick up that life and, if fortunate, carry it on through the many years that have brought this country boy to the Supreme Court of the United States, a circumstance not likely to have been foreseen by any of my Clay County friends or relatives—unless it was my mother.

I

My First Six Years

In 1889, when I was between three and four years of age, my father moved the family from the old farmhouse at Harlan, where I was born, to Ashland, the County seat of Clay County, which had a population of several hundred. While the move was only about ten miles, I recall that to me it seemed a very long journey. I have some dim memories of the old country birthplace. The house was built partly of wood and partly of logs. The kitchen, as was then the custom, was some few yards from the living room, the two being connected by a walkway, covered as I recall. The house was destroyed long ago and the remains of an old house nearby, still referred to as the "old Black place," was my father's country store building. My most vivid memory about the old home is what I remember as a very deep and dangerous gulch on the side of the road next to the house. Years after moving to Ashland I went back to the old home site and was astonished to find that the "deep, dangerous gulch" was nothing more than a shallow ditch on the side of the road cut by running waters after rains.

I faintly recall, or at least I think I do, one occasion before we moved to Ashland when I was taken from my home at Harlan to Alexander City, Tallapoosa County, Alabama, a distance of about twenty miles. Alexander City was the marketplace for the family. My father carried an account there with Herzfeld and Herzfeld. It was probably about the middle of 1887 that my father took my mother and me to Alexander City in the family buggy and while there (family history confirms what I think memory tells me) I saw my first train. It was huffing and blowing as it passed in front of Herzfeld's store, where I still insist I can remember standing and clapping my hands with childish glee. That excellent store is still a prosperous mercantile establishment at Alexander City, owned now by the Frohsins, who are kinspeople and successors of the Herzfelds. I never visit the town without going to the old store where I occasionally heave a nostalgic sigh for old times' sake. The Frohsins, those who are left of the old—and the new who are taking their place—are still my friends. In 1926 when I ran for the United States Senate, the people of Alexander City, Tallapoosa County, where my father was born, and, in fact, that whole area of East Alabama, voted overwhelmingly for me. I am sure those people instinctively knew how dearly I love that part of my native State.

The ten-mile move from Harlan to Ashland was a very big and time-consuming event in my family's life, particularly my father's, who had to plan the change and control the move. Several years before, he ran in the County Democratic primary for a County office, Tax Collector, I think. This was quite a venture for a backwoods country merchant and farmer, but according to my information, he made a very creditable showing. I am confident my father made this race with the hope that, should he win, the earnings from the office he sought would help ease the burden of his move to Ashland. This move was quite a natural one for a man with seven children to educate. My father, brought up in Reconstruction days, had a hard time getting to school himself. He had to walk five miles back and forth each day. People at that time wanted so much to be educated that it is needless to add that there were no student strikes or protests. The school at the Ashland County seat, supported partly by private, partly by public funds, bore the dignified title of "Ashland College." It published yearly catalogues, gave B.A. and B.S. degrees, had students from over the State, and all in all was a desirable school for people genuinely wanting an education. Two of the older members of my family had been boarding students at Ashland before we moved there. Along with the "College," the lower grades were taught too, beginning with the primary.

Before moving there my father went to Ashland and bought a home, which, as I recall, was located on about three acres of ground, was a frame building and painted white. My father also bought a half-interest in a general store, to be operated on the town square under the firm name of Black and Manning. The Manning member had a brother named Joe, who was one of the best known Populists of the period. The Populist Party at that time had a thriving active membership in the County and State. My father was not a Populist, in fact he was always much against that Party. He boasted that he was a Grover Cleveland Democrat, a title he bore with pride until his death in 1899. He was so much a Cleveland Democrat that he voted in the 1896 Presidential election for Palmer and Buckner who were against William Jennings Bryan, the Democratic nominee, *against* "free silver" and *for* the gold standard.

My first two years in Ashland were, I imagine, much like those of all boys from four to six living in small villages. Ashland had at that time a population of about three hundred. Too young to go to school, I began to go to Sunday School, both morning and afternoon—to the Baptist Church in the morning and to the Methodist in the afternoon. These, as you would think, were the most prominent churches in the community, although there were a few Congregationalists (Campbellites) and Presbyterians. There were not, I think, any Jews or Catholics in the County. My family at that time were all Baptists except my father, who declined ever to become a member of that church again after the country church near Harlan "withdrew" from him because he would now and then become intoxicated.

In addition to going to Sunday School each Sunday, I developed an ear for music at an early age, playing all the country musical instruments, fiddle, organ or piano, guitar, and harmonica. A Mrs. Nolen, who became the music teacher at the College, developed an interest in me because at four years of age I had learned to play the family organ. She persuaded my parents to let me "take music" from her. I learned little more than I had before—which was to play by ear—but she did teach me to play an organ duet with her at the school commencement. This gave the commencement crowd much amusement, particularly because my legs were too short for my feet to reach the organ pedals. At any rate, because of my youth or something, the crowd liked our duet and I got my first knowledge of the exhilaration that comes from applause. It was a pleasant experience then and is pleasant to remember now.

It was during those first six years that my political attitudes began to form. Before I could articulate my syllables distinctly I recall how angry people could make me by saying: "You are a Populist, a third party-ite." My reply in those early days, Clay County people tell me, was: "I am *not* a tird party—I a democat."

My first presidential election memory was 1892, when Grover Cleveland came back to win his second term as President. My father must have been one of Cleveland's most devoted followers. He, and I, his echo, talked for Cleveland, fought for Cleveland, shouted for Cleveland, and he, of course, voted for Cleveland. I have taken part in many elections since, in some of which I was the candidate, but even now, seventy-six years later, the sweetness and satisfaction of that 1892 Cleveland victory has never been surpassed. Which reminds me, as have many other apparently natural characteristics, that I am my father's son.

II

My Early School Days

At six I entered the first grade in the primary department of Ashland College. I went to school with excitement and joy. Although I loved my mother and my family and my home, I recall no sense of sadness on that opening school day. This may have been because of the reception given me by my teacher, Miss Lizzie Patterson. She was a *natural* as a teacher. Her smile was constant and contagious. If she knew how to frown I never discovered it. I was hers from the first minute she looked at me and spoke to me. I owe much to many people but to few more than to her. She guided me like a mother. She had the faculty for making me try at least to avoid doing anything she might even in part disapprove. She did not live long after my first year in school. She is buried in the little old cemetery in Ashland, not far from my mother and father. God bless her memory!

In my first nine months of school Miss Lizzie took me through the four first reading year classes. I firmly believe this was not wholly due to any precocity on my part but rather to her expertness in making pupils love to learn. She not only inspired pupils to learn from books, as a leader she made school exercises a pleasure. I can see and hear her now, up on stage leading this song which through the years has never left me:

Now we're tapping with the right foot,
Now we're tapping with the left;
As our feet go tap, tap, tap,
Hear our fingers gaily snap.
Don't you think gymnastics are a jolly sight?

I perhaps have spent no happier or less troublesome years than the first year of school with Miss Lizzie. Many years later, in 1926, when [I was] running for the Senate, Miss Lizzie's brother "L.D.," a prominent and devout Methodist Minister, put a strong endorsement of my candidacy in the Alabama *Christian Advocate,* a Methodist church weekly, which helped me immeasurably in my race.

My second-year teacher was Professor J. H. Riddle, who spent his last years, I believe, as Principal of the Hartselle, Alabama, High School, the birthplace of my friend United States Senator John Sparkman. Professor Riddle was a good, solid, substantial teacher and man who believed that a whipping now and then was a good thing for little men. He whipped me once. It came up this way: I was sitting with a boy my age, Hiram Allen, who served the last part of his life as a Deputy United States Marshal under my selection, and whose cousin is now United States Senator from Alabama. The stillness of Professor Riddle's room was suddenly disturbed by a loud cackle. The cackle was mine, due to a quick jab on my ribs under my arm. Professor Riddle turned around and asked: "Who was that?" Without caring at that crucial moment about the purity of my English, I said: "It was me." He walked over, armed with a rather long, snake-looking switch and said, "Why did you do it?" I said, "Hiram punched me in the side." Without another word the Professor told me to stand up and proceeded to whip me on the part of the body which is most popular for that pastime. Then he had Hiram stand up for his. Looking back on the episode I think of it merely as a part of the day's work or day's schooling. It did neither of us any physical or psychological harm, and in fact was probably good for both of us. I had the great pleasure of telling this story many years later when, at Professor Riddle's invitation, I delivered the commencement address at the Hartselle High School where, as I said, Professor Riddle was then Principal. I consider myself very fortunate to have had the good Professor Riddle as my teacher. He believed in school discipline; so do I. It never occurred to me then or since that my fine old Professor Riddle violated the United States Constitution in giving me that whipping.

In due course, and without further episodes of a whipping nature, I was promoted year-by-year to higher classes, in one of which I took up algebra. All of my prior mathematics courses had been easy for me and as interesting as novels, which I have always loved. That year again I was most fortunate in my teacher. He was Judge Hiram Evans, who had previously served as the Democratic Probate Judge of Clay County. Another boy in the algebra class, Hugh Price, liked mathematics as I did. We began to study together and solved all the problems long before the regular class reached them. After talking over the matter we decided to talk to Judge Evans about it. We did. As a result he told us to go right on and finish, that we need no longer come to classes after finishing the book in our way. We did just that, and I doubt if I have ever had a course on any subject that I learned more thoroughly than I learned algebra.

As can be seen from our algebra experience, Professor Evans, or Judge Evans as we knew him, was no ordinary teacher. He adjusted teaching to the pupil's capacity and did not require rapidly learning pupils to squeeze themselves into one fixed schedule with pupils who required more time to learn. That, I suppose, is responsible for the fact that I have always viewed with favor a division of pupils according to their energy, intelligence, and ability to learn. It is difficult for me to believe that it is either wise or fair to hold some pupils back because others cannot keep up with them.

My course in school at Ashland ran along smoothly until the 1902–3 term. That year the Trustees named two very recent college graduates to be joint Principals of the school, Professors Yarbrough, a Baptist, and Turnipseed, a Methodist. Both were nice people who probably needed more experience before undertaking to manage a school like Ashland College. My only run-in with either one first occurred when Professor Turnipseed thought I had dropped a book on the bench too heavily when I started to the blackboard for some work. The Professor told me with considerable sharpness to go back and lay it down easily. This I did, and nothing further came of that particular incident. I was at that time about sixteen years of age, and had a sister nearly five years older in school. One day in February I was told that because my sister had whispered at her desk Professor Turnipseed had her stand on one foot in the corner of his room. This struck me as being very bad, so I went across the street to my home and reported it to my mother. She told me to go back to the school and tell the Professor to let my sister come home. I did, but to my surprise the Professor, instead of permitting my sister to go home, announced he was going to *whip me.* I went back to my room and took my seat, whereupon Professor Turnipseed came in with a switch and started to hit me. I took the switch away from him and broke it into pieces. He then asked Professor Yarbrough to bring another switch and to hold me. Both of them tried to whip me, but I succeeded in breaking all the switches they had. Other pupils were asked to go out and bring in switches but, as I recall, they refused. About that time my mother, having been informed of what was going on, came into the school building from across the street where we lived and the whipping stopped. After consultation with my mother and other family members, I never went back to that school again but instead went to the Birmingham Medical College for its 1902–3 term. That school episode, however, had an interesting sequel. Before the school year was out the Trustees had some disagreement with Professor Turnipseed and permitted him to resign. He later became a Methodist Minister. Our paths did not cross again until 1926 when I went to Ozark, Alabama, campaigning for the United States Senate. Shortly after my arrival I was told that a Methodist preacher named Turnipseed had been out on the streets pleading with citizens to support me for the Senate. It was my old friend, the Professor! I found him; he was very strong for me, helped me immensely, took me around the City and asked people to vote for me. We became very warm, personal friends. And, to complete the story, one of my first congratulatory messages after my 1926 Senatorial victory came from Professor Yarbrough, then living in Texas, who had held me so that Professor Turnipseed might whip me. This is the way life works out, far more times than anyone would guess. It is never wise to forget that the seeming enemy of today may be the best friend of tomorrow.

Just a few more words about my boyhood life at Ashland, where, I think it is fair to say, my basic life habits were formed. My boyhood was probably much like that of all boys in country villages. My home life was happy. Being the youngest, I was the family pet. At age five I had what our country doctor called catarrhal fever. Now I suppose it would be called the flu or a "virus," or pneumonia. The country doctor (who had never gone to medical college) thought I was dangerously ill and told my mother I must be given whiskey to save my life. My antipathy to whiskey had already become so strong at that age that I refused to take one drop of it. My mother stood by me, however; I did not imbibe, and I did not die. I remember though that I was very thin at the time, being frequently reminded that I had legs like a shikepoke. Because of my thinness (today considered to be a sign of good health), it seems to have been assumed that I was not likely to live long. But look at me—eighty-two years old and today I played three vigorous sets of tennis!

Before leaving my Ashland school days, however, two episodes might be interesting to some who do not understand the indispensability of close cooperation among the members of frontier families. My sister, Ora, was thirteen years my senior. Shortly after the family moved to Ashland some very red calico curtains were put on the windows of the house. I began to love red at a very early age and so the time came when I desperately wanted a waist made out of red calico exactly like our window curtains. I presume I must have urged this desire for the waist with my usual tenacity, *ad nauseam.* Ora finally cut up one of the curtains and made a red waist for me out of it, also making, at the same time, a pair of short britches for me out of an old, black, discarded coat of my father's. I can yet remember the infinite joy and pride with which I wore that suit. This dear sister of mine was always an expert stylist of clothes for boys and girls, men and women.

The second episode about my sister, Ora, relates to her dramatic instincts. In my last complete year at Ashland College I participated in what was then called an elocution contest. Ora selected my speech. It was high drama—the life story of a man born in a devoutly religious, moral, nondrinking home. The story carried me from his innocent childhood through all the degrading ways that led him to drink, lawlessness, and finally to a sentence of death. I can yet hear my sister's voice as she taught me how to repeat this poor fellow's lament:

> Oh Heavens, can such things be?
> Almighty power, send forth thy dart and
> Strike me where I lie!

I recited these dramatic lines with the true artistry she had taught me. But, alas, the audience was overwhelmed, in fact, utterly submerged, when my worthy opponent (later a fine street car motorman) let fall from his lips before that *Alabama* audience the lilting prose poetry of Ben Hill and Henry W. Grady of Georgia which goes like this:

> There *was* a South of slavery and secession;
> That South, thank God, is dead;
> There *is* a South of freedom and Union,
> That South, thank God, is living, breathing,
> growing every hour.

Thus did the future street car motorman crush to the ground the hope of the future United States Senator and Justice of the United States Supreme Court. That defeat, however, served me well. I learned that *what* is said can often be far more important than *how* it is said. For I still believe that had my sister coached me in speaking the words of Hill and Grady instead of the jeremiads of a lost soul, the results of that elocution contest at Ashland, Alabama, might have been quite different.

As a boy I rode horses, fished, swam, jumped, turned hand springs in the air, and walked all over Ashland on my hands; played checkers, dominoes, pitched horseshoes and played baseball as often as possible. I also read a great deal, frequently lying on my stomach on the front porch of our home or somewhere in the shade of trees in the woods close to home. I read everything that was both readable and available. Along with Nick

Carter detective stories, Fred Fearnots, young and old King Bradys, I remember reading many histories, Walter Scott's poems and novels, Dickens' novels, *Pilgrim's Progress,* and many other books generally thought of as too advanced for children. Unless my memory is wrong, I read many of these books before I was ten years old. And, of course, being a Southerner I read and studied the Bible. I should feel guilty of deception did I not admit that, along with good books, I also found and read, even far out in the country where I lived, a number of sheets, pamphlets, and books ranging from the sexually suggestive to the openly obscene and even "pornographic," whatever that term means. Candor, however, compels me to add that an early familiarity with the obscene, dirty, profane, and pornographic language, instead of making me like it, had precisely the opposite effect. I have never liked either to use or read or hear language falling within these vague classifications. Doubtless this personal experience is responsible for my lack of fear of the circulation of the "obscene." Thus perhaps do early habits and views help to shape the views of later life. But although I came out of a home and a community where playing cards, dancing, and reading sexy books were all ranked as "sinful," I nevertheless came out ready to do all these things in moderation. With this attitude I left Ashland, went to what was to me the big city of Birmingham, Alabama, to enter medical college, whence I was to change my life plans within a year and go to law school to begin my life's serious work.

III

I Go to Medical School, Then to Law School, and Then to Practice Law

It is hard for me to remember when I did not want to be a lawyer. This desire increased year by year as I attended the regular sessions of court in Ashland. Few sessions occurred at which a small boy, meaning me, was not present, looking and listening eagerly to find out what the lawyers said and did. Strange and almost fantastic as it sounds, I still remember occasions when I was wholly persuaded that lawyers, frequently good ones, were just throwing away their cases by making stupid mistakes. My views, not completely sound I am now confident, were nonetheless serious to me and doubtless contributed much to my deep-seated boyish yearnings to be a lawyer. But fate was to and did temporarily divert me from the early legal future I so earnestly planned for myself. My brother, Orlando, whom I dearly loved, became a doctor. Because of my affection for him I wanted to walk in his footsteps. After my falling out with the Ashland teachers I did not want to go to school there again, nor did I wish to take four years out of my life to obtain an academic college education. I therefore concluded to go straight to a medical college, believing that by hard work I could finish the four-year course in three years, as was then permitted. With this plan in mind I definitely decided to enter a medical college in 1903. Although only seventeen years of age and without a college degree, I found it was not difficult at that time to gain admission to a medical college. After some investigation I concluded to go to the Birmingham Medical School. It was a small school but had a good reputation. In fact, as I recall, the school closed its doors before very long after 1903 due largely to its refusal to let students graduate who were not sufficiently trained to become doctors. I matriculated without trouble, found a room close to the College on South F Street for eight dollars per month and an eating place close by for fifteen dollars per month. I then persuaded the College to agree for me to take the first two years in one in order to finish the entire four-year course within three years. I worked hard seven days a week, taking time out for Sunday School and church on Sunday, passed examinations satisfactorily for the first- and second-year courses, left Birmingham, and went to Wilsonville, Alabama, to spend the summer with my doctor brother Orlando. After about two months with him my brother advised me that he thought I would make a good doctor but doubted if I could ever be happy in that profession. His doubt was based on his knowledge that I had always had an ambition to be a lawyer. After some discussion of the subject with him I finally concluded that I could be satisfied in no business or profession except the law, went home to Ashland, and arranged to go to the University of Alabama for the September opening.

My purpose was to take the academic course if I were permitted to enter the sophomore class without an examination; if not, to enter the Law School. My year at the Birmingham Medical College had not been a total loss, however. The course taught me how to work long, hard hours and the medical knowledge I acquired proved to be of incalculable benefit to me in the trial of cases in later years. I have never regretted my medical studies. The work there brought me into close contact with a number of the best Birmingham doctors with whom I formed warm friendships that in many instances became closer as the years went by and I was a practicing lawyer in Birmingham.

One of the teachers at the Medical School was Dr. E. P. Hogan, who taught chemistry. He had one favorite quotation that he repeated time and time again. His quotation, as well as I can remember at this time, was:

> He who seeks one thing in life—and but one—
> May hope to achieve it before life is done;
> But he who seeks all things only reaps from the
>   hopes which around him he sows
> A harvest of barren regrets.

This little part of a poem, written by Owen Meredith, has stuck with me through the years. And I am not sure but that it has had a serious influence on my life.

In September 1904 I went to the University without having decided whether I would enter law school or take an undergraduate course. If permitted to enter the sophomore class without an examination, I intended to do so; if not, it was my purpose to take the two-year law course, which at that time one could do without a college degree. My request to enter the sophomore class without an examination was turned down by all officials, including the President of the University, Dr. John W. Abercrombie, who had formerly been President of Ashland College. I explained to him that I was not prepared at that time to take the entrance tests for the sophomore class but that I was absolutely sure I could do the sophomore work satisfactorily if admitted to the class. My proposal was that he let me enter the sophomore class for one semester, at the end of which I would go back to the freshman class if a single one of my professors said I needed to do that. The rule requiring the test turned out to be a rigid one, however, and consequently I entered the Law School at eighteen years of age. Who was right about the rule one can never know. I do know, however, that although I supplemented my Law School work by taking an English class under Dr. Barnwell and a political economy course under Col. McCorvey, I made the honor roll in Law School both years, which, at that time, meant that I made grades of over 90 in every law course I took. Later, I was awarded a Phi Beta Kappa key for my Law School work.

The University Law School, at the time I was there, compelled students to take only one year, but I chose to take the two-year course. We had only two instructors, Judge William S. Thorington, an ex-judge of the State Supreme Court, and Ormond Somerville, a future judge of that Court. Judge Thorington's course was serious, unimaginative, and therefore a trifle dull. Professor Somerville, while equally serious, had a twinkle in his eyes that bespoke a sense of dry humor, and he taught us the dryest subjects with enough imagination to give them life and sparkle. Both were excellent teachers and I have always felt fortunate to have had them for instructors.

I recall at the moment a somewhat ludicrous incident that took place at one of the lectures given by Judge Thorington. One of our law students was named Sartain, a large, freckle-faced, red-haired Irishman, more than six feet tall. His size indicated that he could have been a football player, which in fact he was. Before he entered law school, and after leaving it too, I might add, he was employed as a guard at the Alabama Hospital for the Insane. Before the professors had learned the backgrounds of the students, one very hot summer afternoon, in a very stuffy and sizzling classroom, when air-conditioning was not yet even a dream, Judge Thorington made the mistake of asking Sartain a question, closing with his invariable ending: "If so, why so, and if not, why not, . . . Mr. . . . Sartain?" All the students breathlessly awaited to see how Sartain would ward off this non-football inquiry. He proved equal to the occasion, however, and after the second inquiry answered: "I have no idea." This, I think, completed all the questions ever asked Mr. Sartain. During the entire two years, he played excellent football for our team, adding lustre to our college football record as he did. My good friend Sartain's scholarly achievement could be better understood were I able to give you a list of the classical books when, according to the College paper, Sartain's "valuable library" was destroyed by a fire in his room. My memory of the details is a trifle dim, but I do remember that among his literary treasures were a large number of Nick Carters, Fred Fearnots, Old King Bradys, and others of similar classical categories.

We law students had a debating society that met regularly. I have many reasons for remembering that society, but one particular debate stands out vividly in my memory. On that occasion I was to uphold the affirmative of the question: "Shall capital punishment be abolished?" I gathered together all the sentimental, tear-jerking arguments I could find against what I portrayed as the "barbarous" practice of taking people's lives. On the other side of the debate was a rather round and chubby-faced student who had, I think, been a travelling salesman before coming to law school. He had a glib tongue, was a more or less practical salesman of ideas as well as goods, and all in all was more than a worthy debating foeman against a nineteen-year-old country boy. I can never forget the easy grace and manifest confidence with which he rose to his feet to demolish my very prosaic desultory arguments against capital punishment. He began his speech favoring capital punishment with an exact quotation from the eloquent words of John Temple Graves spoken in eulogy of the great Georgian, Henry W. Grady. He repeated those words without missing a beat or deviating as much as a single syllable. In part he said that he had seen the brilliant light that streamed from the headlight of a giant locomotive; he had watched the beautiful morning light coming in glory over the eastern hills; he had watched with awe the swift morning light that leaped at midnight athwart the storm-swept sky, all of which spectacles he thought were grand. "But"—my debating adversary went on to say, "the grandest thing next to the radiance that flows from the Almighty throne is the light of a noble and beautiful life wrapping itself in benediction around the destinies of man and finding its home in the blessed bosom of the everlasting God." And then my opponent turned from Graves' eulogy of Grady to his own imagery, saying in substance:

> Last night me dreamed that I gave up my cares and woes of this mortal world and flew straightway to the pearly gates and there entered into the ineffable glory of the heavenly realm. There me

> looked and saw the radiant faces of countless angels basking in the beauty of a luminous light emanating from a throne of all the colors of heaven. As me looked there appeared before me a luminous figure and me knew at once that me was in the company and presence of the Son of the Almighty. My gaze strayed upward and me then saw at the top of what looked like an endless pole a beautiful flag blown about by the heavenly breezes. Me saw one side of the flag on which was inscribed in brilliance the words: ETERNAL LIFE. The wind changed, the other side of this heavenly flag appeared before my vision, and inscribed on it me read the heavenly inscription: CAPITAL PUNISHMENT NOW AND FOREVER.

With those last moving words my adversary turned toward me secure in his belief that his heavenly vision gave victory to him without quibble or question. Maybe it did; I do not now know. But I do know that his use of John Temple Graves' Henry W. Grady eulogy taught me for life that my own words, poor though they might be, are good enough for me.

I had many other experiences in law school which made my two years there a precious part of a full life's memories. It is sufficient to say at this time, however, that in June 1906, when I was twenty years and four months of age, I became the proud possessor of an L.L.B. degree entitling me to a license to practice law in Alabama. And this brings me to the days of Hugo Black, the Lawyer.

IV

I Begin the Practice of Law

After graduating from the University of Alabama in June 1906, I spent no time or energy in deciding where I would begin to offer my legal services to the people. The place was Ashland, Alabama, a small town where, as I recall, there were already five lawyers, not one of whom, I am sure, was earning any more than enough to afford him a skimpy living. Nevertheless, I went back there with what now seem to have been rather grandiose plans for my future. My eventual ambition was to practice law in New York. As I look back on it, I can think of no possible reason for that decision other than the fact that New York was the nation's largest city. For I had never been there. My plans for preparing myself to go to New York were too simple to be practical. I would remain in Ashland five years or less, then go to the State Legislature, broaden my acquaintance sufficiently to move to Birmingham, stay there about five years, go to Congress and from there go to New York to practice law. I realize now that the plan was impracticable if not thoroughly impossible. This is what happened to that dream:

My mother, whom I loved dearly, died of pneumonia in the early winter of 1906, several months before my graduation from law school. Pneumonia was very prevalent and the disease, as I remember, was deadly in Clay County where even as late as 1906 people had to depend for warmth on wood stoves. There were no miracle drugs to combat colds and pneumonia. I watched my precious mother gradually pass away because there was no effective way to combat the infection and control her very high temperature. Of course, I realize that nearly all mothers are precious to their children, but I consider it no exaggeration for me to say that no mother was ever a greater inspiration to her child than was mine to me. Looking back, I cannot recall that there was ever a time when I left home, whether for a long or a short period, that my mother did not go with me to the front steps, sometimes to the front gate, take a last look to see if my hair was combed, straighten out any part of my clothing that needed it, and then kiss me goodbye. She was one of a small number of young women of her generation in Clay County who attended one of the few higher academies of learning in Alabama at the time. She was also a woman of superior native intelligence. Rarely did she ever go to sleep without reading from at least one of her two favorite books—the Holy Bible, and Bunyan's *Pilgrim's Progress.* Both have always been favorites of mine.

Shortly after I began the practice of law at Ashland, I went to the Pastor of the Baptist Church, told him I was sure my mother would have wanted me to join that church, and sought his advice. I did so because as an applicant for church membership I did not want to be publicly required to confess a religious faith greater than I had, nor did I intend to follow the custom of pretending that I had been a heavy sinner simply because I had sometimes played cards or danced. The preacher and I easily agreed, and I became a member of the church. Shortly thereafter I became the church clerk, a Sunday School teacher, and the Sunday School organist, playing by ear.

Of course, I had to have a place to live in Ashland. At the time my brother Lee was living in the old family home. I simply moved into his home, paying his wife Hattie six dollars per month board. Today that sum seems like nothing, but it was a fair payment in those days.

For my office I rented a two-room suite upstairs over a grocery store in a building on the southeast corner of the public square. I furnished it nicely, hung up a printed sign: "HUGO L. BLACK, Attorney and Counsellor at Law" at the street entrance to the stairway, and was ready for business. My good friend, Dr. Arthur Owens, joined me in occupancy of the office. The stairway was rickety and the floor of the two offices would shake every time a person of ordinary weight walked on it. I had considerable apprehension therefore each time Dr. Owens came up the shaky stairway and walked across our creaky floor. He weighed over two hundred pounds! I still do not understand how those old offices withstood our joint occupancy without caving in. But they were destined to meet another fate. One night, nearly a year after moving in, I was awakened about midnight by the ringing of church and school bells and the firing of shots—Ashland's customary fire alarm. I jumped out of bed and rushed out into the street, where I could see a huge blaze at the town square. I ran towards it. At the courthouse square I saw that my office and the grocery store below had both burned so completely that not a single thing could be saved, not a book, not even my seven-dollar painted sign. This was quite a blow since I had what I believed to be the best law library in Ashland, paid for with money inherited from my father but on which I had not had the foresight to buy insurance! Judge E. J. Garrison, another Ashland lawyer, was kind enough to let me share his two-room quarters. They were, in fact, the only space left in town suitable for a law office. I sort of "camped out" there for the next few months until I partly carried out my old dream of going to Birmingham to practice law. More about that later.

When I went back to Ashland to practice law, I carried with me a diploma from the University of Alabama Law School which entitled me to be a lawyer, but the people of Clay County saw me not as a lawyer but as the same marble-shooting boy whom they had watched grow up in their midst. Weighing less than 120 pounds, I probably still looked more like a boy to them than like a lawyer. It was therefore no surprise to me that litigants did not crowd into my law office. Anticipating this scarcity of clients, I had planned to utilize my first few years in Ashland by a concentrated study of English, history, and other subjects I had missed by taking no academic course in college. To this end, I bought several good textbooks on grammar, rhetoric, writing, and history, putting in long hours day and night studying them. As was recommended in some of those books, I began writing letters to some of my old friends, letters that must have sounded more like stilted essays than chatty comments on daily happenings. On summer visits to my sister, Daisy Black Rozelle, who lived in the Hatchett Creek Community, I frequently went into the woods along the creek bank near her home and practiced speaking alone. Although my finances did not improve during my Clay County stay as a lawyer, when I went to Birmingham to practice, I had learned far more about writing simple English and talking on my feet than I had ever known before. It now seems to me that I had planned far wiser than I knew when, in mapping out my program, I somehow stumbled upon the idea of spending my first few years as a lawyer in Clay County. They were a people of rugged, sturdy, honest, and patriotic character, and I hope that by virtue of living among them in my early formative years, and also as a part of my heritage, I was able to absorb some of these fine qualities.

Needless to say, perhaps, I had no flourishing legal business during my one year and three months in Ashland. My earliest business, naturally enough, was the collection of old accounts, the first coming from the estate of my father, who had died, seven years before, in 1899. I must say that I had good luck with many of these collections from my father's estate. Men paid debts that they knew were already barred by the statute of limitations. Many of those debtors told me that my father had dealt too fairly and leniently with them for them to be willing to plead a technicality of any kind to escape paying what they owed his estate. They made me very proud of my father.

Of course, every young lawyer is almost certain to be appointed to defend some indigent defendant. My appointment was to defend a murder charge that grew out of a killing that occurred at the end of a crap game at Lineville, six miles from Ashland. One of a half a dozen or more Negro players in the group ended up with all his money in the hands of the other players. This so angered him that he demanded that all the winners give his money back to him. When they refused, he took out a pistol and first fired one shot into the ceiling, threatening to empty his gun into the body of the winner of most of his money. His demand was refused, he did empty his gun, and when the firing ceased the winner was dead. This was the case of the indigent I was appointed to defend. In some localities the killing would have been treated lightly, but not in Clay County. Though young in the law, I knew that no killing in that County could be treated lightly, and I had no yearning to begin my legal record with a death sentence against my client. So I decided to make an effort to get an older, more experienced lawyer to act as co-counsel. Ed Whatley had been a rather successful lawyer at Ashland for many years and was well liked. At my suggestion, as I recall, the judge appointed him to act as co-counsel with me. Ed and I jointly concluded that a partial surrender would be the better part of valor, and it was therefore not long until we had made an agreement with the prosecutor, acquiesced in by the judge, to accept a plea of guilty with a life sentence. Later events proved our judgment was good. At that time, evidence had to be offered in Alabama, in a capital case, before a court could accept a plea of guilty, so we selected a jury. Some of the available evidence was then offered by the State, the jury was told by the trial judge about our agreement, and the jury retired, we thought, to convict the defendant of murder, with a life sentence only. In about half an hour, the jury returned with the announcement that it had not reached a verdict. Inquiry of the judge brought out the fact that the jury, of which my father's long-time friend and former business partner was foreman, wished to know if it were bound by our agreement or whether it was free to impose a death sentence upon the defendant. After some discussion, in which the foreman of the jury plainly stood out in front to impose the death sentence, the judge told them they could return such a verdict if they wished, but if they did he would immediately set it aside. Whereupon, the jury retired again, and in a very few minutes brought in the verdict agreed upon. The jury's position in that case, though adverse to my client, taught me to respect the integrity of jurors. They can, and I have found frequently do, stand staunchly by their oath to do justice, despite biases and friendships.

I shall mention only briefly one other case at Ashland. It, too, was a murder case, but one in which my first cousin, Emory Toland, was the victim. He was shot with a pistol as he started to mount his horse to go home after an altercation at a country dance. This occurred after I had begun to practice law in Birmingham, but his family urged me so strongly to come back and take part in the prosecution that I agreed to do so, without a fee. The family also employed Judge Martin Lackey to join in the prosecution. Although I was still a very young and inexperienced lawyer, Judge Lackey prevailed on me to examine and cross-examine the witnesses. The judge was an extremely heavy man, weighing, I would guess, three hundred and fifty pounds. Like most corpulent men, he was not highly energetic, so while I examined the witnesses he sat in an outside room where he could smoke and listen. Before making the closing argument for the State, he took me into the same outside room and said, "Now, Hugo, tell me all the evidence from beginning to end," which I did. I must say that he amazed me with his grasp of the facts, with the force and logic of his argument, and the power of his eloquence. The jury convicted and sentenced the defendant to seven years in the penitentiary, after the service of which he settled down in a southern Alabama county. Several years ago, someone, recalling my interest in the case, sent me a clipping telling about how the young man (then grown old) who had killed my cousin had himself been brutally murdered in his own home.

But even in Clay County I did get a little law business. My first case, as I remember, brought me a fee of $7.50 for representing a man who had been arrested on a charge by his neighbor of criminal trespass for walking several inches over the neighbor's land line. The value of those several inches of property was very little. Land almost anywhere in the county was valued at less than $100.00 per acre. When I was hired in the trespassing case, the feeling between the two neighbors was at fever heat—at the profane, fighting stage. I still remember that I did not feel wholly comfortable sitting between two feuding litigants. I never knew how long I could keep them apart, as I kept remembering that Clay County people were not always satisfied to fight only with their fists. It was my good fortune, however, that the lawyer for the other litigant wanted to get out of this hornet's nest as much as I did. The result was that we reached a settlement of some kind, but I do not remember the details. Looking back on the case, I am rather inclined to believe that the settlement of the controversy between those two quarrelsome neighbors was about as satisfactory a victory as I ever achieved in my law practice.

I had a collection case later that resulted in a success that neither I nor anyone else could have expected. There was an inhabitant of Ashland who was a modern "hippie," and who, so far as could be recalled, had never shaved his face nor paid a debt in his life. He was thought by everyone, including himself, to be execution-proof, so no one ever sued him. A five-dollar indebtedness against him was turned over to me for collection. A number of requests for payment could not even extract a promise. In response to a happy thought, however, I asked the debtor to give my client a promissory note. Having no fear about being compelled to pay, he rather cheerfully agreed to give the note, which contained a waiver of personal exemptions together with a promise to pay a reasonable attorney's fee in case suit had to be filed to collect the debt. The result was that upon his failure to pay I filed suit before Bud Dean, a rural mail carrier, who was also a Notary Public ex officio Justice of the Peace. I served a judgment for the five-dollar note together with a five-dollar attorney's fee. The debtor owned no real estate and so far as anyone knew, his only personal property was a wheelbarrow not worth enough by itself to pay costs in any case. But one day when lack of legal business had permitted me to engage in a domino game on the public square, I happened by chance to see the debtor with a wheelbarrow filled with goods that he had just bought from several stores. Quick as a flash I hunted for and found the constable, who had an execution in his pocket which he levied on the wheelbarrow and its contents. The coup was successful. The goods were worth more than the five-dollar debt, the five-dollar reasonable attorney's fees, and costs of the suit. For the first time in history this unwilling citizen was made to pay a debt. My reputation as a lawyer was not greatly enhanced, but my reputation as a collector was. Although claims for collection piled in on me, this was not the type of law practice for which I yearned. So I began to consider leaving my boyhood home to go to Birmingham without going first to the Legislature from Clay County as I had originally planned.

V

I Move to Birmingham—September 7, 1907

While attending the Birmingham Medical College in 1903–4, I became very well acquainted with Woodson Duke, another Clay County man from the Mellow Valley Community, nine miles south of Ashland. When I arrived in Birmingham September 7, 1907, to begin the practice of law there, I soon got in touch with Woodson, who was then working as a collector for a furniture store. He, his brother Brooks, and David J. Davis, a recent Yale law graduate from Arab, Alabama, were for twenty dollars per month each boarders at the home of Mrs. Crim on Fifth Avenue North, between 20th and 21st Streets—almost straight across the Avenue from what is now the Tutwiler Hotel. The three occupied one rather small room with two double beds. It was no difficult task for me to get the consent of Mrs. Crim to occupy that room with the others and eat at her table for twenty dollars per month. We four boarders became warm friends from then until the death of the other three. When Woodson Duke died, many years later, he was one of the probation officers for the Federal Court, which position I had gotten for him while I was the United States Senator from Alabama. David J. Davis, the young law school graduate from Yale, became fatally ill many years later while sitting as a United States District Judge, an appointment also made upon my recommendation as United States Senator. I never had more loyal friends than those two. I recall very well that when I first recommended Woodson to be probation officer, the Attorney General sent word to me that he could not appoint Mr. Duke because he did not have a college degree. I telephoned the Attorney General and told him that I supposed, contrary to what I had thought, that all prisoners put on probation were college graduates and therefore officers who dealt with them must also be college graduates. He was frank enough to admit that this requirement had as little common sense to him as it appeared to have to me, and upon my assurance that I knew Woodson Duke to be one of the wisest men I knew, he was appointed. Several years later the head of the Probation Office called to tell me how grateful that office was for my having insisted on Woodson's appointment, because he had rendered invaluable service in his position.

But back to my first experiences in Birmingham. My first job was renting an office, and it soon became clear that I was no expert in that field. My selection was one room in a building which I believe was 1905 1/2 Second Avenue North. I had three neighbors upstairs, one an old-fashioned dentist, his wife, a rather well-fed beauty shop operator, and the third a budding young photographer. Had I searched the City over I could hardly have found an office where a prospective litigant was less likely to come looking for a lawyer. It was about four blocks from the Courthouse and the City Hall. What I needed more than anything else at that time were clients, and no person looking for a lawyer was likely to come to that section or to stumble up the steps to my office even if he did. A month passed and not a single person had come to my upstairs office to find a lawyer. Seeking another office, I then went to the corner of Third Avenue and 21st Street North where, across the street from the County Courthouse and jail, I saw the Lyon-Terry Building, only two stories high and with a large number of signs leading up to the second floor. Most important to me was the fact that every sign at the foot of that staircase advertised one or more lawyers. I walked up the stairs, looked at the offices from the hallway, decided this was the place for me, and went back to the office right at the head of the stairs. On it was the sign: "SHUGART and COMSTOCK, Attorneys at Law." The names meant nothing to me, although I learned later that the name Shugart was a well-known one in Birmingham. Perhaps in as little time as it has taken me to pencil down this incident I had rented desk space in the Shugart office for seven dollars per month, cash in advance. Later I learned that there were two Shugarts—Roland and Curtis. Some time before, Roland had shot and killed a man. The father of the two Shugarts had himself been a widely-known lawyer until he, too, was accidentally shot to death, in a bar room as I recall. One of the best known stories bandied about by their enemies concerning the father had been (whether true or not, I do not know) that invariably when negotiating a fee with a client he would ask whether his services were to be "with or without witnesses." All of my dealings with these gentlemen, I must say, were most pleasant and they were as fair as they could be with me. This is illustrated by the first case that came into their front office, the one I rented.

A gentleman without a collar, and without a shave and obviously a farmer, walked in and asked me if I were a lawyer. I told him that I was, whereupon he wanted to hire me at once. I explained to him as best I could that I merely rented desk space from the firm whose offices these were and that I would have to take him to those lawyers. Under protest he went with me. I explained the situation to whichever lawyer present, Mr. Comstock, I think. He asked the prospective litigant what the case was about and it turned out to be a Justice-of-the-Peace lawsuit at Republic, some miles from Birmingham. There was some controversy over the ownership of a sow. Straightway I was told by Mr. Comstock to go on and take the case if I wished. Naturally I did. We arranged that I was to get a fee of ten dollars, out of which I was to pay my train fare to Republic. There I was to be met by my client and hauled in a wagon to the scene of the trial at the coal company's Commissary, where the Notary Public ex officio Justice of the Peace trying the case worked. My client's story was that about two years before a small, stray, hungry-looking female shoat had wandered into his barnyard where he fed it and permitted it to remain until two weeks before the trial, when the other man in the lawsuit came by his place, claimed to recognize the then sow by a mark on her, and demanded her return. My client assured me there was no identifiable mark of any kind on the sow, and so it was that single factual issue, I thought, that had to be tried out by the Justice of the Peace. Then, too, there was another question as to the ownership of a litter of pigs that the sow had given birth to in my client's barnyard. I arrived at Republic in due time on a Saturday afternoon, went in the wagon to the Commissary, all prepared, I thought, for the trial. Upon arrival I saw a large group of good-sized men squatting country fashion on their toes on the ground. Nearly all of them, it seemed to me, had dangerous-looking guns either in their hands or lying on the ground next to them. On asking my client who were these armed men, he indicated that they were all friends of and witnesses for our adversary —there to back up his identification of the sow. My client had no supporting witnesses whatever and I began to anticipate the sure loss of the sow. I was determined, however, to put up the best possible fight for at least some of the pigs. Giving some study to this issue in the Bar Association's law library, I had unfortunately found that, under the vague and nebulous common law doctrine practically everywhere, the owner of a sow was also recognized as the owner of her pigs. For this reason I deemed it advisable to rely on common sense and reason rather than the common law. Consequently, I took no law books with me to the trial.

On the factual issue of ownership of the sow our adversary literally "slaughtered" us. Witness after witness made out an iron-clad case proving his ownership of the sow. This seemed to me to make it necessary above all things that the judge be persuaded to give at least half of the sow's offspring to my client, who was, after all, the unquestioned owner of the reported father of the pigs. It had somehow ceased to bother me that the common law said the pigs should go to the owner of their mother, since I had by that time persuaded myself beyond all reasonable doubt that whatever might be the general law in cases of this kind, justice, equity, and even morality demanded an equal division of the pigs in *this* case. And so, I pleaded with all my power that the Notary Public ex officio Justice of the Peace decide the case that way. First I told the Judge that whatever side the majority of law books might take on that issue, it was his sacred duty as an acting Justice of the Peace to consider nothing but what his conscience told him to do. That the evidence tended to prove that our adversary owned the sow did not begin, I told the Judge, to determine the equities of the case. I even reminded the Judge that awarding the claimant all the pigs would necessarily remove them from their hog father who up to that time had, most likely with their mother, watched over them. I dropped in a few more ideas along the same line and completed my argument with an earnest plea that he do justice, though the heavens fall! Whether my fervid pleas had any effect of course I do not know and cannot say, but I do know that relying on justice and fairness, as the Judge told us, he awarded the mother sow to our adversary and divided the pigs equally between the two litigants. Suffice it to say, I was satisfied. My client also was satisfied. My client's satisfaction with half the pigs was shown by the fact that two months later he came to my office again, told me that a coal mine under his home and farmland had cracked the top soil, and then signed a contract to pay me as fee half of all I could get above $500.00 either by settlement or suit. As I recall, he had paid only $500.00 for his land. In a very short time the company offered me $1,000.00 in settlement and on my client's strong urging I settled, thereby earning a fee of $250.00. This was a tremendous fee for me, and on the strength of it I moved into another office in the same Lyon-Terry Building, sharing it with another lawyer, each of us paying $15.00 monthly rent. By this time I thought I was really moving! This was not merely because of my pig case and the $250.00 fee from the soil-cracking case.

My loyal friend, Woodson Duke, had caused some people he knew to turn over to me some collections. The most interesting ones, as I recall, were debts alleged to be due to an advertising doctor who treated men and women for so-called "private disease." Most of his patients had refused to pay on the ground that my client, the doctor, had broken his promise to guarantee a cure. I had to fight this issue out with one of the patients. After a rather bitter fight in that case, I won a judgment in the Inferior Court, finally defeated the defendant's claims of exemptions, and wound up actually collecting about $25.00 in cash.

By this time, I had become a good friend of H. B. Abernathy, the Inferior Court Judge, a cherished friendship that continued up to his death. "Ab", as his friends loved to call him, was an eccentric judge. People liked to visit his court to see and hear his latest pranks. Visitors to his court might, in some minor, trifling case, happen to see him render judgment, satisfactory to him and the parties, by the flipping of a coin. Unless my memory is faulty, I recall Ab's telling my good friend Roderick Beddow, then a young attorney who insisted on arguing a case on a very busy court afternoon, that "This case is now passed until 6:30 tomorrow morning to give lawyer Beddow fifteen minutes to advertise." Lawyer Beddow, I should add, was one of Judge Ab's closest friends. With all of his fun and frolicking in the court, however, Judge Abernathy was a highly respected judge in the community.

Near the end of my first year in Birmingham, I became the representative of the Retail Credit Company of Atlanta, Ga., which company paid me 50 cents each for reports on the life and habits of life insurance applicants. This later developed in Birmingham into a business worth $100.00 or more per month to me, a substantial addition to my small income. With this business, and other small fees I picked up in the Inferior Courts, I was no longer worried about making a living. I was, as I thought then, well on my way to success as a Birmingham lawyer.

VI

Building Up a Practice in Birmingham

Probably without appreciation of the difficulties of the task I had planned for myself, I had gone to Birmingham September 7, 1907, determined to build up a law practice by my own efforts. This I knew would be difficult because I was going to that City almost a complete stranger. True, I had attended medical college there for more than six months, but during that period most of my time had been spent in my room, at my eating place, or the medical college—all within a few blocks of one another. My acquaintances in Birmingham, with very few exceptions, were limited to the few doctor instructors I had met at the College and students who lived in other cities in Alabama, most of whom expected to return to their hometown after graduation. I had attended the nearby Southside Baptist Church on Sundays but not enough to form many friendships there. The life of practical seclusion I knew as a medical student was thus in sharp contrast to the kind of life I would have to lead to establish my own successful law practice. I did not, even at that early date, or later, wish to take a subordinate place in a law firm. Neither did I have an entree into any law firm in Birmingham had I wished to work for one. While by no means skilled in building a practice, I was of the opinion that the only ethical way was to meet as many people and make as many friends as possible. This I proceeded to do immediately after arriving in Birmingham.

From my earliest recollections I had for some unaccountable reason wanted to join the Masons. So far as I then knew I had no Masonic ancestors, but, quite coincidentally, several days ago [in 1970] I received from a stranger (who turned out to be a distant relative) a photograph of my maternal great-grandfather's, Hugh Toland's, tombstone at Old Tylersville, Laurens County, South Carolina, on which was a Masonic emblem. In order to become a Mason at the earliest possible moment, and by special arrangement with Ashland Masonic Lodge No. 356, my application for membership went in before I was twenty-one years of age and while I still had my law office in Ashland. On reaching my twenty-first birthday I was initiated into the first or the Entered Apprentice Masonic degree. I had therefore been a Mason some months when I moved to Birmingham September 7, 1907. The night before going to Birmingham, that is, September 6, by special dispensation of the Grand Lodge Knights of Pythias, I took the three ranks in that fraternity. I was glad to join that fraternity particularly because both my doctor brother and my father were members. I had thought of joining the Odd Fellows, too, before moving, but decided to postpone that until after I went to Birmingham. After settling in Birmingham, I immediately began to visit various Masonic and Knights of Pythias meetings with a view to joining one of the local Lodges. I finally decided that question by transferring my membership to Birmingham Temple Masonic Lodge No. 636 and Jefferson Valley Lodge No. 11, Knights of Pythias. I have never regretted those transfers and am a life member of both organizations. Some of the closest friendships in my life were formed among the brethren in these two fraternities, and, to a lesser extent, in the Odd Fellows.

The first night I attended a Jefferson Valley Lodge meeting I met a man who was destined to play a large part in my life and career. He was Herman M. Beck of the Beck Candy & Grocery Company. At the time he was Grand Vice-Chancellor of the Knights of Pythias and slated to become State Grand Chancellor within the next few months. The job, he thought, would be too much for him to handle alone, and it was only a short time after we met that he suggested I become his secretary to help in the new statewide job he was to get. He proposed to pay me the full salary he was to draw, which, as I recall, was $100.00 per month. This, he said, would help me over the lean years of my law practice and at the same time make it possible for him to act as Grand Chancellor without sacrificing too much time from his wholesale mercantile business. Our work together was carried out as planned. During the year I worked with him we became almost as close as father and son, a relationship that continued until his death. I never knew a better or more honest man. In 1918, when I was ordered to go to Europe with my Field Artillery Regiment, I named Mr. Beck to serve, without bond, as Executor of what might be my small estate with absolute confidence that his responsibilities would be met the same as they would have been by my mother or father.

Just another little story about Mr. Beck, and then I shall pass on to other matters. During my year with him, Brother J. Mitt Dannelly, a Methodist Minister and Presiding Elder, was Grand Secretary of the Grand Lodge Knights of Pythias of Alabama. He travelled all over the State with Mr. Beck and me. I once suggested to him that Mr. Beck, being a Jew, did not believe in the Christian faith, and that consequently many devout Protestants thought he could never get to Heaven. Without a moment's hesitation Brother Dannelly answered: "I would not want to go to a Heaven that would not let Herman Beck in." That was my feeling, too.

The first Sunday after reaching Birmingham I went to the First Baptist Church and the Baraca Sunday School Class of that church—a class of men taught by Miss Lula Bradford. She was also a teacher in the Birmingham Public School System. Miss Bradford was one of those dear, good women whose mere presence is enough to inspire a person to try to live a better life. I thoroughly enjoyed going to her class. It was only a short time until I was elected class president. Later I was made Superintendent of the Sunday School. I did not hold that position very long, however, because Miss Lula decided, quite mistakenly I always thought, that the men of the Baraca Class needed a male teacher, and that I was the man they needed. I yielded, began teaching about 1910, and continued to be teacher until I was elected to the United States Senate in 1926. Herbert Grooms, now a Federal District Judge, then became the teacher, and he still is. Although it is no easy task to talk week after week over a period of years to the same group of men, numbering in the hundreds, it was a most rewarding experience for me.

When I moved from Shugart and Comstock's office to a room across the hall in the same Lyon-Terry Building, I rented from Bonner Miller and shared his single-room office with him. Bonner was from a prominent family in Wilcox County, Alabama. One member of the family was later Governor of the State. It was not long after I moved into Bonner's office that Barney Whatley joined us. Barney was an old boyhood friend from Ashland who had moved with his family to Wylam, a Birmingham suburb, where his first job was timekeeper for the Tennessee Coal, Iron and Railroad Company. That Company either then or not too long thereafter became a subsidiary of the United States Steel Company. Shortly after I went to Birmingham, Barney borrowed some law books from me and began to study law. His TCI job enabled him to learn bookkeeping in a very short time and it was not long until he secured a place as bookkeeper at Prowell Hardware Company, which was located in the heart of the business section of Birmingham. At that time he moved from Wylam to East Lake, also a suburb of Birmingham, closer to his work. Much of his law study was done on the street car going to and from East Lake. When he felt himself ready to take the examination then required to practice law in Alabama, he did so, passed with flying colors, and was admitted to the Bar as a full-fledged lawyer. About 1908 I took him in as my partner under the firm name of Black and Whatley.

In addition to having an excellent mind, Barney was one of the best mixers I have ever known. His acquaintance with so many people made him invaluable in assisting me in making Retail Credit Reports on applicants for life insurance. We soon began to earn enough to consider moving, and when the new Farley Building went up on 20th Street and Third Avenue in 1909, only a block from the Courthouse, we rented offices on the second floor. We were about the first, if not *the* first, tenants in the building. Our partnership began a steady and most gratifying growth and ended only when Barney unfortunately developed tuberculosis. His doctors advised him that the only safe thing for him to do for his health would be to go to Colorado and enter a tuberculosis hospital. This he did, made a full recovery, and later entered the law offices of Judge James J. Banks, a former Birmingham lawyer and judge then practicing law in Denver.

One morning Barney, while reading a news item in Judge Banks' Denver Law office, learned that the "entire bar association" had died in Breckenridge, Colorado—the county seat of Summit County. He straightway went to Breckenridge, then hardly more than a ghost mining town near the top of the Rocky Mountains. When Barney arrived he soon discovered that the whole town was desperate because the Colorado and Southern Railroad was threatening to abandon the one railroad that connected Breckenridge with the outside world in the snowy winter months. He was invited and agreed to represent the town to prevent the railroad's abandonment, handling the case successfully before the newly created State Railroad Commission and the state courts. The Supreme Court of the United States dismissed the railroad's appeal. A short time later, probably due in large part to his success in preventing the abandonment of the railroad, Barney was overwhelmingly elected State District Attorney, moved his office to Leadville, Colorado, and later practiced law with great success at Denver, until his retirement some years ago. When Barney had to leave our firm he sold his interest to David J. Davis, one of the three persons with whom I lived when first coming to Birmingham. The firm then became Black and Davis, with the office first in the Farley Building and later in the First National Bank Building.

It can be seen from what I have said that starting from the first day after I moved to Birmingham I began to meet more and more people there. These people regarded me as a lawyer, and as I had anticipated, brought more and more clients to my firm. By 1911 I had small cases in all the courts in Birmingham, most of which, however, were in inferior courts within the jurisdiction of a Justice of the Peace. But some were in the Circuit Court. It was a Circuit Court case I tried before Circuit Judge A. O. Lane that, much to my surprise, brought about my selection to serve as Police Court Judge in Birmingham. It happened this way:

Bonner Miller, a fine, rather shy man, with whom I had an office, did not like to appear in court. Consequently, he wanted someone else to try all his cases for him. At that time a number of counties leased out their county prisoners under a convict lease system which later, as President of the Alabama Anti-Convict Lease Association, I helped get the State Legislature to abolish. Wilcox County, Bonner's native county, leased its convicts to the Sloss Sheffield Steel and Iron Company of Birmingham. Because of a bad system of records, Willie Morton, a colored prisoner from Wilcox, had been held over some time beyond his term of imprisonment. That case came to Bonner and he asked me to try it. I gladly agreed to do so. The case was set before Judge A. O. Lane, who was then about fifty years of age. I had met him several times because he, too, was a member of Jefferson Valley Lodge No. 11 of the Knights of Pythias. The Steel Company sent to represent it in court Mr. William I. Grubb, a leading lawyer in the biggest firm of corporation lawyers in Birmingham. At that time Alabama still chiefly used the system of common law pleading, complaints, answers, replications, rebutters, surebutters, etc. Many cases in court in those days were lost without the jury's ever having heard any evidence because so many lawyers did not know how to plead. Mr. Grubb, later Federal Judge Grubb, was an expert common law pleader, however, and carried me along on the pleading process for about a day and a half. My knowledge of pleading was purely theoretical, since this was my first jury case in Birmingham. But in that case, as always, I had thoroughly studied and considered what kind of pleading could be used to raise the issues in it. My complaint charged false imprisonment, the defense plea to which, in the absence of a prior judgment or settlement, was almost certain to be "not guilty," the equivalent of a general denial. Judge Grubb continued to file so-called special pleas against me through all of the first day and half of the second. Finally, Judge Lane smilingly told Judge Grubb: "Billy, it seems plain you cannot plead this young man out of court, so I suggest you simply join issue and go to trial now." Judge Grubb told Judge Lane he seemed to be right. He stopped trying to trap me with immaterial pleas; we both put on our evidence; the jury returned a verdict in my client's favor for $137.50, plus costs, as I recall; and the judgment was paid. Thus ended my first civil jury trial in Jefferson County.

The course of my life was much affected by the Willie Morton trial in at least two ways. In the first place Judge Grubb became my staunch friend, and about two years later, after he had become a United States District Judge and I had become a candidate for County Prosecuting Attorney, he gave me for publication a written endorsement for the job, avouching my capacity to fill the position I sought. The publication of this statement by the then revered Judge Grubb answered to the complete satisfaction of the voters of the County the charge that I was too young and inexperienced to be the County Solicitor.

Judge Lane's approval of my conduct of the Willie Morton case came earlier and with even more emphasis. The aldermanic government of the City of Birmingham had become so unsatisfactory to the people that the State Legislature abolished it and substituted three Commissioners for the old Mayor and Board of Aldermen. The Governor, anxious for the success of the new form of government, picked out three men, two of whom had played little, if any, part in the old city government, and both of the two deemed by all to be exceptionally well qualified to fill the new positions. Judge Lane was one of them. Shortly after he accepted the place, he sent for me to come to his office, and when I arrived made me a proposition that dumbfounded me. He was to have the city administration of justice under his jurisdiction. There were at that time, as I recall, five City Recorders (Police Court Judges) all drawing salaries from the City Treasury. He suggested that he appoint me to fill all five places. I protested, telling him that I wanted to continue my law practice, which I could not do while doing the work of five men at the same time. Then he told me something that astonished me all the more. He said he wanted me to begin my Recorder's work early enough to finish it before 9:30 A.M., the time the state courts begin their work. Thus, he argued, I could be the City Recorder and continue my law practice at the same time. To help me in this tight program Judge Lane told me he intended to issue an order prohibiting the Recorder from continuing to hear preliminary felony trials for the state courts. I asked for a day or two to consider the matter and went back to him the next day telling him I did not want the position but wanted to suggest my old friend David J. Davis, whom I knew would like to be a judge. Judge Lane promptly told me that he knew and admired "Dave" but did not believe he could do the job, emphasizing that the Commission's first order, which he intended this to be, *must* by all means be successful, and indicating his belief that I was the only person he knew that could carry out his stepped-up program. He explained to me that he would not ask me to take the position if he thought it would interfere with my career as a lawyer, and that if I would take it he would promise to release me at the very moment he thought I had remained Recorder long enough to receive all the advantage from it I could. His arguments persuaded me. I accepted the position in 1911, at age twenty-five, kept it about a year and a half at which time Judge Lane finally agreed that the wisest thing for me to do at that time would be to resign and devote my full time and attention to my law practice. I resigned on October 22, 1912, five years after my arrival in Birmingham from Clay County.

I have never regretted serving as City Recorder. I could easily write a volume about my experience in that judicial position, but that would delay these memoirs too long. I learned much about life in that position. I hope and believe that I administered justice fairly and tolerantly. And, besides, I got to know Judge Lane better, his humaneness, his soft, generous, kindly character. He was so full of sympathy for the weak and suffering that it was easy to persuade him to pardon prisoners if they or their relatives could but get to him to tell their stories. This characteristic brought down on his head much public criticism. But he was the kind of man people not merely liked but loved. With his white hair, white moustache, white shirt and white bow tie, he was the example par excellence of a Southern gentleman, in the best meaning of that term. His unselfish public service inspired me to go and try to do likewise.

VII

Law Practice Continues to Grow— Elected Prosecuting Attorney

October 22, 1912, I resigned as Recorder but before leaving the bench the Chief of Police, George H. Bodeker, asked if I would give him an opportunity to say a few words. I did, and he proceeded to talk about the esteem in which I was held by the entire police force and presented me a solid gold watch from them. I have always cherished it as coming from my friends. I then considered and still consider policemen to be soldiers in the cause of the law.

Under the firm name of Black and Davis, David J. Davis and I kept up our law practice while I served as Recorder. That practice continued to have a moderate increase. I tried practically all the court cases we had and David J. mainly handled office work. Not very long after my resignation David J. told me he had concluded that we should dissolve our partnership. This came as quite a surprise to me since we had roomed together for several years at 1916 16th Avenue South, Birmingham, and had never had any kind of friction. His reasons for wanting to dissolve our partnership were prompted by an eminent sense of fairness which marked his conduct throughout his life. He told me that I attracted more business than he and that I was a better lawyer. For those reasons he said he felt I was worth more to the firm than he, but that he had long before promised himself that he would never be in a partnership where he brought in less income than any other member. I tried to persuade him that he was wrong, explaining my own complete satisfaction with our arrangements. I soon discovered, however, that he was adamant, yielded to his desires, and we dissolved the law partnership. I never had a more loyal and devoted friend, and my affection for him remained undiminished to the day of his untimely death which occurred while he was serving as United States District Judge, an appointment made because of my recommendation when a United States Senator. I shall have occasion to mention him later, for he played an important part in my life.

After leaving David J., I rented a suite of offices in the First National Bank Building, where I stayed until I moved to the County Courthouse the latter part of 1914, after my election as County Prosecuting Attorney. My practice continued to grow up to the time of election. I had acquired a reputation for winning lawsuits, which brought me cases—some of them from other lawyers. I was satisfied with my business. From time to time I had been approached by other lawyers and law firms about forming new associations with them. During that period I was much flattered by one of those offers. Mr. Hugh Morrow, an able and popular lawyer, and a member of the then largest law firm in Alabama, came to see me. He told me he had been sent by his firm to tender me a place as a full-fledged partner. I did not underestimate this offer; it convinced me that I had actually arrived as a lawyer. When I came to Birmingham in September, 1907, I felt no hope or chance whatever of even getting a salaried legal job with any kind of law firm. Now, seven years later, I was offered a partnership in what I rated as one of the best.

I was a great admirer of Mr. Morrow. He belonged to one of the oldest Jefferson County political families, was a man of great personal charm, the son of a very popular ex–Probate Judge, and undoubtedly could have continued his family's successful political career in Jefferson County had he so desired. I reminded him at the time that I had watched him argue cases for the street car company and other companies defending serious personal injury and death cases, and that I had always wondered if he could be wholly happy with that kind of practice. I expressed some doubt as to whether I could enjoy a practice limited to that kind of trial work. He understood my feelings and agreed that I could think the matter over and let him know within a day or two. The next day I told him that I was, of course, much flattered and gratified at the offer, that I liked his firm, but had concluded that I could live a more satisfactory life by continuing the same kind of independent general practice I already had built up. I told him also that I was giving serious consideration to running for County Solicitor, which I could not do if I accepted his firm's offer. So far as I know, my refusal to enter the firm brought about no strained relations between us. I do not now recall that our later contacts were ever anything but pleasant, except for the slight and flitting miffs that aggressive lawyers trying cases against one another frequently have. This quite naturally brings me to my race for County Prosecuting Attorney—called Solicitor—an event of tremendous consequence in my life.

Before announcing for Solicitor I consulted many friends. Perhaps the most important one in helping me decide was William E. Fort, then a judge of one of the criminal divisions of our court system. He had been elected after a stiff fight against the appointed incumbent. I had been one of his most active supporters. Our views about crime and how it should be handled were much the same, both believing in an aggressive but fair and effective enforcement of the law. Neither of us believed that Jefferson County was getting that kind of law enforcement under the then Solicitor. Judge Fort was strong for me, and my first simple written announcement was our joint product.

With my announcement I immediately got busy. Unmarried, I gave practically every minute of my time to my campaign except what I was compelled to give to my law practice. That campaign lasted eight months, during which time I went to every precinct in Jefferson County, some of them many times. Day and night I went where I could see people, to lodges, picnics, basket suppers, stores, baseball games. I recall spending one entire afternoon pitching horseshoes in a county precinct in West Jefferson County, and unless my memory is wrong I got every vote but ten in that precinct when the votes came in—a consequence that spoke well, I should say, for my Clay County skill as a player of horseshoes.

When my campaign started I decided to get as many voters as I reasonably could to sign a written promise to vote for me. This technique proved far more successful than I had even hoped it would, perhaps because of the way I handled it. The first name on my list was Walter K. McAdory, whose persuasion had largely been responsible for my joining Temple 636 Masonic Lodge. Doubtless he was then one of the most popular men in the County, if not the *most* popular. Following his name were those of Frank Hewett, Elbert McClendon, and a host of other friends who were influential county politicians. It was a revelation to me to see how quickly other people would sign my list when they read the name at its head. When election day arrived, I had on my list thousands of signatures from every part of the County and, like most candidates, had not the slightest doubt about winning. Ever since that time I have taken with a grain of salt the trite old saying: "Men will promise to vote for anybody but you cannot believe any of them."

When my campaign was nearly over I had an interesting experience with Frank Hewett, the County Tax Assessor, who, I think, was second on my list of promised voters. Frank had become county campaign manager for Oscar Underwood, our United States Senator, who was opposed by Richmond Pearson Hobson, the hero of the sinking of the *Maine* during the Spanish-American War who had kissed himself into a fame of his own. The Underwood-Hobson campaign was one of the most controversial we had ever had. I announced at an early date that I would take no sides in the senatorial or any other campaign except my own. One day near election, however, I received a call from Frank Hewett asking me to come to his office as soon as I could. Suspecting that his call had something to do with the Underwood-Hobson campaign, I went immediately. I was right about the reason for the call. Almost as soon as I arrived Frank rather brusquely asked me: "What is this I hear about your working for Hobson; I am not going to support a man for Solicitor who is for that . . . It is your duty to support Senator Underwood and I want to tell you right here that I will not vote for a man who disgraces himself by voting for Hobson." I asked, "Who told you that I am for Hobson?" He replied, "Everybody tells me." I said, "You tell me it is my duty to announce for Senator Underwood because that race is so important, but the race for County Solicitor of this County is equally important, especially to me. I will make you a proposition, though. Senator Underwood lives in this County and will vote in the Solicitor's race, I suppose. If you will have Senator Underwood publicly announce for whom he intends to vote for Solicitor, I will at once announce my choice for United States Senator." That ended the interview. Frank Hewett's name remained on my list of supporters, and now fifty-four years later I make my first public announcement that my vote went for his candidate, Senator Underwood, because I thought Senator Underwood the best man for the job. The years have fully convinced me that he was.

There is frequently one incident in every election that has vast influence. That was true in my race for Solicitor. There were four men in the race—Harrington P. Heflin, who had been in office sixteen years; Zebulon T. Rudolph, a good man but with no previous political experience; F. D. McArthur, also a good man who was supported by organized labor; and myself. No candidate doubted that the majority of the County voters was against Heflin the incumbent; the problem therefore was which candidate could beat him. In this situation my friends and I, chiefly David J. Davis, my former partner, and Barney Whatley (who had come back from Colorado to Alabama at his own expense to help me), decided on this plan. We arranged to have distributed simultaneously all over the County, in office buildings and everywhere, small, narrow strips of colored pasteboard, about 1/2″ × 3″ in size, on which was printed on both sides these words: "Black or Hefflin. Which?" These little pieces of pasteboard, as we liked to say, covered Jefferson County like the dew. And we were all convinced that they turned the trick so far as convincing the people that I was the candidate to beat Heflin. Hastily printed and distributed cards stating "Rudolph or Heflin. Which?," "McArthur or Heflin. Which?" did not neutralize the psychological effect of our first distribution. And so, nearly seven years after arriving in the County, I was nominated and later elected its Solicitor. Lest someone think, "How easy," I hasten to add that this victory, like every one I have ever had, was the result of hard, concentrated work, not only during eight and a half months of active campaigning but during all of my first seven years in Birmingham. Few candidates ever get the vote of the people without just such hard work or the expenditure of large sums of money. Neither in my race for Solicitor nor for United States Senator did I ever buy a vote or spend more than the law prescribed. And while I later found that some of my friends had accepted small sums for my campaign, I never spent money supplied by anyone other than myself.

Thus, only seven years after the young hillbilly from Clay County arrived, almost a total stranger in Jefferson, Alabama's most populous county, he was elected its Prosecuting Attorney by the people.

VIII

Prosecuting Attorney to World War I 1914 to August 3, 1917

December 1, 1914, I closed my suite of law offices in the First National Bank Building and moved lock, stock, and barrel to the Jefferson County Courthouse. I had already named as assistants William S. Welch, Walter S. Brower, Ben F. Ray, and James G. Davis. I also took with me Miss Hart, my law office stenographer. I named as court stenographer Morris S. Allen, who had been a fellow student at the University of Alabama Law School. All except Mr. Welch had supported me in my race, and I shall never forget his surprise when I offered him the place of First Assistant. I invited Mr. Welch, who lived at Bessemer, to come to Birmingham to have lunch with me at Hooper's Café. We had not been at the table very long when I suggested that he probably wanted to know why I invited him. I told him right then that I had asked him to come to Birmingham to offer him the position of First Assistant Solicitor of Jefferson County. Without a moment's hesitation he said, "But I did not support you." My reply was that I knew he had not, but I nevertheless believed he was the best man I could get for the job, and that since during my candidacy I had not agreed to appoint as assistants none but supporters, I was free to do what I thought best for the public interest. After some discussion he told me he was sure I knew he would have to make a financial sacrifice to take the position, but that if for the public good I could appoint a man who had fought my election, he not only could but would accept. This pleased me greatly because I was confident that with him as First Assistant my office force would be very efficient. In addition to that force, I was also free to call on the Circuit Solicitor, who had promised the people that if elected he would serve under the County Solicitor. This strange situation existed because the Circuit Solicitor was a constitutional officer who, upon creation of the County Criminal Court with a County Solicitor, was left without any duties to perform.

My first task upon assuming office was to make an assessment of the sort of job that lay before me in line with my campaign promises. There were on the docket over three thousand criminal cases awaiting trials, nearly 100 of which were capital cases. One of my promises had been to clean up those dockets. Due in no small part to the prevailing fee system, the jail was filled to overflowing with prisoners. Costs known as "turn-key fees" were charged against prisoners when they were put in or let out of jail; there were also arrest fees, bond fees, fees for sleeping and eating. These fees were charged to prisoners when convicted, otherwise against a special state and county fund, which did not pay 100%. It was consequently of considerable financial interest to Court Clerks and Sheriffs for convictions to take place. A practice was said to have grown up under which Sheriff's informers would foment payday Saturday night crap games among colored industrial workers, report the games to the Sheriff, and the Sheriff would then raid the games, arresting all participants except the informers. Aware of this practice, I had promised the people during my campaign not only to prosecute vigorously all professional gamblers and informers who instigated crap games but to dismiss all cases against honest-to-goodness working payday crapshooters. After taking office, I found, on making a thorough investigation of prisoners, that a large number were in jail who had not been able to make bond. As a consequence, my first court action of any moment was to seek dismissal of approximately five hundred of the worker crapshooting cases. The Court promptly dismissed all of those cases, causing quite a furor among the beneficiaries of the fee system, some of whom had been my strong friends and loyal supporters. Loud complaints were aired against me. There were even those who talked of impeachment. They got nowhere. I think the most people were in fact *for* what I did. In addition to getting dismissal of the crap-game cases, I also kept in close touch with prisoners who wanted to plead guilty to minor offenses to keep from paying jail fees.

During my campaign I had promised to dispose of all capital cases as soon as possible after taking office. To accomplish this I arranged to have judges from other parts of the State assigned to Jefferson County. As a result, I brought the trial of capital cases almost completely up to date within my first year of office. I particularly recall trying one murder case that was ten years old. The defendant had been convicted of manslaughter in a neighboring county and had served his sentence during the ten years' delay in his Jefferson County case. As I recall, all the eyewitnesses to the Jefferson County crime were dead or had disappeared, and the chief testimony against the defendant was a dying statement of the deceased. This fact illustrates the necessity for trying criminal cases with reasonable expedition.

It would require a large volume to write in detail all of my interesting experiences during my two and a half years as Solicitor. I can therefore mention only a very few of them. During my campaign for Solicitor I ended a number of my published advertisements with this sentence: "Hugo Black believes it is as much the duty of a Solicitor to protect the innocent as it is to convict the guilty." Every assistant in my office was constantly admonished never to try to convict a defendant if there existed in the assistant's mind a reasonable doubt of guilt. Time and again my assistants sent for me as they were finishing cases, told me of their doubts about guilt, we so informed the jury, and the jury acquitted. I remember one occasion, however, in which the jury convicted after we made such a statement. It was one of those cases that turn up occasionally where prejudice of one kind or another has slipped into the record. When the jury brought in its verdict, without a moment's hestitation we asked Judge Fort to set aside that verdict and *nolle pros* [nullify the prosecution of] the case which he did. My record of convictions was rather high, and I have partially attributed it to the fact that the juries knew of my policy against putting to trial defendants whose guilt we doubted.

On the other hand, my policy was to do our best to convict people of whose guilt we were confident. I recall a case where a white man was accused of killing a Negro man. I thought the murder a brutal one but knew very well that, brutal as I deemed it to be, the difference in the races not only made the the job of prosecution an unpopular one with many people, but made conviction extremely difficult. For those reasons I declined to put the burden of prosecution on any assistant but took it on myself. In the first trial the jury could not agree on a verdict. While all were to convict, a mistrial had to be entered because eight stood out for first-degree murder, and four for manslaughter with a small sentence. On the second trial, four jurors were for conviction, eight for acquittal. The third trial never occurred. After the second trial I resigned and it was while [I was] in the army that my successor moved for a *nolle pros.* The motion was granted. I have always had great admiration for the jurors in those trials who voted to convict. Racial prejudice could not blind them to their duty. Perhaps I should not fail to mention that the defendant in the case had been a very strong supporter of mine in my race for Solicitor.

One other case was of such interest that I must record it—a case in which a colored man was accused of the rape of two young white girls. This case stands as proof that there are men in the South who can and do render honest verdicts in race cases even where women alleged to have been raped are white and the defendants charged with the rape are colored.

The defendant in this case was a Negro, about thirty-five years of age, who had been accused of raping two white girls, probably about twenty years of age. To represent the defendant the court appointed John Stone Hoskins, a Birmingham lawyer, who for some years had been claim agent for a steel and iron company in Birmingham. He was just then starting the practice of law on his own. As County Solicitor I knew that my office was going into the case with a strong belief that the defendant was guilty, but with no forewarning that the young, court-appointed lawyer was about to give our office a genuine walloping. The Circuit Solicitor, Joe Tate, who was then acting as my assistant, asked for the privilege of trying the case. It began with nothing to indicate whatever was about to happen. The two young ladies took the stand, each in turn testifying that they had to go home through a rather dimly lighted park, that they were approached by the defendant whom they positively identified, and that he had assaulted them after threatening them with dire consequences if they did not yield. In his cross-examination, John Hoskins treated them with complete courtesy and with near excessive kindness. He neither said nor did anything dramatic. Looking back on this cross-examination one is compelled to recall that out of his mild and gentle questions and the unexcited answers of the girls there emerged these brief but certain facts: This was the second or third night that these young ladies had been reprimanded by their parents for coming home later than they had been allowed to stay out. After the girls' testimony, it was John's time to reveal his witnesses and put on their evidence. To the surprise of everyone his witnesses turned out to be the defendant and several policemen, the latter of whom were all generally recognized to be the most trustworthy on the force. The first witness was the defendant. While, of course, I cannot recall his testimony verbatim, it went something like this:

Q. What is your name? (Name was given.)

Q. What is your business?
A. I am a burglar.

Q. How long have you been a burglar?
A. Ever since I was about fifteen years old.

Q. Where have you practiced your profession?
A. All round in different parts of the country.

Q. Have you ever served in any penitentiary for burglary?
A. Oh, yes, many of them.

Q. Will you name the places? (Here the defendant named a number of states.)

Q. Have you kept a record of your burglaries?
A. Oh, yessir.

Q. Where were you on the night these young ladies were assaulted in the park?
A. I was committing a burglary over on the southside here in Birmingham.

Q. Did you keep a record of the burglary and, if so, where?
A. I wrote it down in this here book, sir. (Taking a memoranda book out of his pocket.)

Q. Will you read to the jury what you wrote down. (Here the defendant read the date, where he was, what time it was and the goods he said he had taken from the homes he had burglarized.)

Q. Where are the goods you stole at that time?
A. Mr. McGill and the other police have them.

After the foregoing and much more of the same kind of testimony about other burglaries, as I recall, Mr. McGill, one of the best officers I ever knew, corroborated the defendant's statement about this particular burglary. His and other testimony coincided precisely with defendant's as to the burglary and the goods stolen. The date and the time of night the burglary took place were the same to the minute and hour that the two young ladies had testified they were raped by the "burglar." Needless to say, the jury, with considerably more than deliberate speed, returned a verdict of "not guilty," showing they were convinced beyond a reasonable doubt that the repeated statements of the defendant, "Mr. Hoskins, I am a burglar, but I ain't no raper," were true. Thus did a young appointed lawyer perform his duty for an indigent defendant and a white Alabama jury prove its merit and its worth.

IX

August, 1917 – I Resign as Solicitor and Go to World War I

Under the law my term as Solicitor was four years, to January, 1919. By the beginning of 1917—half way through my term—I was well pleased with the progress made in carrying out my campaign promises. By that time the Court had, on my motion, dismissed charges against all of the colored payday crapshooters whose games had, under long-established practice, been fomented by hired informers to fatten the purses of officers whose incomes were dependent on the fee system. For these dismissals I had been threatened with various types of punishment including impeachment. My campaign promise to chase professional gamblers to cover had largely been kept. One of these gamblers had sent word to me through his lawyers that I should arm myself because he intended to shoot me on sight. I sent word back to him that I did not and would not carry a weapon and wanted him to know that if he were coward enough to kill an unarmed man he could do so. Instead of bullying me, however, he quit gambling, and to my surprise ten years later, when I ran for the United States Senate, this very man was one of my most active and appreciated supporters.

By 1917 I had practically cleared up the tremendous backlog of cases as I had promised to do if elected. This had been accomplished because, at my suggestion, judges from other parts of the State had been assigned to Jefferson County, and because I had kept a grand jury, served by me personally, in session almost constantly to consider and take care of current court indictments and other business.

Vigorous prosecutions to carry out my campaign pledges could not be and were not carried on, however, without accumulating enemies, particularly in prohibition cases. Alabama's state liquor law was very obnoxious to many people, particularly in two respects. In the first place newspapers quite naturally did not want to obey the provision of that law making it a crime to publish advertisements about intoxicating liquors. They sought to have me agree not to enforce those provisions until they could test their constitutionality. Since I could not see any more reason for that than to hold up all other arrests and prosecutions until new laws had been constitutionally tested, I declined to do so. Finally I was forced to tell the press that if they sent papers on the street with such advertisements, I would regretfully feel it my duty under the law to cause the arrest of all responsible, from the publisher on down, and also to enjoin the violations as the law required. Naturally this did not please those papers that wished to get advertising revenue from whiskey and beer advertisements.

A second group of vigorous opponents to the State's prohibition laws were the brewery interests which made and sold beer. A prohibition State like Alabama found it difficult if not impossible to convict for the sale of beer without proof beyond a reasonable doubt by a chemical analysis that the beer being sold or possessed had enough alcohol in it to be intoxicating. The result was that in Alabama and many other states the "near beer" business sprang up and flourished overnight. Alabama countered by making it an offense to sell or possess beer or any liquid that looked like, tasted like, or foamed like beer. The brewing interests hired Forney Johnston, one of the best lawyers in Alabama. Mr. Johnston filed suit in the United States District Court to enjoin me from prosecuting for the sale, transportation, or possession of "near beer." He contended that the beer provisions of the State's law violated the Due Process Clause of the Fourteenth Amendment to the United States Constitution. This was one of my first serious brushes with the Due Process Clause. My defenses were that the State law made it a crime to possess or sell "near beer," that each separate case raised nothing but factual questions, that the "near beer" law was constitutional, and that the Federal Court was without jurisdiction to enjoin my actions. I defended the case personally before Judge Grubb, we tried it for some days, and the petition for injunction was dismissed.

This case did not end my legal skirmishes with Mr. Johnston, however. It turned out that he was the Attorney for the County Treasurer, whose duty it was to pay my Assistant Solicitors upon warrants drawn by the County Board of Revenue. By this time the Circuit Solicitor, Mr. Tate, had concluded to challenge the constitutionality of the State law under which I was serving as Solicitor. Mr. Tate and Mr. Johnston took the position that the State Act authorizing a County Solicitor was unconstitutional and therefore neither the County Solicitor (my position) nor his assistants could draw any pay at all out of the County treasury. Mr. Tate then employed as his assistants John McCoy, brother of a Methodist Bishop, Wallace McAdory, son of my old friend Walter McAdory, then the County Sheriff, and Jim Davis, brother of Ben Davis of the firm of Gibson & Davis, attorneys for the State Federation of Labor, and for the Board of Revenue, which was supposed to issue checks to pay my assistants and me. We litigated the validity of the Act creating the County Solicitor's Office, the trial judge decided in my favor, and the State Supreme Court upheld the Act. In the meantime I had taken a new look at the duties of my office as set out in the State Act, found it provided that the County Solicitor should represent all the County agencies, and I therefore notified the Board of Revenue that they were without authority to hire Gibson & Davis or any other lawyers—that I was the Board's lawyer. The Board decided otherwise and I, not forgetting the old slogan that "frequently the best defense is an offense," filed a proceeding before State Circuit Judge Sharpe, the oldest and perhaps the most highly respected civil judge on that Court. The case was heard for some days and then Judge Sharpe decided in my favor. The other side took no appeal, as I recall, and I became attorney for the very Board of Revenue that I had been compelled to fight in court to get our pay. That, of course, was quite a satisfactory result for me.

Mr. Tate and Mr. Johnston, attorney for the County Treasurer, then challenged the right of my assistants to draw their salaries. Quite naturally, Mr. Johnston's client, the County Treasurer, refused to pay them. The case wended its way to the State Supreme Court and in due course it handed down a Solomon-like opinion and judgment that I still believe no one could have anticipated. The Court again upheld the validity of the County Solicitor's Act, sustained my power under the Act to appoint assistants, but went on to say that it would be illegal as an abuse of discretion should I not first accept and use the services of Mr. Tate's appointees before appointing or using any others. I publicly announced at once that while Mr. Tate's assistants were nice gentlemen, I did not think I could conscientiously take them as my assistants, that the assistants I had were all I needed, and that I did not want to do anything that would cause the people to pay salaries to men who did not do a dollar's worth of work for a dollar's pay. Consequently I announced my resignation along with a request that the Governor appoint no one in my place but leave the work to be done by the Circuit Solicitor and his assistants. This course was followed. I resigned and Mr. Tate took charge as Circuit Solicitor, using the assistants he had named. For reasons which follow, I had already planned my future course.

World War I had already been formally declared when I resigned. Up to the date of that formal declaration I had been strongly against our getting into war with Germany or any other country. I saw no adequate reason for our entrance into the war then and have not seen one to this day. My views about that war were more nearly in accord with those of Secretary of State William Jennings Bryan, who resigned to keep from being involved in a war. But my views were quite different after our country formally entered the war. Within a very short time I talked over my feelings with my friend Judge Fort. I told him I was undecided as to whether I should enlist, even though I was exempt from the draft on account of both my job and my age. The Judge stated emphatically his belief that my first duty was not to go to war but to continue to serve the people of Jefferson County in the position to which they had elected me. He reminded me also that he felt the call of duty to join the army himself. He believed it was no more his duty to remain in office than it was mine, and told me that he was of the tentative opinion that if I resigned to enter the army he would do the same. I reminded him that his situation was quite different, for he had a family and I did not. But he stuck to his position. The result was that he persuaded me not to resign at that time.

When, however, the State Supreme Court held I must use assistants whom I had not appointed and could not control, I told Judge Fort I felt I could not satisfactorily perform my duties with those assistants and would therefore prefer to resign. He agreed with my decision, agreed that I was then free from further responsibility to the people to remain Solicitor, and further agreed with my decision to join the army. He then continued to serve as judge.

My next move was to talk with the army people about enlisting. I knew absolutely nothing about the army, not even how to march or drill in any way. Everyone to whom I spoke, however, told me that I should not enlist, that the Government needed officers far more than enlisted men. So I took a training course under Crampton Harris, a practicing lawyer but also an officer in the State Militia, applied to Officers Training School, and was accepted to take my training at Fort Oglethorpe, Georgia, not far from Chattanooga, Tennessee. There I was assigned to a field artillery battery commanded by *Major* Crampton Harris, who had by that time been called to active war service. Feeling that my knowledge of mathematics was inadequate to prepare me to be an officer of the Field Artillery, I so informed Major Harris and requested that I be reassigned to the Infantry. When I asked to be assigned to the Infantry training, Major Harris told me that I could get a school trigonometry text book and learn everything about angles that a Field Artillery officer needed to know. When with some fear I protested he said, "You are in the army now and you will go where you are assigned. The Field Artillery needs officers." That ended my protest. I got a school trigonometry text book and learned something about angles. But I was always afraid I did not learn enough.

I never worked harder in my life than I did in those three months at the Officers Training School. Perhaps I also never felt less qualified to learn anything than I did to learn to be an artillery officer. In that training I rode bareback on old army horses until I felt each one was equipped with a razor where I sat, risking my life—I thought—not only in riding bareback but in being blindfolded as well! I can yet remember when, with eyes shut and teeth clinched, I found myself still safely astride a barebacked horse which, much to my astonishment, was successful in having his feet hit the ground after jumping over a fence too high, it seemed to me, for any horse to jump.

Some years before, when I had made the honor roll and graduated from the University of Alabama Law School, I felt I had merely been given that which I had earned. When, however, at the end of the Fort Oglethorpe training I received a Commission of Captain in the Field Artillery, my feeling of gratitude could not be expressed in words. I felt qualified to be a lawyer but not an army officer. With this feeling I was assigned to help train a regiment of old cavalrymen to become Field Artillerymen. Such a job is not an easy one, even for a trained horseman, which I was not. On the first day of my new assignment Sergeant Grady, a longtime cavalry First Sergeant, made me feel at home when, with a sly grin, he took me to the stables, pointed out another "razor-back" horse which, he said, would be mine, but which, unfortunately, he informed me, would not be supplied with a saddle!

X

Captain Black of the Field Artillery

The 81st Field Artillery Unit to which I was assigned for duty, November 3, 1917, was stationed near Chattanooga, Tennessee, a short distance from Oglethorpe. It had been for many years the 11th Cavalry in the regular army. When I arrived, a regular army Major was in command of the Regiment. I was a Captain in the "national" army but our group did not rank very high in the estimation of most "regulars." For war training purposes, however, commissions were granted to so-called provisional Second Lieutenants, which meant that they, after several months of special training, were accepted, like West Point graduates, as members of the regular army. National army officers, however, whether first or second Lieutenants, Captains, Majors, Colonels or whatnots, were never considered by the regular army to be a part of it. So when I went to the 81st Field Artillery I found myself in a battery where, being a Captain, I was supposed to be in command but where I was actually serving under the command of a provisional Second Lieutenant who had taken only a three months' course at an officers training camp, just as I had done. I found that my assignment as a National Army Captain under this type of provisional Second Lieutenant was not exceptional, but customary. And my assignment in this manner continued for several weeks until an old Cavalry Colonel, with a pugnacious, frizzly-looking beard, suddenly appeared on the scene to take command. We later learned that he wore the beard to conceal a scar across his throat which had been put there, it seemed, by one of his soldiers—at least that was the only information passed out to us. He was a West Pointer and his name was William T. Littebrandt. A few minutes after his arrival, notice was given that in less than an hour's time the Colonel would talk to all the officers of the regiment at regiment headquarters. We were all there; and this "National Army" officer, feeling wholly out of place, was practically shaking with fright from an awareness of his ignorance about the army, its workings and its affairs. The Colonel's loud voice, his fierce-looking beard, and his proficient use of army profanity were not calculated to, nor did they, allay my fears. His talk made me feel even more inadequate than I had before. When he had finished speaking, I recall gathering from his remarks that this was a pretty bad regiment, that the bearded Colonel was a rough old officer who would tolerate no foolishness, and that he would straighten out the regiment or kick all of us out of the army. He closed, telling us to go back to our tents and prepare answers to written questions he was submitting to us and to get our papers to his office as soon as possible. The information he wanted was where we had gone to school, our records there, what college degrees we had, what had been our occupations in civilian life, what, if any, political offices we had held, and what had been our annual incomes. My answers, according to my memory, covered less than a half page. From that half page I expected nothing but to be let alone. The next morning our provisional Second Lieutenant took us as usual out on the drill field. Near ten o'clock a messenger from the Colonel sought me out and informed me that the Colonel wished to see me. That really frightened me. I tried to think of what I had done that would cause Jesse James (what we already were calling the Colonel) to send for me. Reporting to my Battery Commander, the Second Lieutenant, I obtained his permission to leave and went on my way. Happily I went by my tent, found my army ritual, memorized instructions as to what one should do and say when approaching a Colonel, and with a fast-beating heart soon found myself standing before him saying: "Sir, Captain Black reports according to instructions." Without even so much as a glance in my direction I heard a mumbling through the beard which, translated into English, I finally made out to be: "Captain Black, you are the Adjutant of this Regiment; hang up your hat on that nail over there" (pointing) "and have a seat in that chair" (pointing again). I answered: "Yes, sir, but I know little about the army and nothing whatever about the Adjutant's duties. What must I do?" His answer was: "Sit down and I will tell you what you have to do and why I selected you. But first I want you to sit down and read these endless pages of a Second Lieutenant's response to the short, simple questions I asked all of you to answer." The Colonel went on to say that the Second Lieutenant's answers were the longest he received and mine were the shortest. "I learned," he said, "that you were a successful lawyer in Birmingham, Alabama, that the people had elected you prosecuting attorney, which office you held until you resigned. You told me what you had been earning. That gave me all the information I wanted. You are the kind of man I want for my Adjutant. I can work with you, but this other man would drive me crazy with his infinite details. I want you this minute to begin to read the answers from all these officers, then I want you to select for me, according to *rank,* a company commanding officer of every battery. I want to utilize the talents that have made these new National Army officers successful in civilian life. Now you know what your duties are. The sooner you perform them and report to me, the sooner we'll have a complete reorganization of the regiment. Now get busy!"

Of course this report of what the Colonel said to me is not verbatim but it is the substance, as nearly as I remember, of my first meeting with this remarkable man. His talk was then, as always, sprinkled with profanity. But such language coming from him did not, to those who knew him, sound coarse, immoral, or obscene, or even irreligious. And I learned to know him well. He kept me with him until the war was over. When the old 81st reached the battle front on September 11, 1918, he was not with them. Nor was I. The War Department had denied his fervent plea to go with his regiment, promising to let him train and carry with him later a new fighting brigade. He had me transferred to his new brigade. Army orders caught me in Birmingham on the way to the port of embarkation, sending me back to Fort Sill, Oklahoma, to report to the Colonel. His first words were: "Mad as hell with me, aren't you?" "Maybe not quite that mad, Sir, but certainly not happy," I replied. "Well," the old man said, "what do you think about me? I graduated from West Point, and have been waiting to fight all of my life. You have not. In spite of that my plan is to make you a Major and brigade Adjutant at once. Then when I take my new brigade to the front (this group of soldiers who have been firing artillery at Fort Sill for years), I am going to take you with me as a full Colonel in command of one of my three batteries."

But such was not to happen! In a very short time, November 11 and the Armistice rolled around and neither my Colonel nor I ever reached the front. We were still at Fort Sill and participated in the Armistice parade in Lawton, Oklahoma. The very day of the Armistice, however, the Colonel told me, "Now you will want to go back to your law; draw up the order for your discharge and go on home." As I recall, my discharge was the second that went through. The first I signed was that of Colonel Morrow of Birmingham. I went back to Birmingham to practice law. Shortly thereafter, Colonel Littebrandt was assigned to Fort McClellan at Anniston, Alabama. There he suffered his last illness. His wife called to tell me to please come over. I arrived too late to see this grand old man again. He is another of the many men I have known whom I respected and loved.

Captain Black of the Field Artillery had tried to serve his country in war. He was a soldier from August 3, 1917, until about September 20, 1918, but never fired a shot against the nation's enemy. Disappointed as he was not to smell the smoke and hear the noise of battle at the front lines, it was not long until the sheer joy of living made him realize how fortunate he had been. There is to me no glamour in war. And I am still optimistic enough to hope that some day, doubtless not in my lifetime, there will be a United Nations of the World with adequate power and force to declare that war will be no more, and thus make one of the world's oldest dreams come true.

XI

Armistice Day: Peace I Return to Birmingham to Practice Law

November 11, 1918, an Armistice in World War I was agreed to. That day my old regiment, the 81st Field Artillery, reached the front line trenches, ready to fight. I was not with them, having been stopped en route at Birmingham and ordered back to Fort Sill to transfer to another well-trained artillery brigade. I was then in Birmingham to attempt to arrange to pay the First National Bank my part of a note, in which I had joined with other Directors of the Commercial Bank, to guarantee the First National against any loss it might suffer from taking over all of Commercial's assets and discharging all its liabilities. Most of the note signers wanted to employ Forney Johnston, one of Alabama's ablest lawyers, to deny and contest the validity of the note. My friend Louis Pizitz and I, however, took the position that we had signed the note in good faith and that the First National entered the agreement in reliance on our promise. For these reasons Mr. Pizitz and I tried from the beginning to obtain an agreement from all the other parties to permit us to pay our part of the note and give us a receipt in full. This we were unable to do. When I returned to Birmingham, however, on my way to France, I was able to settle by conveying to the First National, as full discharge of my obligation on the note, substantially all the property I had accumulated from my law practice. What happened to the lawsuit I do not know to this day. Since I had spent more while in the army than the government paid me, the transfer of my property left me practically dead broke when I went back home to take up the practice of law again. This slight and disastrous foray with the banking business left me with the distinct impression that it is usually true that as a shoemaker should stick to his last, so also should a lawyer stick to his law.

Arriving back at Birmingham as early as possible after the Armistice, I found myself without a job, an office, or a client, without money or other property, and even without a boarding house. Alighting from the train I went straight to the Molton Hotel, which was managed by Harry New, an old friend, rented a room, and for several reasons felt very much as I had when I arrived in the City years before to begin a law practice. One similarity was that the Molton Hotel was at the corner of 20th Street and Fifth Avenue, less than half a block from my first boarding place—Mrs. Crim's. I stayed at the Hotel only a short time, however, for 1918 was the "flu" year. I had been fortunate enough to miss the flu in the army and could not believe that the disease would suddently hit me after leaving the army. But it did. A doctor friend, C. C. Wiley, learning that I was at the Molton, dropped in to see me and discovering that I had a temperature of more than 104, called an ambulance. Over my protest he sent me to the Southside Infirmary, called my regular doctor, Cabot Lull, and within that infirmary I remained nearly two weeks. The "flu" became pneumonia, and, again, as had been the case when I was a small boy, the disease was almost fatal. Having none of our present miracle drugs, a pitcher of ice water, together with torturing ice rubs on my hot body, finally broke my high temperature and I am convinced saved my life. My old friend, Ed Irwin, whom I had served as best man at his and Elizabeth Ramey's wedding in Atlanta, took me from the hospital to their home and kept me there until I had fully recuperated.

After coming back to Birmingham I did not remain broke very long. As soon as I recovered from my illness I rented offices in the First National Bank Building. Clients began to hire me immediately. As I recall the first was George H. Bodeker, who had been Chief of Police when I was Police Court Judge, and who had, for the Police Force, presented me with a solid gold watch the last day I served as Judge—October 22, 1912, when I was twenty-six years of age. Mr. Bodeker, who by 1918 had established the Bodeker National Detective Agency over a large area of the country, retained me to handle all his business immediately after I opened my office. Within a few days of my retention by Bodeker, Goodwyn & Ross, a law firm at Bessemer, twelve miles from Birmingham, came to my office and arranged for me to try all their cases in Birmingham. Having no automobile, I looked around, fell in love with a Paige car, and promised to pay the dealer around $3000 for it. The dealer was Lawrence Pennington, an old member of the County Board of Revenue, and when I bought the car he retained me to represent his company which I did for many years.

Allen and Bell was an old partnership which had long handled a large criminal practice and many civil cases. Mr. Bell had died while I was in the army and about the time I returned Mr. Allen was suffering from an illness that later caused his death. He asked me to join him under the firm name of Allen & Black and I did, keeping their Allen & Bell's old offices in the Farley Building. One of my old commanding Field Artillery officers, Colonel Crampton Harris, had by this time returned and I hired him for a time, later taking him in as a partner. That my business had become very lucrative in a short time was shown by the fact that within about three months from purchase I paid for my Paige car in full out of my earnings and in addition repaid my doctor brother's widow three hundred dollars I had borrowed to pay my hospital bills.

XII

Law Business Prospers

It did not take me long to learn that in agreeing to represent the Bodeker Detective Agency on a regular retainer I had undertaken quite a job. Almost immediately they brought me two cases, spectacular in nature and involving many dangers. Both cases were front-page news for quite a time. In the first, Bodeker's agents had been themselves arrested for conspiring with the mother of a child in Fayette County, West Alabama, to kidnap her own child. In the second case, Bodeker's agency, which had a protective contract with the Tutwiler Hotel at Birmingham, had caused the arrest of a Birmingham lady on the charge of stealing some bonds from under the bed of a hotel room where she was a week-end guest. Under our agreement I, of course, had to defend the agents charged with kidnapping, and Mr. Bodeker insisted that I should help the State prosecute the lady charged with stealing the bonds.

The kidnapping case occurred in a small town in a rather small county. The kidnapped child's father, who was divorced from the child's mother, was a widely popular doctor who lived in Fayette. The mother, on the other hand, was living in California and found Fayette County feeling was against her. The local judge convicted and imposed the maximum punishment, which we, of course, appealed. Finding out that a prior controversy between the father and mother over the child's custody had been tried in Birmingham, I hitched the new case onto the old and asked for custody for the mother. The Supreme Court of Alabama refused to grant the father's motion to bar the Birmingham case, and the lawyer for the father and I went to California and took quite a bit of evidence. A Birmingham

Circuit Court Judge tried the case and finally awarded the child to the mother. The State Supreme Court affirmed, and this prompted the child's grandparents not to push the criminal case further. This, of course, was a victory for my client, the Detective Agency.

The second case did not turn out so well for my client. I could not convince my client that having a special prosecutor against a woman might not help to bring about a conviction, and so I had to prosecute against my own judgment. If having a lawyer is sometimes good for his client, this case proved beyond the shadow of a doubt it is not always so. I had a number of real close friends on the jury that tried this case. My good friend, Reese Murray, a former FBI Agent, was representing the defendant. Reese started after the "Special Prosecutor for Money" at the very beginning and kept up his attacks to the very end. The lady whose bonds were alleged to have been stolen cannot truthfully be said to have strengthened her case. She was a richly dressed widow who came into the courtroom with black silks that swished as she walked. In her hands she carried a lorgnette, which now and then, especially when looking at the jury, she put to her eyes. When asked if she owned the bonds, her answer to me was: "Mr. Black, you will have to ask my broker for a description of the bonds. You know I do not keep up with things like that." Suffice it to say, her broker did give the jury an accurate description of the bonds, and the description was that which other evidence showed to be the same as bonds the defendant sold at the races in New Orleans.

After the jury came in with its prompt verdict of acquittal, a friend on the jury who had borrowed three dollars from me at the Knights of Pythias Lodge came by my office to pay me the loan. I asked him how the jury returned its verdict. His answer, which I think I shall never forget, was: "Hugo, do you think the jury would convict a woman for stealing from that damned old bitch."

This story may be thought by many to present an irrefutable argument against the jury system, but who can say such a result would not have been accepted by the Founders, who provided for such trials by the friends, neighbors, and acquaintances of the defendants?

The Women in My Life

Shortly after I returned to Birmingham, an old friend, Val Cobb, invited me to live in a "bach" located adjacent to Niazuma Avenue, South. Val, a member of the old and well-known Cobb family of Georgia, more or less ran the bach. He and I had been good friends since I met him when he was secretary to the President of the Tennessee Coal, Iron and Railroad Company and while I was canvassing in that office for Solicitor of Jefferson County in 1914.

To reach the bach from Highland Avenue it was necessary to go up a steep hill. Along in December, while going up that hill, I saw a beautiful young lady struggling up the hill. She was wearing, as was then the style, a long, very tight-fitting dress. As I learned later, it was the uniform of a "Yeomanette" in the Navy. And I also learned later that this Yeomanette was Josephine Foster, daughter of Dr. Sterling J. Foster, whose home was just around the corner from the bach. She had been released from government service in the Navy, as I had been released from the Field Artillery. I began to see her from time to time at various places, and the more I met her the better I liked her. Before long I began to talk to and see her as often as she would let me.

From these experiences I soon learned there were many other men who were also captivated by her beauty and charm. So that when I decided that she was the person I wanted to marry, it was not surprising to learn that there were other—nice, promising, attractive—young men who were pursuing her diligently with the same serious purposes that were mine. Suffice it to say that she finally made me supremely happy by accepting my proposal, and we set February 23, 1921, the day after Washington's birthday and four days before mine, as our wedding day. Only a few very close relatives, the boys at the bach, and my good friends Albert Lee Smith and Hugh Locke were present at the wedding. By that time I had a very prosperous law practice for a Birmingham lawyer, and my Josephine and I decided to spend a month's honeymoon in sunny California. From then we lived together a little more than thirty years. They were grand years. During that time we had three children, Hugo, Jr., born in 1922, Sterling Foster, born in 1924, and Martha Josephine, born in 1933 and named for her mother and mine.

My wife's health was not good during the last years of her life and her sweet, kind, gentle, generous spirit left this world sometime during the night hours of December 6–7, 1951. I was a most fortunate person to win and keep this lovely person as my wife for so long a time, and my children are equally fortunate to have had such a lovely lady for their mother.

For a number of years after she went away, this was a dark and dreary world for me. In fact, I often thought the sun would never shine again. But five years after her death another Alabama woman, Elizabeth Seay DeMeritte, with an equally sweet, kind, gentle, and generous spirit, came into my office as my secretary. Less than a year and a half later she agreed to come into my home as my wife. She is still here and radiates her sweetness, beauty and charm—day after day, week after week, month after month, and year after year. My fervent hope is that when my remains are put to rest close to Josephine in the Arlington National Cemetery on the little hill that overlooks the beauty of our Nation's Capital, my sweet and gentle Elizabeth will sometime join us on that sloping hilltop. I cannot believe that any man has been or could be more grateful for the women in his life than I am.

PART TWO

The Years Between

In this section of the book I would like to briefly bridge the gap between the time when Hugo's memoirs end, in about 1922, and when my own pick up, in 1964. There are several good biographies available for the reader who is interested in a more complete account of Hugo's life. I will do no more here than sketch in the main events so that the remainder of the book will be understandable.

Hugo ran for the office of United States Senator from the State of Alabama in 1926. The seat was being vacated by Senator Oscar W. Underwood, and the other candidates were John Bankhead, son of the former U.S. Senator; Thomas E. Kilby, former Governor of Alabama; Breck Musgrove, a wealthy coal operator; and Judge James J. Mayfield of Birmingham.

Hugo had saved $10,000 by the time he entered the race, and he refused to spend more than that during the thirteen months he campaigned. In fact, he spent only about $7000 in all. Hugo had some wonderful stories about that race, and no wonder. He had set aside his law practice and visited every county in the state in his Model T Ford, working from farmer to farmer, merchant to merchant, and meeting to meeting. One day he was riding through the countryside in search of votes. He approached a farmer out in a field and, handing him a campaign card, introduced himself and asked the man to vote for him. The farmer looked at the card, turned it over, and read every word on each side. He then returned it to Hugo, saying, "Sorry, but I can't vote for you. I've already decided to vote for John Bankhead."

When Hugo asked him why, the farmer answered, "Well, his father was a good Senator, so I just thought I ought to vote for the son."

Hugo conceded that the senior Bankhead had indeed been a good Senator, but then he asked the farmer if he had a son himself. When the farmer said he did, Hugo asked, "Do you plan to educate him and try to see that he gets opportunities in life?"

The farmer said that he was going to send his son to college and give him the advantages he himself didn't have when he was growing up.

Hugo then asked, "Do you think that someday your son might become, well, Probate Judge of this county?"

"Sure," replied the farmer, "if my son qualifies for Probate Judge there is no reason why he shouldn't get that job."

"He can't do that!" Hugo said. "Wilbur Nolan is Probate Judge of this county and he has a son. According to your theory, *his* son should get the job. Wilbur has made the county a good Probate Judge."

The farmer squinted at Hugo for a moment and then said, "Let me see your card again." He reread the card carefully and asked, "Do you have any spares? I'd like to give them out to all my friends."

Hugo's campaign slogan came out of this encounter. "Does the son of a Senator always have to be a Senator and the son of a farmer *always* have to be a farmer?"

He won another precinct in the state by beating a county checkers champion, and he bested the front-runners, Bankhead and Kilby, in a big debate they had in North Alabama even though he hadn't been invited to participate. Hugo hired an old man who owned a broken-down dray and a horse that looked about half dead. He got someone to paint two large signs and to get the old man a permit to sit outside the auditorium.

The afternoon of the debate, the hall was packed and the two candidates attacked each other pretty vigorously. After a couple of hours, the townfolk filed out of the building hotly discussing the issues presented by their candidates. The moment they stepped out of doors, they came face to face with Hugo's dray. On either side there was a large sign: "Bankhead says that Kilby will not do. Kilby says that Bankhead will not do. They are both right. Vote for Hugo Black." Everyone broke into gales of laughter and all the newspapers picked up the story. He may not have been invited, but Hugo managed to turn the entire event to his own advantage.

In his years in the Senate, though he was a strict prohibitionist himself, Hugo participated in the repeal of the Eighteenth Amendment because he felt that though prohibition worked pretty well in Alabama, it didn't in the rest of the country. He supported Al Smith for President when he became the nominee of the Democratic party. That position didn't win

Hugo any friends in Alabama with Al Smith being a Catholic *and* a wet. He held vigorous investigations into public utility holding companies and the Air and Ocean Mail contracts. The result was the Merchant Marine Act of 1936 and the Public Utility Holding Company Act of that same year. Hugo was responsible for the first lobbying reforms in the history of the Senate. The first wage and hour bill, the Fair Labor Standards Act, made a thirty-hour week the standard in an effort to spread jobs during the Great Depression. The bill was proposed by Hugo and passed in the Senate on July 31, 1937, but was defeated in the House. The precedent had been set, and in 1938, after Hugo had left the Senate, a Wage and Hour Bill was passed by both Houses of Congress.

In 1937, because the Supreme Court had consistently struck down legislation for social and economic reform, President Franklin D. Roosevelt proposed to enlarge the Court. Hugo was in favor of that plan, called the Court-Packing Plan, and made a radio speech for it on February 23, 1937. The furor caused by the proposal is well known.

The next open seat on the Court had been promised to Joseph Robinson of Arkansas, the Senate leader in favor of the Court-Packing Plan. Robinson died suddenly in July, 1937, and with the retirement of Justice Willis Van Devanter, President Roosevelt nominated Hugo to the Supreme Court on August 11, 1937. Hugo was confirmed by a vote of 63 to 16. There was, however, a lot of opposition, largely from big business interests and a few powerful newspapers. Hugo told me he took the Constitutional oath immediately, in the office of Ed Halsey, Secretary of the Senate, because "I wasn't taking any chances. I knew that my enemies in big business and the press would inflame the public against me so much that they might get a judge to enjoin me from taking the oath. After I had taken the oath, my enemies would have to impeach me for something I had done *since* taking the oath of office."

Chief Justice Charles Evans Hughes administered the judicial oath on the first day of Court, despite a motion that was attempted to keep Hugo from taking the oath and despite a demonstration outside the court of about 400 people marching around the building with mourning bands around their arms for the "death of the Republic."

On September 13, 1937, the Pittsburgh *Post Gazette*'s reporter Ray Sprigle wrote an "exposé" revealing that Hugo had been a member of the Ku Klux Klan. Although it was hailed as a disclosure, that same information had been reported in Alabama a number of times. As a result of the furor that arose, Hugo made a public address in October, 1937, explaining his Klan membership. At the end of his talk he said that he would never again speak publicly about the matter, and he never did.

Years later, however, in December, 1968, Eric Sevareid and Martin Agronsky conducted a television interview with Hugo in which the matter was discussed. It seemed to me that his answers to the questions about the Klan were innocuous enough, but before the interview was broadcast Hugo requested that the program focus on the Court and not on the Klan. It turned out that the decision had already been made to eliminate that part of the program, so Hugo's request was academic. For the sake of history, however, it seems appropriate to give the gist of those deleted remarks here.

Mr. Sevareid asked if the great crisis in Hugo's life came at the time of his Supreme Court appointment when it was revealed that he had been a member of the Klan. Hugo explained that it hadn't been a crisis and that the information had been published before by politicians who had run against him in the past. He said that he felt that the Klan had been a different organization when he was a member than what it was at the time of the interview. The Klan in Alabama, Hugo said, was organized largely by Masons and he had been a Mason since he was twenty-one years old. "I also joined the Knights of Pythias before I left home in Ashland to move to Birmingham to practice law. I joined an organization from Texas called the Pretorian. I joined the Odd Fellows. I joined many groups."

Hugo, in response to another question, said that undoubtedly some of the members had been racist, but then, it was like any other lodge: "Nearly all the preachers belonged to it."

Hugo sometimes spoke to me about joining the Klan. He said that most people thought the reason he joined was that he was politically ambitious. Hugo said that, in fact, the Klan, as an *organization,* never backed him for any office, though of course many individual members were for him. He said that the main reason he joined was so that he would have an equal chance in trying cases before jurors who were largely Klan members in Alabama at that time, and because most of the defendants as well as most of the lawyers who represented corporations and who opposed Hugo were also members.

Hugo also told me that he resisted joining the Klan for a long time. Finally, however, when his Jewish friend and benefactor, Herman Beck, urged him to join, he gave the matter a second thought. "Hugo," Beck had told him, "if good men like you don't join the Klan it will be left to some of the roughnecks." It was at that point that Hugo submitted his application for membership. Hugo told me about a speech he had made to the Klan and said it "was one of the strongest speeches that I ever made urging respect and obedience to the Constitution and the Bill of Rights."

Many other people have given reasons for what they believe motivated Hugo, in their effort to seek an answer to the paradox of one of this century's most widely known liberals having joined the Klan in the first place. I think that Hugo's words, as I've reported them, should stand.

Chief Justice Charles Evans Hughes welcomed Hugo warmly as a brother on the Court, even though Hugo had, as a Senator, voted against Hughes's confirmation on philosophical and economic differences.

The Chief Justice encouraged Hugo to dissent whenever he wished, and Hugo—a natural challenger—did so in his first year on the bench as well as throughout his judicial career. His opinions, both majority and dissenting, were forceful. They were couched in simple and concise language and delivered with vigor and passion. He had the pleasure of seeing a great number of them eventually become the law of the land.

Among the more notable of his dissents* was in the *Betts* v. *Brady* case (316 U.S. 455) in 1942. Hugo said in his dissent that "no man shall be deprived of counsel merely because of his poverty." Twenty-one years later, Hugo had the satisfaction of delivering a majority opinion of the Court in the landmark *Gideon* v. *Wainwright* case (372 U.S. 335 [1963]) overturning *Betts* and ordering a retrial for Gideon with Court-appointed counsel.

Another outstanding dissent was *Colegrove* v. *Green* (328 U.S. 549) in 1946. Hugo dissented to the majority's denial of equal representation in voting.

A case in which people are always interested is *Korematsu* v. *United States* (323 U.S. 214), written by Hugo in 1944 shortly after the attack on Pearl Harbor. It has come in some disrepute as racist because it resulted in putting over 100,000 Japanese-American citizens and their relatives in concentration camps.

This opinion was written long before I knew Hugo, and he didn't speak of it to me, but I sat in on his occasional meetings with various groups of students. Almost invariably they asked Hugo about that case, and invariably Hugo would answer the same way.

He stoutly maintained that if the circumstances were the same now as they were then, he would do it the same way. "The Japanese had just attacked Pearl Harbor and we were in a state of war with Japan," he would tell them. "There were fears that California would be infiltrated and taken

*A full list of the cases on which Justice Black wrote is to be found starting on page 317.

over by the Japanese. Hysteria was everywhere. Some Japanese people had been attacked on the streets by fearful citizens. The Japanese were distinguishable by their features and were also in danger. Reports were coming in through the press and radio that Japanese planes had been sighted close to New York. Yes, given the circumstances, I would still write *Korematsu* the same way." That seemed to satisfy the students.

Another surprising decision that Hugo and William O. Douglas were always asked about was *Minersville School District* v. *Gobitis,* the famous Flag Salute case of 1940 (310 U.S. 586). Hugo, Bill, and Frank Murphy joined Felix Frankfurter in the opinion that the children of Jehovah's Witnesses could be compelled by the state to salute the United States flag.

I spoke to Bill Douglas about this in 1977, after Hugo died, and his version of what happened was very much the same as what Hugo had always told me. Bill said that he and Hugo had great respect for Felix when he was first appointed to the Court. Through his writings and public statements, they had put him down as a flaming liberal. "But," said Bill, "it was the first Flag Salute case that disillusioned us."

"Yet didn't you and Hugo vote in favor of that decision?"

Bill replied, "We all joined the opinion to that effect. The first time around Felix wrote the sole opinion and, to the end, Hugo and I could never understand why we agreed to it to begin with. It gave legislatures pretty broad control over all First Amendment rights."

Bill then said that three years later in *West Virginia State Board of Education* v. *Barnette* (319 U.S. 624 [1943]) they rescinded their vote and righted the matter.

During the 1940s, Justices William O. Douglas, Frank Murphy, and Wiley Rutledge were often with Hugo to form a majority or to register dissent, but in 1949 both Justices Murphy and Rutledge died, leaving Hugo and Justice Douglas again often in the minority.

In the early fifties, during the so-called "McCarthy Era," Hugo and Bill Douglas were busy upholding the rights of the individual, mostly in dissenting opinions, and by so doing were earning a lot of unpopularity with some elements of American society. Epithets such as "Pinko" and "Commie" were hurled at them. Hugo was used to this abuse because back in Alabama when he was introducing new and creative ideas, many were calling him a "Bolshevik." However much abuse he received, he never wavered in his belief that the First Amendment to the Constitution protected the right of those who spoke or wrote ideas inimical to our form of government as well as of those who loved and revered it. In a brief dissent in the case of *Dennis* v. *United States* (341 U.S. 494 [1951]) Hugo expounded the thesis that freedom of speech affords the best and strongest safeguard against sedition.

Hugo's dissent in *Adamson* v. *California* (332 U.S. 46[1947]) was the one that he himself selected as the most powerful—and the one that had had the most effect. Alan Barth, in the piece he wrote about Hugo's death published in the Washington *Post* on September 26, 1971, described that case as follows:

> Black argued throughout his career on the bench that the due process clause of the 14th Amendment was designed to make the articles of the Bill of Rights (originally applicable only to the federal government) binding as well upon the states. This view was set forth by him in a major dissenting opinion in a case called *Adamson* v. *California* decided in 1947.
>
> He never succeeded in persuading a majority of the Court to accept this view. One by one, however, through a process of selective incorporation, the Court has ruled over the years that the 14th Amendment protects against infringement by the states the liberties accorded by the First Amendment, the Fourth Amendment, the Fifth Amendment's privilege against self-incrimination, the Sixth Amendment's rights to notice, confrontation of witnesses and the assistance of counsel, and the Eighth Amendment's prohibition of cruel and unusual punishment.

The majority opinion that Hugo considered his best writing was that of *Chambers* v. *Florida* (309 U.S. 227), a 1940 case wherein Hugo, for a unanimous Supreme Court, voided the death sentences of Chambers and other blacks who had been picked up by the local police in Florida after the brutal murder of a white man. These blacks had been questioned night and day for eight days, were not allowed to see family or friends, and when questioned had each been surrounded by four to ten men. On the morning of the eighth day, the petitioners confessed. The death sentences were based on these confessions.

Hugo wrote in that opinion:

> Under our constitutional system, Courts stand against any winds that blow as havens of refuge for those who might otherwise suffer because they are helpless, weak, outnumbered, or because they are non-conforming victims of prejudice and public excitement.

Hugo felt so strongly about the *Chambers* case that he could never read aloud from his opinion without tears streaming down his face.

Roosevelt is said to have called in some of his newspaper friends after the *Chambers* case was announced and asked them if they were not now ashamed of themselves for making such an outcry against Hugo's appointment.

As a matter of fact, despite the controversy surrounding Hugo, he was acknowledged by a majority of the people and much of the media as a Justice of intelligence and integrity, one who followed the precepts of the Constitution as he saw it.

During his busy years on the Court, Hugo still found the time to continue his program of self-improvement by intensive reading. He loved the Greek and Roman classics, essays, history, and philosophy. He read continually about the history of the Constitutional Convention in Philadelphia, and always he read with pencil in hand, so that he could annotate in the margin his own ideas, whether in agreement or disagreement with the author. He penciled his own index in the back of many books for easy reference when writing an opinion or a speech.

His reading and hard work were a source of solace to Hugo during the "lonely fifties," when not only was he in the minority on the Court much of the time but he also lost his wife, Josephine, in 1951.

The coming of Earl Warren as Chief Justice in 1953 marked the beginning of a brighter era for Hugo. After Warren, there came the appointment in 1956 of William J. Brennan, Jr., who with Justice Douglas and Hugo formed the nucleus of a new liberal majority in the Court.

Chief Justice Warren handed down for a unanimous Court the *Brown* v. *Board of Education* case (347 U.S. 483) in 1954, outlawing segregation in the public schools, which caused a tremendous upheaval in the South. Even before 1954 Hugo's popularity in Alabama was at an all-time low, but after the *Brown* decision he was reviled and despised by many of his former friends in the South. They complained that their way of life had been disturbed and destroyed by the villainous Supreme Court, aided and abetted by their fellow Southerner, Hugo Black. Hugo was called a renegade and a traitor.

It was in this atmosphere of hatred and resentment that I came to work for Justice Black on March 15, 1956.

I had met Hugo for the first time in Washington, D.C., in 1954, at his office in the United States Supreme Court. I was then working for the Federal District Court in Birmingham, Alabama, and stopped in to pay my respects. In 1956, through his son's recommendation, I became Justice Black's secretary. For almost the first seventy years of his life, therefore, I did not know Hugo Black. For the next fifteen years of his life I was successively (and sometimes simultaneously) his secretary, his wife, and his unabashed hero-worshiper.

For fifteen years I had been a deputy clerk in the office of Mr. William

E. Davis, clerk of the United States District Court for the Northern District of Alabama at Birmingham. Among the lawyers I met on my job was Hugo Black, Jr., who had come to Birmingham, fresh out of Yale, to practice law.

One day in mid-February of 1956, my friend Mary Tortorici walked into the office and said excitedly: "Elizabeth, little Hugo just came by to see me and asked if I wanted to go to Washington to be his father's secretary." Mary couldn't leave Birmingham, but she did recommend me for the job. My husband, Fred DeMeritte, and I had decided to separate, but because he was running for Mayor of Fairfield, Alabama, we were being discreet about it. Still, the timing of this job possibility seemed perfect for me.

The next day Hugo, Jr., came by the office and told me he had called his daddy to tell him he wanted to send Mrs. Elizabeth DeMeritte up the following week for an interview. Hugo, Jr., had said, "Daddy, she is the best I can get down here."

I learned much later, as reported to me many times, that Hugo, Sr., had at first demurred, telling his son, "I don't want a woman with middle-age problems on my hands." But Hugo, Jr., (bless him) had answered, "But *Daddy,* she's so good-looking!"

On the morning of February 27, 1956, I sat nervously in the secretary's office in Justice Black's chambers. I watched young men coming and going into the Justice's office, among whom were several Birmingham lawyers I knew. They were all former law clerks of the Justice who had come to honor him on his seventieth birthday, the day of my arrival at the Supreme Court.

After a rather tense wait, I was called into the inner sanctum. My heart was pounding as I walked in. Justice Black was sitting at his desk rocking gently in his chair. He put me at ease as he rose and greeted me. With his beautiful sparkling and penetrating eyes and his Roman nose, high-arched and proud, Hugo Black looked for all the world like a Roman senator.

The Justice shook hands with me and asked me to sit down. We laughed and chatted about Alabama, and I began to feel completely at ease. The Justice continued to rock, and as he did so he put the tips of his fingers together in a characteristic gesture.

"Hugo, Jr., told you I want a secretary from Alabama."

"Yes, sir, he did," I replied, "and I have lived in Alabama all my life."

"What was your maiden name?"

"Seay," I replied. "I was Elizabeth Seay. My father was Dr. James E. Seay and practiced medicine in Birmingham."

"Yes," Justice Black said, "I knew your father very well. I also knew his brother in Pratt City, Dr. Cleveland Seay. Your uncle was one of my warmest supporters in my race for County Solicitor and later for the United States Senate. Your father never was for me; we were on opposite sides of the fence politically. I was a strong prohibitionist and he was anti-. However, I liked your father."

I was glad he added the last sentence, because the conversation had taken an uncomfortable turn.

Swiveling his chair around, he faced an old black safe, opened it, and unlocked a small compartment. From it, he withdrew a little black book, explaining that it was his old campaign book with a list of supporters and notes about their efforts on his behalf.

"Here it is all right," he said. " 'Cleveland Seay, doctor, well liked and known in the Western District. Took me over the Bessemer Cut-off to introduce me to his friends when I was running for County Solicitor.' "

He flipped the pages a bit. " 'Dr. Mark Seay.' Was he any kin to you?"

"Yes, sir, he was my great-uncle who lived in Lamar County," I answered.

"Well, he was also my good supporter. He put up posters for me all over Lamar County when I was running for the Senate and helped me a great deal."

By this time I was feeling reassured. Two out of three supporters in the family seemed to be a pretty good percentage. Suddenly getting serious, Justice Black said to me, "Now about the job. Hugo, Jr., tells me you have been highly recommended, and I know you can do it well. However, it seems you have a personal problem. You and your husband are separating, and I do not want to contribute to that. What I want you to do is to go home and have a serious talk with your husband. If he is willing to let you come to work for me, then you can let me know. I want you both to understand, though, that should you decide to return to him one day, one week, one month, or one year from the time you come to work for me, you are free to do so."

The interview was over. As I rose, Hugo Black got up to follow me to the door. This relaxed, easy-to-know man, a legend in Alabama for some thirty years or more, had been so kind and understanding to me that I felt a surge of emotion. Tears came into my eyes as he extended his hand. I took it in mine and impulsively put it to my cheek, then turned around and quickly left.

Justice Black was on the bench hearing cases being argued the week of my return to the Court as his secretary. This left time for me to learn the ropes of my new job from Gladys Coates, the departing secretary, who told me, "The Judge will take a great interest in you, but if I were you, I wouldn't tell him anything about my personal life. He gets very involved with people. He'll take over and try to change your life, your personality, and everything about you. He gets these extra bright boys as law clerks from the top schools. Most of them are already men, but he starts working on them patiently, trying to get this one to work harder, that one to play more, and softening down another's personality."

Hugo Black always lunched with his office staff when the Court was not in session. The two clerks for the 1955 Term of Court when I came on duty were Harold Ward III, from Orlando, Florida, and Vernon Patrick, who by strange happenstance came, as I did, from Fairfield, Alabama. How could a Supreme Court Justice select *two* people who did not know each other, from the same little city of Fairfield? Although I had met Vernon's parents there and I knew that Vernon knew all about my husband Fred's race for Mayor of that city, by an unspoken agreement he never mentioned it to the folks back home. He kept my secret well. Therefore I felt at ease with Vernon and Harold when we lunched with the Judge. Usually we were all wrapped up over writing an opinion for the Court, or a dissent. If the Judge was about to unload a dissenting opinion on his brethren, the talk around the table would be especially lively. At other times the Judge would regale us with his Alabama stories about his days practicing law in Birmingham, or trying cases as a police court judge there, or his running for the United States Senate. One day the Judge came out of his chambers, said he was going to lunch, and asked all of us to come along. He stood in line in the cafeteria carrying his own tray, just like the rest of us, and when one of the boys took dessert, he raised his eyebrows and teased: "Trying to put on a little weight there, are you?"

When we sat down at the table, the Judge remarked that I had on a pretty dress.

"Thank you," I said. "It's new."

"How many new dresses do you have?" he asked curiously. "Every time I mention it, you tell me your dress is new."

I laughed a little and then confessed, "Eight."

"Eight new dresses?" he asked incredulously. "Why, I never owned eight new suits at the same time in my whole life! You make me think of Dr. Hugh Grant, my former administrative assistant when I was in the Senate. I had Roosevelt appoint him minister to Albania. When I met my tailor on the street one day, he thanked me for sending Dr. Grant to him. 'Why,' he said, 'he has bought twelve new suits: a morning suit, an evening suit, a tuxedo, a smoking jacket, and eight business suits!' "

Then, observing my reddened and swollen arm, Hugo Black asked me, "What is the matter with your arm?"

"It's just the after-effects of my tetanus shot," I replied.

"My goodness," the Judge exclaimed, "where in the world did you think you were coming? Eight new dresses and a tetanus shot!"

I rose bright and early Monday morning, April 2, the day Gladys left, so I could leave home in time to beat the Judge to the office. This took some doing, as he usually was there by 8:30.

Daniel Berman, a student at Rutgers who was doing a master's thesis on the Judge, came in. I asked him to sit down. We talked nervously and spasmodically, but I soon heard the now-familiar brisk step and whistling of the Judge in the marble hallway as he approached his chambers. He walked right up to my desk and stopped. Almost eagerly he said, "Josephine wants me to invite you to dinner either tonight or tomorrow night."

I must have looked eager, too, as I replied, "Well, I'm free tonight, but, er . . . maybe . . ." I hesitated, thinking I should really accept for tomorrow.

"Fine, why not tonight, then?" he said. "I'll call Lizzie Mae and tell her to expect you. Do you like fish or steak?"

"Fish," I replied, although I didn't really prefer it. I later learned that Hugo Black liked steak *every* day in the year. So my first decision turned out to be a wrong one.

I gestured toward Mr. Berman sitting on the sofa, and the Judge smiled and told him to follow him in.

A very excited new secretary sat alone at the desk in Hugo Black's outer office. With the breaking-in period behind me, the work no longer seemed quite so formidable and my first day passed quickly. The Judge could not have been kinder or more considerate.

Around four I went into the Judge's office to ask directions to his house.

"Oh, I'll come by and get you," he said quickly. "I never let the ladies in my family go out alone at night."

I went home and put on a soft pink silk dress. When I heard the car door slam in front of my apartment, I got up and peeped out the pane in the door. I saw the Judge almost running up the sidewalk, his battered old hat jammed on his head. He looked as though he had been away on a long journey and was coming home at last.

The Judge's house, 619 South Lee Street in the old port section of Alexandria, was mellow and beautiful, bearing its two hundred years almost regally.

Josephine, the Judge's only daughter, was a pretty young girl, gracious and charming, and she had her father's knack of making a person feel at ease. I was also introduced to Mrs. Elizabeth Howie (Lizzie Mae), their housekeeper and long-time friend.

After dinner, we went upstairs to the Judge's study, his favorite room in the house. A large desk and his big chair dominated the room. His well-worn books lined two walls almost from floor to ceiling, and little wagons of books were within his reach as he sat at his desk. There were easy chairs and a large roomy sofa. Josephine explained that her father always liked to bring guests to this room.

We sat talking pleasantly until around 10:30, when I rose and the Judge took me home. On the way, by sympathetic questioning, Hugo Black drew from me the story of my life, which I'll shorten a bit here: After graduating from Bellevue Medical School in New York, my father, Jim Seay, and my mother, Attie Austin, were married. My dad took his bride home to Lamar County, Alabama, where he joined my grandfather in the practice of medicine. After nine months of country doctoring he decided to move to Pratt City, a small mining community outside of Birmingham. He and my mother had two sons, Erskine and James, who were seven and six years old when I, the only girl, arrived on the scene in Pratt City.

When I was about three years old my parents moved to Southside, in Birmingham, which was called "Silk Stocking Row" when we lived there.

My dad's practice was thriving and he was a surgeon on the staffs of two hospitals, but he died suddenly when he was only forty-one years old, just three days after my twelfth birthday. My mother put me in private boarding school in Birmingham until she could wind up my father's estate.

After two years my mother and I moved to Tuscaloosa, where my brother James was taking a premedical course at the University of Alabama. My brother Erskine was a cadet at the Naval Academy at Annapolis.

I enrolled in Tuscaloosa High School and soon entered into the happy dancing, dating life of a high school flapper of the Roaring Twenties. One day my brother James brought home a fellow medical student by the name of Fred DeMeritte. Fred came frequently after that, and sometimes after I returned from a date or party with kids my own age, he would be waiting for me in another room, talking to James and Mother. He was about twelve years older than I, but I didn't consider him anything but a friend at that point. During the fall semester of my junior year in high school, Fred dropped out of medical school to go to Miami, which was then in the middle of the big Florida real estate boom.

My mother suffered dreadfully from the cold weather in Alabama, and as a result of Fred's calls and letters she finally decided to move to Miami, over my vehement protests. After three months of Miami, she was disappointed and wanted to go back to Tuscaloosa just as soon as I finished my junior year at Miami High. By that time, Fred and I had developed a romantic interest in each other.

After school one day, Fred was waiting for me in his car, and as I got in with him he said, "Your mother is going to take you back to Alabama. You know that I am in love with you and don't want you to go. How 'bout you and me driving up to Fort Lauderdale this afternoon and getting married?"

Getting married seemed like a novel thing to do, so I agreed to it. We drove to Fort Lauderdale, went to a justice of the peace, applied for a marriage license (Fred upgraded my age from sixteen to eighteen), and there we became man and wife. Ten months after my marriage and one month before my seventeenth birthday, my son Fred was born. I was young, inexperienced, and a little miserable and asked my mother to come and live with us. I stayed married for thirty years, but there were many ups and downs in my life that led finally, in 1956, to Fred's and my decision to end our marriage.

After this long, complicated story was told, the Judge saw me to my door and drove off. The next morning the telephone rang at about 8:00 A.M. On the other end of the line I heard his cheery voice.

"Last night I thought a lot about your situation. What you need is to develop a philosophy of life for yourself."

"What do you suggest?" I asked.

"You need to go on a reading program. I'm going to bring you some books to read: John Dewey, Bertrand Russell, and others I have here."

I thanked him, told him I'd see him at the office, and hung up. I stared at the phone for a minute. "John Dewey and Bertrand Russell on top of coping with that electric typewriter? I'll never make it!" I thought.

Later that spring the Judge was scheduled to make a speech at Yale. Since I could see no preparations for a speech going on, I finally asked him if he intended to write one.

"No," he replied, "I never write a speech unless it is to be published. I just shoot from the hip. I do have something I am going to use that I want you to copy for me, however. I'll bring it to you as soon as I can find it."

Soon the Judge appeared in my office with a paper in his hand. "Here is the quotation I want you to copy," he told me. "It is one of the most beautiful things I have ever read. Make me about six copies. I want you to put one copy in my Bible, one in my dictionary, and then you can think of other places to stick them around, so I can always find a copy when I need it. It is Virgil's Song and it expresses my feelings so exactly that I want it read at my own funeral."

Seeing the look of distress on my face, the Judge widened his eyes, raised his eyebrows, and in mock seriousness continued, "Should that remote and unlikely event ever occur!"

Then he read it to me, standing there at my desk:

> As Virgil sweetly sings, me let the sweet muses lead to their soft retreats, their living fountains, and melodious groves where I may dwell remote from care, master of myself, and under no necessity of doing every day what my heart condemns. Let me no more be seen in the wrangling forum, a pale and anxious candidate for precarious fame; and let neither the tumult of visitors crowding to my levee, nor the eager haste of officious freedmen disturb my morning rest. Let me live free from solicitude, a stranger to the art of promising legacies, in order to buy the friendship of the great. And when Nature shall give the signal to retire, may I possess no more than I may bequeath to whom I will. At my funeral let no token of sorrow be seen, no pompous mockery of woe. Crown me with chaplets, strew flowers on my grave, and let my friends erect no vain memorial to tell where my remains are lodged.

As he finished reading this passage in his beautiful voice, tears were in my eyes. As I looked up, I was not surprised that his eyes, too, were moist.

Those early days were tumultuous ones for me. The Judge was giving me books to read, then leaving me with little time to read them. I tried to scan the ones he brought, but I found it much more enjoyable to let him expound them to me. Hugo Black was a born teacher, infinitely patient and yet argumentative. He would always take the opposite point of view from the one I had and argue it vigorously.

Things were slow during the summer, since the Court was not in session. For the Judge, the work was routine and consisted mainly of keeping up with petitions for *certiorari,* which are applications asking the Court to review decisions of lower courts.

The Judge spent his summers catching up with his "outside reading": reviewing the many books that were sent to him during the year; inspecting the latest law review articles; and rereading, often out loud, a few old favorites such as *The Works of Tacitus* or Diogenes Laërtius' *Lives of Eminent Philosophers.*

While the Judge relaxed playing tennis and enjoying his yard that first summer, I was feeling anxious and depressed on account of the general upheaval in my life. Early one summer morning, the Judge called me on the phone. My voice was husky and he detected at once that I had been crying. "What in the world is the matter with you?" he asked.

"Oh, Judge, I get so frightened when I think of life, I feel really depressed."

"Depressed?" he said. "You mustn't feel depressed. Why, it's a beautiful morning. Look outside. The sun is shining and the birds are singing and *you* are going to be all right."

Despite my preoccupation with my own personal affairs, I was seeing the Judge more after hours now. After my first trip out to the Judge's home for dinner, his daughter Josephine invited me back rather frequently. If Josephine sensed her father was becoming interested in me as a person, she never gave any sign of resenting it. In fact, I thought she did a pretty good job of aiding and abetting the situation.

The summer passed rapidly. I had to go back to Alabama twice, to see about my mother and to vote in the Democratic primary in which my husband, Fred, was elected the nominee of the party for mayor of Fairfield. In earlier years, becoming the Democratic nominee in Alabama was tantamount to election. This particular year of 1956, however, was a different story. Eisenhower was sweeping the country, and a restless South, frightened by the 1954 Supreme Court *Brown* decision, was leaving the Democratic party. That year Alabama's three largest cities, Birmingham, Montgomery, and Mobile, went Republican.

After the primary, the Judge told me how he thought Fred could get elected. "Tell him," he said, "to announce that his wife has gone career-mad and has gone up to Washington to work for that reprobate Hugo Black. He will pick up a lot of sympathy votes."

Perhaps it might have worked. I don't know. Fred wouldn't try it. He was narrowly defeated in the November general election by an overwhelmingly Republican vote that swept the Birmingham area, of which Fairfield was a part. I was free then to get a divorce, which was granted in November, 1956.

This time when I returned to Washington I brought Mother with me and put my house up for sale. My Alabama phase was ended.

Back at the office, the hustle and bustle of the new 1956 term of Court was beginning. Two new law clerks had come in earlier in the summer, Bob Girard, from the state of Washington, and George Freeman, from Birmingham, Alabama.

At the office I often listened to the Judge arguing with George and Bob over a case. His voice would rise and fall in beautiful cadences, as though he were arguing a case before a jury. "The boys," as he called his law clerks, would join issue with him so vigorously that I sometimes thought they were all mad at one another. But this give and take was just what the Judge wanted and enjoyed in his clerks.

Although there were many pressures on him, Hugo Black never lost his kindly, patient manner with his office personnel. Sometimes he would call Spencer Campbell, his messenger, and me into his office and read us an opinion he was working on, explaining he just wanted a layman's point of view. "Were you able to understand what the case was about, and the meaning of every word I used?" he would ask. If the answers were affirmative, he would then go on to ask if we agreed with his position. In the event either of us did not agree with the Judge, he would quickly extract our reasoning and proceed to demolish it.

Although the Judge was confident of his views, his confidence in vote-getting among the other Justices was never absolute. He always "ran scared." In some cases, everything would go smoothly and the votes would come in quickly, often indicated by a line written on the back of the Judge's circulated opinion. "Hugo, count me in" was a typical notation.

In order to iron out a case, one or another of "the brethren" (as they called each other) would come into the Judge's office to go over an opinion —line by line, word by word—until there was a meeting of minds. If there could be no agreement, then the other Justice might decide to write a dissenting or a concurring opinion. Sometimes it happened that the Judge would lose his Court, and his opinion would turn out to be a dissent or a concurring opinion.

Throughout all of the Judge's excitement about opinions, one fact came out clearly. He had a deep respect for all his brethren on the Court and for the convictions they held.

The Judge's zest for the fight, his enthusiasm for hard work, his high regard for his brethren—all were contagious and spilled over on us. I found this period as Hugo Black's secretary one of the most exciting of my life. I felt I was touching the skirts of history.

As the Judge's seventy-first birthday February 27, 1957, approached, the law clerks and I decided to have a little surprise party for him. We asked Josephine, Lizzie Mae, and Spencer to conspire with us to have it at his home, since that was the place where he always seemed happiest.

After Lizzie Mae's New York steaks, eggplant casserole, hot biscuits, and a slice of birthday cake, we all went upstairs to the study. The Judge always liked to tease the staff, and after he made a gibe in my direction I announced, "You hired me exactly a year ago today. I hope you have no regrets about bringing me up here."

He looked at me quizzically and replied, "The only thing I regret is that I am not twenty years younger!"

Hugo Black was an intense man, and he concentrated all his powers on whatever he was doing at the particular moment—working, reading, writing, playing tennis, courting, socializing—whatever. At the same time, he had a light-hearted, joyous quality about him. He liked to sing, and as a boy he entertained at church and at school socials by singing and by playing the fiddle.

"The difference between the fiddle and the violin," he told me, "is that the fiddle is held out from the body, while the violin is tucked under the chin."

Often, as we whizzed over beautiful Mount Vernon Parkway, Hugo Black would sing to me. Sometimes there were romantic songs, such as "All I Want in All This World Is Just a Little Rocking Chair and You." Sometimes the songs would be religious ones, mainly Baptist, and frequently we would sing the beautiful Negro spirituals of our Southland. Hugo Black's voice had a lyrical quality about it, and he sang the old songs with soul:

Heard a rumblin' in the sky,
These bones gwine rise again!
Must've been Jesus passin' by,
These bones gwine-a rise again.

Or another favorite:

I fee-yul like,
I fee-yul like,
I'm on my jourr-huh-ney home.

And so the summer of '57 flitted away happily. Hugo and I spent long hours in searching talks. He told me about his life. He talked about how much he had loved his first wife, Josephine, and about his hopes for his children.

In regard to my own life, Hugo stated flatly that he did not think it wise for parents, meaning my mother, to live with their children, and he said that at his age he could not take it. I realized Hugo Black was moving slowly toward marriage and that he wanted to approach it analytically. At this point I had not given any serious thought to the direction in which we were drifting. I found his company pleasant, we liked working together, we laughed a lot with each other, and it was an enjoyable time in my life. But marriage had not entered my mind.

On the night of September 9, 1957, at about 8 P.M., I was shampooing my hair when the telephone rang. I wrapped a towel around my head and flew to answer. It was Hugo.

"Josephine and I were sitting at the dinner table," he said, "when suddenly out of a clear blue sky she said to me, 'Daddy, why don't you and Elizabeth get married?' I said, 'Whatever gave you an idea like that?' and she replied, 'You're in love with her and she's in love with you. Why don't you get married!' "

Giving me time to digest this fully, Hugo paused and then added, "What are you doing? I'd like to come over right away and talk to you."

"Right away?" I wailed. "I'm in the middle of washing my hair!"

Hugo was disgusted. "Why on earth is it that right in the middle of every crisis in a woman's life she's got to be washing her hair?"

I relented. "Oh, well, I'll do it up in a towel. Come on over."

It took only the minimum time for Hugo to arrive: "twenty-five minutes with the traffic lights, twenty-eight against them!"—as he often told me.

I watched the Judge as he came up the sidewalk, with his quick light walk and his hat crushed down on his head. I opened the door before he reached it. He came in, closed the door, and grasped me by the shoulders. He gave me a penetrating look as if wanting to see right down into my heart and soul.

Hugo seemed satisfied with what he saw. He took me by both my hands and sat me down on the sofa next to him. Hugo Black did not speak of marriage. He spoke of love and the Supreme Court.

"Who knows what love is?" Hugo asked me, musingly. "It is a chemical blend of hormones, happiness, and harmony," he went on to say. "But I have had a prior love affair for almost twenty years now with an institution. It is with the Supreme Court. I have a tremendous respect for the prestige of the Court. We have to act on so many controversial matters, and we are bound to make some people mad at every decision we make. Therefore, in my personal life I have to be like Caesar's wife: above reproach. I have to know that the woman I marry is a one-man woman. The woman I marry will be around extremely attractive intellectual men. I am seventy-one years old. You are twenty-two years younger than I. In another five or ten years you may not find me as attractive as you do now. If that were to happen and you wanted a divorce, I would give you one. But I think it would finish me and hurt the prestige of the Court."

My reply was that for fifteen years before coming up to Washington I had worked in the federal court system. During that time I had acquired tremendous respect for the federal judiciary, and my year and a half at the Supreme Court had caused me to care for it just as Hugo did.

"But why," I asked, "are we talking about the Supreme Court?"

We kissed, and then we sat there with our emotions in a jumble for about a half hour. As Hugo stood up to go, he held me at arm's length and again looked deep into my eyes.

"You'd be wonderful for a man in his twilight years," he said. "With you, I could sail into the sunset—with glory!"

Hugo left abruptly, but in thirty minutes—the traffic lights must have gone against him—he called me on the phone. "I forgot something. I forgot to tell you I love you, darling—and good night!"

We were married on Tuesday, September 11, 1957. Before the wedding, the Judge and Hugo, Jr., went to the Court to see Chief Justice Earl Warren, the only member of the Court in whom Hugo confided the news of his marriage.

The Chief Justice, after hearing the news, told Hugo he felt relieved. "Seeing the serious look on your face, Hugo, made me think for a moment you had come to tell me you were going to retire, and that was the last thing on earth I wanted to hear."

Hugo, Jr., laughed and said, "No, Mr. Chief Justice, an old man retires and Daddy is too young for that. He's going to take on a young man's duty."

PART THREE

From the Diaries of Elizabeth Black

As the diaries that follow make clear, neither of us ever regretted our marriage for a minute. Under Hugo's tutelage I learned to watch my weight religiously, to exercise vigorously, and to play tennis—constantly. After my first tennis lesson I told Hugo, "Here I am, a Southern girl who never lifted anything heavier than a magnolia petal, and you're making a muscle-bound athlete out of me."

We shared a lot of fun and a lot of love. I think Hugo drew from me the strength of his roots. The spark that flared between us almost at sight was our common background. I gave him back Alabama, which he was hungry for when I came on the scene. Hugo had missed the speech, the softened manners, the colloquialisms of his Southland.

What Hugo often wanted from me was the lay point of view. Of course, in our early days together, when I was just up from Birmingham, I certainly had a Southerner's way of thinking about things. For example, one time he was writing on a case that had come up from Birmingham, concerning Ollie's Barbecue Restaurant and the question of whether or not it was involved in interstate commerce (*Katzenbach* v. *McClung,* 379 U.S. 294 [1964]). If the decision was made that it was, then provisions had to be made to serve people of all races. Now, I frequently went to lunch at that restaurant and I thought they made the best barbecue in the world. I kept telling Hugo, "They just have local people coming in for lunch. Nobody is a stranger in that place." Hugo just laughed that one out. I never influenced him on that case or any other. He always demolished my arguments and came out with his own views. On the other hand, I was brainwashed by him—because of course he was right. Hugo said that more people in the South got mad at him for introducing the Wage and Hour Bill in the Senate than they did for his work on integration, because they had to give up their six-dollar- or ten-dollar-a-week butlers or maids.

The diaries are detailed because I kept careful notes of conversations like this one about Ollie's Barbecue Restaurant, and because I had a lot of opportunity to talk to Hugo and observe him. Hugo Black didn't often sleep nights through. He was a wakeful man and he always wanted someone to talk to. Many times I would be exhausted and might have preferred to sleep, but when he'd turn on the light I knew he needed to talk. I also knew that he was a great man and that I was lucky he was sharing all these ideas with me. Sometimes he would talk about a case and then get up at 2:00 in the morning and go sit at his desk and begin to write on a yellow pad.

During the day we often worked together in the study. Hugo's desk was at the rear and I would sit across from him with my typewriter and desk facing the window.

Hugo and I spent an enormous amount of time together. Sometimes when I might want to take my mother back down to Alabama for a visit, Hugo would say, "Wait until I can go with you." Once when Hugo's son Sterling and his wife were expecting a child, Sterling asked his father if he could spare me to go to New Mexico to help for a few weeks. Hugo told him, "No, I married her for better or worse, until death do us part, and I'm going to stay with that—until death do us part."

The pages that follow are the fruits of that closeness. I present them not as my own diaries but for whatever light they may shed on the life and work of my beloved husband, Hugo Black, the Magnificent Rebel.

1964

Monday, May 11 Hugo had promised the Unitarians he would meet on May 7 with their Men's Club in an informal exchange of ideas. Poor Hugo had been working literally night and day trying to get his last three opinions of the year written in final form. He had written the Sit Down[1] cases in Florida, but because of the intense feeling and infighting at the Court on the issue, he was finding himself having to answer dissents every day. First, [Associate Justice] Arthur Goldberg circulated a dissent referring to "the good old common law," which forced innkeepers and others to serve whosoever of the public wished to be served, and read into the Fourteenth Amendment the right of all, regardless of color, to get such service. Hugo practically demolished Arthur's dissent by careful research of the *Globe* [an early version of *Congressional Record*], in which no member of Congress even mentioned such an intent or hoped-for result of passing the Fourteenth Amendment. The Chief [Chief Justice Earl Warren], and [Associate Justices] Bill Brennan and Bill Douglas agreed to Arthur's first circulated dissent, but under Hugo's withering fire, each, though still joining Arthur, decided to write his own dissent. The Chief wrote, saying he could not in good conscience deny to anyone the right to be served solely on account of the color of his skin. Bill Brennan was saying the Court did not have to reach the constitutional question involved. Hugo tried to say very plainly that though the Constitution itself did not tell merchants and innkeepers not to discriminate in its customers, Congress could pass a law to that effect.

Among Hugo's soldiers, [Associate Justices] Byron White, John Harlan,

Potter Stewart, and Tom Clark—a scant and scared majority—there was a difference of opinion on how plainly that could be said. Byron wanted to put it down in black and white. John Harlan said that would be prejudging. Both said they might write, although all recognized the advantages of unanimity among the majority. Hugo has had to make innumerable phone calls and has had to submit many rewrites, both to please his army and to answer the minority dissents. Even today, May 11, as we leave this afternoon for Fort Worth, Texas, to attend the Fifth Circuit Judicial Conference, Hugo is uneasy about going and says we most surely will have to return Thursday instead of Friday, as planned. Dick [A. E. Dick Howard], his law clerk, thinks, as Hugo believes, that if Hugo is not back for Friday's Conference, the case will not come down. Hugo has had his opinion written since January—he wrote it in Florida—and the other side admittedly has delayed due to the fight in Congress to pass the Civil Rights Bill. The minority felt that Hugo's enormous prestige would work adversely on the bill's passage. Hugo disagrees and feels Congress needs to know and the Negroes need to know, especially the latter, since they continue to break the law in the belief the Supreme Court will sustain the legality of their claims. Hugo thinks Potter Stewart is getting nervous and edgy due to the infighting. We are hoping it will come down on Monday the 18th.

On May 7, the day of the Unitarian address, Hugo sat at his desk at home all day long bending over a yellow pad, wearing down pencil after pencil. He was very tired. I told him as we left that I hoped he would make a tiny speech, since they had him listed on the program as giving "Informal Remarks." He said positively he would *not* do it, that he would only answer questions. We arrived at 6:30, and they escorted us to Dr. Duncan Howlett's study in the church, where Selma and Harold Burton [Associate Justice, served on the Court 1945–1958] were waiting. Hugo and I sometimes go to this church, and Hugo says he's going to hold on to Dr. Howlett because he's his closest connection to God. Dear Harold, in the last stages of Parkinson's disease, stands as a living monument of the indomitability of man's spirit over the ravages of disease. Although his spine is curved with the rigidity that sets in, when I entered the room he tried to stand up. After a few moments, we all went to the Fellowship Hall for punch, and in so doing we had to go down two flights of stairs. Harold, with a cane, and with Selma at his side, laboriously and painfully made his way down. We soon left for the dining hall, where I sat next to Dr. Howlett. I confided in Dr. Howlett that Hugo was exhausted and had said he would *not* make a speech.

The presiding officer had a nice introduction of the two Justices; then Harold, much to my surprise, stood up to introduce Hugo. He spoke in a voice that often trailed off into a high key, and once or twice his face would go blank and Selma would prompt him, but in the main his remarks about Hugo were beautiful and touching and very coherent. It was as though he had summoned all the willpower at his command to direct his mind and voice into this channel. When he finished his gallant address, all stood up, and I could see how moved Hugo was. As he came to the microphone I knew he was going to make a speech. He started off by saying one of the greatest rewards of his twenty-seven years on the Court was working with a gentle, kind, wise, and noble gentleman like Harold Burton.

Then Hugo told one of his rare old jokes, about getting lost on the road to Andalusia and asking a child for directions. "Andalusia, or Montgomery—which way is which?" The child didn't know. Finally Hugo said, "You don't know much, do you, son?" The boy replied, "No, but I hain't lost."

From that, Hugo went on to say he was a Baptist; his father was a Baptist; his grandfather was a Baptist; his grandmother was a Baptist. "In fact," he said, "I am somewhat like the Democrat who moved up to an East Tennessee Republican county." Soon word was noised about that there was a Democrat in the neighborhood come to disturb the peaceful atmosphere of the Republican community. A meeting was called, and after the fashion of Andrew Johnson, the chairman laid his pistol on the desk and announced that rumor had it that a Democrat had moved in, and the chairman wanted that Democrat to stand and identify himself. After repeated requests from the chair, the Democrat reluctantly stood up. "Reckon I'm your man, Cap'n," he said. Then the question: "Why are you a Democrat?" "Well, never thought about it much, but my father was a Democrat; my grandfather was a Democrat; my great-grandfather was a Democrat." "Why, that's no excuse!" cried the chairman. "What if your father had been a fool; your grandfather had been a fool; your great-grandfather had been a fool—then what would you have been?" "Well," drawled the recalcitrant, "then I guess I'd have been a Republican."

This took down the house. Then Hugo gave the sweetest talk I have ever heard him give. He spoke in defense of Southerners. He spoke on why he liked the Baptist and Unitarian churches. He said to his liberal audience, "Southerners aren't *bad* people; they're just like you. They have some views you detest; you have some views they detest!"

Next Hugo told of the Baptist ministers visiting him at the Court: how some seventy of them sat on the floor of the Conference room asking him questions and talking about things that troubled them as ministers, in connection with the hatred and lack of respect some of their congregations had in regard to the Supreme Court. Hugo told them they would have to educate their people, but, in the main, to "just let 'em talk." He told of the many nice letters he had received from them. And he told the story of the letter he received after the Prayer decision [see page 95, *Engel* v. *Vitale*] had been handed down. In part, it was as follows:

> During the reign of Bloody Queen Mary, a woman lay on straw in a jail at Litchfield, England, sentenced to die by burning as soon as her child, which she bore, was born. Her sin had been that she had sheltered her brother-in-law in her home. Her brother-in-law was a heretic. For that crime she was soon to die. The baby was born and the woman, named Joy, or Joyous Lewis, was taken out and burned at the stake. The child was a boy whose name was Thomas (Thomas was the third child of Joyous Lewis). He grew up and named his third child Thomas. In that family, every third child, where possible, has borne the name of Thomas. The writer of that letter was named Thomas, and he had known why since he was only knee high.

Needless to say, the writer had appreciated Hugo's Prayer decision. Then Hugo closed on a note of sentiment and unity between North and South, by quoting this poem:

> Here's to the Blue of the wind-swept North
> When we meet on the fields of France.
> May the spirit of Grant be with us there
> As the sons of the North advance.
>
> Here's to the Gray of the sun-kissed South
> When we meet on the fields of France.
> May the spirit of Lee be with us there
> As the sons of the South advance.
>
> But here's to the Blue and Gray as one
> As we meet on the fields of France.
> May the spirit of God be with us all
> As the sons of the Flag advance.

There was not a dry eye in the house, including Hugo's, when he sat down. Dr. Howlett leaned over to me and said: "I knew this was a great man, but I didn't know he was an orator, too!"

After much handshaking, we left the room and finally got Harold up the stairs, out into the street, and into our car. Every step was an agony of effort for him. His walking cane was a hindrance rather than a help, but with monumental willpower he overcame the rigidity of his body and with the slight assistance of all of us he made it. Dr. Howlett said this was an evening the Unitarians would long remember: these two great spirits—one weakened by nature and disease, his mind struggling to be clear; the other, Hugo, fortunate in having his physical strength and mental ability still intact.

When we arrived at the Dodge, the Burtons' hotel, it turned out that Harold was on the street instead of the sidewalk side. Hugo was afraid to let him out with all the cars zipping by, so he asked Harold to move over to the sidewalk side. Harold was almost completely unable to do that, so Hugo reached over and picked Harold up and in three little jolts got him over to the sidewalk side where he could get out without danger. Hugo—at seventy-eight, three years older than Harold—lifted that gentle soul almost like a baby.

Though Hugo didn't go into it that night he had felt deeply and passionately about the Prayer case, *Engel* v. *Vitale.*[2] This was the New York Regents' attempt to force schoolteachers to read every morning in the classroom a prayer the Regents had written. This offended Hugo's deeply held view that there should be absolute separation between church and state. He pointed out to me that people had been tortured, their ears lopped off, and sometimes their tongues cut or their eyes gouged out, all in the name of religion. He advocated many religions of a diverse nature, because, as he said, when one religion gets predominance, they immediately try to suppress others.

I went to Court to hear Hugo deliver his opinion in this case. He stated it in a low-key sort of way, pointing out that this did not mean that songs with the word "God" could not be sung. In fact, I thought his opinion sounded almost like a sermon because he had drawn on his long period of teaching Sunday School class in Birmingham. Headlines came out in the papers, written by many reporters who had not even had time to read the opinion, screaming that the Court had outlawed God in the schools, and other absurdities.

The publicity produced a deluge of mail to Hugo about this case. Some people praised it, but a lot thought it was terrible. One woman condemned Hugo to Hell, without a hearing, he told me, and he wrote an answer telling her a bit sarcastically, I thought, that if she would go to the library (as he was sure she would not have it in her own house) and ask for a book called the Bible, she could turn to the chapter and read where it said "Pray in your own closet." He answered some of his Protestant correspondents with the question "How would you like it if the Catholics were to force you to say 'Hail Mary' every morning in the schools?"

Written much later. Tom Clark deserted on the *Bell* case and wrote an opinion for the Court which they were all reluctant to agree to. Finally, it was determined that, to keep Tom's from coming down, Potter Stewart would join Bill Brennan's four (not to reach the constitutionality) and thus Bill would give the Court's opinion. Bill Douglas and Arthur Goldberg reached the merits and voted to reverse the judgments outright, although they concurred in Parts II–V of the Court's opinion. Arthur wrote, joined by C.J. [the Chief Justice] and Bill Douglas. Hugo dissented, joined by John Harlan and Byron White.[3]

1965

Friday, January 1 In Miami, Florida. New Year, 1965. I have the usual feeling that I must grab the spinning wheel and stop the swift passage of time which is bringing such a full and happy life to Hugo and me.

Monday, January 4 We are now watching television while Hugo keeps one eye on the book he is reading, *The Great Rights* by Edmond Cahn. The President [Lyndon B. Johnson] is supposed to give the State of the Nation Address at 9:30, which we will watch.

Hugo and I listened to LBJ's State of the Union Address. It was not delivered as forcefully as we have seen Lyndon talk. He looks tired, but he had a magnificent ending about the Pedernales River: "State of Union is good, restless, and growing."

Wednesday, January 6 Hugo sat up until 12:00 last night and when I awakened this morning at 8:00, he had been writing in the parlor since 6:00 A.M. I fixed breakfast and straightened up the apartment, and by 10:15 A.M. he was ready to mail his dissent.

Tuesday, January 12 It is now 11:00 P.M. and Hugo is just finishing writing a tribute to Dean Edmond Cahn for the *New York University Law Review.* He had me read it aloud, and it is so moving we both had tears in our eyes when I finished.

Wednesday, January 13 On arriving home in Alexandria, we found some wonderful homemade bread and Texas honey from the LBJ ranch delivered for Christmas. There was a notation that we would be in the Presidential Box at the Mayflower for the inaugural ball and Hugo *almost agreed!*

Thursday, January 14 Hugo brought home from the office a beautiful print from the President and Lady Bird called "President's Levee or All Creation Going to the White House, Washington," by Robert Cruikshank, published in London in 1840. It was inscribed in the President's own handwriting, "To Hugo and Elizabeth Black with all our love, Lyndon Johnson," and in her writing, "Lady Bird." Hugo called Lady Bird to thank her. I shall write.

Monday, January 18 I went to Court with Hugo, leaving home a little late. Hugo was two minutes late but got there in time to go in with the Court. I had as guests Frances [Mrs. Thurman] Arnold and Jinksie Durr, Hugo's sister-in-law. Arthur Goldberg gave the opinion of the Court in the *Cox* case (Negro preacher arrested for picketing courthouse in Louisiana) finding Cox not guilty. Hugo dissented vigorously to this[1] and also to the Texas Breach of Contract case.[2] Hugo was magnificent in his delivery and wording. Jinksie Durr disagreed with Hugo on *Cox* but commented on his vigor and youthfulness of voice. After dinner Hugo fell asleep reading *certs.* We went early to bed, for both of us were exhausted.

Tuesday, January 19 Hugo and I went to Katharine Graham's house for dinner. Mrs. Graham is owner of the Washington *Post.* Her husband, Philip, committed suicide about two years ago. He was an ex–law clerk for Felix [Associate Justice Frankfurter, 1939–1962] and very brilliant. We saw lots of old friends and interesting people. Joe Alsop, the columnist, stopped and talked. Joe said Hugo, Robert La Follette, and George Norris were giants of the Senate. Saw Luvie [Mrs. Drew] Pearson; the Alan Barths; worlds of newspaper personalities; the Fred Friendlys from New York—he's the CBS Senior Executive Producer who wants Hugo to do a broadcast on television.

Wednesday, January 20 *LBJ's inauguration.* What a day! I had on a green three-piece woolen suit with woolen drawers and undershirt beneath (as did Hugo), a heavy black Persian lamb coat, and Mother's black hat with wrap-around scarf to keep the ears warm. We got to Christian Church at 14th Street and Thomas Circle and the principal speaker was Billy Graham, who almost exhorted the Supreme Court, or so I thought. Very dynamic but like a country evangelist. The Presidential party was two rows down from us. Services were over promptly at 9:30 and we, with our driver, whose car was very splendid with two small American flags waving from the radiator and we sitting a half block behind it, soared off to the Court. The swearing-in and all the ceremonies were most impressive. Lady Bird held the Bible for Lyndon to take the oath, although Mr. Davis, the Clerk of the Court, must have been disappointed at the departure from tradition. Prior to that day, the Clerk had sworn in the incoming President. Went to the parade, sitting in the President's Reviewing Stand. Early in the parade the President came over to greet us all, shook hands warmly with Hugo, and leaned over and kissed me lightly on the forehead, knocking my hat off as he did so. He didn't notice, but television did—much to my family's delight. We came home tired, but had to dress for the ball. Went to Andy and Potter Stewart's home for dinner and from there to the Mayflower. Hugo took me down to the dance floor, which was roped off, to dance. The President cut in on me and we took a few turns. Andy Stewart was laughing but protested that he didn't dance with her!

Saturday, January 23 My birthday—the fifty-seventh—ugh!

Sunday, January 24 I helped Hugo revise his memorial speech for Dr. Alexander Meiklejohn of St. John's College in Annapolis. Then he dictated a final draft, which I took in shorthand and typed for him. We looked over tax returns, which precipitated a few words over what disposition we'd make of next year's overpayment of taxes. I got my feelings hurt and it is now 1:00 A.M. and we are both working away. I'm too burned up to sleep.

Monday, January 25 Hugo likewise got his feelings hurt. The raw, naked force of Hugo's intellect and will is usually concealed beneath that kind, gentle exterior, but, believe me, on the few occasions we have had a clash of wills since we first met, I have seen the County Prosecutor, the Senate Investigator, the Attorney Cross-Examiner, and the Justice's analytical powers all rolled into one. Although I thought, and still do think, that I had a justifiable complaint, I ended up apologizing to Hugo. I asked him for an apology, but I never got it. However, when he summed up our conflict, he did it so sweetly by saying, "I have told you and others many times that the period I have been married to you has been the happiest of my life." After that, I just melted right down. We talked away our disagreement and then he went off to Court. I went to Seven Corners to buy a pair of lamb-lined slippers for him to wear on the bench. I also bought black dye and dyed them, as the brown looked too conspicuous. Hugo came home early and the quarrel was over.

Thursday, January 28 Hugo was so tired last night he couldn't hold out and went to bed around 9:00. However, he woke up at 3:00 and read *certs* for an hour or more and got up at 6:45 to dictate. Said he'd had it on his mind in the intervening time between 3:00 and the time he actually got up. Hugo has to go over all the "flimsies" [*forma pauperis* petitions for *certiorari*]. He also has to prepare to state the cases at Conference tomorrow. Hugo came home at about 5:30 this afternoon and he is working tonight, but there is a wonderful thing about him: when he is through with his work Hugo can relax.

Sunday, January 31 Today we started off by being lazy. I wanted to go out and sweep the light, frosty snow from the sidewalk, but Hugo insisted he'd go too if I did. I do not want to expose him to another cold.

Tuesday, February 2 *White House dinner.* Arrived at White House right at 8:00. There were about 150 guests; tables were round, each seating ten. I was thrilled to see I was on the President's left, Mrs. [Hubert] Humphrey on his right. The President was gregarious and expansive. Before many minutes, and without my asking, he had autographed his place card, my menu, my place card, and my matches with "Love, Lyndon." I asked if he was doing that for everybody at the table and he said, "No, just for you." However, several others at the table, seeing him with pen out, passed up various things for him to sign, which he did very graciously.

Monday, February 8 We are in Miami. Hugo and I watched a Western on television until 8:30. He is now working on the Louisiana-Mississippi Voting Rights cases [see page 105].

Tuesday, February 9 We didn't go to bed until 1:30 this morning, so we were slow wakers. However, we finally got the paper (Hugo's job) and I snoozed a little on his shoulder as he read the news. Then he woke me and read the funnies.

Wednesday, February 10 Hugo worked all morning long and so did I, doing housework and writing letters. We went to the Royal Palm at 4:30 to play tennis. Hugo's mind still being on his dictation, he said he played a horrible game. We stopped back by the store and bought a steak, which I cooked. Hugo went right to dictating his Louisiana Voting case and finished it at 12:30 A.M. I was dead tired and went to bed early, or he would have had me go down and mail it with him.

Saturday, February 13 I worked industriously until noon, when we put on our "business clothes," i.e., tennis shorts, and away we went. We played until 5:00 with Hugo, Jr., Graham [his wife], and one set with Hugh [Hugo III, their son]. Came back and barbecued steak. Midnight, and Hugo is now reading the *Louisiana* briefs. Now to bed.

Sunday, February 14 Hugo, Sr., is very tired. He took something to make him sleep so he can work hard tomorrow dictating the *Louisiana* opinion.

Monday, February 15 Hugo woke up about 7:30 feeling a little disturbed about Hugo, Jr. We talked a long time about it during breakfast. He thinks Hugo is so fine but two things bother him: (1) his mimicry of people in politics whom he is against, and (2) his telling of stories about his father which exaggerate the facts to make Hugo, Sr., appear a shrewd and calculating person. We talked about it quite a while and Hugo decided he would talk to Hugo, Jr., before he leaves.

Tuesday, February 16 Hugo and I went to Hugo, Jr.'s, for dinner and had a nice time with the family. Hugo, Sr., again talked to Hugo about his criticism and mimicry of other people, which Hugo, Jr., took very well except, actually, I think Hugo, Jr., does it so seldom he felt it was unjust criticism. Hugo, Sr., feels so proud of Hugo's many fine qualities and has so many high hopes for a fine future for him that he ever strives to make him as perfect as possible. Also, he feels Hugo, Jr., will succeed him as the head of his family.

Wednesday, February 17 Hugo mentioned at dinner, apropos the hours of the waitresses, that his Wage and Hour Bill [the Fair Labor Standards Act of 1938, originally introduced in the United States Senate by Senator Hugo Black and popularly known as the "Black-Connery" Wage-Hour Bill] was one of the finest things he accomplished for people in his public service. He said William Green, then President of AFL, fought the bill because it would discourage many people from joining the union, as there wouldn't be very much incentive if government limited hours and fixed minimum wages.

Sunday, February 21 Leave for Orlando. Rainy and dark.

Tuesday, February 23 We drove up to St. Augustine to eat breakfast and bought a paper. As we sat down at the table Hugo opened it and glanced at the headlines. Immediately he said, "Ohhh, Felix is dead!" His eyes filled up with tears. We both read then that Justice Frankfurter had died yesterday about 5:40 P.M. We were surprised the news hadn't reached us because we had watched the news on television. After breakfast as Hugo drove, he composed a statement, I writing it down, to give to the papers. We stopped at Jesup, Georgia, about 10:30, where he telephoned the office and gave it in. Frances [Lamb, Hugo's secretary] said they had wanted to call him at 10:30 last night but she advised against it. Hugo filled up a little as he gave the statement to Frances. He is very sentimental. We drove on until about a quarter of 5 and called Frances to find out when Felix's funeral would be. She said at 3:00 P.M. the next day, so we decided to drive on until dark, so we could make it in to Washington by then.

Wednesday, February 24 *Felix's funeral.* Rainy, cloudy, cold. We woke up at 5:30 and got away by 6:00. It is now 10:25 A.M. and we are about 53 miles south of Richmond. Should be home around 1:30.

Went by Mother's [Mrs. Seay lived a few blocks away] and found her in pretty good spirits, then we rushed home and dressed to go to Felix's memorial services. We arrived just at 3:00. All the Court except Bill and Joanie Douglas were there. The President came in at the last moment. They were wheeling in poor Marion [Frankfurter] as we arrived. The room in their apartment was filled with former law clerks, special friends, Dean Acheson included. Paul Freund made a touching address, calling Felix "FF"; Moose Isenberg, Hugo's former law clerk, played the clarinet and was accompanied on the piano and by a violinist; very sad and penetrating music. A man read the Kaddish, the Hebrew prayer for the dead. After the service we brought Paul Freund and Dean [Erwin] Griswold of Harvard by the airport, returned home, and I went down and sat with Mother an hour. We went to bed right after dinner, dead tired. Hugo almost had a chill.

It's ironic that Marion outlived Felix, because she has been ill so long. In 1957, when the picture of the Court wives was taken, Marion, as usual, was bedbound. Felix insisted that an empty seat be shown in exactly the right place according to protocol. (See photo insert.)

Friday, February 26 Hazel Davis's [Hugo's brother Lee's daughter] book *Uncle Hugo* came in the mail, all published and everything. A charming book, complete with old letters, tickets, political cards, Sunday School cards, clippings, etc., and Hazel's own beautifully written narrative holding the theme together. We all competed to look at it.

Saturday, February 27 *Hugo's seventy-ninth birthday.* We had a late breakfast and dressed for Marx Leva's [Hugo's second law clerk] luncheon. Associated Press and Alexandria *Gazette* came at 12:00 to take pictures. Hugo got phone calls and telegrams all day. At dinner we were sitting around talking when the doorbell rang. An aide from the White House in a big black limousine stood there with an envelope. It was a beautifully written two-page letter from President Johnson and two pictures of Hugo and Lady Bird at the Inaugural Ball. Hugo read the letter aloud, and before he finished his voice broke a little and his eyes were moist. He was not alone in this. How thrilling at age seventy-nine—or any other age—to receive such a letter of affection and pride written by one's President! In it he quoted from Hugo's *Chambers*[3] opinion: "Under our constitutional system, courts stand against any winds that blow as havens of refuge for those who might otherwise suffer because they are weak, outnumbered, or because they are non-conforming victims of prejudice and public excitement." The President said that Hugo had done honor to his native State of Alabama and to his Country.

Monday, March 1 Hugo came home about 7:15. He is now, at 10:30 P.M., dictating. Hugo has certain steps to warm up for writing either an opinion or a dissent. First he reads the record of the case exhaustively and painstakingly. Then he talks it over with his law clerks for hours—searchingly and argumentatively. Often he has the clerks come to the house and spend the day. It's exciting to hear the give and take that goes on. Hugo always tries his best to convince them he's right. Sometimes he does, but once in a while he doesn't. If he feels pretty hopeless about it, he might say, "I'll dictate the first draft myself." Sometimes he has the objectors to his ideas write the first draft of the opinion, and then, when they have to use Hugo's reasoning, they become convinced he's right. Sometimes the law clerks put a doubt in his mind, but I think they would agree with me that this has been very rare. Often at the clerks' reunions one or another of the clerks will say, "Judge, do you remember that maritime opinion you were so wrong about?" Hugo will come right back at them and say, "Yes, you thought you were a great admiralty lawyer then, didn't you? Man, you were going to set the record straight!" Whereupon they will all laugh heartily and the clerk will murmur, "I still think I was right, Judge!"

Almost invariably, on an opinion he thinks to be very important, Hugo awakens in the middle of the night thinking about it. Soon he pulls the chain to turn on the light. "Darling," he says to me, "are you awake?" By that time I am, of course, fully awake. "I am bothered about a case." "Tell me about it," I say. "Well, this is what it is all about . . ." Then he recounts in detail and with passion the horrible injustice being perpetrated on a person because of his brethren's failure to see it his way. "I will have to write it on very narrow grounds if I want to get a Court," he says, naming those he has with him and those against.

Sometimes this unwinds him, sometimes not. If he doesn't feel he can go to sleep, he says, "Now it's three o'clock in the morning and I have just got to be fresh for the Conference tomorrow. I need sleep. What do you think I ought to do?"

Then I suggest, "Why don't you take a little bourbon to make you sleepy?" (Hugo is terribly inhibited about taking liquor and usually wants me to be the one to suggest it.) And so he pours a splash of bourbon on ice, fills the glass with water, and soon is sound asleep. The next morning he awakens as bright and clear-minded as can be, and he approaches the day with his usual eager zest for life and vast good humor. He is like a spirited racehorse, held back only by the firm reins of his own self-control, but once on the track and running, giving the race everything he has!

After these nocturnal discussions about a case, Hugo comes home from the Court, maybe lies down for a little nap, and after one of Lizzie Mae's good dinners, comes back upstairs. He sits at his desk thinking about his case and then gets out a yellow lined pad and starts to write. As he becomes more immersed in his work, he takes sharp breaths which are audible all over the room. My own theory is that instinctively he inhales more oxygen to fuel his brain. Often as he starts to write I might get up and turn the television off, or stop typing at my desk in the far corner of the study, but he tells me not to bother—nothing I do bothers him. And such are his powers of concentration that once he starts writing, nothing does interfere. The sound of his quick intakes of breath and the soft scratching of his pencil continues until the task is finished—sometimes a period of four or five hours of steady writing. To borrow a phrase from one of his law clerks —Chuck Luce—Hugo is up on Mount Olympus communing with the Constitution.

Wednesday, March 3 *Joan Douglas's twenty-fifth birthday party.* Joanie told of a cabdriver's conversation. The cabbie was knocking the Court and said, "That Douglas is a real creep, married a twenty-five-year-old girl," and she replied, "Yes, I'm that twenty-five-year-old girl." *Eeeeeee,* his car went out of control and back. "Nothing personal, ma'am."

Sunday, March 7 Hugo repaired to the study to write his draft of a thank-you letter to President Johnson and spent practically the rest of the afternoon on that. When Hugo got through with his letter, I typed it and he copied it in pen. At 6:00 we delivered it to the White House.

Monday, March 8 Hugo left for Court at 9:00 and I followed at 9:30, arriving just in time to see the Justices come into the Courtroom. Several opinions came down, then Hugo's, giving the unanimous Court decisions declaring Mississippi and Louisiana's voting registration laws in regard to Negroes unconstitutional.[4] John Harlan sent a note from the bench. "Hugo looks fine," it said. "Don't let him misbehave!"

Wednesday, March 10 Everything is buzzing because of the Selma, Alabama, law enforcement and state troopers' brutality to the demonstrators marching on behalf of the Negroes. Jim Reeb, the white Unitarian preacher who married Josephine [Hugo's daughter] to Mario [Pesaresi], was clubbed by four or five white men in Selma and was carried to Birmingham in critical condition with no hope held out for his life. It all seems so needless. The Congress will pass the laws the Negroes are demanding anyhow, and though the courts are "not as glamorous as the streets," nevertheless Hugo thinks they are the route by which the only lasting civil rights will come. My poor Alabama!

Friday, March 12 Heard on television last night that Jim Reeb died; his family, with four young children, are prostrate with grief. How my heart goes out to them. The whole country is in an uproar with civil rights demonstrators marching in Chicago, sitting in the U.S. Attorney's office in Boston, blocking traffic at the White House. California to Maine seems to be in a great uproar of protest. And yet the Government is moving toward a bill guaranteeing all the right to vote. Was it imperative for Martin Luther King to organize this march from Selma to Montgomery? Was it necessary for King to plead with all clergy to come to support his march? Whose fault—King's or Wallace's? I asked Hugo again at dinner if we shouldn't have the Howletts over and give them an anonymous donation for Mrs. Reeb, whether one of us should write, whether we should send flowers, and I got from Hugo almost a cry of agony and impatience, begging me not to bring it up again, as it worries him that I do. If he does what I ask, he says, and it is published, he will probably have to sit out of all those cases. I was contrite.

Saturday, March 13 Hugo has spent almost all day on writing his article about Felix for the *Harvard Law Review.* About 6:00 he finished it and let me read it. It was a beautiful tribute and I said so. He said, "Well, now that I have written about my deep and sincere friendship for Felix, I feel free to write my views on how mistaken his views were."

Here is a transcript published in June, 1965:

There is a widespread belief that men whose views about some things differ sharply must be enemies. During our long service together Felix and I did have disagreements about the law and the meaning of the Constitution, many of them, and we frequently expressed these differences with vigor and emphasis. But he never was the kind of person to bear personal enmity toward others merely because they differed with him, and after a heated dispute when we passed on to the next case he was ready to ally himself cheerfully with his former adversaries. Out of our discussion and our association I learned that he loved this country with a passionate devotion and that long before I had ever met him, he had dedicated his life to its service. I learned also that he had this same devotion to our judicial system. I could not have, even if I had tried, harbored ill will toward a man I knew to be so dedicated to our country and its ideals. And so my initial respect and friendship for Felix survived all differences of opinion, in fact grew with the years, and left me with a feeling of great loss when he died.

I am happy to have had the opportunity and good fortune to have served with him for twenty-three years and seven months; to argue with him; to agree with him; to disagree with him; and to live a large part of my life in the light of his brilliant intellect, his buoyant spirit and his unashamed patriotism. This was a man. We need more like him.

Monday, March 15 I talked to Frances Lamb about 3:00 and she asked me if we were going to the Special Session of Congress tonight to hear the President give his Voting Rights Bill speech. Hugo came on the phone and said he was not going, that he, John Harlan, and Potter Stewart thought it inappropriate to go because the bill would soon be in their laps, most likely. Bill Douglas had a previous dinner engagement and couldn't go. The others, the C.J., Byron White, Bill Brennan, Arthur Goldberg, and Tom Clark, decided to go. Hugo and I watched it on television. It was a good speech but didn't end until 10:00 P.M., and I was glad we were here instead of there.

Tuesday, March 16 I decided to go to the Memorial Services for James Reeb at All Souls Church and hurried to the Court to see if Maggy Bryan [Chief Justice Earl Warren's secretary] would go with me. We got a cab and arrived about 2:00. Soon the Vice President and Mrs. Humphrey, Teddy and Joan Kennedy, and members of the family came in: his widow and fine-looking son of thirteen or so, his mother and father, and others. The Memorial was well done, but too long. There were three preachers and Dr. Howlett said his eulogy, which was the best, I thought.

Thursday, March 18 We had to go out to the opening of the new Washington Hilton. Hugo is supposed to be honorary chairman of their tennis courts, and naturally he wanted to see the courts and the manager. Dinner was slow and confused. They served soup, appetizer, and dessert, entirely skipping the entrée.

Friday, March 19 *Chief's birthday.* I went to the Safeway and got up a box of fruit to give the C.J. for his birthday. Hugo doesn't approve of a birthday gift tradition but preferred to give fruit over flowers.

Monday, March 22 What a thrilling day! Astronauts Grissom and Young went into orbit and landed safely. To show how blasé people are now about such miracles, my mother said, "Why are they coming down? I thought they were landing on the moon." She had in mind the *Ranger* 9 that is supposed to hit the moon tomorrow. We watched television until they safely "ditched" at about 4:00. One announcer said it cost us 45 million dollars to do one two-man Gemini flight today. We had more maneuvering today than in the past, and we are one step closer to the moon.

Wednesday, March 24 We had the Arthur Keeffes over for dinner and bridge. Art is a professor of Law at Catholic University who has sort of taken Hugo over to hero-worship. When we played bridge, Art and I opposed Hugo and Mrs. Keeffe. Hugo bid us up disgracefully, later admitting he had only *three* points. Keeffe said, "He's a fighting player. I hate pleasant people at the bridge table!"

Thursday, March 25 We both felt sluggish on awakening. We had gotten the giggles way in the night, as we often do, over a triviality, and we were both wide awake at 2:00 A.M.

Friday, March 26 Lizzie Mae and I got together a good dinner—steak; fresh asparagus (I hand-picked 100 stalks from store); biscuits; and strawberry shortcake. Tom Corcoran and Ben Cohen [advisers to Franklin Roosevelt] came first. Tom is always a fascinating conversationalist and talked of Roosevelt and legislation of the day. After dinner we went up to the study and Hugo again tried to get Tom to say he would run for the state senate or Governor of Rhode Island, that he had too fine a mind to "waste" on making money. Tom said the states were nothing now; hardly anyone is interested in office at the state level. Besides, it took "chips" for people to run. He'd make the chips and let his children run. Drayton Nabers, the coming law clerk, just finishing Yale, said he'd take Hugo's way and be Governor of Alabama in 1972, just going to the people.

Saturday, March 27 Hugo had developed a cold and spent nearly all day in pajamas, reading Alpheus T. Mason's book on Chief Justice Taft [*William Howard Taft: Chief Justice*], which he found fascinating. He would stop now and then and read passages of it to me. He said Taft stood for everything he was opposed to, though he respected him for being honest in his views. Taft wrote many letters reflecting on his Court brothers, mostly Stone, McReynolds, Brandeis, and sometimes Holmes and others. Hugo said, "Thank God I've never written one word reflecting discredit on one of my brothers!"

Sunday, March 28 Hugo was still somewhat under the weather and spent most of the day in bed and finished his book on Taft. These are good days of rest, catnaps, and reading aloud, one to the other. Since he wants me to stay right with him, I don't attempt to do much other than necessary chores.

Monday, March 29 I took two friends into the Court to hear them argue the Connecticut Contraceptive case.[5] When we arrived, they were arguing the case where a man named Brown had been elected an officer of a labor union and was an admitted member of the Communist Party. The Solicitor General, Archibald Cox, argued it, and afterward his wife, Phyllis, went to lunch with us. She said Archie has three nightmares: (1) he would be late to Court; (2) he would forget his argument in the middle; and (3) he would look down someday and discover he was in his BVD's with no pants on! When Phyllis went back to Court, Archie told her he had had a hassle with Justice Black. We had heard Hugo question him keenly on several points.

The Contraceptive case started at about 1:00, and Ethel and Joan Kennedy came in and sat next to us. Thomas Emerson, a professor at Yale Law School, opened the arguments. The bench, already lively, really came to life, leaning forward, all asking questions 'til the poor man said he had tried to reach their points but couldn't.[6]

Wednesday, March 31 Washington *Star* reported Texas Congressman [John] Dowdy said that the A.G. [Attorney General], Nick Katzenbach, had been told by someone that five Justices of the Court had looked over and approved the draft of the Voting Rights Bill. Hugo said C.J. told them of the rumor. It was *absolutely* not true but they talked of whether they ought to issue a statement of denial or let it ride.

Thursday, April 1 A special April Fools' Day joke. The C.J. leaned forward to question a lawyer who was answering a question put by Arthur Goldberg, saying, "You didn't answer Justice *Goldwater's* question." Everybody laughed. Hugo came in at 6:00. He wasn't sure as yet whether he'd have a case coming down on Monday. I had hoped he would because our meat cutter and his wife want to come to Court. Hugo said he had one almost for sure, but Arthur Goldberg told him late this afternoon he had decided to write a concurrence, so that means John Harlan might want more time to write a dissent.

I liked [Senator Everett] Dirksen's denunciation of Dowdy: he said the lie about the Court conferring with Katzenbach was as monstrous and large as the State of Texas!

Friday, April 2 We went to Tom Clark's cocktail party in his apartment, taking John Harlan with us from the Court. Had a nice little visit. After that, Hugo and I slipped off and went to dinner at Parchey's, where we used to go often before we were married. Hugo was so sweet and dear. Said I'd made music for him now for nine years, and I told him he had made life just as beautiful for me. I suggested that we go see the movie *My Fair Lady,* but I could see that Hugo preferred to talk, and this we did. He talked of the Court, of his two current opinions—oh, of many things. For the first time we viewed the two really excellent color photographs of Hugo hanging in Parchey's.

Monday, April 5 *Last Monday opinion day.* A busy, busy day. Up at 7:00, to the office with Hugo by 9:30. Had the meat cutter at Giant, Bob Tarno and wife, as my guests. Court session short but interesting, with Hugo giving an important opinion that the Sixth Amendment is now applicable to the states by virtue of the Fourteenth, thus giving his *Adamson* dissent of fifteen years ago the virtue of becoming the law.[7] The C.J. also announced that henceforth opinions would be given when ready and not just on Mondays—a break with tradition.

[Hugo's son] Sterling went with us to Franklin D. Roosevelt, Jr.'s, home. They live very modestly, in comparison with my ideas of how a Roosevelt lived. Harvard and Radcliffe students were there and Hugo parried their questions. Hugo showed them that they were pro–civil rights and against Southerners. Finally, at 7:30, I dragged Hugo away. He would have made a grand teacher. He is wonderful with kids.

Tuesday, April 6 Rainy. Hugo did lots of reading in bed.

Friday, April 9 Shay Minton died [Associate Justice Sherman Minton, served on the Court 1949–1956].

Sunday, April 11 Hugo and I left for the funeral. We caught a plane for Louisville, Kentucky. The C.J., Stanley Reed [Associate Justice, served on the Court 1938–1957], the Marshal of the Court, and the Clerk also went. Tom Clark met us in Louisville. We were met by photographers and two limousines. The newsmen told the C.J., "There is great growth of the John Birch Society here. Do you care to comment?" The answer, of course, was no.

Monday, April 12 *Shay Minton's funeral,* New Albany, Indiana. Gertrude and Shay's children greeted us at the funeral home. Shay had become a Catholic two years ago and so it was a Catholic Mass. Shay's messenger, Hood, came from Washington to attend the funeral. He came up to the Chief, who was on the front seat of our car, and remarked on how sad it was. "And to think," he said, "it's opening day of baseball!" —referring to Shay's complete devotion to the game.

Tuesday, April 13 Today has been a packing day for me, getting ready for the Fifth Circuit Conference in St. Augustine. Hugo has worked all day, dictating and passing on petitions they've been sending out from the Court. We are on the 6:25 P.M. plane now, tourist class, waiting for dinner. It is 7:10 and still no supper nor sign of a drink even. I don't mind, but Hugo gets grumpy. We landed at Jacksonville, rented a U-Drive-It, and drove down to the magnificent old Flagler Hotel in St. Augustine. Went in and it was like "Old Home Week" with all the judges coming to say hello.

Thursday, April 15 Hugo, Jr., and I took on Hugo and Graham in tennis. Judge Seybourne H. Lynne, bless his heart, came out and sat on a bench and watched, soon to be joined by Judge Elbert Tuttle. For a while we had a big audience, and we were the envy of the others who usually had given up tennis years ago. At 6:00 all the Alabama judges and lawyers came to our room for a drink. I was most impressed by Howell Heflin and his wife, Elizabeth Ann. Also the Godbolds from Montgomery, Frank Johnson, who seemed lonely and courageous, Judge Hobart Grooms, and his little sweet honor, Judge Lynne, who told us he was going to invite us to the Christmas party in Birmingham. I do pray that we go.

Friday, April 16 Hugo and I had breakfast in the room, as he wanted time to think about his speech. We went down at 9:10, and when his turn came he was just simply magnificent! His voice rises and falls and is beautiful in its resonance. His talk was about how the judges and lawyers would meet the problem of the new law. It was so uplifting, so inspirational. He holds his audience in the palm of his hand. I forgot to mention that they elected Judge Herbert Christenberry from New Orleans as a delegate to the Judicial Conference for the next three years, and when Judge Tuttle asked for votes I absentmindedly voted "aye." Hugo turned, surprised, and looked at me, and then he opened his speech telling all that the election was illegal because I had voted! Was my face red! Hugo gathered in the loose ends of the whole conference and summed it up skillfully, complimenting the City, the Chief Judge, the weather, the subject matter, and so forth. His peroration was to walk humbly as servants, rather than as masters. He is a great speaker. We all had goose bumps.

Saturday, April 17 After the huge breakfast Hugo ate—orange juice, cereal, prunes, eggs, sausage, half of my hot cakes, toast, jelly, and one hot-cross bun—I thought he would eat no lunch. To my amazement he ate soup, salad, a club steak, and four cookies! Hugo always teases me by asking whether I can afford the calories and I have to admit I can't. He can eat all that with no problem.

Sunday, April 18 *Easter Sunday.* We are home and Hugo is swamped with work. He sat up until 1:00 A.M. and dictated two opinions (one dissent and one concurrence).

Friday, April 23 Hugo went in town to the Conference and Mother and I went to Kleins, a big discount store out on Duke Street. I tried on dresses galore and I found a cocktail dress of flowered polished cotton for $13. Hugo told me it was pretty. Said it reminded him of window-curtain material his father used to sell for 7¢ a yard—oh, well.

Sunday, April 25 Hugo disturbed over *cert* note where woman shot her lover. He mused at length at the tragedy of women who have strong sex urges and get themselves mixed up with too many men.

Tuesday, April 27 On Sunday night Hugo got up from sleeplessness and read a chapter in the Bible and was so thrilled with it he brought it to the breakfast table Monday and read it to me—about Samuel, whose two sons were named judges who proved to be corrupt and so the people came to Samuel and asked for a king. Samuel asked God and God told him to warn the people their burdens would be doubled. Samuel did so, but the people still wanted a king, and so they got one. Samuel's prophecy came to pass. Hugo feels the people in this country subconsciously want a change in government, since all seem to want a "government by demonstrations and marching." He remembers Hitler took to the streets before he took over.

Thursday, April 29 This morning at 4:30 A.M. Hugo awakened me sniffling and sneezing; said he had been awake about an hour. He was animated and said that the Intellectual man and the Physical man were all tied together, that the Intellectual was in high crescendo and therefore the Physical cooperated by waking up the Intellectual with sneezes so the latter could think. Hugo proceeded to talk about an opinion Bill Douglas was circulating with which he could not agree. This always bothers Hugo because he and Bill are usually so close in their thinking. He talked it out, I raised the window, and he took a nap until 6:30 A.M., when I woke up and turned on the television. Hugo wanted to listen (as we have been doing) to Professor Casson of New York University lecture on Alcestis. The Professor has been doing a series of lectures on the Greek tragedies. Hugo awakened brightly, got up, shaved, dressed, and went to work. I am dragging.

To Skelly Wrights' for dinner, with the Charley Fahys and David Bazelon [Judges Wright, Fahy, and Bazelon of the U.S. Court of Appeals for the District of Columbia]. Lovely conversation, but Hugo's opinions on many things are more conservative than theirs.

Saturday, May 1 Hugo and I sang some wonderful old hymns at dinner—"Abide with Me" and "At the Cross." Hugo tried to think of an old tear-jerker sung at funerals, but neither of us could recall it.

Sunday, May 2 I made soup for supper. Hugo worked. We watched *Profiles in Courage* showing George Mason's part in passing a "Bill of Rights" resolution in the Virginia Assembly. Hugo talked to me at dinner about those men—Jefferson, Mason, Patrick Henry, Randolph, *et al.* I wrote letters until 12:00 and Hugo sat up dictating an opinion 'til 2:30.

Monday, May 3 Went to Court with Hugo. A jillion attorneys were introduced; then came opinions. There was one about a citizen who wanted to travel to Cuba, but the State Department denied him a passport. The Court upheld the denial, and Hugo gave an eloquent, expressive dissent.[8] Marion [Mrs. Byron] White was in Court, and John Harlan, after verifying from Potter Stewart we were there (poor John is almost *blind!*), sent us a cute note addressed to "Mrs. Black and Mrs. White." It said "Happy May Day" and was signed J.M.H. Viewed the new portrait of Hugo—very good but not quite Hugo. Hit balls with Hugo in the boiling 90° sun.

Wednesday, May 5 I was so mad! The artist insisted I come to the Court this morning to give him criticisms on Hugo's portrait. We went down to see it and he had worked it over slightly. When I told him the face was too fat and the right eye off, he told me in no uncertain terms he would not change a line no matter who wanted it. Said it was a masterpiece and he would sometime sell it to a museum. And to think I gave up a round robin at the club to have him tell me this.

Monday, May 10 Dinner at the Skelly Wrights'. Hugo was dreadfully tired. However, he woke up when he mentioned how proud he was of the ten men on the Hayneville, Alabama, jury who wanted to convict on the trial for the murder of Mrs. Viola Liuzzo of Detroit on the Selma March. Two jurors held out and there was a mistrial.

Tuesday, May 11 We got up at 6:20 to hear Hugo's program—Dr. Casson's lecture on Aristotle's *Poetics.*

Wednesday, May 12 Hugo always wakes up now in time to hear Greek lectures. This morning it was Russian literature, in which he was not much interested. Hugo worked late tonight—2:30 A.M.

Monday, May 17 Hugo is the most rewarding man to live with. He worked until 2:00 A.M. When he came to bed he wanted to talk. He told me how happy I am making him and we reviewed for the jillionth time the miracle of our romance and marriage. We got to sleep very late, or I should say very early. We both got up at 8:00 and since my car was at the Court I drove him down. Hugo gave a vigorous dissent to the California Offshore Lands case.[9] I left before he gave his opinion of the day. Came back to rest and get out clothes for White House. Spencer drove us and we arrived at the southwest gate at 7:55. We were escorted to the East Room. The Presidential party came down at 8:15. LBJ hugged Hugo and kissed me. We both sat at the head table, I with Hubert Humphrey on my left. I loved talking to him and I felt completely at ease. Hugo sparkled between Mrs. Humphrey and Mrs. Henry Jackson, wife of the Senator from Washington. Hubert Humphrey wrote on my dinner menu, "To a Southern belle from her dinner partner." He said he wanted a dance, but Hugo and I were both tired so we slipped away early.

Friday, May 21 Hugo came home and worried that I was wearing myself out. He said Bill Brennan was really mad with him because of one of his opinions and dissents and was very snippy to him in Conference. Hope the Brennans come to my dinner party!

Saturday, May 22 Hugo worked until 1:30 this morning and is still going strong. He's having *lots* of dissents!

Sunday, May 23 Couldn't sleep last night. Worrying about Chianti: should I return and get better, etc. Hugo woke up at 2:00 and talked at length about Court. I decided my worry was trivial.

Tuesday, May 25 Well, the party was marvelous, as I knew it would be when everything seems to go wrong beforehand. I was tired, but pushed myself; Hugo shut himself in the study to dictate his last opinion (he hopes) of the year. All members of the Court except Goldbergs (at their Circuit Conference) and Douglases (in Puerto Rico) came. After dinner, we *sang!* Potter Stewart was darling! He has a splendid voice and hammed it up. Hugo also was adorable and sang several solos. All joined in. When Stanley Reed left, he said he had been going to Supreme Court parties for thirty-five years and this was the gayest he'd ever attended. So all ended quite well, and Hugo's tensions seemed to vanish.

Thursday, May 27 This was a scorcher—97°. Hugo and I hit balls about two hours in the morning. I nearly dissolved in my own sweat.

Monday, May 31 Memorial Day holiday. Today has been a day of gentleness and peace. We slept late, ate a leisurely breakfast, picked up Mother, and drove into the Court to get an opinion Hugo needed. Lizzie Mae had dinner ready about 8:00—good old turnip greens, poke salad, salt pork, corn, cornbread, steak, and strawberries for dessert.

Tuesday, June 1 I had to go to the Court by 12:00, as Hugo and I were going to the White House at 12:30, where Hugo was to swear in nine presidential appointees. We all went to the Rose Garden at 12:30 and the President came out and greeted Hugo warmly. (I was out in the crowd.) The President, fresh from his daughter Luci's high school graduating exercises, looked tan and well, although I read he did not arrive back in

D.C. until 2:00 that morning and had a rigorous schedule all day. When he introduced Hugo to give the oath he called him "my beloved old friend, Justice Black." After the ceremonies, the President called for me (by name) and the wives of the swearees to come into his office. He greeted me with a kiss and asked, "Did he beat you yesterday? At tennis, I mean!" and laughed.

Wednesday, June 2 Hugo has refrained from our "daily drink" for two days now. I told him I'd join him in refraining, except when we go out or have company here.

Thursday, June 3 Hugo went to the office at 10:00 and came home at 5:00, and we hit balls until almost 7:00. We are now watching television about the space flight. Such a miracle! Too bad! Some Southerner took a pot shot at two Negro deputy sheriffs at Bogalusa, Louisiana, killing one and injuring the other. How incongruous in the space age.

Friday, June 4 Libby and Douglass Cater [journalist and author, former aide to Lyndon Johnson] came over at 6:30 for "tennis and turnip greens." Our mint juleps were delicious, though Hugo had ginger ale. The discussion after dinner ended up with Hugo's telling Doug how sad and wrong he thought the Viet Nam and Dominican intervention was on our part.

Sunday, June 6 Andy and Potter Stewart came over for a few minutes for Andy to see the garden. I fixed ginger ale and lime sherbert. Hugo still working, and it is now 10:30.

Monday, June 7 What a day! My headlines would be as follows: COURT ENDS TERM. ASTRONAUTS MCDIVITT AND WHITE LAND SAFELY. HUGO BLACK DELIVERS A POWERFUL DISSENT TO CONNECTICUT CONTRACEPTIVE CASE.

The two cases in which Hugo dissented were very important to him. One was the *Linkletter* case, in which the Court held that the *Mapp* case[10] did not apply retrospectively and all defendants convicted on evidence seized in an unlawful search and seizure prior to *Mapp* were denied relief. Hugo thought this was a miscarriage of justice and said so vigorously.[11]

But his main dissent was to the Court's holding in *Griswold* v. *Connecticut* where the Court held that the Connecticut law against selling contraceptives violated the Constitution because it intruded on an individual's privacy. Hugo thought the law itself very foolish, but thought that nowhere in the Constitution could there be found any prohibition against it. All but Potter Stewart went with the Court, which adopted Felix's balancing concept that where a law offended the conscience of a community, or judges, then the Court could overrule it, thereby making the Constitution current with changing times. Hugo was eloquent. Wish everybody could have heard him. I think it will be one of his great dissents![12]

Tuesday, June 8 Yesterday during the introduction of attorneys, a man who was introducing another gave his spiel about being satisfied so and so was qualified to practice before the Court, and ended up proudly by saying that so and so was from Houston, Texas, "home of *Gemini IV.*" This, of course, referred to the spacecraft which had just completed its successful mission. The Chief was apparently annoyed and said, "Does *Gemini IV* have anything to do with it?"

Wednesday, June 9 Lizzie Mae got us out of bed with the shout that Jigger, our dog, had fallen into the fish pond and she couldn't get him out. I had visions of his drowning and rushed down in robe and nightgown, very agitated. Hugo was right behind me. There was poor Jigger, wet as a drowned rat, standing up in the box of water lilies vainly trying to get out! I took off my robe, vaguely thinking I'd have to get in the pool. However, the three of us lay down on our tummies and with a mighty heave pulled him out.

Alan Barth called later and apologized for having talked one way to me on the Contraceptive case and writing an editorial directly opposite. Alan, the editorial writer for the Washington *Post,* sat next to me yesterday in the family box listening to Hugo's dissent in the Contraceptive case. We went to the cafeteria together for lunch, and he expressed great admiration for the dissent. "He is absolutely right," he told me. I was surprised to hear him say this because Alan, good friend that he is, usually reflects the Harvard viewpoint in his editorials. To my consternation and amazement this morning's *Post* editorial, written by him, was *opposed* to Hugo's dissent. Hugo was surprised, too, in view of what I had told him about Alan yesterday. When Alan called at 7:30 this morning he said, "I was so carried away with Hugo's eloquence yesterday that I thought I was for him. But when I went back to my office and did my homework I found I was against him." In response to his apology, I answered, "It is all right." Hugo was right beside me reading the morning *Post*'s editorial, and he said he wished I had let him speak to Alan. "I would have told him that Felix was still running the *Post* after his death just as he did during his life."

Wednesday, June 16 Had dinner at the Thurman Arnolds' [appellate court judge and Justice Department attorney]. Thurman's book *Fair Fights and Foul* is just out.

Sunday, June 20 Played tennis with Marx Leva and his daughter, Lloyd. They beat us with lobs, Hugo said, but I don't know; I get discouraged. I volleyed badly and didn't kill balls when I could. We watched *Judgment at Nuremberg* from 9:00 till 12:30.

Hugo had opposed the Nuremberg trials, and he also was opposed to President Truman's sending Bob Jackson [Associate Justice, 1941–1954] over to Nuremberg as special prosecutor of the Nazis' war crimes. He did not believe that a President should appoint a member of the Supreme Court to any Commission that would take him away from his duties at the Court. However, his dissent was that he believed the crimes the people were being tried for were *ex post facto* and that no one should be tried for acts committed before there were any laws on the books defining those acts as crimes.

After seeing the movie, Hugo said he thought it propaganda on behalf of the trials, although it purported to show the prosecution in an unfavorable light from time to time.

Saturday, June 26 We always listen to *Sunrise Semester.* Hugo thinks the professor of political science who teaches is very good but said the professor did not understand today's topic, "Search and Seizure and the Fourth Amendment," as set out in *Wolf* v. *Colorado*[13] and the *Mapp* case.

Wednesday, July 14 We are at the Circuit Conference in Sun Valley and have heard that Adlai Stevenson died suddenly. Sadness everywhere over death of a great man.

Friday, July 16 Conference ends. Hugo's speech at the banquet was just great. He told several good stories, and then gave a very inspirational talk ending with Virgil's song about burial. Everybody listened with rapt attention, including some of the kids in the kitchen, our Alabama waitress included.

Sunday, July 18 Caught plane. Pleasant flight to Chicago, but Hugo and I had coach tickets from Chicago to D.C. We were in a section of three seats and a man who weighed 200 pounds sat next to us. Hugo disconsolate.

Monday, July 19 Am listening to eulogies to Adlai Stevenson: "Let me be an instrument of Thy peace."

Tuesday, July 20 *Arthur Goldberg goes off the Court to succeed Adlai Stevenson in U.N.* The big news broke at 11:00 A.M. today. Frances Lamb called to tell us about it. Hugo immediately called the office and got Arthur and Dorothy. Dorothy, Hugo said, was almost in tears, and Arthur apparently was fearful that Hugo would disapprove because he hadn't earlier called him and because he knew Hugo's view that a Supreme Court Justice should not take jobs other than the Court, or go off on other missions. Hugo reassured him and became convinced from what Arthur told him and what he later heard on television in regard to the President's and Arthur's statements that Arthur should have responded to the plea of the President.

John Harlan called about 6:45, much disturbed at the news, but Hugo reassured him. He is now talking to John and they are speculating as to the replacement. They are mentioning Abe Fortas as the replacement, or possibly Thurgood Marshall from the Second Circuit. I must admit I'm hoping Abe will be the one because I'm very fond of the Fortases and I hardly know the Marshalls.

Still much racial trouble in Bogalusa, Louisiana. University of Mississippi admitted a Negro today without incident.

Wednesday, July 21 Hugo talked to Abe Fortas on the telephone today and told him he and the C.J. both hoped he'd take the position on the Court vacated by Arthur. He replied his office was meeting at that moment to talk it over. Much flurry and editorial comment (favorable) about Arthur.

Monday, July 26 *Arthur Goldberg sworn in as U.N. Ambassador by Hugo at the White House.* Today I felt truly a part of history. Hugo and I had Spencer drive us to the White House. Some fifty to seventy-five people were standing in the Rose Garden in the blazing 90° heat. The President talked seriously of the Viet Nam situation and that we must stand by our commitments. Then he introduced Hugo, calling him "a great humanitarian." Hugo read the oath to Arthur with most impressive emphasis, and Arthur repeated it in like vein, very seriously. Already, it appeared to me, Arthur was taking on the awesome burdens of his job. Hugo's hand shook visibly as he gave the oath. Then Hugo surprised us all, while still holding Arthur's hand, saying a few words on behalf of the Court, telling how highly they respected Arthur and how they gave him up with reluctance only for the cause of peace. Arthur was visibly moved by his words. Arthur read his letter of resignation from the Court and the letter he had written his brethren. He spoke impressively of his determination to inch toward peace. We stood about for a few moments shaking hands with many Senators and others of the Cabinet. Then Hugo signed the oath for Arthur and we left.

I got home in time to rest ten minutes, then dressed, and Hugo and I went to Court (I driving while he did *certs*). We joined Byron White and went to the Federal Bar Association, where they presented the first copy of *Equal Justice under Law,* the new book on the Supreme Court, the sister book to those on the Capitol and White House, done by the National Geographic.

Abe later called Hugo to say he was not accepting the Court job at this time, that he felt a duty to advise Johnson that he personally was pushing for Walter Shaeffer, Chief Justice of the State of Illinois.

Wednesday, July 28 *Abe Fortas appointed to Court.* At noon the tremendous news came that Abe Fortas *would* be our next Justice. We were not cheered, though, to hear the President say the Viet Nam War had to continue and 50,000 had to be called up through the draft.

After the President's announcement, Abe called again and said the President said, "Now look, Abe! They need you on the Court. You may never have the opportunity again. *Take this job*!" So Abe said he felt he had to accept. We are all glad!

Sunday, August 1 To the Doug Caters' for a swim. The Jack Valentis and their three-year-old came by. Jack Valenti is Johnson's main assistant, practically. He and Hugo talked very interestingly of history and Hugo got in a few more licks on how wars often cause defeats of Presidents.

Thursday, August 5 Hugo worked on checkbook and I thought we'd be late for the *Sequoia,* the Presidential yacht. Many Cabinet members were already on board. I saw Mrs. Dean Rusk and Mrs. Robert McNamara, whose husbands [the Secretary of State and the Secretary of Defense] came on later, intact with briefcases. There was a spirit of camaraderie among the guests. Hugo and I felt a little outside, as indeed we were. The sun hung low, a big red ball of fire over the Potomac. Since Humphrey was aboard, the Secret Service tender followed us along. The Veep bubbled over, as usual, and said that Muriel was still put out with him because they had to get married in the morning. "Papa didn't want to close the store in the afternoon," he explained. Suddenly we heard violent sneezing from across the way. Arthur Goldberg had told McNamara the Waldorf Astoria charged the U.S. $14.10 for every luncheon guest they had. They kidded McNamara, saying the thought of spending so much money for lunch had given him an allergy attack. Dorothy [Goldberg] swore she was going to send Arthur out to the Automat with a shopping bag to bring back food for lunches. McNamara, who has just written a paper on economy for the Pentagon, laughed and sneezed for quite a while. I was surprised when we left to hear Hugo say he was going to drive home because I had more to drink than he had. I said, "Do I look tipsy?" "No," he said, but insisted on driving. Since I always drive after dark (he sees very poorly at night) I was rather put out with him and a little frightened. I was annoyed because he is so very rigid and I started to talk to him about it but decided the best course was to drop it entirely. He seldom is relaxed when out like that and we miss a little fun that way, but he is so dear and sweet in other ways, he more than makes up for it.

Saturday, August 7 I keep thinking of discussion at the Caters' *in re* the rash of stories about Kennedy now appearing, "telling all." Jack Valenti said that people who are chroniclers are a menace. For instance, he said he might get impatient and say "Cater is a damn fool and an idiot." He said he wouldn't actually feel that way about it, but if he had told his wife that and she had written it down, it might go down in history that he considered Cater an idiot and a fool when nothing could be farther from the truth.

Tuesday, August 10 Today Hugo sat down and dictated his memories about [Louis] Brandeis [Associate Justice, served on the Court 1916–1939] and said he was going to dictate on other subjects from time to time. I believe he intends to write his memoirs. I do hope so. His memories are so rich.

We had invited Carol and Abe Fortas for dinner in answer to an SOS by Bill Douglas, saying they were having a serious crisis about Abe's going on the Court. Carol told me they had several big things going that now have to be given up, that they can't live on the small Court salary and may have to give up their new home. Later Hugo talked to Carol in that dear, straightforward way of his. I was almost in tears at the things he was saying and it did have a great softening effect on Carol, I could tell. He told how he had deliberately chosen public service; how invaluable his first wife's role was in his work; how unproductive he was in the years when he was alone; and, bless him, how much he was able to do after he married me. How a man needs a wife, in short. Carol asked indignantly if he was suggesting that she give up her law practice which was her life, and Hugo said, "Certainly not." And as to whether Abe would have to sit out of some cases because of Carol's involvement, they were only a minute percent of cases. I do believe Hugo's advice helped. They stayed until after midnight.

Thursday, August 12 At last, a lazy day! Hugo and I woke up to hear our 6:30 lecture, read the paper in leisure, went to breakfast about 8:30, came back up and went back to bed for a while and read. As I lay with my head on his shoulder, he pulled me closer and said, "This is my idea of heaven." That *is* his idea of heaven. To read his paper and eat his breakfast laden with blueberries, peaches, and figs. To lie down after breakfast and read; to go out and hit balls for a couple of hours on the tennis court. Then to go out in the yard and pick figs, have lunch, then for a long nap with me beside him. To read in bed, to eat dinner, sometimes having a drink before, but lately only beer. Then work at his desk until sleepy and time to go to bed again. This is the summer schedule Hugo loves. He enjoys his comfortable little rut, his tennis court, his home-grown food, his well-tended gardens by Spencer, his well-cooked food by Lizzie Mae, and his wife's presence. He is a grand and wonderful man and so rewarding to live with.

Friday, August 13 There are terrible riots by the Negroes in Los Angeles. They have been going on two nights already and are expected again tonight. The Los Angeles riots got started because it was alleged that police brutality was used in arresting a man and woman for drunk driving. Hugo has been saying that the demonstrations would lead to riots and anarchy and he is borne out, to some extent, already.

Sunday, August 15 The horrible race riots in Los Angeles are still going on after three days, about 37 killed and 750 wounded and stores burned and looted. Horrible! Part of the lawless spirit of the times.

Saturday, August 21 The astronauts, Cooper and Conrad, went up to begin eight days in space! Another miracle under our very eyes!

We cooked out even though it was sprinkling. Hugo, good sport, standing out with raincoat and hat turning steak.

Tuesday, August 24 Hugo had been asked to swear in Thurgood Marshall, the first Negro Solicitor General, and I went with him. Tom Clark was also present, as were Roy Wilkins [of the NAACP]. and others. The President came out, shook hands with Tom, kissed me, almost kissed

Hugo, and made a nice speech about Marshall. Hugo swore Marshall in and said a few remarks about him, very sincerely and movingly—that he would represent *The People,* that he had seen him cross swords with a great lawyer, John W. Davis, and that he had never lost his temper or showed bad spirit, etc. Afterwards the President took us into his office, sat at his desk and told us a story about Ernest Gruening [Senator from Alaska] and FDR. The punch line was that FDR had never seen Ernest before, but that he reached over with cigarette holder in mouth, tilting up as usual, and murmured, "Ernest, where have you been?" As he did that the President mimicked FDR and looked for all the world just like him. He heaped souvenirs on the two Marshall boys and presented Mrs. Marshall and me with some White House Lyndon Johnson playing cards.

Wednesday, August 25 Dean and Jimmy [Dean DeMeritte, Elizabeth's grandson, and James Black, Hugo's grandson] and I arrived ten minutes late for a tour at the FBI. When I asked a guard where Mr. Hoover's office was, there was a special agent waiting to take me up. I arrived to find J. Edgar Hoover standing in his office waiting on me, a photographer to take a picture of the four of us. Then a grand tour in which we went behind the glass windows into the labs, saw a bullet under a microscope, saw the file on bank robbers, and the little boys handled tommy guns, etc. They were quite thrilled. At 6:00 that evening a special messenger delivered three autographed photos of the pictures made that day!

Thursday, August 26 Sterling [Black, Jr.] mailed the black snake and lizard he had hoped to carry on the plane straight home by air mail special delivery. Hugo told him he would not sleep in the same house with a snake.

Friday, August 27 Such a long day. Jimmy was anxious for plane time and could hardly wait. Sterling, when he was not teasing Jimmy, was flopping in a chair or going to lie down. Hugo talked to both boys at some length about taking advantage of educational opportunities, etc.

At 3:00 we left to go to the Court, where Hugo presented a gift to Johnny Warren, the messenger of many years of the Clerk's Office, who came to the Court the same year Hugo came, 1937. In Johnny's written reply, which he read, he broke down and cried. I was touched, as he was the messenger of the Clerk when I was secretary. Got boys on plane. Whew, what a relief!

Saturday, August 28 Tom Corcoran came over at 10:00 to talk to Hugo about his daughter, Margaret. He told him he wouldn't take her as *his* law clerk and didn't want Hugo to take her on his account. Hugo said to send her over to talk to him. I am weary in bone, spirit, and emotion. A real strain to look after children. So glad to be back in my usual rut with Hugo.

Tuesday, August 31 Hugo checked with the Library [of Congress] and they found my great-grandfather, Rufus King Williams, was Chief Justice of the Supreme Court of Kentucky about 1868. Mother had always heard it but had not verified it. Why did Grandfather Williams leave a wife and five children (grown by then) in Kentucky in 1879, and go to Ogden, Utah, to start life over again? He married a widow ten years his junior, became City Attorney in Ogden, took part in politics, and died in 1889, at age seventy-two. Life is stranger than fiction!

Wednesday, September 1 Hugo asked me if I thought we should pay off the last $3000 he owed on insurance. I told him I thought we should and so we did. Hugo said it was the first time he had been out of debt in forty years. Quite a good feeling.

Thursday, September 2 Margaret Corcoran telephoned, saying she wanted to see Hugo about being his clerk next year. Said she and Ben Cohen would come over to play tennis and later she could talk to Hugo about clerking.

Saturday, September 4 Went to Sears and while there Hugo followed the Navy doctor's advice and bought their cheap $10.95 shoes, the first he had bought since I have known him, over nine years ago.

Monday, September 6 We loaned Nils Anderson [an old friend and tennis partner of Hugo's] our *Bet a Million Gates,* written by Hugo's friend Herman Kogan, to read while he was here this week. When he came into the study he was nostalgic of the many talks he and Hugo had had there. Hugo shows the way to the stars to so many human beings by being so good, so philosophical, so inspirational. He must have been a profound influence on the lives of more than he dreams of!

Tuesday, September 7 Hugo and I went to the Court, he dropping me in town to look at a pin which he will give me for our anniversary present on Saturday, a pretty fourteen-carat gold bow with three small diamonds. Then went to Court, where Hugo, the C.J., and the law clerks were in the cafeteria eating—I think this was about the second time the C.J.'s ever been there. The cashier didn't even recognize him! I ate with

Maggy and the secretaries. Then went to Library of Congress where I found three letters written by Lincoln in regard to Grandfather Williams. Also read many of his judicial opinions.

Saturday, September 11 *Our eighth anniversary.* A warm day, emotionally speaking and weather-wise. We rested during the morning and received messages, cards, visits, telephone calls, and congratulations. Hugo gave me my lovely pin and I gave him the best tennis racket that money could buy: a gut-string Kramer Wilson. Hugo told Hugo, Jr., over the phone it was the only expensive racket he'd ever owned except Hugo, Jr.'s, hand-me-downs. I cooked dinner, dressed up in my wedding dress, and did my hair as I did then and, when Hugo came down, I surprised him with candlelight and Italian champagne. We spent long hours remembering, and talking about the miracle that brought us together.

Monday, September 13 The Library sent me out another Kentucky law book (*Duvall's Kentucky Reports,* vol. 63) and there is a thrilling dissent in the case of *Corbin* v. *Marsh* at page 202. I think I will be proud of this dissent. Hugo said, "He can write! He is quite a fellow!" I think Hugo felt a kinship with him because Rufus Williams had suffered in Mayfield, Kentucky, for siding with the North just as Hugo suffered in Alabama over integration. How eerie to steal backward a century and peer into the mind of my great-grandfather! Another coincidence—John Harlan's grandfather, John Marshall Harlan, practiced before Chief Justice Williams as State Attorney General.

Wednesday, September 15 Up at 5:45, arrive Denver 10:20. Futile call to Breckenridge but finally got Barney Whatley's Denver home. Ride to Breckenridge is breathtakingly beautiful. Barney [Hugo's first law partner] was delighted to see us. Two Clay County boys reunited: near eighty, Hugo young and vigorous, with face unlined; Barney erect, slim, past eighty.

Thursday, September 16 This morning Barney took us on "Whatley's Boulevard," a jeep trail around his house and property (about 500 acres in all). It was a breathtaking experience in two ways—fright and beauty. The jeep would go up a hill at almost a 45° angle, then we'd wind over a bumpy trail through pines and spruce and golden shimmering aspens. Going down the steep slopes frightened me into a new batch of gray hair. Barney drove with great nonchalance and a complete indifference to the danger involved. I'd squeal now and then but we lived through it. Hugo and Barney swapped wonderful stories of Clay County. Both these country boys were great speakers and talkers; both successful. Barney is worth over a million dollars and has given widely to philanthropic causes. Fresh fish from Barney's private pond for dinner and bridge until ten, Gertrude [Whatley] and I beating the boys.

Friday, September 17 We said our goodbyes to Barney and Gertrude, with always the nostalgic twinge that perhaps we'd never see them again. Gertrude wanted to send Lizzie Mae some of their wonderful turnips grown in their garden, but Barney didn't want to go get them.

The long flight came to an end and it looked mighty good to see Spencer, sharply dressed as usual, in a dark suit and chauffeur's cap, standing at the gate waiting.

Monday, September 20 Hugo awakened around 2:00 A.M. and I woke up too. When he has these wakeful spells he seems to have a lot of talk penned up in him that he has to let out. Even though I am a bit sluggish, these are moments to cherish. He talks of what is bothering him, the Carpentier Lectures for Columbia University at the time, then he talks of how happy I have made him and he sang me a song—"I only want my little rocking chair and you." So dear!

Wednesday, September 29 Returned at 2:30 from Mother's to get Hugo and a possum we had caught in the squirrel trap. The possum played dead and we took him to Mount Vernon. Hugo had to shake the cage to get him out and then Brer Possum turned and snarled at Hugo before waddling up the hill.

Thursday, September 30 I suggested to Hugo that he work this morning and hit this afternoon, because our program of hitting all morning leaves little time for him to work. We hit, have lunch, then he is tired so he takes a nap. Up around 3:00, but the few hours before dinner hardly get him started on his work. Today he did his work this morning.

Friday, October 1 John and Ethel Harlan to dinner. They brought us a fifth of "Rebel Yell" whiskey—a very good brand, too. I am so sad about dear Ethel and John. His eyesight is so very, very poor and her health is bad too. She can't help him much. He needs a reader. Such dear people.

Monday, October 4 *Court opening. Abe Fortas sworn in.* Wives only and Fortas friends in Justices' Section. As Abe took his seat, I wondered how his thoughts ran. The C.J. eulogized Arthur Goldberg; then Abe's commission was read. The Clerk administered the oath and Potter Stewart (next to Abe) simply turned, shook hands, and said, "Welcome, Mr. Justice." Abe seemed a bit bemused. As we went out I made a chance remark to a guard who had just been promoted from garage to Courtroom plainclothesman, saying, "Are you going to be in the Courtroom now?" To his affirmative, I said, "Bet you'll wish you were back in the garage." What a stupid remark. It hit Hugo the wrong way, I could tell.

Monday, October 11 Hugo thought that since Thurgood Marshall, the first Negro Solicitor General, would be introduced to the Court, it would be rather historical and that I should go in. I did and saw the welcome and stayed through the introductions of attorneys admitted to the Bar.

Tuesday, October 19 Hugo couldn't sleep and we talked till after 2:30. These night talks are so dear to my heart. We tell each other of the wonder of our eight years of married life. He frightens me a little, too. He said that nobody had the power to destroy him but me! *Me!* And I'd give my own life to save him if it were necessary.

Tuesday, November 2 Voted Democratic. Went down early to vote, and there had been brisk voting before I came and stood in line.

Thursday, November 4 Vernon Patrick [Hugo's law clerk in 1955] brought an editorial from the *Wall Street Journal* about Hugo's being more conservative (Connecticut Contraceptive case and Sit Downs).

Hugo and I talked to about 2:00 this morning, one of our wakeful nights. He says time is so short with me that he hates to go to sleep and leave me. I love him so much.

Thursday, November 18 Hugo is home now (5:30 P.M.) and I plan to read the book he wants me to read but which I have to get back to the library tomorrow. It contains Mary Wollstonecraft's essay on "The Rights of Women," and John Stuart Mill's essay on "The Subjection of Women." Hugo thinks they are the best things ever written about women. He says he doesn't agree with Wollstonecraft's proposition, however, that women should not make themselves attractive to men as an important principle of life.

Sunday, November 21 Hugo hired Margaret Corcoran as his law clerk. I think she is the first or second woman to be used as a law clerk in the history of the Court. Margaret Corcoran and Ben Cohen came over to play tennis with us. After that Hugo gave Margaret a straight-from-the-shoulder talk about how much work there was to being a clerk; he told her that she wouldn't have time for dating and having fun if she were his clerk. Ben and I made fudge pie while they were talking in the study.

Monday, November 22 Had lunch with Eleanor Bumgardner [a secretary at the Court]. When I think of "Lady" Bumgardner I remember the priceless faux pas she made when she substituted for me when I was Hugo's secretary. Hugo dictated on the machine—something about "a case which we summarily dismissed." Lady typed it "which we so merrily dismissed."

Hugo showed me a letter from Judge Lynne urging him to bring me to Birmingham for the Christmas party. I hope and pray we can go!

Wednesday, November 24 Last night Hugo capitulated by degrees and finally decided to take me to Birmingham. It will have been ten years since the last Christmas party I attended. I would be *so* proud to produce him and show him off to my dear friends. Judge Lynne plans to keep it a complete surprise. Later Hugo called Judge Lynne at Decatur. Judge Lynne, not knowing who it was, seemed a little cross at being awakened and Hugo had his good hearty wholesome laugh at him. Judge Lynne said he would take care of everything and said we could spend the night at his house. Glory be! I'm so deeply moved I dare not think about it lest it go away.

Met Steve Susman, the new law clerk, who will serve with Margaret Corcoran. They are going to work tonight.

Saturday, December 4 Read *Fanny Hill* this afternoon. *Some book!*

Monday, December 6 Hugo was stimulated and we talked until 4:00 A.M. I hardly slept at all after that. Hugo read where one can add six years to his life by sleeping six instead of eight hours a night, so he decided to work. When he does he always gets himself stimulated and wants to talk.

Hugo came in at 5:00 tonight, very tired and sleepy.

Monday, December 20 Getting ready for Birmingham. Today we made a dry run to airport. Hugo dictated his opinion while I got my hair done. He finished it by the time for dinner. Wrote my poem. All set, ready. Go!!

Tuesday, December 21 I dared not believe we'd make it and sat on the plane in a daze. The clerk's office in Birmingham had brought me back to life when I first went there to work in 1941. The other women in the office and I were kindred spirits, a little zany and full of ideas. We'd even write birthday plays and put them on at lunch. Once we put one on in the courtroom for the judges. I couldn't wait to get back to see my friends, but I was afraid Hugo would never let me go back. He always wanted me by his side. I copied my poem until it was time to change planes in Atlanta. Again I kept my fingers crossed. Don't be too happy, I told myself—it won't come true. But it did come true! Judge Lynne at the airport to meet us. Went home with the Judge, driving on detours to see where Hugo and I lived before we met. On arriving, Mrs. Lynne greeted us graciously, and I changed into my black velvet dress. Judge Lynne had ordered the halls of court cleared and everybody seated in the courtroom by 1:30. When Judge Lynne went in, he thanked the committees and said they used to have someone who added so much to their parties and that he had persuaded a notable Alabamian to bring her back. He then announced, "Justice and Mrs. Hugo L. Black." What a thrill!

Judge Lynne insisted we stay with him rather than in a hotel because he felt it was less dangerous for us to do so on account of the *Brown* decision.

The judge had planned a stag barbecue for the judges at his home while the "girls" in the office wanted to take me to our old haunt, Joy Young's, for dinner. But Hugo would have none of that. "I'll decline the stag and go with you. You're my wife and I want you with me." So I declined the girls' party and as a result Mrs. Lynne had to invite the judges' wives to her house.

Saturday, December 25 Christmas Day in Miami with Hugo, Jr. The children all opened their "Santa Claus" toys, though Margaret, the youngest, advised us there was no need to keep up the pretense any longer about old Santa.

Friday, December 31 Hugo took a lesson, his first, from John Hammill, the tennis pro at the Royal Palm Tennis Club. John pounded the ball at Hugo for almost an hour. Hugo hit some beautiful balls back. John kept saying to himself, "Incredible!" After fifteen minutes he went up to Hugo to ask if he was tired. (What a laugh!) When he finished the lesson, John told Hugo he could only remember three men over forty who could take the terrific pounding he had taken and that he must be in superb shape.

I didn't believe we would go anywhere that night, but Graham had made a date, way in advance, for me to go to get my hair fixed. Hugo hated for me to "waste" a hair-do; he told me to decide where I wanted to go. We made up our minds to go to the Royal Palm Country Club with Hugo and Graham for their party.

Hugo, Sr., as usual, outdanced everybody; and in the arms of my sweet husband, as the New Year came in to the tune of "Auld Lang Syne," I thought how happy the New Year would be.

1966

Sunday, January 2 Every day that goes by I count myself very blessed in having the dearest, kindest husband who ever drew a breath. He has been sweet and considerate of me. I know he went to the football game yesterday solely on my account, and I love him for it, among other things! Hugo dictating tonight.

Monday, January 3 Hugo worked 'til 3:00 this morning dictating five records on a dissent in the Louisiana Library Sit-in case [see page 135, *Brown*]. I sat up with him and wrote about five letters.

Tuesday, January 4 Norman Redlich from New York University Law School came to see Hugo about 11:00 A.M.. Hugo was expansive and vastly entertaining. He talked freely about the law. He told a delightful story about Richmond Pearson Hobson ("Remember the *Merrimack*"), who was a "kissing congressman" while Hugo was a senator. Hobson went wild on the subject of narcotics and asked Hugo to put a speech in the record. Later he wanted Hugo to put almost a whole anti-narcotics book in the record for him. When Hugo refused to do this at government expense (so Hobson could send it free all over the country), Hobson asked Hugo's secretary, "Confidentially, is the Senator a narcotics addict?" Hugo said he told his Administrative Assistant, Hugh Grant, "That's funny, yesterday he asked me the same thing about you!"

Saturday, January 8 Lately I have been having the strangest dreams of people in my childhood, many of whom are long since dead. Last night it was of Miss Maude Walker, my music teacher. Other nights it was of Uncle Jep, Aunt Eunice, and Salla Mae (all three been dead twenty years or more).

Wednesday, January 12 Leaving Florida for home at 1:30. At the airport I came out of the ladies' room and saw Hugo "stealing a weigh" on the airline scale. He was so cute with feet on the scale, derrière stuck out behind, and head peeping around at scale. Told him I wished I had his picture, with that yellow overcoat and jaunty hat in that undignified position. Got in at 4:30 P.M. and we went to Mother's; she told us all the terrible things that happened while I was gone. Then we got ready to go to State of the Union address. Met the other members of the Court in the garage at 8:20 and glad-handing all around. Went in a group over to the Capitol. Lady Bird in front row and Dorothy Goldberg right next to her. Both looked great! Cabinet wives in front of Mary Clark, Dotty Warren [Earl Warren's daughter] and me—Nina Warren, Andy Stewart, and Marion White also there. Joanie Douglas getting divorce, Brennans had other engagement.

The President came in dressed for color television with his blue shirt and light gray suit and tie. After the first round of applause, the Republican side of the House sat on their hands. The Democratic side received his message cordially, but not too enthusiastically. The Chief and Tom Clark applauded each time there was an applause. None of the others on the Court did.

Monday, January 17 *Court.* Hugo was in "rare" form, making us all laugh with his dissent to Abe Fortas in the *Yazell* case, holding a married woman not liable when signing a note for borrowed money.[1] Hugo had Carol Fortas in mind, as cool and competent a lawyer as ever put foot in a courtroom. The idea of *her* having to be protected from the male world was laughable. Hugo dissented on the Court opinion that the City of Macon, Georgia, could not resign as trustee under the will of a man who left the land as a park for the exclusive use of white people.[2] Then the Attorneys General from South Carolina and Virginia got up and argued on the power of Congress to pass the Voting Rights Act of 1965. Later Alabama and Louisiana argued against the law. A historic argument but I had to leave—too much to do.

Thursday, January 20 Mother says she got upset yesterday over the photo of Hugo in the hall and nearly fainted and worried about it all night. She didn't like it. Said it was *not* he! I told her she was crazy and I was so aggravated—me on the top rung of the ladder and she down there making noises about a picture! Anyway, I was sorry. Hugo had busy day. He presided. C.J. went to Truman's party.

Friday, January 21 Brennans, Harlans, Wrights to dinner. Black tie. We started a gay evening by singing "Auld Lang Syne." We really had fun and John got up at the end and told how great Hugo was and that I was the best thing that ever happened to Hugo and the Court. Bless his heart!

Sunday, January 23 My 58th birthday.

Wednesday, January 26 *White House dinner.* Snow eight to ten inches. I sat in Blue Room, with Lady Bird at my table, Hubert Humphrey on her right and C.J. on her left. I was on Humphrey's right and [Senate Majority Leader] Mike Mansfield on my right. Gosh, Mansfield is a hard man to talk to! But Hubert Humphrey won me over. When the big controversy over civil rights took place at the Democratic Convention in 1952, the South walked out. Humphrey was known as one of the young Turks, and being an Alabama resident all my life, I was prejudiced against him. When I told Humphrey about that tonight, he laughed and said, "That's fine. If people don't like you before they meet you and you tell them that you brush your teeth at night, they say, 'Well, he's not so bad after all.' " Glamorous dinner even without Jackie Kennedy's French chef. During program the President came over and knelt down and asked me if Hugo could still beat me playing tennis.

Sunday, January 30 Blizzard. Three to four feet of snow. O weather! We awakened to a beautiful but fierce world this morning—drifts of snow in windblown mounds almost six feet high in spots. What a day to work indoors! Instead I ran out and Hugo and I dabbed with the shovel, cleaning our front steps. I worked my way to the back and put birdseed in the feeder. Rewarded by a bunch of redbirds partaking.

Monday, January 31 *Still snowbound.* Hugo and I awakened feeling pretty helpless against the elements. We cooked breakfast and then an unwelcome belch from the sink threw back a bunch of second-hand tea leaves and coffee grounds from the disposal. Hugo worked on it about an hour and then I went to the basement and found the hand suction pump. We would flush with water, turn on disposal, and up they'd come! Then we'd bail the water, Hugo would use the pump and repeat. I finally said I was tired and we'd wait on a plumber. Not he! He said he *knew* he could open it and he stuck with it until he did!

Hugo could not go to Court and asked the C.J. to announce his opinion. About noon Hugo called the Street Department and told them he would like to get out that afternoon, that we were leaving for Florida in the morning. The man said they'd send a plow in an hour but for us not to come back as more snow was in prospect. The neighbors came and shoveled us out onto the street. Then the plow came by and we got out. We went to Court and Hugo conferred with C.J. about assignment of opinions. Spencer then took us to the White House to see Mrs. Roosevelt's portrait.

When we arrived there was a big fire in the Green Room and Mrs. Johnson was already down. Elliott Roosevelt and his sister; Reverend Kidd, pastor of church in Hyde Park; and Bess Abell [Lady Bird Johnson's social secretary] were there. Mrs. Johnson asked each about their memories of Mrs. Roosevelt.

Hugo told Lady Bird a couple of things to tell her University of Alabama audience in her forthcoming speech. "Tell them that Southerners were responsible for holding the Constitution together," Hugo told her.

Tuesday, February 1 Spencer expected to be out at house at 7:30 A.M. even though plane not due to leave until 9:45. Hugo was tense and so was I. He kept saying, "He'll never make it" as he stared at our great mounds of snow. I asked him to use the same faith he showed in unplugging the sink, but he said no—he had faith in that because he was depending on himself. He didn't have the same faith in depending on others, though he knew Spencer would get through if anybody could. Spencer got to our house about 9:00, and we inched through traffic and finally arrived at the airport. We need not have worried. The plane was an hour late in leaving.

Saturday, February 5 In Miami. Definitely not our day. Started off with a puncture in one of our "puncture-proof" tires. I went to the beauty parlor and while I was waiting to be rolled up, one sour-looking lady started sounding off about judges. Said she didn't believe in appointed judges. She believed they were corrupt political appointees. She thought judges who sat on the Supreme Court should have at least practiced law. I knew what was coming. I said most of them have either practiced or taught. Felix Frankfurter, I said, taught, and she said, "Oh, but there are Hugo Black and Earl Warren, who never practiced law a day in their lives." I told her I was Mrs. Black and that my husband had been a successful trial lawyer in Birmingham for twenty years before going to the Senate. She looked flustered but kept right on spluttering: "Earl Warren never practiced," she said. "Oh yes he has," I said. "He was County Attorney, District Attorney, and then Attorney General of California before becoming Governor." I was a little upset, but my friend was very, very upset. I cooled off, and she went under the dryer. Before I left, I went over, took her hand, and said, "You'd like Hugo Black, too, if you knew him." She smiled and apologized but went on to say, "I'm an Alabama person and I know him."

Tuesday, February 8 I talked to Louis Oberdorfer [Hugo's law clerk in 1946] yesterday about a present for Hugo's eightieth birthday party, which is being given by Hugo's law clerks. Lou says they are having each clerk write up his most vivid memory about working for Hugo. They will then get them printed. He asked if I wished to contribute to the book and I said no, I thought it should be from the clerks.

Hugo worked until very late—or early—in dictating the *Surowitz* case [see page 139]. Then his mind was driving forward and he couldn't sleep. He woke me up and wanted to talk about many sweet and intimate things and he asked if he was too exacting. I told him no—he was the most wonderful husband in the world. And Hugo said, "You suit me 100%." Then he said, "When I ruminate on it—and I don't allow myself to do it often—I find myself in a terrible position. I hate to leave you and yet I can't bear the thought of your leaving me first!"

Wednesday, February 9 Hugo talked long into the morning hours, this time about what an impossible situation the gambling and obscenity laws were. Some people had been arrested for "transporting in interstate commerce gambling certificates put out legally by the State of New Hampshire." Then he talked about the *Ginzburg* Obscenity case [see page 140]. He said, "Here is a man getting five years in the penitentiary and there was no way in advance for him to know he was committing any crime." On the other hand, *Fanny Hill,* which was terribly obscene, was deemed not "utterly worthless" in social values.

Friday, February 11 Hugo dictated a dissent on *Ginzburg* case.

Saturday, February 12 We were packing to go home from Florida and Hugo couldn't find his driver's license. We both searched under the seats of the car, through every pocket, everywhere. Hugo says that if he were caught without a driver's license in any minor traffic violation in Virginia they would surely put him in jail. Hugo telephoned the boys [law clerks Drayton Nabers, Jr., and John W. Vardaman, Jr.] and told them to have Richmond (which was closed for Saturday, naturally) wire him authorization to travel. No good. Finally, George Freeman [Hugo's law clerk in 1956] came through and had the Governor's aide teletype the police in Miami. They made a mistake and wired authorization for the "Chief Justice of Virginia" to travel, and, of course, Hugo said that that was grand because they would never dare arrest the Chief Justice of Virginia.

Sunday, February 13 Found driver's license in bag of tennis balls.

Tuesday, February 15 We had a long hard drive over mostly two-lane highways with heavy traffic going both ways. I get so frightened trying to pass when a car is hurtling seventy miles per hour toward you and vice versa. Hugo says I must learn to control my nerves and be stoical.

Wednesday, February 16 We got home by 2:00 P.M. and Hugo immediately called the boys and told them to come out, which they did. Hugo worked with them until 7:15, then we had dinner and he sat up and worked past midnight. Found Mother in unusually good spirits, due in large part to the card the Judge wrote her on Sunday.

Thursday, February 17 Hugo had the boys come out at 9:30 and they worked with him all day. Hugo worked late after the boys left. He has so much work to do. At this time he is largely in dissent and has to write on nearly every case.

Wednesday, February 23 What a day it's going to be for Hugo. He got up at 6:00 to attend a Masonic breakfast. He has the *Brown* dissent and has promised to sit for photographers and give interviews for his eightieth birthday. I went to the Court. Abe Fortas gave the opinion on the *Brown* case where five colored men sat in on a library even though they had been served. Hugo's dissent was magnificent, spine-chilling, and thrilling.[3] How eloquent he is, as his voice rises and falls. The master of the spoken word! Everybody sat on the edge of their chairs.

Saturday, February 26 Clerks' dinner for Hugo. The big day dawned and I rose early and went to the store to do errands. Sam Bradberry, Hugo's distant cousin, and Ed Best, manager of the supermarket, brought Hugo a large birthday cake shaped like Alabama with eighty cherries, showing Clay County, Montgomery, and so forth and indicating footprints from Alabama to Washington. All morning flowers and messages were being delivered. A pound cake from Mildred Faucett [Hugo's niece], flowers from Harlans, Douglases, Brennans, and others. By 6:30 we all were dressed and on our way to the Sheraton Carleton Federal City Club.

Clerks were all there except three out of the country (Robert Girard, Dan Meador, and Guido Calabresi), one sick (Charles Reich), one too far away moneywise in California (Jack McNulty), and only one not heard from. They presented Hugo with a printed book. Each had written his memories of his year or term with Hugo. Buddy Cooper, the first clerk, presided. He did so beautifully, with the proper mixture of humor and sentiment. Then Hugo arose and in a conversational tone told them how much he loved each one of them, of his pride in their records, and of his confidence in their integrity. It was so sweet and personal that their faces were shining with love and radiance. I read my poem. It was a sort of "This Is Your Life" going through his stages of development. The first two stanzas were:

Happy Birthday, Mr. Justice!

To wish you happy birthday, Judge,
We've gathered on your day,
To sup and swap a friendly word,
And love and tribute pay.

And as we gather round you, with
A minimum of fuss,
We know you've brought enrichment to
The lives of each of us.

Then, after talking about the Senate, the Court, *and* tennis, I ended with:

We know that we can get a Court!
We announce it to the town:
Our unanimous opinion is
That *you* are "Handed Down!"
'Tis the verdict of this court, and
The jury is not hung—
That your capacity for growth
Will ever keep you young.

We rank you as a truly great—
On this we'll never budge.
We wish you health and happiness—
A joyful birthday, Judge!

Sunday, February 27 The caterers came at 12:45 and quickly put out the food. About 4:00 Arthur Goldberg and Dorothy and the Skelly

Wrights came over. Tom Corcoran, Ben Cohen, and Margaret [Corcoran] came around 4:30. After we sang "Happy Birthday" to Hugo, Arthur asked to speak and he told how dearly Hugo was loved by his colleagues on the bench. Tom Corcoran spoke and said he had clerked for Holmes when Holmes was eighty-one and that Jim Rowe [later Corcoran's law partner] had clerked for Holmes when he was ninety-three and Tom wanted Hugo to stay on the Court at least thirteen more years. I was requested to read my poem again, which I did.

Dorothy then graciously spoke and after her tribute to Hugo she said, "Elizabeth, you have become a person *in your own right,*" and Tom Corcoran echoed that several times—"in your *own* right." How sweet that sounded.

Margaret Corcoran made a wee but sweet speech and Skelly Wright, with tears in his eyes, wished Hugo a happy birthday. Ben said a few words. Tom played the piano and we all sang a few numbers. Jo [Hugo's daughter, Josephine] and her dad jitterbugged a bit and then they asked me to do it with him, which I did.

Various pictures were taken until Hugo was exhausted and refused any more. Hugo went upstairs and shut himself in the study until all the guests had left. Then we came down to sit around the back bedroom fireplace and talk together. Hugo and I went up at 9:00 because he had a chill. We heard laughter floating up from downstairs until all hours and Hugo said one of the best things about his birthday was what a grand time his children had together.

Monday, February 28 We took Sterling to the airport, Hugo still coughing. Arrived home and there was a call from White House inviting us to a birthday party for Hugo on Tuesday. We called Sterling at the airport but he couldn't stay, because of his qualifying to run for the Senate in New Mexico the next day. Jo said she and Mario would come back. Hugo, Jr., and Graham would come back. Fred and Janice [DeMeritte, Elizabeth Black's son and daughter-in-law] were treading on clouds! We suggested Helen and Skelly and Doug and Libby Cater, in addition to the others the White House had already contacted. We were sorry only four members of the Court were invited and Hugo told Bess Abell, Lady Bird's Social Secretary, if it were left up to him he would invite the *full* Court. Bess explained they wanted to have it in the family dining room and to keep it small and intimate.

Tuesday, March 1 *White House birthday party.* Spencer drove all six of us stacked in our car to the White House. Mrs. Johnson, lovely and gracious in a short formal, was waiting for us in the second-floor sitting room. Chief Justice Warren and Nina, Tom and Mary Clark, Bill Douglas, and Abe and Carol Fortas were already there. Other guests included the Thurman Arnolds, Paul Porters [law partner of Thurman Arnold and Abe Fortas], Skelly Wrights, Douglass Caters, Tom Corcoran and Ben Cohen, Hugo, Jr., and Graham, Jo and Mario, Fred and Janice, [Senator] John Sparkman from Alabama, Mrs. Bob Jones, wife of a congressman from Alabama, and the President and Lady Bird. The President, a little late arriving, showed up at the door laden with gold-wrapped presents, including a medallion for me and one for each child, two watercolor portraits of himself, one of them inscribed "To Hugo Black, 80 years young and every one of them fighting for the people," another medallion for Hugo, cuff links, a tie tack with the Presidential seal. The Marine Band was playing in the hall as we arrived upstairs. Then we went into dinner and the menu included filet of beef "Justice," which was Lady Bird's way of personalizing the menu to fit her guests. The President gave a beautiful toast to Hugo. Then everyone looked at Hugo and he arose and responded in his own inimitable way. Later Tom Corcoran called to say Hugo had jumped the gun, that he had asked Lady Bird for permission to speak and sing a song to me. Lady Bird had said yes and he was all set to sing "I've Grown Accustomed to Your Face," but Tom said it would have been lese majesty to speak after Hugo. Nearly everyone was wiping away tears when Hugo quit.

After dinner, Bird took us to see the Lincoln Bedroom, the Treaty Room, and the Queen's Bedroom. What a feeling of the continuity of history!

Thursday, March 3 Hugo had to stay home, though he was due to sit on the bench, and was miserable all day, sneezing and coughing. The boys came out and he sat at his desk working with them on the Voting Rights Bill case.[4]

Friday, March 4 Hugo woke up still coughing. We went out to Bethesda Naval Hospital, where Dr. Taylor examined him but decided not to keep him. He ordered bed rest. Hugo followed orders, except he stayed on the phone a long time with the boys about his concurrence and dissent in the Voting Rights Bill case. Hugo is dissenting on the part that requires certain states "hat in hand" to come to ask the Attorney General of the United States or a federal district judge in the District of Columbia for permission to pass laws regarding voting.

Saturday, March 5 Hugo is still running a temperature and feeling weak. Poor thing! There has been too much pressure on him and although he loved all the birthday festivities, what he really wants most is to just do his job on the Court.

Monday, March 7 I went to Court and Hugo, though his voice was still husky, announced the *Surowitz* case.[5] Then the C.J. gave the Court's opinion sustaining the constitutionality of the Voting Rights Act of 1965. Hugo concurred in part, but gave a great dissent on the section that requires the states, certain of them, to come to Washington to ask permission to pass voting laws.[6]

Tuesday, March 8 Hugo is feeling rotten and discouraged. No fever but very languid and fretful over the mountain of birthday mail he must answer, as well as thank-you notes for gifts he received. He had hoped to write lectures these two weeks. On top of everything else, Frances is out with the flu too.

I spent the day composing a letter to the caterer because Lizzie Mae was so steamed over the way the head waitress drank, stole a bottle of our liquor, and took home a whole turkey, rolls, fruit, cake, and heaven knows what else! What a bunch of thieves! I told Frances Arnold, who says Washington waiters frequently get stewed, but she thought it was bad when the waiters get as drunk as the guests! I also composed an eight-page letter describing in detail the three birthday parties, which took quite a lot of doing.

Wednesday, March 9 Hugo asked me to go to the office with him this morning. I stayed in the outer office and acted as his secretary all day long. It was fun but tiring. He had a girl from the pool do his letters, but I had to write several things for him, too; and being unused to an electric typewriter, it took a little time.

Ralph Brown Buick, in person, came to deliver our gorgeous new Black Buick with gray seat covers. It set us back some $3300 plus our 1963 Buick. List price, Brown says, is $5800 with all additions we got.

Hugo and I got home about 4:30 and he is still discouraged about his mail. His dictating machine is broken. So I volunteered and he dictated about twenty letters to me and I got them out.

Thursday, March 10 Hugo home all day and still feeling languid. He was a little stronger, though, and stuck to his desk all day writing notes of thanks, including two to his former girl friends, which sizzles me a bit, but I repressed it.

I went to Mother's and stayed quite a while making out her income tax, a tedious operation, and I didn't get home till 4:30. Hugo said, "I thought you'd left me."

We got ready and went to the Lawyers Club to the unveiling of the Chief's bust. Tom Clark presided and was very clever about it being Earl Warren's first "bust." The C.J. responded by saying that when a portrait of himself was hung in the State Capitol in California, the portrait appeared in the newspaper with headlines under it saying "TO BE HUNG TODAY." Tom responded he was glad the Chief was busted after he was hung.

Monday, March 21 I went to Court and the Obscenity cases came down.[7] I thought Hugo was going to take note of the C.J.'s seventy-fifth birthday and kept waiting and even told Nina he was. After some note-writing back and forth from the bench I found the C.J. had vetoed it, so Hugo didn't do it.

Hugo's words on this case were so beautiful—"No words need be spoken in order for people to know that the subject [sex] is one of the creation of life itself." And it was so witty! "It is a subject which people are bound to consider and discuss whatever laws are passed by any government to try to suppress it."

Hugo got home around 7:30, full of pep and bounce, and yet tired too. He said Bill Douglas had worked all day Saturday on Hugo's dissent to Bill's Poll Tax case and Bill circulated his revised opinion this afternoon and he wants it to come down Tuesday! Hugo and the boys got their revised dissent down to the printer and Hugo feels exhilarated by that—but tired withal.

Wednesday, March 23 I had to go with Hugo to Court because my car was in the garage there. He did not know whether Bill Douglas's Poll Tax opinion was coming down until we got there. Since I learned it was, I stayed to listen. Bill delivered the Court's opinion; John Harlan gave a very eloquent dissent stating his grounds; and then Hugo gave his dissent.

Hugo was determined not to be charged with "shaking with anger" as the press had reported some of his other dissents. And so he talked with a half smile on his face and without the usual passion, though now and then it would creep in at the turn of a phrase. It was a matter he felt very strongly on—not just the demise of the poll tax, but of Bill Douglas's splitting with him and "writing new law" by construing it under the Equal Protection Clause.[8] He, Bill, had pushed Hugo unmercifully on this case all week and Hugo was relieved after it came down.

After lunch I came upstairs and Hugo had Max Lerner and a group of about thirty Neiman Scholars from Harvard at a question-and-answer session. He was answering with his usual clarity and sincerity. When Hugo saw me peeping in, he invited me to come and sit in.

Friday, March 25 The President sent scrapbook of pictures made at White House dinner honoring Hugo's eightieth birthday. Aline and Dan Berman [a professor of economics at Washington College] arrived for dinner at 7:00, Dan with a sort of new beatnik beard, though he declared it was a Charles Evans Hughes beard. Dan and Hugo had *lively* arguments throughout the evening, Hugo explaining his position on the Court. They are extreme pacifists about Viet Nam.

Saturday, March 26 For a change Hugo hasn't got a pressing case to write, so he decided to read Harry Golden's book *A Little Girl Is Dead,* about the Leo Frank case in Atlanta.

Monday, March 28 I went to the Court in my own car and met Frances Arnold. Heard Abe Fortas give the decision remanding the Mississippi cases (the three civil rights workers killed in Mississippi) for a new trial. We also heard the Penn case remanded to Georgia. Hugo got a call today from a man who wanted him to speak to the Georgia Bar Association in June, but Hugo declined.

Thursday, March 31 Went out to Bethesda with Hugo at 11:00 for eye examination. Our fears that Hugo has started cataracts were confirmed. If he was depressed he did not show it. In his usual breezy way he told me he would go back for another exam in six months. When he got to where it was preventing him from doing what he needed to do, he would get an operation. Might knock him out of tennis for three months, he said. Bless his dear brave heart! I will be his seeing-eye woman, if need be.

Friday, April 1 I was busy this whole day; as a matter of fact, for the first time I can remember, I didn't even try to play *one* April Fools' joke on anybody.

Saturday, April 2 *Our tenth anniversary. Pure heaven.* This is a nostalgic day for Hugo and me, though it's not our wedding anniversary. It was ten years ago that Hugo came trotting into the office to say, "JoJo wants me to invite you to dinner either tomorrow night or tonight, tonight preferably." And I said, "Well, I don't have anything to do tonight."

Whereupon it was settled. "What time do you want me to be there?" I asked. He said, "I will come and get you. The ladies in my family do not go out alone at night, and I won't let you!" I shall never forget watching for him out of the front door and seeing him almost running up the sidewalk! We remembered much. We sang songs we had learned as children.

Monday, April 11 We hit balls from 11:30 to 1:00, and Hugo got a bad knee from it. He stayed in bed with heat and books.

Tuesday, April 12 Drayton came by at 9:00 to talk about the case he is writing. Hugo is letting him try his hand at it so as to teach him. Hugo says he himself could have had it out a week ago, but he wants Drayton to learn.

Wednesday, April 13 I can't shake the feeling of depression. Hugo and I talked about friends in his past and I felt an unreasonable jealousy, partly because I was not of it. Hugo and I love each other so dearly, yet our lives came together at such a late date. I wish I could shake this depression. He is so dear and it is all my fault.

Thursday, April 14 I am still in the dumps. Hugo and I hit balls at about 5:00, and soon Sam Bradberry came and Hugo went in to talk to him, which he did like a father, about his chances at Giant [a supermarket chain], what he should do to improve himself and get in the management end of it. He advised him to study and go to night school. I am sure it was good for Sam. Hugo and I talked late.

Saturday, April 30 Naturalization ceremony at Mount Vernon. Drippy and rainy, but we rode from the gate to the door of Mount Vernon in great style. The ceremonies were performed on the porch. Hugo made a splendid talk. The Governor of Virginia, one of the original massive resisters to integration, gave Hugo a fine and courageous introduction.

Tuesday, May 10 Leave for Fifth Circuit Judicial Conference, San Antonio. Large reception committee to meet us, a dozen roses, television and cameras, motorcade. Hugo was asked to be the last to get off the plane. This gave him the opportunity to finish reading and to jot something down on Tom Clark's opinion so he could mail it at the airport. Dinner with Judge Elbert and Sara Tuttle.

Friday, May 13 Hugo felt disturbed because he had had no time to prepare his speech. He planned to think about it during the program. We ordered breakfast in our room and ate with Hugo, Jr., and Graham. Judge Tuttle called and said so many had to catch an 11:00 A.M. plane that he wanted Hugo to speak first on the program. Hugo went into the bathroom with a Gideon Bible out of the hotel bureau drawer. He said, "I've always heard it said, 'When in trouble, read your Bible.' " He came out and said with relief, "I'm not going to make a speech. I'll just talk and thank them for the hospitality." "Oh," I said, "honey, you have to say something inspirational!" I was distressed. So he said no, he was just going to talk. Hugo, Jr., and Graham, Mrs. Tuttle, and I all went in to hear Hugo talk. He got up and made a wonderfully inspiring talk, telling the judges how important their role was and what a grand and courageous job they had done. He quoted the Bible, using his favorite passage: "Faith, hope, love, these three; but the greatest of these is love." He said some of us might not be back next year and if he were to be one of those he wanted them to remember that and he truly believed they loved him. I was in tears!

Saturday, May 14 Leave for Washington by way of Corpus Christi, Texas. We heard a gentle rap on the door this morning and it was Hugo's eighty-five-year-old Aunt Lida Toland bringing us coffee and tea and the morning paper. Hugo granted the paper an interview at Aunt Lida's request. Then we looked over the Toland scrapbook she had put together. Saw the cradle Hugo's maternal grandfather had made and the one in which Hugo had been rocked as a babe.

Monday, May 16 American Bar Association dinner at State Department. Hugo was annoyed that he had accepted because he was very tired, very desirous of cleaning up some of his work, and also he felt he owed the American Bar Association nothing. As he said, they had predicted the world would come to an end when he went on the Court, and they had been extremely rude and critical of him and the Court at various times since. When the President of the Bar Association arose and gave the two toasts, "To the President of the United States," "To the Supreme Court," Hugo responded with "To the American Bar Association, who we all like to think represents the lawyers of America."

Tuesday, May 17 John Frank [Hugo's law clerk in 1942] came to dinner. There was some question as to whether we should go out or have John here to eat turnip greens (which I had labored over for two hours in picking yesterday). Turnip greens won out and John came to dinner, giving Hugo several provocative questions on freedom of speech, such as using profanity and cussing out a lady, inciting to murder, etc. John wanted Hugo to touch on it in his Columbia speeches.

Wednesday, May 18 I finally made it to the Court at 11:00 A.M. after stopping by Apex Liquors and buying liquor for our dinner party to the tune of $105. After debating as to whether to transfer it to the office and to take it home four bottles at a time, I decided to risk getting caught and to take the entire amount to Alexandria in the trunk of my car. I felt the trail was cold by the time I left the car in the garage a couple of hours. [It is a violation to transport out of the District more than a gallon of liquor at a time from the inexpensive stores in Washington, D.C.]

Monday, May 23 Sequoia *party.* The entire Court was present. Abe toasted "Elizabeth Black's house in which she permits Hugo to live"—as we passed by our house. Hugo got pretty peeved at Bill Douglas for affectionately putting his arm around me. Other than that, everything went fine.

Wednesday, May 25 *The Great Party for the Great Society.* I awakened to a mist of rain. Peered out anxiously and must have called weather twenty-five times but always same reply: "Rain Wednesday and Thursday." It clouded up but stopped misting at 7:00 just as the first guests arrived at our house, all the Court coming except Mary Clark, who was sick.

The President arrived about 8:00. Lady Bird was most apologetic and insisted we have our dinner as we wished. Some of the members of the Court were completely surprised by having the President and Lady Bird present. Marion White said she'd have worn a different dress. We ate indoors. I had the President on my right, the C.J. on my left. Conversation was centered with everybody talking to the President. He liked well-done roast beef and adored ham. He took a quarter of our mold of rum dessert and then urged the Chief Justice to "take a lot of that dessert, it's good." Since I only had one more small mold I passed it up. Later at dinner the C.J. told the President that he was going to Heidelberg tomorrow "to talk to some of your soldier grads of the University of Maryland commencement [extension program for the military]." "How are you going?" asked the President. "By commercial airline," replied the C.J. "The hell you are. You're going to take my plane. Get up your own party, and that's an order!" And soon we had been invited. Hugo, after an overnight worry about the propriety of accepting, finally capitulated and agreed to go.

Sunday, May 29 Commencement exercises, University of Heidelberg. The C.J. spoke well despite a bad cold. A degree was conferred on him.

Monday, May 30 We took the C.J. and his daughter "Honeybear" to Mickelstraub. Such a quaint medieval German city, with its narrow winding streets and its thirteenth-century City Hall all decorated for Pentecost. Home at 9:30. Spencer met us at plane.

Tuesday, May 31 Hugo had an antitrust opinion.

Sunday, June 5 Felt awful. Hugo says it's better to play tennis for a cold. Anyway, it didn't kill me!

Monday, June 6 The *Sheppard* case came down, Tom Clark giving the opinion of the Court at great length and almost like an argument to the jury. Hugo dissented without an opinion. He was the only dissenter.[9]

Monday, June 13 Mother called last night about 11:00 P.M. and I got scared and went down and spent the night with her. I had to forego going to Court to take care of her and clean her apartment. Hugo hated for me to spend the night away but thought I should.

I missed an exciting day in Court. The C.J. gave the *Miranda*[10] opinion holding a suspect cannot be questioned unless his lawyer is with him. There were some hot dissents.

Tuesday, June 14 Hugo is tense and nervous over the enormous amount of work he has to do between now and Court's ending next Monday. He had the boys out working all day.

Wednesday, June 15 Hugo woke up at 3:00 A.M., wide awake and wanting to talk. He talked about last Monday's case, *Miranda* v. *Arizona,* and the 101 related *cert* petitions that he had to examine and said they had to have a conference Thursday, Friday, and possibly Saturday because all the judges had made commitments, so they *have* to adjourn next Monday. Bill Douglas has already left for the summer, saying he had made commitments to speak. Finally Hugo talked himself out, got up and fixed himself a Scotch, and went back to sleep. I was wakeful for a while longer.

Monday, June 20 *Last day of Court. Hugo presiding in absence of C.J.* Judge Elbert Tuttle from the Fifth Circuit was present at the Court and sat with me. Potter announced two civil rights cases, one of which said that state criminal prosecutions could not be removed to federal court if they involve such offenses as blocking streets, disturbing the peace, inciting to riot, or assault and battery by biting a police officer.

Hugo had two dissents very important to him, which he filed but did not announce in view of scarcity of time and a desire for harmony in the Court at its close. One of his dissents was to Abe Fortas's Communist case, to which Hugo wrote a wonderful dissent. "Never since the McCarthy Era," it started off.[11] The other was to Bill Brennan's Blood Test for Drunkenness opinion.[12] Bill announced all his opinions at great length and it was almost 12:30 before we quit. I took Judge Tuttle back to say hello to Hugo, and Judge Tuttle seemed relieved to have the removal questions settled, although he got reversed on one and affirmed on one.

Tuesday, June 28 We voted absentee ballot for [former State Senator] Army Boothe and [William] Spong [junior Senator from Virginia]. Hugo cast his first vote in some thirty years, ever since he's been on the Court. But he decided to qualify to see if he could help Army beat the Byrd machine. He was so cute when the registrar was taking our personal descriptions. When she asked Hugo what color his hair was he stated very positively "brown," although the little hair he had left was definitely white.

Tuesday, July 5 Hugo and I got off to drive to Alabama.

Wednesday, July 6 On the way down through South Carolina Hugo said he'd always wanted to go to Laurens County to see where his mother was born. Hugo had always told people that his mother was born in "Laurens County Courthouse," and my literal mind thought that meant she was born in the actual building. I found out later that the *area* was known as "Laurens County Courthouse District." When we arrived, sure enough, there was a big old dilapidated courthouse, built around 1840. It showed signs of past grandeur. Hugo could get no information about its history from the old fellow in the courthouse, but he was directed to the Library, which, together with all the stores, closes at noon on Wednesday. It was then 1:00 P.M., so I took several Polaroid and Instamatic shots of the courthouse, much to Hugo's embarrassment, only to find I had taken the rear of the courthouse. Hugo observed that the statue in front, like all the Confederate statues, turned its back on the North and faced the South. He said, "No wonder we lost the war. We never *would* face the enemy."

Hugo, age twenty.

Hugo's brother Orlando.

Hugo's brother George Pelham.

The Seay family, 1903; James, Elizabeth's father, is seated on the banister at right.

The Seay home in Birmingham, 1914, with Elizabeth (*left*) and her cousin Martha Ashbrook.

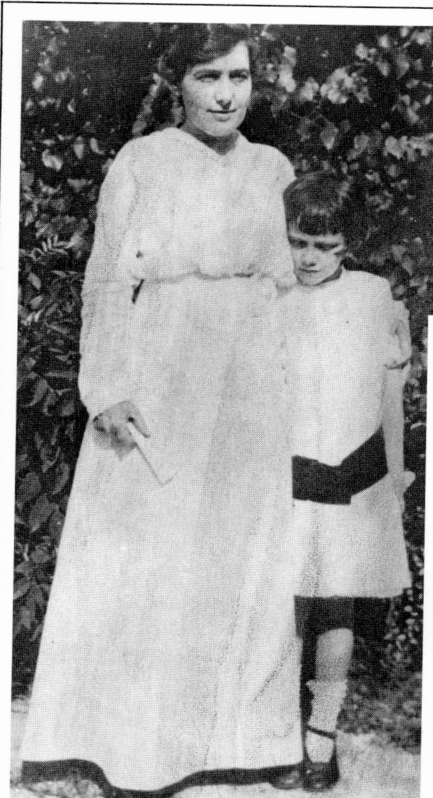

Elizabeth and her mother, Elma Atkins Seay, in 1914.

Elizabeth at eight.

HUGO BLACK
FOR YOUR NEXT
U. S. SENATOR
ALSOP PRINTING CO. Birmingham
aid Political Adv. by Hugo Black, Bir ingham, Ala.

The Senate race of 1936.

The Ku Klux Klan broadcast, 1937. (BY THE COURTESY OF THE CURATOR OF THE UNITED STATES SUPREME COURT)

August 19, 1937—arriving for a White House lunch just after the Supreme Court appointment. (BY THE COURTESY OF THE CURATOR OF THE UNITED STATES SUPREME COURT)

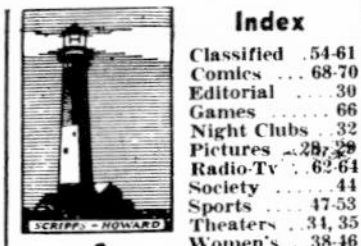

Index

The WASHINGTON DAILY News

36th Year—No. 265 DI. 7-7777 Entered as Second Class Matter at D. C. Post Office

FINAL EDITION THURSDAY, SEPTEMBER 12, 1957

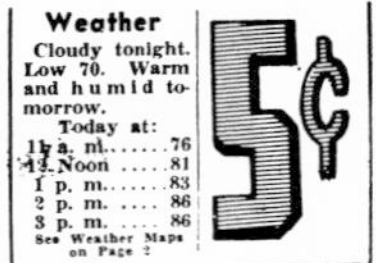

Weather

Cloudy tonight. Low 70. Warm and humid tomorrow.
Today at:
11 a. m. 76
12 Noon 81
1 p. m. 83
2 p. m. 86
3 p. m. 86
See Weather Maps on Page 2

5¢

JUSTICE HUGO BLACK WEDS HIS SECRETARY

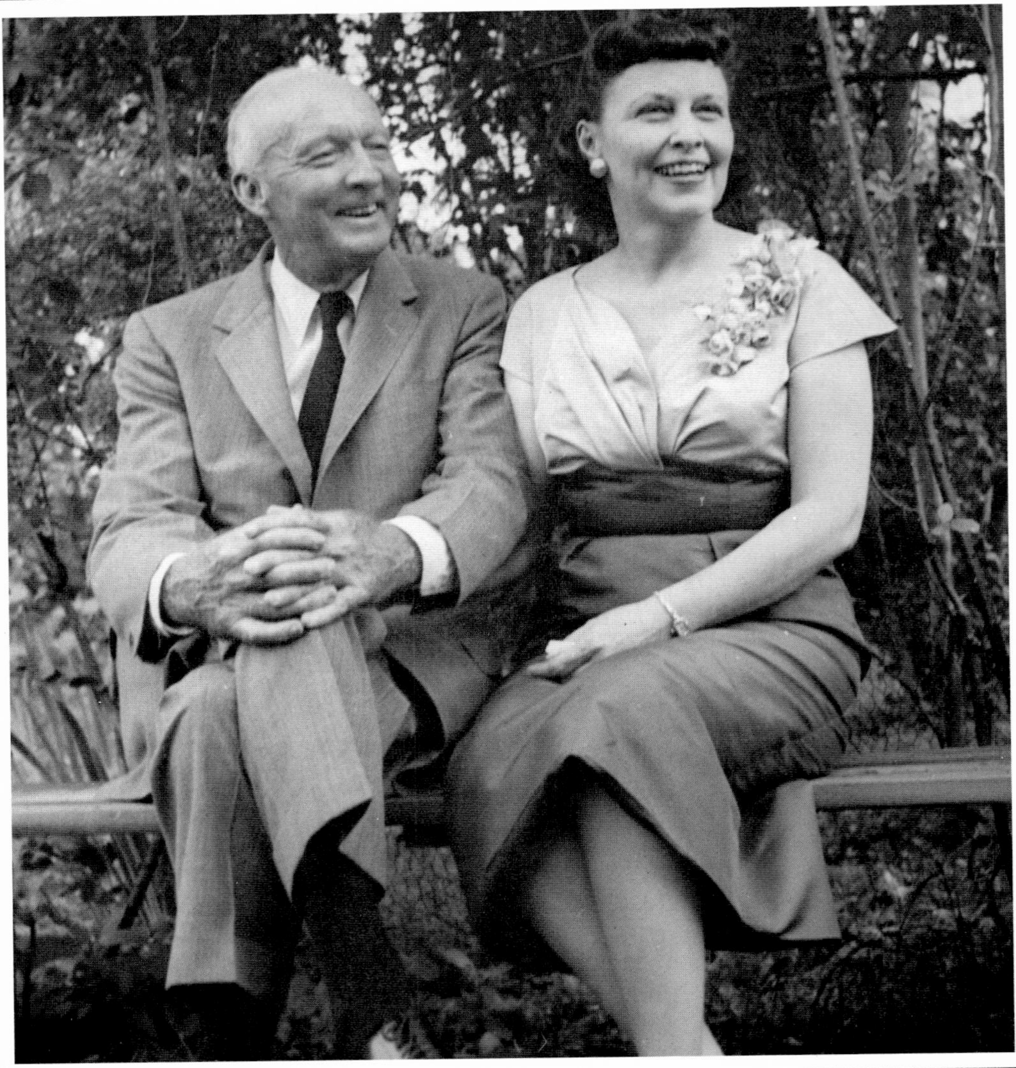

A wedding photograph.

Hugo and Elizabeth, 1971.

Tennis, Bridge & Bermans

FRIDAY, OCTOBER 21 (294)

A.M. Such an exhiliarting day — Mary Taylor & I were the #4 team (Bottom was #5) & we went to Washington Golf & Country Club at 10 — After getting beaten 6-0 the 1st set we came back & beat the opponents ~~8~~-6 — 6-3 — Were we thrilled! Especially since some of the "better" teams were defeated. Then I came home & changed & Mary, Marian Gifford & I played bridge with Helen Ran — I was lucky & drew cards!! I was the winner until I tried Mary's gimmick of bidding 3 no trump after 3 passes & got clobbered — down 6 tricks! Glad I learned that lesson quickly.

P.M.

We went to Berman's for dinner & after a few bad moments thinking I had got us lost, we arrived — Fred Graham (Reporter for N.Y. Times) & wife were there, also several profs & the dean of American U —

A page from Elizabeth's 1966 diary.

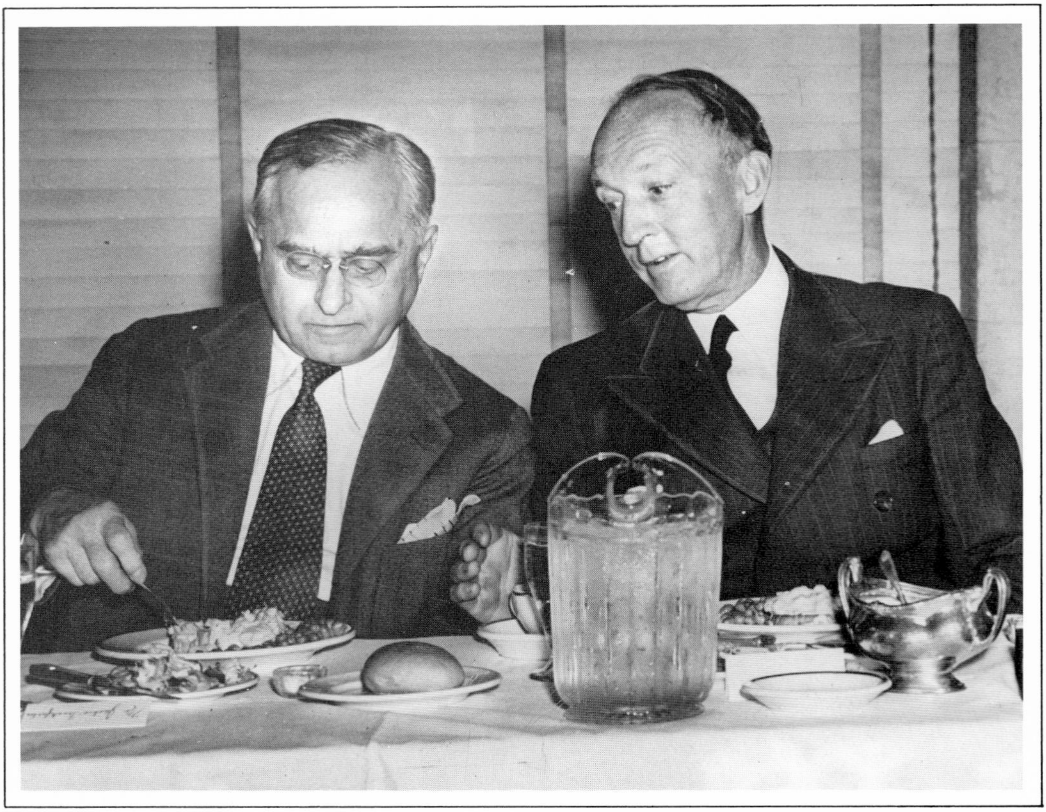

With Associate Justice Felix Frankfurter. (WASHINGTON POST)

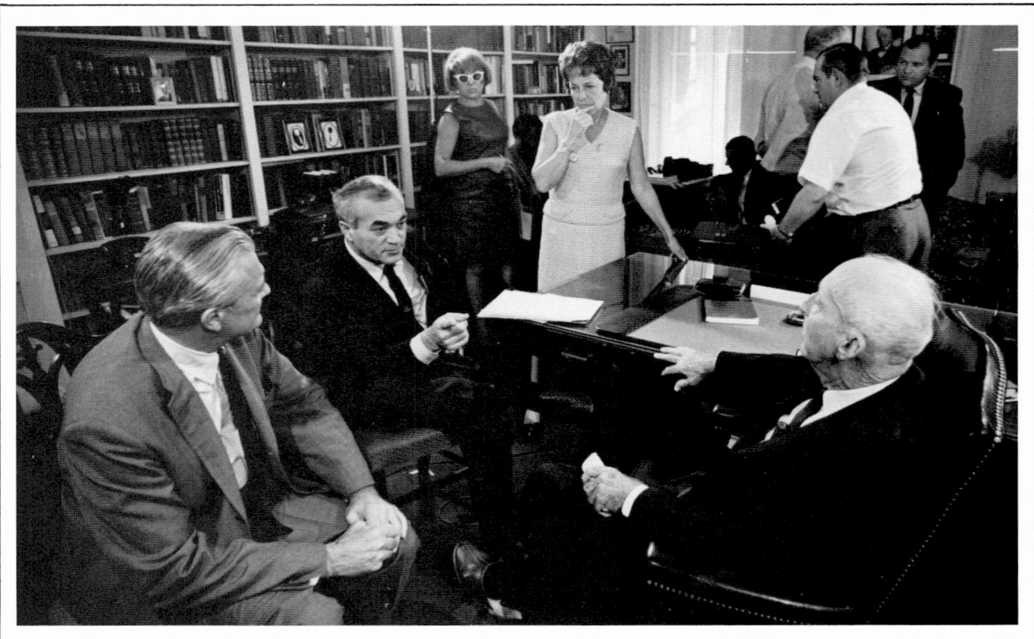

Taping of the CBS News special "Justice Black and the Bill of Rights." *Left to right*: Eric Sevareid, Martin Agronsky, Elizabeth and Hugo. (CBS)

A

Supreme Court of the United States
Memorandum

C

Supreme Court of the United States
Memorandum

B

Handwritten notes from Hugo: A, on his statement on *Bryan* v. *United States*, 338 U.S. 552, 560 (1950); *B*, from the bench to Elizabeth; *C*, to Justice Douglas on an antitrust case.

On the tenth anniversary of Earl Warren's appointment to the Court (September 1963). *Seated, left to right:* Tom Clark, Hugo L. Black, Earl Warren, William O. Douglas; *standing, left to right:* Byron R. White, William Brennan, Jr., Potter Stewart, Arthur Goldberg. (John Harlan was not present.) (LONNIE WILSON)

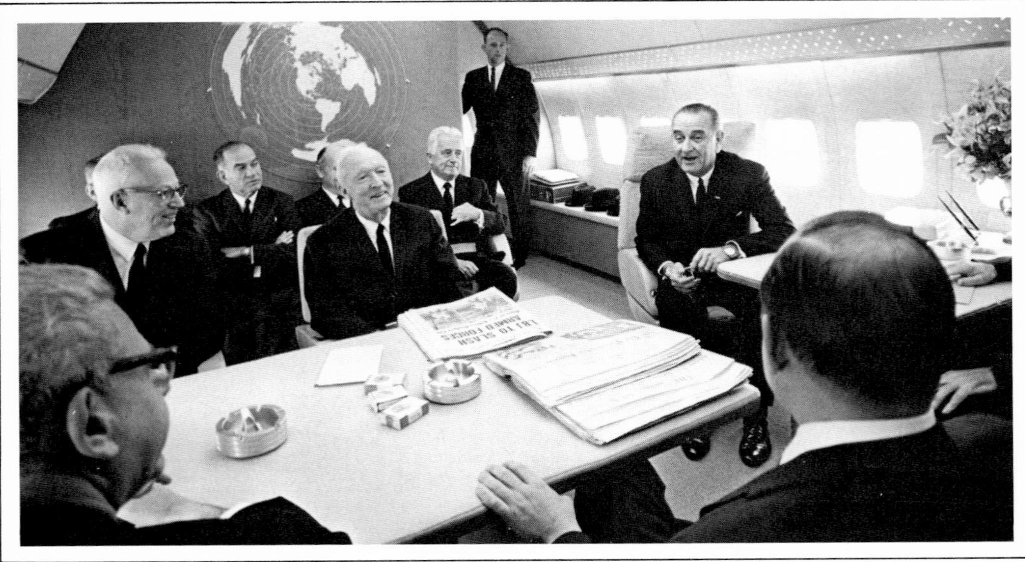

On the presidential plane to attend former New York governor Herbert Lehman's funeral, 1963. *Foreground,* Arthur Goldberg, Abe Fortas; *center row,* Earl Warren, Hugo Black, Lyndon Johnson; *rear,* J. William Fulbright, Jacob Javits (partly obscured), Kenneth Keating.

The 1957 Court wives' portrait. At Justice Frankfurter's request, a chair was left empty for Mrs. Frankfurter, who was ill. *Seated, left to right*: Mercedes Douglas, Elizabeth Black, Nina Warren, Selma Burton; *standing, left to right*: Marjorie Brennan, Mary Clark, Ethel Harlan, Winifred Whittaker. (MAXWELL COPLAN)

The White House dinner for Hugo's eightieth birthday, 1966: Hugo Black, Lady Bird Johnson, William O. Douglas.

Elizabeth and Earl Warren at William O. Douglas's Anniversary Convocation, November 3, 1973. (CAPITAL AND GLOGAU PHOTOGRAPHERS)

At Winterhaven, Florida, 1962.

The White House party for Hugo's thirtieth anniversary on the Court. *Left to right:* Hugo Black, Jr., Hugo L. Black III, Graham Black, Mario Pesaresi, Josephine Black Pesaresi, Elizabeth, Hugo, Lady Bird Johnson, Hollis Black, Gladys Black, Janice DeMeritte, Fred DeMeritte, Anne Black, Sterling Black.

On the tennis court, 1971, three months before his death.
(LIBBY BLACK)

Elizabeth's mother on her ninetieth birthday, 1967.

619 South Lee Street, home of Hugo and Elizabeth Black.

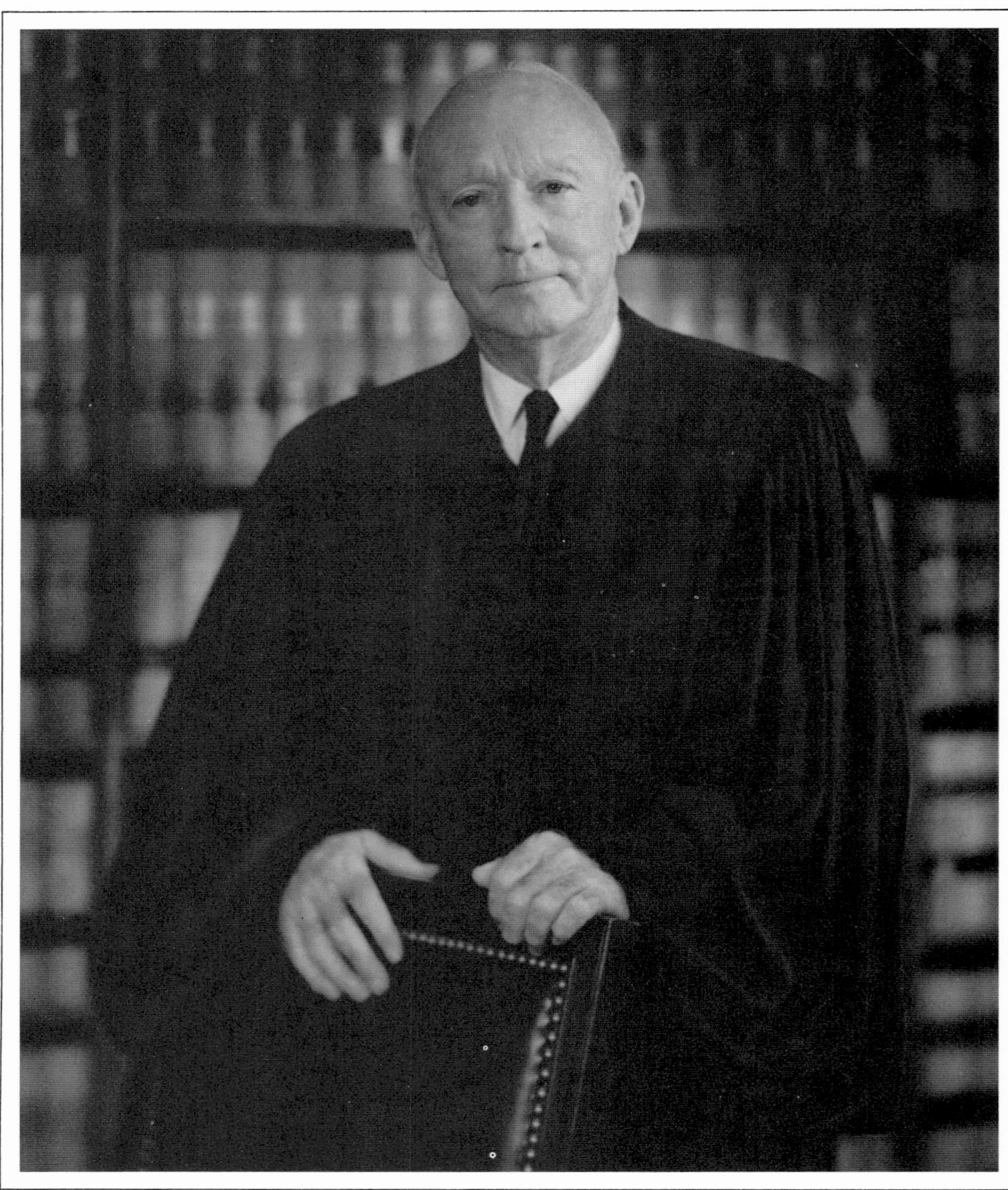

Thursday, July 7 Arrived at Fort Payne, Alabama, about 1:30 our time. I am in the car in front of DeKalb County Courthouse, where Hugo has gone in to see his relative Jay Black, County Solicitor. Got in touch with Irma Black Scruggs, who runs Black's Department Store. Then her sister Bessie came, then brother Jay. We all went to Macedonia Cemetery at Geraldine, Alabama, where George Walker Black, Hugo's granddad, is buried.

Friday, July 8 Lucyle (Hugo's niece) and Aubrey Taylor's home, Sylacauga, Alabama. Hugo is having such a good time. It is spiritually refreshing to him to go back to his roots, and he loves Lucyle dearly. Mildred and her husband Lewis Faucett came about noon. Lucyle's preacher came and stayed about an hour. Later Hugo's nephew Robert Black and his wife Kittie came, then his cousins Thomas and Bunyan Toland, then Martha Seay Crawford, my cousin. Hugo sparkled, talked, and convulsed them all by singing in his nasal twang "How Tedious and Tasteless the Hours." Then Mildred demonstrated how old Aunt Such-and-Such would sing off at a tangent when everybody else was singing a hymn. It was all good fun and true happiness and we were loath to go to bed.

Saturday, July 9 Drove to Alexander City to see Judge Jack Coley, a staunch friend of Hugo's through the years, and President of a local bank. He had us sit in the board of directors room and brought various people to see us. One old lady with a safety pin in her dress came up to Hugo and told him she'd been voting for him all her life. Carey Harlan, cousin to John Harlan and to Hugo, came in. Visited Harlan graves. Arrived at Buddy Cooper's, in Birmingham at 6:00. Dinner with officers of Birmingham Bar Association, judges, and old friends. Hugo made a great speech. He was at his *best.* As someone said, it was funny and sad, beautiful and stirring. Abe Berkowitz [a Birmingham lawyer] said, "Why, he's back down here running for the Senate again!" I was so proud of him, especially to have my dear friends hear him! We sang all the way home.

Sunday, July 10 Family reunion at Thomas Toland's (Hugo's nephew), Ashland, Alabama. Went to Ashland Baptist Church, same one Hugo attended as a boy. Number of old hymns sung, and Hugo requested Thomas to have them sing "The Old Rugged Cross." As I sat there I thought to myself, "This is what true happiness is made of." After church we stood and shook hands with many old friends and their now grown children, many of whom were named Hugo. We visited the graves of Hugo's mother and father at the First Baptist churchyard in Ashland.

After lunch we went in a motorcade to Mt. Ararat Cemetery. Then saw Hugo's birthplace and his father's store. It was a general merchandise store with a post office in the back. Hugo always thought his mother was the postmistress because she did all the work, but he recently checked with the Post Office Department and they told him his *father* was the postmaster—for a dollar a year! At the Tolands' dinner Hugo was at his best, scintillating, sparkling, and warm. If any had ever had doubts about his Court decisions, they melted away right there.

Friday, July 15 En route home. We are now full of gas and full of food just north of South Hill, having come 202 miles since we left Charlotte. Only event other than lunch was when we stopped at a roadside outlet place in North Carolina and Hugo engaged in a conversation with the man who owned it. In the course of the talk religion came up and the man complained that the Baptist Church was not like in the good old days! Hugo, as usual, took issue, and he sang in full the old hymn "Dear Wife I've Found a Model Church." I had to go back before leaving to exchange the size of my sweatshirt and I couldn't resist telling the man whom he was talking to. The man said, "If I ever need any judging I'll get him. He's a nice man."

Observations on the trip: At no relatives' home we entered, Hugo's or mine, did they fail to ask the blessing before eating. At no place were we offered any alcoholic beverage.

Monday, July 25 Charlie Reich [Hugo's law clerk in 1953, now an author and attorney] came to dinner and he seemed to so enjoy being "at home" again. 619 South Lee really represented a happy phase of his life.

Wednesday, July 27 JoJo and I went to the matinee of Liz Taylor and Richard Burton in *Who's Afraid of Virginia Woolf?,* which Hugo refused to see because he heard it was filthy.

Saturday, July 30 Hugo is so strict and demanding with children, especially about diet and table manners. I approve in one way because he is so anxious to help, but it seems to do so little good, and I hate to be thought of as a nag. Hugo has a way of coming right out and saying what's on his mind because he thinks the person—child or adult—*needs* to hear it. He is that way to me and I know he did correct his own children whenever he thought they were out of line or needed improvement. He'd say about the children, "But if I don't tell them, who will?" Though he can be very critical, he says it in such a nice way I don't see how a grown-up can take offense. He really doesn't talk to his acquaintances that way, only to the people he loves.

Monday, August 1 After dinner Hugo played a long time on the harmonica, on which he is really excellent.

Tuesday, August 2 Hugo, Jr., and I hit balls for a while. Hugo, Sr., wanted his lunch upstairs so he could work on *certs.* We had a nice family dinner and Hugo exerted his charm, reminiscing about family matters. Hugo hopes to start working on his Carpentier Lectures [Hugo Black's book *A Constitutional Faith* (New York: Knopf, 1968) was based on these lectures] right away.

Wednesday, August 3 I drove to Sears and bought a new mattress and box spring for Mother's bed. She's been sleeping on lousy beds for the past twenty years! Hugo had a Harvard applicant come up to Court and argue with him about his views. It helped Hugo in the lectures.

Saturday, August 6 *Luci Johnson's wedding.* Spencer was waiting with our spic and span black Buick and we whisked to the Court, where we were supposed to go in a motorcade to the wedding, those invited being the C.J. and Nina, Tom and Mary Clark, Bill Douglas and his new bride, Cathy, and the Fortases. I met Bill Douglas's bride for the first time in the elevator and managed to wish them both much happiness. The C.J. kissed her and wished them happiness and Nina said, "Welcome to the Court." When we arrived at the great Catholic cathedral called "The Shrine," the newspeople called to Bill, "Mr. Justice, look over this way," and Bill had Cathy, a very immature-looking pretty blonde with a tomboy haircut, stop and smile into the television cameras. Abe Fortas said to Carol, "That's the very thing I didn't want him to do!"

Hugo isn't too much fun on an occasion like this. Pomp and ceremony almost nauseate him. We were sitting about six rows back, behind the family section. I watched several flies, uninvited and irreverent, light on first one august head and then another. The music was grand but almost oppressive in its volume. Then came the excitement as the wedding march began. Lynda Bird carries herself like a queen. Then came Luci, radiant, sweet, and girlish-looking, on her father's arm. The President looked sober, proud, happy, and sad all at once. Lady Bird was seated before the procession, looking poised, serene, and lovely in her bright yellow dress.

Hugo and I went to the White House for the wedding reception. Hugo hates to take a drink in the middle of the day, hates champagne, and hates to stand. However, we went through the buffet (by then it was 2:30) visiting with various couples and saw Dorothy and Arthur Goldberg. We were in a long line waiting to go through the receiving line. An attaché came out and got Arthur. I held on and said, "Take us with you," and he got us in. Attachés hardly ever recognize Hugo. As one newspaperman said, "He looks like the lively little man next door." We shook hands with the President, who made jokes about Hugo's tennis and kissed me. I spoke to Lady Bird, who introduced me to the Nugents [the Johnsons' in-laws], and I wished Luci and Pat happiness. We visited awhile with the Warrens and the Clarks and Hugo very much wanted to go, so we left. I felt a bit cheated in not getting to see the cake cut or the bride and groom leaving. And so endeth another chapter.

Thursday, August 11 Hugo and I arrived at Marjorie Brennan's at 8:00, loaded to the gills with camera equipment, figs, and a birthday gift for Mickie Bazelon. Other guests were Drew and Luvie Pearson, Mickie and David Bazelon, and the Brennans. We stayed until after 12:00 so they could drink to Hugo's twenty-ninth anniversary of his appointment to the Court. Drew and Hugo reminisced about the times of FDR and conversation went to the new Daniels book about FDR's love affair with Lucy Mercer.

Sunday, August 14 Jack Vardaman came out at 6:00 and we took him over to the Club for dinner. He and Hugo are now talking and it's 10:30. Hugo just told Jack the one thing he is sure that he has accomplished on the Court: caused the Bill of Rights to be recognized as a part of the Constitution. Jack stayed until almost midnight, and as he left, Hugo told him how much he had enjoyed having him as his law clerk. Jack looked as though he might cry and he said, "It's been the best year of my life." He's such a nice boy.

Monday, August 22 Hot. Whew. 100°+. Hugo has been working until around 1:30 every night and last night was no exception. He is working on this case he is so interested in. It's one that Abe Fortas got out about a week before Court adjourned; Hugo told them he was going to write a dissent this summer, so they agreed to get it reargued this fall.[13] When Hugo writes his opinion he'll put it in his file in readiness for when Abe circulates again after the case has been reargued. After this, Hugo plans to start on his lectures. He is still working and it's 11:30 P.M.

Thursday, August 25 Hugo worked on his Carpentier Lectures until 1:30 A.M. last night. We went to the Court at 10:30. I had the Court car (the first time I, personally, have ever called for it) take me to Fred's building. I saw his office at NASA. His door read "Fred J. DeMeritte, Chief, Space Vehicles, Aero-thermodynamics Division." I felt so proud of him.

Tuesday, September 6 We worked 'til 1:45 A.M. I at last completed my Alabama scrapbook. Hugo, bless his heart, read it word for word and picture for picture and we turned off the lights at 2:30 A.M. Neither of us slept too soundly. We got on the tennis court by 11:00 and hit until 1:30. Hugo's knee was sore, so he said he was anxious to play tennis to see if it would help it! *Not* appreciably. After lunch Hugo went right back to work on the lectures. He says he won't do them if he can't get them to his satisfaction.

Wednesday, September 7 We worked again 'til 1:30 last night, Hugo working on his lectures. I don't believe he's going to give them. He's worried. The Atlanta race riot took place yesterday and he thinks he would have to mention his views on keeping order in the streets. He's worried too about making slashing attacks on the Due Process concept the Court now seems to have adopted. The lectures would be no good if he pulls his punches, and he doubts the wisdom of doing it.

Thursday, September 8 Hugo just about definitely decided not to do Carpentier Lectures at this time. He's afraid of it. Doesn't want to hurt the Court.

Friday, September 9 Hugo wanted to go to the office this morning, so we hit early and he got ready and went in. He wanted to talk to his clerks about the lectures, his *Time* case dissent [see page 153], and other things. Hugo is still going to work on his lectures and have them ready in case he decides to give them. We went to bed about 1:30.

Sunday, September 11 *Our ninth anniversary!* Hugo and I have been remembering nine years ago when he asked to marry me and I went out and bought my wedding dress with Maggy Bryan. Went after Mother at 4:00 and Helen and Skelly came out at 4:30—without tennis clothes. They had misunderstood. We broke out the champagne and even Hugo took some.

Tuesday, September 13 Chuck Luce [Hugo's law clerk in 1943] called for us at 8:45 to take us to the Department of the Interior, where he was sworn in by Hugo as Under Secretary to [Secretary of the Interior Stewart] Udall. A good many former law clerks were there: Marx Leva, Buddy Cleveland, Frank Wozencraft, and perhaps others.

Tuesday, September 20 Very lazy, and laziness begets laziness. Hugo is full of affection and loving kindness. He is never too busy to have me sit with him, love and comfort me. He's such a joy.

Monday, September 26 Hugo had a morning visitor, Tom Clark. He wanted to talk to Hugo about "What if?" "What if Ramsey [Clark] is selected as Attorney General?" Should Tom get off the Court? "Yes," Hugo told him. He thought it would make for a bad situation for the Attorney for the Government to prosecute cases before the Attorney's father, among others.

Thursday, September 29 Helen and Martin Agronsky [the journalist] arrived at 7:30 for dinner. Martin and Hugo talked politics mostly. Martin was a little startled to hear that Hugo thinks Ronald Reagan has a good chance over Pat Brown, although hoping for the latter.

Monday, October 3 *Court opens.* Yesterday's Washington *Star* said that Bill Douglas was dropped from the Social Register—a blow I'm sure he doesn't even know hit him.

This morning I went to Court for the opening. I drove my car and followed Hugo. He's a pretty fast man to keep up with! Most of the wives, with the exception of Ethel Harlan, were there. Cathy Douglas sat next to me and got a note from Tom Clark almost before she sat down; then one from Bill Brennan, and another—I think possibly from Abe. Then one from Bill, at which they exchanged loving glances.

Monday, October 10 I watched Hugo read last night and my heart was torn to see him try to manipulate the lights and magnifying glass. He is so brave and so lacking in self-pity.

Sunday, October 16 We went over to the Douglases' at 6:00 for dinner. A story appeared in the Washington *Post* this morning that Bill draws $12,000 a year from the Parvin Foundation, which derives much of its income from Las Vegas gambling casinos. Made us sick! I finally decided *not* to wear a long dress. Nobody but Cathy had one on. A nice evening: same house, same food, same people—different wife.

Monday, October 17 We got to Court and heard arguments in a case where a marijuana seller had sold the dope to an undercover agent who did not take the precaution of obtaining a search warrant before entering the house, disguised as an addict, and buying the marijuana. I can see it now: the undercover agent takes off his slouch hat and mustache and says, "I'm an undercover agent for the Government and I hereby serve you with this search warrant." Then he quickly dons his mustache and slouch hat and enters into negotiations!

Thursday, October 20 Hugo said Abe came to see him, hurt and angered about his dissent in the *Time* Magazine Libel case,[14] but that they talked it out and Abe left feeling O.K.

Sunday, October 23 Hugo told me he had assigned *five* cases Friday.[15] He evidently got the Court on his *Time* Magazine case! How he has worked. Abe and the Chief only ones against him.

Monday, October 24 *Cleaned library books.* I got started about 10:00, after getting Mother to help Lizzie Mae and me. We washed all the bookcases behind Hugo's desk, dusted all the books, and I even vacuumed the space above. Mother was in her glory and dusted all the books in the carts. When Hugo came home from Court at 4:00 we were still going strong; but we finished, thank goodness. Now we won't have to disturb his use of the study. He'll be out of Court for the next two weeks. Tired though I was, I took a hot bath and put on an evening dress. I was fearful to go to the Isaac Stern concert because Hugo had worked last night until 2:30 A.M. writing an opinion and I was afraid he was too tired also. We went and enjoyed it, however. The C.J. and Nina were in the box adjoining and we saw Bill Douglas and Cathy several boxes up. We skipped the State Department reception.

Tuesday, October 25 Spent two hours looking over and evaluating law clerk applications for Hugo.

Thursday, October 27 Hugo chose his two clerks for 1967. One was the number one student at Harvard, Steve Schulhofer; the other Joe Price, now in Viet Nam, from Montgomery, Alabama.

Friday, October 28 Here it is Friday again! The weeks fly and our yard is breathtaking, with our chrysanthemums, all colors, in full bloom; pyracanthas in full plump red berries; hollies in bloom, and fragrantly so. Hugo is so pleased that he is *up* with his work. He wrote all the applicants for a clerkship today telling them he has already selected.

Tuesday, November 1 I took Hugo by the Court and went downtown to look at magnifying glasses for him. I selected four glasses, but they were not what I had hoped to find. I got back to the office about 4:00. Guido Calabresi, looking far more settled, was there waiting. Now Professor Calabresi of Yale Law School, he was recruiting law clerks to teach at Yale next year.

Monday, November 7 Court resumes. Hugo was worried because his volleys were so poor yesterday and he feared it was his sight. However, he hit very well today.

Wednesday, November 9 Hugo came home at 3:00 and I practiced him again on volleys. His eyes are getting so bad and I keep my fingers crossed that he can continue to hit.

We are sitting here listening to the election news. We got the sad news [Senator] Paul Douglas of Illinois was defeated by [Charles] Percy. [Ronald] Reagan won [as governor of California]—that's bad. We got two out of three in Virginia: [Harry Flood] Byrd, Jr., out of our yellow-dog Democrat loyalty, and Spong. We lost DuVal to old [Joel] Broyhill. *Lurleen* Wallace is the new Governor of Alabama—to our sorrow. John Sparkman returned to the Senate, hurrah! [Lester] Maddox and [Howard] Callaway tied for Governor in Georgia, one about as bad as the other! Hugo called Sterling at noon and found he had squeaked by for the [New Mexico State] Senate over the Republican "Mother of the Year" of five children. He said he won by five or six hundred votes.

Sunday, November 13 Hugo is finally going to get down his Florida case where the people stormed the jail, were arrested, and appealed.

Monday, November 14 *Hugo's opinion affirming Florida judgment and jailing civil rights demonstrators around jail in Tallahassee.* I had invited wives of two former law clerks, Helen Luce (Chuck is now Under Secretary of the Interior) and Shirley Wozencraft (Frank is now legal counsel for the Department of Justice) to go to the Court for Hugo's court opinion, which was his first victory on the Civil Rights demonstrations wherein the Court affirmed a judgment of the lower court of conviction for thirty-one who crowded a jail to protest the jailing of people demonstrating to desegregate a theater.[16]

Saturday, December 3 Gridiron stag honoring the Supreme Court. Hugo said Arthur Goldberg charged the Court with crimes committed by him when he was on the Court, the C.J. pleaded *forma pauperis,* and Abe defended the Court.

Sunday, December 4 At 5:00 Hugo and I left for the matinee of the Gridiron party at the Statler. Nearly all the Court was present. Walter Trohan, the incoming President of Gridiron, was our host. He and Hugo chatted amiably and I was surprised to learn later that Hugo had once told Trohan of the Chicago *Tribune* that he would *not* give a statement to the *Tribune* about his Ku Klux Klan involvement, that his paper would distort and lie about it to its own satisfaction. The Court was kidded in the songs.

Monday, December 5 Hugo got up this morning full of zip. After breakfast, he went right to the office. I was about in as big a hurry since I had to pick up Frances Arnold. Hugo had three short opinions and the Chief gave the opinion affirming that Julian Bond should be seated in the Georgia Legislature. The C.J. took about forty minutes to announce the opinion. Then followed the Georgia election argument, which was fabulous! Hugo and Bill Douglas practically argued the case through counsel. Hugo was full of bounce, asking cogent questions and pouncing when some other Justice would ask a leading question.[17]

Hugo's eyes are getting worse with the cataracts coming on. He let Spencer drive him home after dark for the *first* time. He also let me read three of his *cert* notes to him for the *first* time!

Tuesday, December 6 When Hugo got up this morning he said, "Now I am glad I have not retired from the Court," and so was I! Last night when he came home he said, "I have my opinion on the Georgia case at the printers!" On Sunday night, working until 1:30 A.M., he had written a "dissent" to it which he could easily change into an opinion of the Court.[18] So he was ready! I came home about 4:00 and Hugo arrived soon after, saying he kept Bill Brennan on his opinion only overnight, as there was a dissent to the Georgia case on his desk this morning (after spending a long time yesterday with Bill in which he incorporated some of his suggestions in the opinion).[19]

Wednesday, December 7 Hugo came home tonight full of vim and bounce. He has circulated a memo saying he thought the Georgia case should come down Monday. Whereupon Bill Douglas circulated a memo saying he needed a *month* to write his dissent. Whereupon Hugo circulated a memo stating Bill was well known for his quickness in writing an opinion and besides (in answer to Bill's saying in his memo they might be able to get another vote) Hugo said that he thought *all* the Justices were of sufficient maturity that they would be able to stick by their original vote. The C.J. called tonight and said for Hugo *not* to worry, that the case would come down on Monday and not on January 9 as Douglas proposed, because that was just three days before the Georgia Assembly was due to meet. Hugo says that if the Court rules that Georgia must *not* follow its Constitution, the State's rights will be absolutely nil. He is really wrought up over this case. It appears now we won't leave until Monday.

Once before, Bill Douglas gave an unusually sharp attack in his dissent to Hugo's *Arizona* v. *California* case.[20] I was in the Courtroom and I recall being shocked as Douglas literally spit out his words. He said, "The present case . . . will, I think, be marked as the baldest attempt by judges in modern times to spin their own philosophy into the fabric of the law in derogation of the will of the legislature."

Some people think that Hugo and Bill's occasional disagreements are caused by Hugo's disapproval of Bill's fourth marriage. Also, several times Hugo has been accused by columnists of "reasoning" with Bill Douglas in trying to dissuade him from marrying again, whichever time it was. This is not true. Hugo has told me that the only time he was involved in the slightest was when Bill was about to divorce his first wife, Mildred. Hugo and Josephine had a big party at their house, inviting Bill and Mildred, and several of their closest friends, in an effort to solidify the marriage. But such was not to be. Hugo then was reconciled to the divorce and when Bill married Mercedes Davidson, he asked Hugo to allow little Josephine to go around the world with them when they took a trip. Hugo consented and Josephine went along with them. When they got to Rome, where JoJo had a friend, Bill told her she should just continue her visit there and he went on to Russia, taking Bobby Kennedy with him but leaving JoJo behind. Hugo and JoJo were greatly disappointed but nothing was said to Bill.

Thursday, December 8 Last night neither of us slept. Hugo said he was up with his work, that now he felt he was at the peak of his writing ability and he must decide whether he will just loaf in Florida or whether he would write the Columbia essays and his memoirs. We voted in favor of the latter, as I knew he would want us to.

Friday, December 9 Hugo was on pins and needles for fear he would lose his Court on the Atlanta case. He was uneasy about Tom Clark, but

Tom vowed he would stick and he apparently is going to. It's now 6:10 P.M. and Hugo is home. At the Conference today he was told that Abe Fortas was sulking and said if Hugo changed *one* word in his opinion, he'd refuse to let it come down on Monday. Hugo did want to put in one word —"possibly"—but he didn't *dare.* Bill Douglas circulated a memo a few days ago saying he didn't want to be rushed, whereupon Hugo circulated an answer saying that the State of Georgia was entitled to a decision, and waiting until January would be at the opening of their General Assembly, and that Bill Douglas *never* takes over half a day to write.[21] Tense days!

Saturday, December 10 Hugo went in to confer with Earl Warren. He told the Chief that despite their differences of late, he still thought he would go down in history as a great C.J.

Monday, December 12 The Georgia case came down. Hugo was superlative. Whew! What a day! Hugo, after a very restless night for us both, awakened fresh and bright at 5:30 A.M. He announced to me he had made up his mind that he would state his case! He would not follow his written opinion exactly, but would say it in his own words. We got up and he got the encyclopedia and looked up Georgia and had me read some of its history, but we couldn't find anything pertinent.

Hugo then went to the foot doctor and I helped Spencer get the big Buick packed for us to leave for Florida. Then we drove to Court, as I did *not* intend to miss this day.

Andy Stewart and I were the only wives present. Potter had three opinions, including *Hoffa.* An electric shock went through the Courtroom when he announced that! He was very good in his delivery, affirming Hoffa's conviction, 5 to 4. Abe had one, so did John Harlan, and then Bill Brennan announced for Tom Clark.

Hugo got to the Georgia opinion and stated it very eloquently. Bill Douglas gave a sort of nasty dissent saying just because the Constitution of Georgia was old it was no sign it was good. Slavery was traditional in Georgia, Bill said, as was coercing confessions and segregation. And so he went on! Abe was flushed with anger and stated his dissent with more heat than usual. All he said was under "one man–one vote" rule the people should hold an election and not allow the Georgia Legislature, which is malapportioned and under orders to reapportion by May, to elect the Governor. In stating his opinion, Hugo said, "This Court, *this* Court, this *Court,*"—he said it three times—"is not allowed to write laws. We are here to interpret only!"[22] Well, and so it ended, but Hugo had the better of it by far.

We started off for Florida, Hugo driving, at 1:40 P.M. John Harlan had written me a note asking me to do all the driving during Hugo's temporary eyesight difficulty, and I was nervous as a cat. Hugo can't read the speedometer and I had to mention to him several times he was going 80 mph. Once I had to warn him there was a barricade ahead. His reactions are great, but I was relieved when he let me take the wheel. Usually I get very tired, but I guess the Lord gives people strength when they need it most. I love Hugo so dearly and lately I'm beginning to sympathize with "Mr. Sam Weak Eyes" in Li'l Abner, the gent who is constantly about to step over a precipice. I pray Hugo doesn't get hurt and that his eyesight will soon be restored.

Tuesday, December 13 Today has been very tense and I thank the dear Lord for keeping us safe. Believe me, I talked to Him continually. Hugo drove about 1 1/2 hours before lunch and about the same after lunch. I drove the rest of the time. Although he still drives well and does not tend to go off the road, I am so unnerved by his failure to see such things as curbs and "Barricade Ahead" signs, to say nothing of road signs. I have not written one Christmas card, as I usually do in the car, but feel I have to keep my eye continually on the road.

Wednesday, December 14 We awakened and Hugo announced we should *not* try to make the 600 miles into Miami today, and then we spent all morning and half the afternoon trying to make Miami! Hugo drove (after I did my early morning stint) and he went like a demon. Again and again I told him, "You're going eighty"; "You're going eighty-five"; and twice I said, "You're going ninety." He was almost like one possessed! He was passing everything on the road. We stopped at the Welcome Station right over the Florida line to get free orange juice. I lectured him gently (this is where I blame myself!) telling him it was dangerous, particularly with his eyesight so bad, to travel at such speeds. He agreed, but after lunch he went right on doing it. I was terribly worried but finally got out my crochet and quit looking, except when a state trooper caught up and had Hugo pull over to the side. He was polite and told Hugo he had followed him for fifteen miles and he had fluctuated from seventy-five to ninety all the way. He gave Hugo a ticket and put him under a twenty-dollar bond. In a way, it was a relief to me. Hugo was very pleasant and so was the trooper. Hugo asked him where we could find a good place to eat. If the cop recognized his culprit as he wrote "Hugo Lafayette Black," he never flickered an eyelash and Hugo never let on. This really chastened Hugo and afterwards we set the cruisematic on the speed limit, which was seventy, and we never went over the mark again. Even when I was driving, Hugo would urge me on to eighty but I never went over the limit. By late afternoon Hugo began saying, "How far to Miami?" or "Only four hours to Miami." I thought I saw the handwriting on the wall and I was prepared to go in feeling resentful and mad. Suddenly, however, Hugo capitulated, was charming, and even took me over to Vero Beach to spend the night at a fancy fish place called the Ocean Grille, which was right on the ocean. I was so happy. A big cloud rolled away.

Friday, December 16 Hugo is very disturbed that his mail sack hasn't arrived here yet and he called the office. He was quite upset to find that Margaret [Corcoran, a law clerk] wasn't there for the second day! He told Frances and Steve he wanted her at the office and to call and tell her so. I think he feels a bit weighted down with problems: his eyesight, which is getting so much worse so quickly; his inability to read as much as he wants; his tennis—all the things, as he says, which he has taken for granted for so long. He hates to call on me for doing so much for him, which I have tried to get him out of, but it hurts his pride.

Saturday, December 17 Hugo wrote Margaret Corcoran a very serious letter tonight telling her he expected her to work or quit. It was a nice letter in the end, though.

Monday, December 19 Hugo is having a very hard time reading his records tonight. We have turned on every light and he is still having trouble, but he doesn't want me to read to him yet.

Tuesday, December 20 This morning when Hugo and I were doing "jumping jacks"—throwing up the arms and jumping the feet apart—Hugo threw his left arm out of socket and it has been very painful ever since. This trip has been a bit unlucky so far, but this is bound to be the end of it.

We were going to the tennis court at noon and the mailman came with the mail sack—at last! We hit about two hours. Hugo can't see the ball when the clouds come over. I can beat him for the first time, a very hollow victory. But when he does see the ball he socks it hard.

I am reading *Lyndon B. Johnson: The Exercise of Power* by Rowland Evans, Jr., and Robert D. Novak.

Thursday, December 22 Hugo went right to work on his opinions and by noon we mailed two back to the office, the one he wrote last night and the one he wrote this morning.

Friday, December 23 I was out Christmas shopping and got home a little late. Hugo was worried and afterwards told me, "I'm just like your mother, always worrying about you. What if you got killed! What would happen to me?" I felt so bad about leaving him.

Sunday, December 25 A fine Christmas! We went to church with the family. Went back to Hugo, Jr.'s, and opened presents. They gave the Judge a rawhide jump rope, three books, pajamas, etc. I got a tennis dress and false eyelashes!

Tuesday, December 27 Hugo is keeping up his running in place and this morning did 300 runs. I am beginning to jump rope and did ten without stumbling.

Wednesday, December 28 We played doubles, I with Margaret and Libby [Hugo, Jr.'s, children] with Hugo. They both wanted Hugo, so I told them we'd switch after a set.

I fixed bacon and eggs for dinner and have been writing letters. I copied one of Hugo's pen-written letters to his cousin Charley Toland, in which Hugo suggested that Charley remarry. I was touched and gratified when Hugo said, "I married the second time at seventy and it is one of the wisest things I have ever done. No part of my life has been happier or more productive than those nearly ten years now." God bless him!

Thursday, December 29 My Hugo is still running in place and hit 250 tonight.

Friday, December 30 Hugo got in a load of work from the office so when Graham called to see if we wanted to hit, Hugo told me to go on, as he had to work. His legs are sore from running, too.

Saturday, December 31 Well, here it is again! The last day of the year. At 6:30 we went to Hugo, Jr.'s, for a cookout, three delicious porterhouse steaks. We left right after midnight and returned to find our apartment project "swinging," which kept us up until after 4:00 A.M.

Hugo decided to do 150 "runs in place," thus starting 1967 off on an athletic note! Hugo, Jr., and I have been encouraging him to take up some other form of athletics or exercise until after his eye operation. All in all, it has been an exciting and happy year, highlighted by Hugo's eightieth birthday parties, the White House party for Hugo, our Spring Supreme Court party at home with the President, and our trip to Germany. Welcome 1967!

1967

Sunday, January 1 As I look forward to 1967, I can see some shadows on the horizon: Hugo's impending eye operations and possibly Mother's, who will be ninety on her birthday in May. Yet the operations give promise of renewed hope, too, with restored vision. I just must find ways of keeping Hugo in good physical shape, so his strong and sinewy body won't weaken and fail.

Saturday, January 7 Clerks came out to work.

Monday, January 9 For the first time, Hugo says he is not going to drive until he can get his eyes fixed, a wise decision, I believe.

I wrote letters after dinner and Hugo worked. His spirits are very high since he decided to have his operation.

Tuesday, January 10 *State of the Union Address.* Heavy security and riot squad called out due to Congress voting out Adam Clayton Powell. Came home exhausted. Took Bufferin.

Tuesday, January 17 *White House dinner.* I labored long over putting on my false eyelashes. Hugo came home in the middle of it and told me not to wear them. Hugo sparkled in his tux. We stopped by to show Mother how we looked. At the White House a number of the members of the Court were already there and we kissed all around. Bill and Cathy Douglas stood a little aloof but were soon joined by the Harlans. Hugo and I danced after dinner.

Friday, January 20 Hugo came home early, about 4:45, seemingly unperturbed about his impending operation. Spencer drives him all the time now.

Monday, January 23 My fifty-ninth (ugh) birthday.

Thursday, January 26 I arrived at Bethesda Naval Hospital at 8:50 A.M. They had my Hugo on a stretcher ready to wheel him to the operating room. He was in fine spirits. He told me not to worry, that he would be back and his eye would be all right. At 10:30 I was sweating it out and doing some strong praying. About 10:45 the stretcher with my Hugo on it came back. He was wide awake with his left eye bandaged. He said, "Now I'm ready for the second one." He was bright and perky. He had to stay awake while they cut his eye, removed the cataract (which all came out), and stitched it up again. He talked to the office and to Mother less than an hour afterward.

Thursday, February 2 Hugo released from hospital. He is exhilarated to get home.

Sunday, February 5 Louis Oberdorfer and Hugo had a lively argument about the state's right to pass a law prohibiting people from assembling on state property. I had to warn Hugo to quit shaking his head so vigorously (waving his eye around, I told him).

Friday, February 10 Hugo back at work. Spencer came out in the Court car to fetch him for the Conference. He came home at 5:00, feeling mighty bad. He had forgotten to put drops in his eye.

Saturday, February 11 Hugo spent all day in bed. We watched a movie on Abe Lincoln's young life.

Monday, February 13 I left for the Court about 1:00. Found the arguments dull, so I waited for Hugo in the office. He came out at 2:15 and we went to the hospital. Hugo felt much better after his stitches were out.

Tuesday, February 14 Hugo had to write Harvard and Yale Presidents regretfully declining offers of honorary degrees. He has turned down so many he could not afford to accept one from them. We were both sorry, knowing how certain friends have knocked themselves out getting it offered.

Monday, February 27 Hugo's eighty-first birthday. Quiet and happy. Hugo presided over Court because the C.J. was in South America. Flowers, telegrams, and telephone calls poured in. We were very loving with each other all day.

Tuesday, February 28 I weighed myself and with clothes had gained to 135! Decided to get some lard off, so ate salad only for dinner. Tom Clark called Hugo and told him Ramsey was appointed Attorney General, but not a word that he was retiring, which was later announced on television.

Thursday, March 2 Hugo was interviewed by a young man from the Birmingham *Post Herald* on his birthday, and a Mr. Tom Dowling from *Time* wanted to talk to me about it too. But I handed him over to Hugo after Hugo told me all the things *not* to tell him. No freedom of speech here! I complained about my First Amendment rights.

We had a simple dinner—steak, turnips, turnip greens, cornbread, and buttermilk. I ate moderately.

Friday, March 3 Spent all morning right with Hugo. He tells me how fortunate he was to find me and how I suit him in every way. I always tell him I am the fortunate one. He is so loving and sweet.

Saturday, March 18 The clerks worked with Hugo all morning, but his eyes are so bad. Hugo just doesn't get discouraged, though. He has an *indomitable* spirit!

Friday, March 24 Hugo had his abscess removed—a deep root canal involving an abscess that wrapped around three teeth. He was doing remarkably well, no swelling and very little pain. He has an almost exhilarated attitude after some painful experience. He has a great spirit, and a very healthy attitude toward illness. It's almost like a personal victory over adversity.

Saturday, March 25 Les Carpenter made a positive statement in the paper last Sunday that Hugo was retiring August 17. It put the press in a furor. Hugo talked to several reporters and there was a mean article in the Baltimore *Sun,* and denials in other papers. Hugo went in to see the Chief, and Mother and I tagged along, sitting in the outer office. The Chief asked Hugo and me to go to Geneva, Switzerland, with him in July to the World Peace Through Law Conference. Hugo told him we might go, and later travel on to Athens and Rome! Whoopee! Chuck Luce called to say he was leaving the Under Secretary of Interior job to take the Presidency of Con Ed in New York, one of the largerst power companies in the country.

Monday, March 27 Hugo gave an opinion on the Chicago Bus Transportation case.[1] He gave it very well. I was glad on account of that mean article about his denial of retirement the Baltimore *Sun* carried.

Tuesday, March 28 Hugo's tooth is doing fine, thanks to five shots, ice bags, and the exhilaration of victory over a foe.

Hugo told Frances that I was going to write his first draft of his 5000-to-7500-word article on freedom of speech for the new *Yearbook* of *Encyclopaedia Britannica.* I was flabbergasted, scared, flattered, and excited. I've always wanted to write. Maybe here's my big chance.

Wednesday, March 29 Yesterday I was thrilled to hear Hugo so surefooted and positive in his arguments with Margaret. His eye trouble has caused him to proceed so cautiously, and he fails to see so much, that it was thrilling for me to see how surefooted he is in his own field. How I love him! And he tells me all the time how much he loves me.

This morning Bess Abell called to tell us the President and Mrs. Johnson would like to give a reception for Hugo on April 25 honoring him for his thirtieth year on the Court. We accepted. The whole Court will be invited and about twenty-five or thirty of our friends. Who?

Thursday, March 30 Hugo was home when I got back from the store. The doctor gave him glasses, and he was reading in bed—first time in a year! The doctor wants him to wait until after Geneva for the second operation. I think Hugo will agree to go with only one good eye.

Saturday, April 1 I tried to evolve a list of invitees to the White House. Hugo and I sweated blood over it. We'd add this one and strike that one, and Hugo said he was sorry because he has to leave out so many he wants so much.

Monday April 3 Hugo and I were terribly restless and sleepless last night. My mind was racing, and I tried to go to sleep by dwelling on the book Hugo gave me to read: Bury's *A History of Freedom of Thought.* Hugo has given me three or four very dull books to read to help me in my first draft of the *Encyclopaedia Britannica* article on "Freedom of Speech."

Tuesday, April 4 What are we going to do about the List! Hugo talked to Bess Abell, and she said he could invite all his clerks. Hallelujah! Also any others he wanted to a limited degree.

Hugo had a letter from *Encyclopaedia Britannica* saying that if he wished to write a longer article, they would give him another $1000. Oh, boy! Get busy! Read more of Bury's *Freedom of Thought.* Each paragraph I had to read twice to keep my mind on it.

Thursday, April 13 Dreamed vividly last night that I was in Birmingham filing a bankruptcy petition.

Friday, April 14 We had Mary and Tom Clark, Ramsey Clark and Georgia, his wife, and Helen and Skelly Wright to dinner. It was good to see how proud Tom is of his tall, good-looking, dignified son. Hugo talked about Tom's notes to everybody. Then he said, getting serious, "We love him, we'll miss him." Said if a charwoman died, Tom was at the funeral.

Saturday, April 15 Hugo's feet were giving him fits, so I took him to the foot doctor, who altered his innersole and advised Hugo to walk, walk, walk to get his feet back doing their work.

Sunday, April 16 Hugo and I took an eight-block walk, and he was surprised at how exhausted he became. His feet didn't hurt, though, which was good.

Monday, April 17 Louis Oberdorfer called and asked if the clerks could come over here after the White House reception, and would the reception be a good place to give Hugo a "chair" in the University of Alabama. Hugo and I took about a nine-block walk and today Hugo didn't get as tired. It made me feel better too.

Thursday, April 20 The President is going to [former West German Chancellor Konrad] Adenauer's funeral, much to everybody's consternation, and will be there on Tuesday, the day of our party. Everybody is in a state of uncertainty as to whether the party will be postponed. Hugo and I walked twelve blocks.

Friday, April 21 This afternoon a call came for me from the White House. I was not at home so they said they would call the Justice. They called Hugo out of Conference to talk to Lady Bird. She asked if he would accept her as a substitute, as she and the President were both terribly sorry developments prevented the President's being there. If not, she would postpone the party. Hugo told her she would certainly be acceptable—his admired Alabamian. Hugo always refers to Lady Bird as an Alabamian because she spent her summers in Selma, Alabama, with her aunt, her deceased mother's sister. Lady Bird asked if it was O.K. to ask the C.J. to stand in line and act as her host in the President's absence.

Saturday, April 22 Went to the Court for Hugo to meet C.J. on assignment of cases.

Tuesday, April 25 *White House reception honoring Hugo's thirty years on the Court.* Hugo spent part of the day in bed letting the excitement swirl about him. I got Mother at 3:30, as she wanted to see us after dressing. Mother was invited but would not go because she was too proud to go using a walking cane. A bit of an argument over whether we should leave at 5:00 or 5:15. Hugo wouldn't let us leave 'til 5:30. We piled into two cars, Spencer, Hugh III, and Annie [Sterling's daughter] in the front seat of our car, Lizzie Mae, Hugo, and I in the back. Sterling, Jo, and Mario went with Hugo, Jr., and Graham. Spencer insisted on wearing his chauffeur's cap. When we got there the guard told him where to park. I said, "Oh, no, he's a guest." The guards died laughing and said, "In that case, we'll park it ourselves."

Hugo and I were escorted into the Red Room to wait for Mrs. Johnson. She arrived, meeting the C.J. and Nina in the hall. Pretty soon an aide came in and said, "Almost a hundred guests are waiting below," whereupon we went into the Blue Room to form a receiving line—the C.J., Lady Bird, Hugo, me, and then Nina. After the line we all went into the East Room, where refreshments were served. The Vice-President made a delightful small speech and paid Hugo a touching tribute. Buddy Cooper, as senior law clerk, spoke next and told of the Hugo Black Fund for the Law School of the University of Alabama the clerks were establishing for him. Then David Vann, the secretary and moving power behind the Fund, spoke briefly, and Dan Meador, who is now Dean of the Law School at the University of Alabama, accepted it. Hugo was deeply touched and made an eloquent and moving speech of gratitude.

Senator Lister Hill and Henrietta, and Senator John Sparkman and Ivo, were both present—the first time Lister has come around Hugo in almost ten years.

After the reception the gang went to our house. We had plenty to drink but only things like olives, Fritos, crackers, and the like to eat. Whereupon, on leaving, lots were happily high. Tom Corcoran played the piano and we all sang. Dr. and Mrs. Howlett, Sara Tuttle, and Potter Stewart were among those really enjoying the singing. They all left around 11:30 P.M. and the family made a bee-line for the kitchen to raid the refrigerator. We were all starving.

And so ended the day which will become one of the favorite memories of many people, certainly of Hugo's and of mine.

Sunday, April 30 Changed time ahead. We ate breakfast on fast time, it being 9:00 instead of 8:00, came back to lounge heavenly in bed, napping and reading the paper. Hot Shoppe for dinner, after Hugo and I had walked our mile. Hugo wrote three cases (dissents and concurrences) via yellow pad and pencil. He stayed up till 11:00. I went to sleep reading at 10:00.

Wednesday, May 3 I had invited Mother to go with me to a lunch at the Congressional Club. Hugo and I went to her house and I took her a slip, my hat, and her jewelry. While Hugo worked on *certs* we had Mother dress up. She put on her clothes, and Hugo said we should buy her some navy blue stockings (she had on his black socks and I guess Hugo thought she was going to wear them to the luncheon). Mother got out her regular hose and showed them to him.

Thursday, May 4 I picked Mother up. She looked smart in her new dress, and she was so proud. She told Spencer, "Now I look like the wife of a doctor from Birmingham!" What courage she has, at almost ninety. I'm proud of her.

Sunday, May 7 Hugo is working on a case he dreads to work on. Says it will emasculate the juvenile delinquency laws.

Tuesday, May 9 Left for Atlanta, Fifth Circuit Judicial Conference. Ahh, what luxury! Lying in bed in the swank new Regency Hyatt House in Atlanta; not to have any pressures; to have a silent phone. Hugo put in a heavy day's work at the office, several opinions, *certs,* etc. He worked till 1:30 last night.

Friday, May 12 Heard a speech on bail and the concluding business of the Conference. Then Hugo got up for his remarks, paid tribute beautifully to both Sara and Elbert Tuttle, and spoke of the duty of judges to keep their eyes on that charter of liberty, the Constitution. Hugo told how most judicial appointees come fresh from the political arena, how their hair changes color or disappears, how their stomachs may get larger, but they all grow in mind and spirit. Then he ended by talking of going over the crest into the sunset, and by that time there wasn't a dry eye in the house. Sara Tuttle and I frankly were crying.

Saturday, May 13 Home sweet home. Hugo had stacks of opinions to read and act on waiting for him. We walked just under a mile.

Sunday, May 14 We were awake from 3:00 till 5:00 this morning. Hugo talked some and said he saw now that he had to work hard to pack a lot into a short time. He said he was going to dictate a series of word pictures, one of Walter White, the NAACP man. Also he has to write the article for *Encyclopaedia Britannica* (with my help, he says) and a speech for Geneva for the World Peace Through Law Conference.

Monday, May 15 *In re* the Court: I walked down the hall with John Harlan and I said, "John, aren't you going to state your dissent?" And he said he was just going to have it announced, and I said, "If you don't state your dissent, Hugo won't state his concurrence." Later in Court, John wrote me a note saying, "I will state my dissent; you shall have your show!" He did, and Hugo delivered a long discussion against the Due Process concept. It was all in the Juvenile Delinquents case.[2]

Tuesday, May 23 Hugo and I took the longest walk to date—eighteen blocks. No pain in the chest, but Hugo did complain of his right hip hurting before it was over. I'm sore from tennis.

Wednesday, May 24 Dash dash, push push, drive drive! We left home about 10:15 so Hugo could see a newspaperman who wanted to do an obituary! They do these from time to time.

Friday, May 26 Conference. Hugo was still upset because Margaret flew off the handle and said she could not do thirty-five *certs* on the weekend. She had to go to parties with her daddy. Hugo told her he would either do all of them, or part. She did take twenty-one, and Hugo took the rest. He feels disappointed in Margaret, and I feel I made a mistake to urge him to take her. Tom Corcoran came over after dinner (I'm sure he was disturbed!) and talked, finally bringing up that young people won't work now; they have too many choices. He apologized for Margaret without ever mentioning her name or seeming to refer to her at all.

Saturday, May 27 Hugo worked on *certs* and opinions till 12:00 A.M.

Sunday, May 28 Mother, who was ninety yesterday but only admits to eighty-nine, wanted to dress up for her birthday party today; she really looked forward to it for the first time I can ever remember. Hugo came down in time for the cake-cutting.

Thursday, June 1 Dr. Fox thinks the chest pains Hugo gets from walking are a form of angina. He says that losing out on tennis has put Hugo back a long way, health-wise, and he hopes to get him back at tennis as soon as possible. He insists Hugo continue his walks, and he gave him nitroglycerin for the first time. Walked two miles this evening.

Friday, June 2 Hugo woke up at 3:30 A.M. and told me he had had a horrid dream. We were at a picnic and I was flitting from man to man talking to each and, finally, when time to go came, Hugo went and got in the car and I didn't show up and he was furious. He woke up and, still mad, went to the bathroom and saw a note on the mirror reminding him to take his medicine. Then he came back and told me this horrid dream and laughed at himself. Said here I was, nearly dead with a cold and running around and doing everything for him, waiting on him hand and foot, and he gets mad at me in a dream!

Saturday, June 3 Roses at peak. I brought Mother up for lunch. She stayed for about two hours, sitting in the sun and walking in the roses. I took her home, came back, and typed Hugo's dissent on the New York Eavesdropping case, which he fed me, page by page.[3]

Sunday, June 4 I had to have Hugo at Dr. Alexander's at 9:00 A.M. in an effort to save his abscessed tooth. Dr. A. worked on it an hour, bored a hole in it, and drained it. Hugo came home and worked on his Eavesdropping dissent, feeding out handwritten yellow pages to me as I typed them and retyped the corrected ones. Got through at 2:15 and Steve came out to rework them with Hugo. At 3:30 Grover Hall, Jr., arrived and we sat out under the grape arbor. He is a sincere admirer of George Wallace (and evidently of Hugo too!) and tried to sell us on George's chances to be President. Hugo, without saying anything against George, was magnificent. He defended the Court forcefully and debunked Grover's assertion that George wasn't running on the race issue. Grover's father was the publisher of the Montgomery *Advertiser.* When Hugo joined the Ku Klux Klan, Grover's father had published a notice in his paper, like a social note.

Years later he told Hugo that if anybody got a Pulitzer Prize for that story, it should be he.

Monday, June 5 War between Israel and Arabs broke out.

Wednesday, June 7 Hugo came home and wrote a dissent, dictating it on the phone both to Frances and Bill Douglas, and he got Bill's vote right on the phone *(Curtis Publishing Co.)*.[4]

Thursday, June 8 Hugo got home at 7:00, exhausted from the Conference.

Monday, June 12 *Last day of Court.* Last day for Clarks. I went into the courtroom, but since they had twenty-nine opinions, dissents, and concurrences in all, they agreed to announce the results only, a lackluster and boring procedure. The C.J. noted Tom's resignation; then to our surprise the Chief took note of Hugo's thirty years on the Court. Hugo saw people until 2:00, and we then went into the Conference room, where Tom and Mary were hosts to their clerks and the Court. Saw all the Justices and wives. Mary looked so sad. They are leaving Wednesday for a trip around the world.

After the party Hugo came home and rested an hour. We rushed back to Court at 5:30 to a reception Ramsey was having for U.S. Attorneys. Hugo was supposed to make a toast to Tom at the dinner, but he was so tired he said he was only going to say two sentences. I kept nagging and worrying. When Hugo did get up he made a beautiful speech. Swept everybody to their feet in applause and had nearly everybody in tears by the power of his oratory.

Tuesday, June 13 We had to be at the dentist at 9:15. Thence we walked to Remington Razor place where Hugo showed them his World Wide Razor and asked for explanations. Hugo can be so dumb about mechanical things. He doesn't understand them at all, and he pinpoints and confuses the store clerks with a number of staccato cross-examining questions. If I open my mouth he silences me with "Let her explain it" (if she can, is implied). If I didn't know he was the smartest man in the world, and if I hadn't heard him make that eloquent speech last night, I'd think he was pretty dumb.

Monday, June 19 Honestly, Hugo is such a small boy at times. Last night I had him squirt a spray can of medicated powder on my itching back. It was so cold I shrieked and shuddered, whereupon he started spraying it (laughing) up and down my spine. I had to flee into the bathroom with him in hot pursuit to give me a cold bombing.

I tried my best to do more research on the "Freedom of Speech" article. I took Hugo to the office about 1:30 (he had finished his Geneva speech) and dropped him off. The Court car (which has a standing date with Douglas at 5:30 every day he is at the Court) brought Hugo home at 4:45. Hugo had to fit it into Douglas's schedule. We walked a mile, came home and ate supper, and I read Hugo my eleven-page resume of what I had read. We talked about Anaxagoras, *et al.*, and the concept of free speech, and my use was at an end.

Tuesday, June 20 Hugo saw a man who is doing an article for *Esquire* on him, and another reporter at the office.

Hugo has taken over the free speech article completely now, and I have dismally failed. Hugo said that I helped him gather his thoughts together, and my efforts were not wasted.

Sunday, June 25 Leave for New York and Athens. At 10:00 P.M. we were still circling New York at 5000 ft., anxious that our Olympic flight would leave without us. Finally, as we deplaned we saw a welcome Greek face awaiting us. They said they held the plane for us. They asked if we were willing to go without our baggage. I said yes. Hugo said he didn't think so. We got aboard, and the young man said he would do his utmost to get our bags. What a mess! Traffic and planes coming in all directions, Air Canada roaming around the field like a wounded dinosaur with five or six emergency vehicles following it. The steward finally arrived breathlessly to say our luggage was aboard. What a relief!

Monday, June 26 Arrived Athens at 4:30 P.M.

Tuesday, June 27 A man from "Horizon Tours" came at 4:30 and took us to Piraeus to catch the ship, the *Stella Solaris.*

Sunday, July 2 The Acropolis. Hugo managed, though poorly, to negotiate the hill, but he had to stop and wait before we got to the top, as it was rough, slippery, and uncertain footing. We have seen the Minoan palace on Crete, the island of Rhodes, and Ephesus, where Saint Paul was imprisoned and Saint John is buried.

Tuesday, July 4 Left Athens. Arrive in Rome.

Wednesday, July 5 To St. Peter's and Old Rome. We ate at the Café Paris; Hugo asked for a grilled cheese sandwich and queried plaintively if they had New York sharp cheese. The waiter told Hugo, "When in New York, eat New York cheese; when in Rome, eat Riviera cheese!" We saw the Pantheon, the Capitol Hill, the Old Roman Senate. We made it to St. Peter's as the Pope was having an audience. It was pandemonium, with different groups cheering and applauding as their sections were called out. The Pope spoke in five or six languages, and I stayed for the blessing. Hugo went over to a little chapel and sat down.

Thursday, July 6 I had a very sore throat and dreaded giving it to Hugo, who suffers so dramatically. We were taken to the Palace of Justice to meet the C.J. of Rome—the "President" of the Court. We were told he was an admirer of Hugo's and a scholar of the American Constitution. He had been on the committee to draft the Italian Constitution and now he was interpreting it. He was eighty-one years old, but he looked far older than Hugo. Hugo spent about an hour and a half conversing with him. Hugo promised to send him the book *To Secure These Blessings* [*The Great Debates of the Constitutional Convention of 1787,* edited by Saul K. Padover].

Saturday, July 8 One of those perfect days that grow richer in memory. Giovanni, our driver, and Joan Corcoran appeared at our hotel at 9:30 and we were off to the races! Giovanni, a typical Roman and a typical Roman driver, must have made 90 passing everything on the road until we asked Joan to slow him down. We arrived at the Spoleto Music Festival about 11:30, just in time for the chamber music. I felt refreshed as we left. Giovanni drove us to a hilltop restaurant, where Ingrid Bergman sat at the next table. Then Joan took us to a limpid lake described in one of Pliny's letters, where Pliny and Cicero had walked together. What a thrill this was for Hugo.

Sunday, July 9 Geneva. Dinner in the "Continental Room." When the tiny pumpkin-shaped melon came, Hugo almost ate the skin! Filet of sole was marvelous. When Hugo wanted seconds, the waiter sent for a new plate. "We don't want to confront you with the same plate, sir." "I've been confronted with the same plate all my life!" Hugo exclaimed.

Monday, July 10 Opening session, World Peace Through Law Conference, Palais des Nations. They persuaded my reluctant Hugo to join in the procession of judges. Robes were requested but of course Hugo had none. Some of the Black nations had regal red velvet trimmed with ermine and woolen wigs. Very picturesque. They tore Hugo from me and said I should sit in the diplomatic corps. Hugo was seated on the front row. Many long speeches. Got out forty minutes late mainly because one French gentleman assigned five minutes took thirty.

Tuesday, July 11 Hugo's speech. The C.J. gave Hugo a most gracious introduction, and Hugo came up with a great and inspirational speech, departing considerably from his text—the real inspiration of the day.

Saturday, July 15 Paris. Had a beautiful drive through the country with our tennis friends from home, Asa and Jacqueline Bates. We visited La Grange, Lafayette's chateau. Hugo's middle name came from his father, who was named for General Lafayette. The name was Alabama-cized so that it is pronounced La-FAY-ette, and his father was called Fate. His sister Ora chose the name Hugo, after Victor Hugo, because she was a great admirer of that writer.

Sunday, July 16 At 8:00 this evening we proceeded to the Club Lido by car. The floor show opened with a number of tall girls wearing flesh-colored G-strings and dressed in glittering stuff that did not hide their naked breasts. Hugo looked as solemn as an owl (with his big thick glasses), but I really think he enjoyed the show. While he hates what he calls "privy jokes," he likes to look at beautiful women.

Tuesday, July 18 Leave Paris for London. On arrival at hotel we had a bunch of messages; one from Lord Sellers [a friend of Justice Harlan's] to go to court and for Hugo to lunch with him at Gray's Inn. When Hugo found out no ladies were allowed at Gray's Inn, he declined lunch but said we would like to see the court anyway.

Wednesday, July 19 House of Lords. When we got to the Peers' entrance, the clerk missed us at the door. I wanted to call the office of Sir Edward [an acquaintance of Justice Harlan's], but Hugo is always fearful of being too forward so we just sat in the visitors' room for about forty-five minutes. Then Mr. Skelton, who had missed us before, came and showed us the library where they housed historic documents. Here was the death warrant of Charles I, the Petition of Rights, the first printed Bible, and other treasures. We saw the elaborate throne room, with its exquisite art and ornate throne. We got to the hall in time to see the Lord Chancellor, in wig, hat, and robe, parade in. I had to go to the rest room and was taken to the Peeresses' room. They had the most beautiful toilet—a sort of wooden bench with a hole and a blue delft, china-looking chamber pot, which I felt it too bad to desecrate. Heard abortion law debated. In court upstairs heard a milk price-fixing case argued. Tea with Sir Edward; cocktail party with Ambassador David Bruce; Savoy Grill for dinner.

Saturday, July 22 I scooted down early to look at shops, much to Hugo's dismay.

Sunday, July 23 Home sweet home. We arrived a half hour late, and just as we cleared customs Spencer appeared. He dropped us off at Mother's. She really has done beautifully, to my great relief. Hugo and I walked home and explored the garden.

Tuesday, July 25 Hugo is a bit discouraged because he still has to polish a speech, answer mail, make inquiries as to his Georgia ancestry for his Athens, Georgia, speech in November, see to resurfacing the tennis court, and a million other things before he enters the hospital for his eye surgery.

Friday, July 28 I have searched everywhere but cannot find the eleven pages of copy I wrote for the free speech article. Hugo wants it to help put flesh on the bones of his article, which he thinks is pretty good now that he has reread it. They are running stories all over the country about Hugo on his thirtieth year on the Court. The AP has a very nice piece, and I liked Grover Hall's insofar as it pertained to me. It said I was handsome, buoyant, and had an excellent voice. Hugo liked the article, except as it pertained to his brethren on the Court who believe in the "shocks-the-conscience" Due Process method.

Wednesday, August 2 To the hospital. Nurse Sullivan made Hugo welcome in her nice Irish way. After blood chemistry and much conferring, it was decided to go ahead and operate for cataracts tomorrow. I stayed until almost 4:00, and Hugo's spirits were good. He always gets bouncy when one of his ailments is remedied, or about to be.

Just before I left he asked me to shut the door and come over and sit beside him. He told me, as he took my hands in his, that he had had something bearing on his mind for several days and he must speak out. With his eyes looking enormous and with some emotion, he told me if he should die in any of these various illnesses he's been having, that more than anything on earth he wanted me to be buried beside him. But if he should die (and he said he didn't intend to for years and years yet), he wanted me not to be a frustrated woman and if I ever decided to get married again, I was not to have one qualm of conscience. I nearly wept; in fact, I did. I told Hugo I would be sixty on my next birthday, and after ten years of happiness and more with him, I'd never ever marry again.

Thursday, August 3 Hugo was operated on at 7:00, and by the time I arrived he was back in his room and had called to see what was keeping me. Fortunately, I walked in about fifteen minutes later. He was much groggier than after the first operation, and at noon was in very severe pain. He said in no uncertain terms that he wanted Demerol by injection. They gave it to him and he likened it to an umbrella spreading over him, and talked a bit drunk the rest of the afternoon, making love practically to his Irish nurse, Miss Sullivan, and speaking in raptures of his 3:00 to 11:00 nurse—the wretch!

Friday, August 4 Hugo is not dopey today. He kissed Miss Sullivan's hand when she told him goodbye at 3:00.

Wednesday, August 9 Hugo complained I was shortening up on my hospital hours with him, that I came later and left earlier each day. He asked me instead to come earlier and to leave later, so I did.

Thursday, August 10 Hugo home today. Hooray!

Sunday, August 13 Hugo and I went out and spent a couple of hours picking figs.

Tuesday, August 15 White House for dinner. I was proud of Hugo. He looked sparkling in his tuxedo. No one would ever suspect he was just thirteen days from a major operation. Both Hugo and I were at the head table for a change. The President often looks like his liquor is heavy upon him, but after sitting with heavy eyelids, he can get up and make a remarkable toast, as bright as a dollar. Guess that's what makes him an extraordinary man. He also used a toothpick discreetly at the table. The German Chancellor chatted in English with Lady Bird all evening, but responded to his toast in German. An interpreter then read it and twice the German Chancellor corrected him in English.

Friday, September 1 Hugo told me there was a possibility that Thurgood Marshall [Associate Justice, 1967–present] would be sworn in today and for me to keep in touch. I arrived at the Court about 2:30 and found the Supreme Court Marshal, Perry Lippitt, sitting in the guard's box in the driveway. He didn't know when Marshall was due to come in and he didn't intend to miss him. Perry escorted the Marshalls—his wife Cissy, Thurgood, Jr., age eleven, and John, age eight—to Hugo's office. Hugo called Bill Brennan, the only other Justice in the building at the time. Hugo asked Thurgood if he had a favorite chapter in the Bible, and Thurgood said he couldn't think of one, so Hugo said, "What about I Corinthians 13: 'And now abideth faith, hope, charity, these three; but the greatest of these is charity.' " Thurgood loved it, and Hugo swore him in on his white Gideon Bible bearing an insert saying it was from the U.S.S. *Arizona.* I suggested that Hugo present the Bible to Thurgood. We all wrote our names in the margin of the page of I Corinthians 13. Thurgood wished his daddy could have been there, but said he knew he was on some street corner in heaven shaking his finger and saying, "I knew my boy would do it."

Monday, September 11 Our tenth anniversary. I spent two hours hollowing out oranges and making orange cups. Hugo laughed, shook his head, and said, "Women!" Bill Brennan started the toasts rolling by giving a dear and sincere one to us both. Hugo then got up and gave one to me that made me cry a bit, about how eleven and a half years ago I had come to run his office and then ten years ago his home. After a few humorous remarks about how he proposed, Hugo told how sweet I was then, how sweet I'd been ever since, and how happy I had made him. I think everybody was weeping a little.

Wednesday, September 13 Hugo came home at 4:00 and for the first time since last December was on the tennis court again. He couldn't get a service over, and for a while not even a dropped ball. Finally I started serving and he then knocked a great many back to me. He has far to go because he has been so unbalanced—his sight is so different, and he is rather weak from lack of exercise, even though we have walked a great deal. When he finished hitting, he jogged the length of the court twice, and then he was all in. The man has real guts!

Sunday, September 17 We sort of rested today. At 9:00 we went out and hit balls for an hour. Hugo couldn't serve one over until I put a little competition in it and played him a few games. His serve started coming in pretty good. We hit an hour and he ran three lengths of the court, tiny slow steps but brave steps in the face of hurting knees.

Monday, September 18 Took our watches to the engraver. He will engrave mine: "Elizabeth with love from Hugo 9-11-67." He will engrave Hugo's: "Hugo with love from Elizabeth 9-11-67."

Tuesday, September 19 Hugo took the Buick and drove to the office. My heart sank, but I feared it was the feeling one gets when baby birds leave the nest. He has asked me not to destroy his confidence in his driving, so I must swallow hard and let him go. He got home safe and sound, thank goodness, and we went out and hit until 6:30. Again he ran a couple of lengths after his game. My heart always swells with pride to see him gamely trying to run, with both knees bandaged against the pain. Bless his heart!

Wednesday, September 20 Hugo and I hit until 11:30, then I went in to bathe while Hugo persisted and practiced his serve, achieving, he said, thirty good ones out of forty-eight.

Monday, September 25 Hugo and I went to the airport to pick up Dean Cowan of the University of Georgia Law School, who came up to help Hugo decide what to say on November 18th when Hugo dedicates the new Law School at the University of Georgia. Hugo asked Dean Cowan a number of questions, such as "What real good is it to have a fine new building?" "What are you trying to teach your students?" "Why do you think lawyers are necessary in the community?" and so forth, until 11:45, at which time I got up and went to bed.

Friday, September 29 John Frank to dinner. He wants to be Solicitor General, and Hugo wants him to be. John wants Hugo to call the President, and I believe Hugo will when the President comes back from Texas.

Saturday, September 30 Hugo walked right over to the phone last night to call the President to ask him to appoint John Solicitor General in response to John's telling him Abe Fortas thought it would be a good thing.

Sunday, October 1 We saw in the paper where the President named Dean Griswold of Harvard Law School as Solicitor General—a *Republican,* when John Frank has so loyally supported LBJ in Arizona longer than anyone! Hugo is depressed over it because Griswold is against everything Hugo is for. John Frank called up to thank Hugo, saying it was worth a lot to him to have Hugo reach for that phone. Hugo told John he was almost tempted to get off the Court, but John said, "One of us has to be there in Washington." This Solicitor General's job has been almost a life-long dream of John's. We were both terribly sorry.

Monday, October 2 There was the suppressed excitement that accompanies knowing the President is going to be in Court. I sat on the back row with Winifred [Mrs. Stanley] Reed, Ethel Harlan, Marion White, Andy Stewart, and Cathy Douglas. Winifred has got so she whispers loudly in Court, and she kept saying (*in re* the 250 applicants for admission to the bar), "Where does all that money go to? We're making a lot of money," and so forth. Thurgood Marshall's family was on the front row: his wife, his two sons, his wife's sister, and I believe his mother. The President came in exactly at 10:00, watched while the C.J. announced that Marshall had taken the first oath before Hugo and would now take the Constitutional oath, and saw him installed in his seat. Byron White now sits between Thurgood and Bill Brennan. John Harlan has moved next to Hugo in Tom Clark's old seat, and Potter and Abe are on the far side of the bench. The Justices were all in good form today.

Friday, October 20 Our party for C.J., Douglases, and Thurgood Marshalls. Lizzie Mae cleaned, waxed, and polished for two weeks in anticipation of the party. The C.J., Nina, and Hugo all drank fresh apple cider. Bill Douglas suggested if I would put a little bourbon in the apple cider when I served the C.J. and Hugo, it would liven up the party. Thurgood Marshall is the first person of his race I have ever entertained in my home. His grandfather was a slave! He has so much to tell. He knows every good judge and every bad judge in this country, I think. He must have had many affronts and yet he has been buoyant. Cissy is a lovely person. She hovers over him protectively.

Tuesday, October 31 We had lunch at the Court—Mother, Hugo, and I. Hugo put in a call for Professor [Walter E.] Dellinger (then in North Carolina) to tell him he has been selected as Hugo's clerk. Dellinger was almost speechless.

Wednesday, November 1 Hugo told me he has been invited to speak to the Alabama Bar Association in Tuscaloosa in July. He also has been invited to speak to the Birmingham Bar Association, but he finds the subject of the meeting, "A Lawless Society Never Creates a Better Society," unacceptable. I am a bit put out.

Friday, November 3 I took up the hem of my black woolen dress, over Hugo's protest. I told him if I listened to him I'd still be wearing my dresses below the calf of the leg.

Monday, November 6 Hugo reported that he had had another letter from Red [James E.] Clark, President of the Alabama Bar, saying he heard Hugo had already been asked to speak before the Birmingham Bar and he wanted to assure him that the Alabama Bar still wanted him. Hugo, bless his heart, then consented to speak before the Alabama Bar, and he also wrote the Birmingham Bar that he disagreed with the theme "A Lawless Society Never Creates a Better Society," as witness the American Revolution, but if they still wanted him in view of his non-sympathy with the subject and in view of his speech at the Alabama Bar in July, he would come. I love that man!

Tuesday, November 7 Hugo came home at 3:00 and we went to vote. This is one of the first times he's voted since he's been on the Court. Both of us were frustrated because the voting machine does not distinguish between parties or mark candidates Democratic or Republican. I voted for three I knew were Democrats and guessed at the other. Hugo refused to vote for the other, saying he wasn't going to ruin a lifetime record by taking a chance on voting for a Republican.

Monday, November 13 Hugo and I ran eight rounds of the tennis court—2400 feet, he figured it. Hugo sent in the title for his speech at the University of Georgia Law School: "There Is a South of Freedom and Union." Oh, brother! Bet that makes 'em jump!

Tuesday, November 14 At the C.J.'s dinner party for Thurgood Marshall the talk turned to football, and Byron White, alias "Whizzer," told us interesting tales of his football days. He played pro football for the Green Bay Packers and went to Yale Law School at the same time. Once his owner sold the entire first team with the exception of Byron. They came out third from the bottom that year. Nice party; excellent eats.

Saturday, November 18 Hugo's speech at the University of Georgia. Outdoor ceremony; platform under big oak tree; high wind. Acorns rained down like machine-gun fire; yet somehow they avoided Hugo's dear bald head. Hugo's speech, "There Is a South of Freedom and Union," was good but not up to his standard, in terms of moving people emotionally. He read it, only ad-libbing here and there. I was disappointed, but others liked it.

Sunday, November 19 Before we went back to Washington, the University of Georgia arranged for Hugo to see the site of the old homestead of his great-grandfather, Lemuel Black. It was up in Oglethorpe, Georgia, and it developed that the grandfather of Lyndon Johnson had been sheriff of Oglethorpe. We walked through the tall brush and finally found the remains of the old house and a well. Hugo got stung by a yellowjacket. We teased him and said it was his great-grandfather Lemuel Black reincarnated and coming back to run him off his property for getting the South so messed up with integration. We left the property all covered with beggar's lice and cockleburs.

Saturday, December 2 Today was blustery and cloudy. Hugo wrote on his dissent all day, something about telephone eavesdropping not forbidden by the Constitution.[5]

Friday, December 8 Brown Whatley [first cousin of Barney Whatley] called and dropped a thunderbolt! He said he read that the Pennsylvania Railroad case was before the Court, and he thought Hugo should know the railroad is one of the largest stockholders in Arvida Corporation, which owns the Boca Raton Hotel. We naively thought Brown owned it. Of course, we can't stay there. Hugo, Jr., is going to try to find us another place in Miami.

Saturday, December 9 White House. Lynda Johnson's marriage to Captain Chuck Robb. Bird looked gorgeous in ice blue and jeweled neck. Lynda was regally beautiful. The President looked subdued, tired, and dissipated. Hugo was so sweet. He stayed until after the cake was cut and Lynda tossed her bouquet. We danced to Peter Duchin's music.

Sunday, December 10 Last night Hugo got to talking to me and said he didn't know why he should care, but he just wanted his "dirt" to lie next to my "dirt" when we both died. I told him, "Puhleeze do not refer to my *dust* as dirt," and, of course, our dusts would lie side by side at Arlington Cemetery.

Tuesday, December 12 Traffic monstrous. Hugo had to be on the bench by 10:00, and we just barely made it to Court. I then went to the liquor store, got eight liquors, and went back to Court to put half in Hugo's car to make carrying it into Virginia legal.

Wednesday, December 13 Drew Pearson's seventieth birthday party. Frances called at 5:45 to say Hugo was still in Conference. I put Hugo's tuxedo in the car and away I went! Hugo was very tired when I got in, as they had been on bench until 2:30 and then into the Conference. Hugo said all his brethren had speech dates and this was the only day they could meet; Bill Douglas left his votes and left anyway.

The party was great. It would have been a surprise except Humphrey called Drew to say he couldn't make it!

Thursday, December 14 Hugo and I were a little rocky all day after not getting to bed until 2:00 A.M. I drove Hugo over to Bethesda Naval Hospital in the morning. We took Mother along, and I had to sit idly by until noon when Hugo finally came out in an expansive mood. He had had a long talk with the skin doctor about affairs of the Nation.

Friday, December 15 I got up and went to packing in earnest. Hugo for his part worked hard too. He wrote a long-overdue note to the President. He said, "I just called him 'Dear Lyndon'—that's what I've always called him!" He had never written him to thank him for his thirty-years-on-the-Court party, though I had written Lady Bird. He also wrote notes to every contributor to Steve Strickland's book about him, *Hugo Black and the Supreme Court* [Indianapolis: Bobbs-Merrill, 1967], including Aline Berman, whose husband died in India.

Saturday, December 16 Well, it's 9:00 A.M. and we're sailing down the road seventy-five miles out of Washington. Hugo, Jr., and his dad are sitting up front. Margaret [Black] is curled up sleeping in the left corner and I am holding down the right. Hugo, Sr., drove twice on the way down, and I am afraid I was unduly tense. I told him I had confidence in Hugo, Jr.'s, driving. This hurt my Hugo and he said I had lost confidence in his driving.

Sunday, December 17 We got up at 5:30 and left without breakfast. Everybody was a little cross. Hugo, Sr., announced that he would drive no more. To have achieved what I wanted, I felt terribly upset. My Hugo's eyes were filled with tears. Later he said, "On this trip," and I felt relieved. I love him so. I hate to hurt his feelings; but I would hate to see him get killed, too.

Monday, December 18 Miami. Our apartment seems to be a nice roomy one, on the fourth floor. They call it "The Penthouse." Hugo is relaxed and happy, and we are having a good time. As long as we can be together, we always have a good time. Hugo has been reading a bit.

We went to Hugo, Jr.'s, for dinner last night. Hugo III now taller than his granddad. Libby has a pet mouse named Nibbles.

Wednesday, December 20 Hugo hit on the ball boy about an hour and then we hit together another hour. He is hitting very well. In fact, he beat me on the twenty-five-count on his serve, the first time since the eye trouble.

Tonight Hugo closed the bathroom cabinet and part of the mirror crashed. Every day something new falls apart.

Thursday, December 21 Hugo is reading toward his Columbia lectures. He doesn't have any case assigned to him because he has already written four to almost everybody else's three.

Monday, December 25 Christmas Day, 1967. Another typical "Black Christmas."

Tuesday, December 26 We got a notice today that our tax assessment is raised again, to something like $85,000. It will mean about $300 a month! How much longer can we keep that place at that rate!

Sunday, December 31 And the sands of time have run through the hourglass once more without bringing any drastic changes in my life. Hugo and I are spending a quiet evening here in the apartment.

1968

Monday, January 1 Dear 1968, I wonder what you have in store for us? If you treat me as well as your predecessor, 1967, I shall have no complaint. When you came in last night Hugo and I were sitting here in the parlor of our Miami apartment—he working and I writing letters. As the fireworks popped and the people in the neighborhood behind us shouted, "Happy New Year," Hugo and I gave each other a sweet kiss. I then made us a drink and we toasted you, dear 1968. I had a letter to Mother in my typewriter and I was able to say I was writing her at the stroke of midnight. It was all so pleasant and cozy that I was happy we hadn't gone out among strangers to celebrate.

Tuesday, January 2 Hugo and I went out to the Monkey Jungle to get tangelos. In passing we saw a sign in a tomato field saying, "All the tomatoes you can pick for three cents a pound." We got out and picked seven pounds for twenty-one cents—Hugo being the world's highest paid and most competitive tomato picker!

Hugo called his office telling the boys he was sending in his first Carpentier Lecture for them to rework.

Wednesday, January 10 Arrived home from Florida. We stopped by to see Mother, came home, and plowed into the mountain of mail.

Thursday, January 11 Hugo tells me he will not drive while I am in the car, since I'm so fearful, but he will drive himself. I keep assuring him that it is he for whom I am fearful.

Friday, January 12 Spencer's car won't work. Hugo said for me to look around for a new car, so I can give Spencer my Buick Special.

Sunday, January 14 Hugo worked quite a while, mostly on his Columbia speech, which is sounding good! I went to Mother's for about an hour, and Hugo said he'd go to sleep—that way he wouldn't miss me as much.

Tuesday, January 16 I conceived the notion of getting a pen and pencil box—black tooled leather, imitation variety—and pasted Hugo's picture on it saying, "I'd rather be hung than to say hanged." Hugo is always arguing over lunch at the Court about the correct way to say it. I also got a pocket dictionary and pasted in a quote that "*hanged* is preferred to *hung* in the death penalty." Then Scotch-taped a dime (his betting loss) to the box.

Wednesday, January 17 *State of the Union Address.* The President's delivery was very good, I thought, though he is still holding out for the Viet Nam War.

Thursday, January 18 At Helen Wright's suggestion we drove over to Bethesda, Maryland, to see her contact lens man about contacts for Hugo. Although Hugo said the man looked like a motorman on a streetcar, we stuck it out and Hugo was delighted with what he learned. His resolve to wear contacts was pepped up considerably, and with his usual enthusiasm Hugo wanted to get them immediately so he could start right in.

Sunday, January 21 Hugo keeps coming back again and again in the wee hours of the morning to the fact that he wants me to be happy and if I want to marry, should he die, he wants me to. But his strongest urge is that I do nothing that would jeopardize my being buried beside him. I assure him I am fulfilled in every way and will want no part of another marriage, but he says he loves me so, he doesn't want to interfere with my happiness.

Tuesday, January 23 My sixtieth birthday—Elderly Elizabeth! A more soul-satisfying birthday no one has ever had, be it the sixteenth or the sixtieth! My remembrance of my sixteenth is so frightful that I try to forget it. I had a hard time, to say the least. But my sixtieth has been great. Hugo woke me up singing to me. I spent the day with Mother, writing letters and cheering her up. I came home at 4:00 to find a dozen red roses from "An Admirer." How thrilled I was that Hugo remembered! He even called in the order himself, Frances told me later.

Thursday, January 25 *White House dinner.* There was tension in the air about the capture of the *Pueblo.* Two or three units of the Army Reserve have been called up. Security was tight. No dance music due to the war scare. My, the President looked tired with lines etched deeply in his face, his eyelids heavy with fatigue.

Friday, January 26 Hugo was in the Conference all day. He had a victory by writing two hot dissents on a Fourth Amendment case (search and seizure). They were going to reverse without argument, just summarily reverse, in a case where an affidavit was deemed insufficient to support a search warrant for a dope peddler about whom there was no doubt of guilt. John Harlan and the Chief were hot on the other side. Hugo got the Court to deny *cert.* The district judge and six of eight appellate judges below had decided the affidavit was sufficient. Hugo was like the cat that swallowed the canary.

Monday, January 29 Return to Florida. Hugo came home at 2:30, having had his contacts in since 9:00. We hurried into the car, the last time it would be my car since I was transferring title to Spencer.

Thursday, February 1 Two law students from the University of Miami called to ask Hugo to visit with the law school and answer questions, but Hugo declined. I wished he would.

Friday, February 2 "If I beat you up on the hill, Elizabeth, I believe I'll know when they bring you," Hugo said to me a few minutes ago. At first I didn't understand what he meant. Then I said, "Darling, I believe we'll go up the hill together, but if not, I'm sure you'll know or I'll know when they bring the other."

Later, Hugo was taking off his contact lenses and succeeded in getting them both out by himself. "I'll give you a ninety-five on that only because you forgot to have your glasses next to you," I told him. "No, give me one hundred," he said. "I have you next to me, and as long as I have you next to me I'll be all right." Hugo held me in his arms tenderly, with his eyes looking into the future—"to the hill," as he said. I love him so dearly.

Monday, February 5 We went to the Golden Nugget Pancake Palace for the Early Bird Special: 55¢ for one egg, two strips bacon, and two pancakes. Then to Post Office to mail Hugo's third Carpentier Lecture.

Thursday, February 8 Date with dentist. Dr. Haggard's maid, Thelma, was cleaning up the sitting room. The hygienist introduced me as being from Birmingham. Thelma, too, was from Birmingham, and it was like old home week. I asked her if she knew Justice Black. She said no, and then I asked if she knew Senator Black. "Yes ma'am, did I know Senator Black," Thelma answered. "Lawyer Black, Lawyer Black, what a lawyer that man was! He'd strut into his office, sling his hat on a chair, and strut on in." (She demonstrated the movements as she talked, which was hilarious.) "Why," she said, "that man would strut all over the 'cote-house'! That man was a *strutter*!"

Friday, February 9 Hugo wrote a dissent last night on a rape case. He went with me to Dr. Haggard's office and telephoned his dissent to his office from there.

Thursday, February 15 Joe Price [a law clerk] and Hugo worked until noon on some tax case Abe Fortas has written which overlooks some of Hugo's previous opinions on the subject.[1] After tennis, we rested while Hugo entrusted the job of writing the tax dissent to Joe, although Hugo said he had it in his own mind and could have written it in forty-five minutes. When Joe came for dinner, they worked over Joe's draft and mailed it to the office.

Monday, February 19 Hugo's speech to Miami Bar was great. Hugo, Jr., introduced his daddy and he did a beautiful job. He is an excellent, relaxed speaker, like his father. It was a touching tribute. When Hugo, Sr., responded he looked emotional and said, "If it is not sacrilegious, I would like to say, 'This is my beloved son, in whom I am well pleased.' " Hugo, Jr., got the ball to rolling by asking his father if he considered himself an "activist." Hugo spoke eloquently on that. Later, a television reporter asked Hugo if the Supreme Court was responsible for crime. They set the lights and camera on Hugo, who with his new contacts could see nothing. Hugo asked them to turn the lights off, greatly disappointing the reporter, but he complied. Whereupon Hugo gave the most eloquent, impassioned speech for the rights of man I have ever heard. When he finished, the room was on its feet applauding.

Friday, February 23 Left Florida for home. Hugo drove about seventy-five minutes. He drove all right but my stomach was in knots.

Monday, February 26 Hugo drove a while and we had a few words over his going over the speed limit, whereupon he told me to quit watching him. I told him I preferred him to remain within the limit but would say no more. I clammed up in hurt silence, and he watched the speedometer. He drove about two hours, then Joe took over. We arrived home about 6:00. We found Steve had sent a lot of last-minute *certs,* much to Hugo's dismay.

Tuesday, February 27 Hugo's eighty-second birthday. Lots of telegrams, calls, flowers—the usual.

Sunday, March 3 Hugo is busy writing a dissent to a "horrible" opinion of John Harlan's.

Tuesday, March 5 Frances Arnold says she believes her beloved Thurman is dying. I have prayed all evening and have been reading Thurman's autobiography, *Fair Fights and Foul.* Hugo came home at 6:00. Watched special on Clark Gable.

Wednesday, March 6 The dean of Columbia University Law School, Bill Warren, and his wife, June, came down to spend the night with us and to make plans for Hugo's lectures at Columbia. We are to alternate Broadway plays and Hugo's lectures for three days.

Tuesday, March 12 Twelve years ago today since I started to work for Hugo. What a day! Snow all over everything. In Court, Carolyn Howlett (Dr. Duncan Howlett's wife) was already there. She was interested in the Religious Establishment Taxpayer's case, which was a protest to taxes being used for helping parochial schools.[2] All the judges were actively questioning each lawyer during his argument.[3] At five to twelve we slipped out and went to lunch. I noticed that Mrs. Griswold, wife of the Solicitor General, was already in the lunch room in her wheelchair. Right behind us was the Solicitor General, in his long-tailed coat, coming through the cafeteria line getting his and his wife's lunch. What a difference between the British and the American way!

Hugo has told me all day that my coming here twelve years ago today was the best thing that ever happened to him. He said I had made his seventies and now two years of his eighties the happiest of his life. Sweet darling!

Wednesday, March 13 To Court. The arguments were dull, and I nearly went to sleep. I would see Hugo fighting off sleep on the bench too, which worried me, but he conquered it.

Thursday, March 14 Hugo came in about 5:30, brought by Frances Lamb. On 3rd Street, S.E., he had been driving toward the throughway and a car coming close to him caused him to swerve and hit a car parked parallel at the curb. No one was in it. He asked me to drive him back to the scene of the accident, where we met an AAA wrecker that towed our car to the Buick place. A policeman asked Hugo to report in the morning to the Corporation Counsel's office. Hugo seemed unperturbed. The man whom he hit came out, introduced himself, and Hugo shook hands in a cordially forgiving manner.

Friday, March 15 Hugo would not allow me to go to Municipal Court with him, and he refused to get any of his clerks to accompany him. Hugo said the Corporation Counsel told him that he assumed the insurance companies would settle the loss and let Hugo go.

Sunday, March 17 Thurman Arnold better, thank Heaven. Hugo writing a dissent to Harlan tonight.

Monday, March 18 I got up with Hugo early, although we both had a miserable night. He worked 'til 1:00 A.M. and I couldn't go to sleep. I felt pretty bad all day but made it to Court to hear Hugo's vehement dissent to John Harlan's opinion in a suppression-of-evidence case where a man swore that he owned certain property yet the Court ruled that the affidavit could not be used against him in a trial.[4]

Tuesday, March 19 To N.Y.! Dinner at Laurent's. *Rosencrantz and Guildenstern.*

Wednesday, March 20 First Carpentier Lecture. Hugo's lecture had to be moved from Columbia Law School to the McMillin Theatre on Broadway because of the demand for tickets. Hugo wore a necklace mike and his voice came through great. Bill Warren gave Hugo a gracious introduction. The audience was Hugo's all the way. They rose as he came on stage; they rose as he began and when he quit. They broke into applause at several points. Hugo spoke for an hour and twenty minutes, sometimes speaking, sometimes reading, on the topic "The Role of the Courts in Our Constitutional System." Hugo attacked the "shocks-the-conscience" Due Process interpretation. He disclaimed the label of "judicial activism," and he proved by quoting from his Senate speeches that he had not changed his views.

Thursday, March 21 Weather warm. Hugo tremendous. Hugo's second lecture was at 12:00 noon. This one was on "Due Process of Law" and Hugo fought his battle to keep judges from striking down laws on the "shocks-the-conscience" test of Due Process. He received two standing ovations from a crowd of 1500 people, and ripples of applause throughout.

Friday, March 22 New York *Times* luncheon with Arthur Ochs Sulzberger, President and Publisher, and six of the editorial staff, including Turner Catledge, Executive Editor. They asked Hugo many questions and Hugo talked brilliantly. Hugo told me before we went in that he wanted me to look pretty but act dumb, and I think I succeeded in the latter. I think Hugo taught them a thing or two about freedom of speech and of the press. He also talked about promotion of judges from lower courts to the Supreme Court. He said he thought the Supreme Court could survive a few such promotions. They were astounded.

Saturday, March 23 Hugo's final lecture. Hugo read over his lecture. At 2:30 in the afternoon we went to the McMillin Theater, which had all 1500 seats packed. They greeted Hugo enthusiastically as he came out, with that sweet shy smile, looking very slight against the huge stage. His voice was strong and resonant, though, and he gave a tremendous lecture on "The First Amendment," saying it does not cover conduct such as marching and demonstrating. A very emotional ending left everybody in tears. The standing ovation lasted and lasted.

Monday, March 25 Before he left for the office, Hugo took me by the shoulders and looked me in the eyes and said, "Do you know why I've been able to accomplish so much work this past year? It's because you have taken such good care of me and made me so happy and caused me no anxiety." He is so very dear.

Wednesday, March 27 Here I went sound to sleep at my desk, and Hugo awakened me at 1:45 A.M. when he finished his work.

Thursday, March 28 Hugo said he dozed on the bench several times today, to my dismay. When he can't keep awake, I am inclined to think he should retire, regardless of how tired he is.

Sunday, March 31 At 9:00 in the evening, Hugo and I tuned in on the television to hear the President make a speech on Viet Nam. His concluding words were, "I shall not seek, and I will not accept, the nomination of my party for another term as your President." It was a great speech, I thought. Hugo said it was one that would make LBJ a hero. He has stopped the bombing of North Viet Nam and offered to hear peace proposals. It was almost with relief that I heard the President announce this, because much as I like him and Lady Bird, I would hate to see them face the acrimonious and hurtful treatment they would be subjected to if he stays in the race. Hugo and I are against the War, although we like LBJ very much. The television announcers were stunned, thus giving the President the last word in his desire to surprise people. I believe he has done the best he could and that he is convinced the War is necessary.

Monday, April 1 The big news about the President is on every tongue. There is much praise and some deprecation, such as "He knew he would get beaten so he quit." But I think it will go down in history as a hero's speech.

Wednesday, April 3 I sat between Marion White and Nina Warren at the Cherry Blossom Luncheon. Marion asked me quietly if I thought the Chief would retire so Johnson could appoint Abe Fortas Chief Justice. I had talked to Hugo about the possibility, but Hugo didn't think so, said even if the C.J. wanted to, Congress might not confirm him since that should be the plum of the new President and Congress.

Thursday, April 4 Just heard on television that Martin Luther King was assassinated in Memphis tonight.

Friday, April 5 All hell has broken loose in Washington. We got up this morning to the mournful account of the shooting of Dr. King last night in Memphis. Hugo went to the Conference, and all the Court went to the memorial services at the National Cathedral. The C.J. then went to the White House for a conference. There has been looting of stores on 7th and 14th Streets all night by Negro mobs, and a white man at a gas station was taken out of his car and beaten to death, just because he was white. At noon today the rioting broke out again. I left at 2:45 to go to the Court. A heavy pall of smoke and the stench of burning wood hung over the Capital. Spencer rushed home to see if his kids were in, since he couldn't rouse them on the phone. Television was incredible, showing mobs of Negro men, women, and children making off with armloads of clothes, small radios—even one man hauling off a record player on a dolly—all turning and waving gaily to the cameras. Spencer called at 8:30 to say the mob had arrived in their neighborhood and had wrecked and burned a store across the street. He and Lizzie Mae are appalled by the whole thing. Phones are jammed and it is incredible that the Nation's Capital is in the hands of lawless mobs. Curfew from 5:30 P.M. to 6:30 A.M. in effect; troops called out. Shocking!

Saturday, April 6 Rioting continues to rage. Spencer came out to the house. He had watched a gang loot the liquor store across the street from him—little kids ten years old. He sat up all night expecting his block to be set on fire. His heart was sick. I told him to bring his family over here until the danger passed, but he wouldn't.

Monday, April 8 As I drove Hugo to Court this morning at 7:00, the heavy pall of smoke over Washington had lifted. We saw youthful troops—not at all menacing—posted at the entrances to the Capitol, or groups of eight to ten slouching down the street eyeing pretty girls. The C.J. came into Hugo's office at 11:00 to get Hugo to help him assign cases. Hugo urged the C.J. not to retire even in the face of having Nixon or Kennedy appoint his successor.

Tuesday, April 9 Hugo is in the hospital today for correction of his left eye, which has developed a blister. At about 7:00 he called and said he wanted me to know before he went on the operating table that the past twelve years had been the happiest years of his life and that he loved me devotedly. I arrived at the hospital about 9:30 to find Hugo with a patch on his eye and eating a big breakfast. We watched the Martin Luther King funeral all day. They started televising it at 10:00 and at 4:00 P.M. they were still delivering the eulogy. Music impressive. Dr. King will probably be the Messiah for his people.

Wednesday, April 10 Hugo home from hospital.

Friday, May 3 *Hugo Black comes home to Alabama.* Spencer got us at 8:00 A.M. and we were ready though Hugo suddenly wanted to get his Georgia speech, which of course was at the office, and we had no time to get it. When we landed in Birmingham, Judge Lynne, Buddy Cooper, and the President of the Birmingham Bar were waiting to meet us. We checked into the Tutwiler Hotel and had the Presidential Suite, though I suspect it has been some years since a President occupied it. The old familiar hotel looked a bit down at the heels. The Law Day Committee came to escort us down to the reception, which was jammed. The dinner had been sold out and over 750 people were there, including many of Hugo's old friends. Judge Lynne gave Hugo a beautiful introduction and Hugo spoke on the part Southerners played in writing the Constitution and the Bill of Rights, and their responsibility to uphold them. He ended with his poem about "The Sons of the Flag." Hugo spoke at length, but he was eloquent and used not one note. He was witty, and there were ripples of laughter throughout. I am sure these Southerners would have preferred hearing Hugo's views on demonstrations (he's against them), but he saves that speech for New York. At home, in the South, he goads them into following the Constitution.

Monday, May 6 I took Hugo to Court because I wanted to hear his opinion upholding the *Miranda* rule in a case where a man in a state penitentiary was interviewed by Internal Revenue without being warned he could have a lawyer present. Hugo was in fine fettle, delivering his opinion with vigor and eloquence.[5] Byron White, who dissented, joined by John Harlan and Potter Stewart, was goaded into answering Hugo.

Tuesday, May 7 *White House Judicial Reception.* The President is *far* more relaxed and stopped Hugo to talk to him at length.

Monday, May 13 It is now 11:30 P.M. and Hugo is still working. I, being an athlete with a tennis match tomorrow, am going to bed.

Tuesday, May 14 Hugo sat up until 2:00 A.M. writing an opinion.

Sunday, May 19 Hugo woke me up at 2:00 A.M. He had been restless and wanted to talk. During these wakeful periods he talks of his dissents or opinions about which he feels outrage if they are going down the wrong way. He talked of the article in *Esquire* about him, which he thought was very well written and excellent—"An artist painting with broad strokes," he said. He always comes back to the theme of how lucky he is to have found me for his twilight years, how he can sail on into the sunset.

Monday, May 20 Hugo gave two spirited dissents to (1) an antitrust case which after eleven years was disposed of by a summary judgment;[6]

(2) the Court's opinion that pickets could march on a store's pick-up area (Weis grocery store);[7] and a concurrence to Byron White's opinion extending the Bill of Rights to the states by requiring a jury trial.[8] John Harlan wrote me a note asking me what I fed Hugo for breakfast. "He is in fine fettle!"

Thursday, May 23 Hugo is working on his last dissent to Potter Stewart's, saying they should have asked the jury "Can you render a just verdict even though you have conscientious scruples about the death sentence?"

Sunday, May 26 Mother's ninety-first birthday party. She only admits to ninety, but I've got the proof on her. She looks much younger than her ninety-one summers.

Monday, May 27 Court. Little Nina Warren (about three) called out to the C.J., "Grandpa," and Nina whisked her out. The Court decided by way of the C.J. that a draft-card burner had to go to the clink. The "Freedom of Choice" school case came up. Bill Brennan rendered the opinion, and it looked like nobody had freedom of choice, especially the school boards.

Tuesday, May 28 Yesterday, when he was eighty-two years and three months old exactly, Hugo began writing his memoirs.

We read in the paper where Hugo had passed another milestone. He is now the third oldest man ever to serve on the Court. Holmes was ninety and Roger Taney eighty-seven. Brandeis retired at eighty-two years and three months.

Hugo was at home until 12:30 completing his preface to his memoirs, over which he said he dropped a tear or two. He can stir passion within himself, and I suppose that is why he can stir passion in others.

Wednesday, May 29 Hugo called me from the Court and said, "We're getting picketed!" It seems the Indians of the Poor People's March were protesting Monday's decision that Indians, like everybody else, had to abide by the state's ban on net fishing. The Negroes, Indians, and others ran down the flag, broke windows in the basement, dived in the fountain pool, frolicked on the lawn, and did other disgraceful antics. The court doors were locked, but they finally let sixteen in to see the Clerk. Reverend [Ralph] Abernathy's statement, according to the *Star,* was, "I won't say Earl Warren hasn't been all right, but the Court's swinging the other way and we've got to get 'em back."

Thursday, May 30 At Ethel Harlan's birthday dinner, we discussed the disgraceful picketing of the previous day. John said that during the disturbance he went down to the record room and saw Thurgood Marshall looking out at the crowd in a disconsolate way. He said to John, "To think they would do this after what you fellows did for them on Monday." The Court on Monday nullified the freedom of choice plan of integrating schools, which had meant, in effect, segregation.

Monday, June 3 *Two hot dissents.* According to a memo by the C.J., all attorneys to be admitted were to remain in the Courtroom until after all opinions were given—thus to keep demonstrators out of the Courtroom. The memo also said that in case some of the demonstrators got into the Courtroom and caused a disturbance, the Court would file out until order had been restored. Potter Stewart had two opinions that Hugo thought were terrible. One involved a man convicted five years ago, whose case had been taken off the Special List by Potter, and whose conviction was overturned by the Court because all the prospective jurors, having been queried if they had conscientious objections to the death penalty, were not then asked if despite their objections they could render a fair decision.[9] The other was a search and seizure case where a man was given a life sentence because of rape and attempted murder of the boy and girl involved and who was convicted because they had found the rifle in his grandmother's house; the grandmother verbally admitted she told the searchers to go right ahead, and the sheriff had said he had a search warrant but she didn't ask for it. This man's conviction was reversed because she hadn't really consented, though she affirmed she had consented.[10]

Tuesday, June 4 Hugo worked solidly on a dissent he's doing to John Harlan's opinion, for three and a half straight hours.

Wednesday, June 5 All of us were rushing home to hear the outcome of the California primary in which [Eugene] McCarthy and Bobby Kennedy were so hotly contesting. Hugo worked another hour before bed, while I had on the television, but no definite outcome due to Los Angeles' new electronic system of voting. So at 6:30 A.M. I turned on the television again and heard Bobby's victory speech, 46% to 42% over McCarthy! But then I was devastated when the announcer said, "This was just before Senator Kennedy was shot down as he was walking through a kitchen passageway on the way to a press conference." Oh no! It *couldn't,* it just could not happen again to that poor family! We were encouraged to know he was taken to the hospital. We had high hopes and prayed his life and mentality would be spared, as he was shot through the brain.

Thursday, June 6 We got home at 5:00 and listened to television reports on Bobby Kennedy. A young and obviously demented Jordanian shot him at five feet. What is becoming of this country? He died at 3:45 P.M., California time.

Friday, June 7 The pall of poor Bobby Kennedy's death hung over us. Hugo was in Conference all day. Said he had a few minor fights.

Saturday, June 8 We watched hypnotically and sorrowfully the complete funeral services televised all day. The music was especially stirring—Handel's *Messiah.* Teddy Kennedy in his eulogy was superb. Never have I seen the immediate family so actively participate in the funeral. We watched until they buried Bobby by candlelight, so poignant, so sad, so tragic.

Monday, June 10 The Court said taxpayers can now sue if they think the government is helping religious establishments. Seems to me the Court was inconsistently holding the government could help parochial schools by furnishing free textbooks, and in the same breath saying taxpayers can sue if they think the government is helping "the establishment of religion."[11]

Thursday, June 13 Last Conference of the year, except for tomorrow's continuation. Hugo told me the C.J.'s secret (confidentially).

Friday, June 14 Hugo had to go to the Conference at 10:00, the last one of the year, continued from yesterday. He spent all afternoon writing a dissent to deliver Monday.

About 3:00 A.M. neither Hugo nor I could sleep well, so finally I turned on the light and put my head on his shoulder. Then he opened up. He is tormented by what course he should follow, and I think for the first time now he is considering retiring. The C.J. told them yesterday that he had sent in his letter of retirement to the President. This means Abe Fortas will be sure to be the next C.J., and Hugo, though he loves Abe, doesn't like his judicial philosophy.

Sunday, June 16 I was too worn out to sleep much last night. Hugo got up and read two hours because he couldn't sleep. He is still disturbed because the C.J. is retiring. He fears he will give his age (seventy-seven) as his reason to retire and Hugo is five years older than he. The *Post* is sniping at old and "senile" judges of the past and saying old judges ought to voluntarily retire. Hugo has always said he didn't mind retiring, but that was belied tonight when he said in an anguished voice, "But what will I do!" I told him a number of things, all of which he rejected. But he does want to write his memoirs.

Monday, June 17 I felt the possibility that this may be Hugo's last appearance as a member of the Court, and certainly it was Chief Justice Warren's last day. All the wives were there except for poor Ethel Harlan. A number of opinions, and very important ones too, were read: the case extending open housing by saying a seller cannot discriminate; the Alcoholic case (can they be punished for the "crime" of being drunk?)[12]; and others. Hugo had two dissents and one opinion of the Court. He gave his with vigor and preciseness. There was also Bill Douglas, fresh from the hospital, having had a pacemaker machine inserted in his body to regulate the heartbeat, looking weak and drawn and pale. (His complexion is so florid ordinarily.) He gave an impassioned dissent to a "stop and frisk" case, and everybody was relieved he got through it without dying. I studied Nina and the girls. How sad they looked. I studied Hugo, the C.J., and Bill Douglas and thought fate might decree none of the three would be there next year. Truly the end of an era.

Tuesday, June 18 Hugo talked to John Harlan this morning and John, who is leaving for Connecticut tomorrow, begged him not to do anything rash over the summer, like retiring. I would hate for Hugo to retire, yet I want him to go off the Court with his image of a great Justice untarnished. One never knows when something will hit that will incapacitate him. I love him and feel so yearningly sympathetic.

Wednesday, June 19 Television was full of the Solidarity March of the Poor People. Mrs. King was the most impressive of the speakers, singing a spiritual and reading her late husband's "I Have a Dream" speech. There were 50,000 people here for the march. It is predicted the poor people will now go into civil disobedience.

Thursday, June 20 Poor People are starting "Phase II," the militant nonviolent part, by lying down in front of the Department of Agriculture doors and in the streets. Some sixty-five have been carted off to jail.

At 11:00 P.M. there is news of trouble in Resurrection City (or Insurrection City, as it was called on television today). Tear gas bombs were thrown by police.

Sunday, June 23 Hugo is still deeply disturbed about the C.J.'s retirement and the furors in the papers. He says he won't be a part of a mass retirement.

Monday, June 24 Hugo got in a slow, inch-by-inch traffic jam on the 14th Street Bridge because the police were vacating Resurrection City, arresting those who would not go. We had to detour Constitution Avenue because Reverend Abernathy [who led the Poor People's March] was having a confrontation with the police because he wanted to go on the Capitol grounds. Abernathy was arrested.

Hugo and I had a big argument as to whether we could replace our thirty-year-old gas stove which has a semi-rusted oven and no thermostat on it. We stopped by Harris plumbing to see if the old stove could be fixed, and Mr. Harris laughed heartily when Hugo was so insistent that our stove was perfect. Hugo said if people made stoves to last only thirty years they ought to be arrested.

Tuesday, June 25 Hugo wrote on his memoirs until 12:30 A.M. We never mentioned the stove, and I went on as though we had decided to get a new one. I think it very important to get Lizzie Mae nice things to work with.

Wednesday, June 26 Abe Fortas and Homer Thornberry named as (1) Chief Justice and (2) Associate Justice. [Thornberry did not receive Senate confirmation.] Hugo came home from the office. Abe had come in to see him and had said many nice things about Hugo. Hugo offered him sage advice.

Thursday, June 27 Hugo talked to me finally about the stove, reiterating his opinion that we do *not* need a new stove, but if it would make me happier he'd get it for me. I told him it would, and so he agreed, reluctantly. Hugo is writing tonight on his memoirs.

Sunday, June 30 Lazy day. Hugo and I were almost too lazy to go out for tennis. We finally made it and stayed until close to 1:00, in the searing heat (97°). Once Hugo fell and scared me to death, but as he fell I saw him make himself into a ball and roll gently. How many people at eighty-two could fall down hard from a standing position without breaking bones or spraining joints! John Frank was in town and came out for an hour. He urged Hugo not to retire, saying that law and order was important, and they had to have somebody to rally to.

Monday, July 1 Hugo called me in for a talk, saying he did not approve of modernizing the kitchen, but if I wanted it badly he'd go along with me to look at new kitchen ranges. Hugo does not approve of throwing things away before they are worn out: "They don't build things like they did thirty years ago." We went to look at stoves and I decided on the Modern Maid.

Tuesday, July 2 Hugo still writing his memoirs. Now looking at news at 11:20 P.M.

Friday, July 5 Hugo and I were stunned to hear over the radio that the Chief Justice had announced he *would not* retire until and unless Congress confirmed Abe Fortas. Hugo thought it a very bad thing for the Court, an effort to put the Chief Justice on a higher and different plane from the Associate Justices and an effort to force Congress to appoint Johnson's man. It was also a dig at Hugo, since the C.J. called a press conference and in it said the age factor was the only reason and there ought to be a cutoff date, and so forth. Hugo would automatically be Acting C.J. in case of a vacancy.

Saturday, July 6 Hugo and I are still gravely talking of the implications of the C.J.'s press conference. Hugo says they may attack him openly in the press before it's over and he has never run away from a fight and doesn't intend to now. I have told him over and over that I preferred for him to get off the Court and to take the rest that is his due, for his long and arduous labors on behalf of his country. I fear, with attitudes on his age, his image will lose some of its luster, but not, I think, in the overall picture of history.

Sunday, July 14 We advertised our dishwasher and stove in today's paper. I got three calls but all lost interest when they heard the respective ages of the appliances. Hugo said I was no salesman and suggested he talk to the next one.

Monday, July 15 Hugo tonight working on his Tuscaloosa speech. By "working" I mean he is thinking about it and getting little things like Virgil's Song about life and death typed. They want him to reminisce.

Wednesday, July 17 Abe Fortas testified before the Senate Judiciary Committee today and admitted he was Johnson's adviser in many matters but none pertaining to the Court.

Hugo is reading to clear his mind of everything, after which he may think of his speech.

Thursday, July 18 Arrived in Tuscaloosa at 12:00 noon. Hugo was asked if he desired security but he declined.

Friday, July 19 Red Clark asked Buddy Cooper to escort Hugo to the platform, and the packed auditorium gave Hugo a standing, enthusiastic reception. Truman Hobbs [Hugo's law clerk in 1948] introduced Hugo and told the story about [Senator] Will Bankhead's advance man wanting to put out posters in the stores in Jasper, Alabama, the day after he came home from Congress the first time saying: "Will Bankhead, Welcome Home." And one old storekeeper said, "Go ahead and put the poster in, but let me ask you this: Whar's Will been?" Truman said everybody knew where Hugo Black had been the past thirty-one years.

Hugo's speech was a review of his early days as a student and a lawyer. He spoke for forty-five minutes, ten over time. They gave him three standing ovations. These were the children and grandchildren of Hugo's contemporaries. The "middle generation" had been violently opposed to Hugo's Wage and Hour Bill and also the *Brown* decision. *Their* children were more liberal and were more susceptible to Hugo's charm.

Toward the end of his speech Hugo made a forceful statement that any judge worth his salt would enforce the Constitution, and that brought down the house. This would have been the ideal stopping place, but he wanted to read Virgil's poem about death beginning "Me let the sweet muses lead to their soft retreats." It was difficult for him to read and he showed emotion. Mildred [Faucett] punched me to ask me if he was O.K. His hands trembled and I think all of us were a bit worried. However, the speech was tremendous, and he had come back home to the arms of the Alabama Bar. He began his speech by showing a photostatic copy of the Mobile *Register* in 1934, his last visit to the Bar Association, when Leo Oberdorfer was President. It showed a riot in San Francisco, robbers chased on land, sea, and air—the usual violence. At the Alumni luncheon that followed, Hugo was presented with a Phi Beta Kappa Key and a record, "Here Come de Judge."

That evening we went to the banquet and I sat on Governor Brewer's right, with Hugo on my left. Alabama's Supreme Court Judge Ed Livingston made the outrageous statement in his short remarks that he was to the right of Wallace. Wallace stood in the school door but Livingston's folks in Notasulga, Alabama, burned the schoolhouse down. Everybody was relieved when the old fool sat down.

I meant to mention that earlier in Hugo's speech he recited from the beautiful poem "Thanatopsis": "So live, that when thy summons comes," etc. Hugo's speech, he said, "was like hash—a little of this and a little of that." His theme that ran through it though was to live so you can sleep well at night, and when death comes you can lie down to pleasant dreams.

Sunday, July 21 Family reunion. We had a great time singing old Baptist hymns. Hugo, Mildred Faucett, and Bunyan Toland recorded "How Tedious and Tasteless the Hours."

Tuesday, July 23 Northport, Alabama. We went down to Lewis's store (Faucett Hardware) and bought Hugo a straw hat. Came home for a huge vegetable lunch, fresh corn, butter beans, the works. We got away by 2:30 and had a drive through the beautiful Alabama countryside—red clay, and the kudzu covering trees and bushes impartially. Arrived at Sylacauga about 5:30. Talked largely of family history—until midnight. Sentimental journey!

Wednesday, July 24 Alexander City, Alabama. We drove out to Horseshoe Bend Military Park, where the Battle of Horseshoe Bend took place. Davy Crockett had scouted for Andy Jackson and told him there were too many Indians to win, but by strategy Andy won the battle. The Creek Indians were fighting for homes and families, yet we called it a great victory for freedom.

Friday, July 26 Ashland, Alabama. We went by to Hugo's mother's and father's graves to pay respects.

Monday, August 5 Home. I got Hugo to the Court, where he met a young student who had written a paper on Hugo's use of history in his opinions based largely on Fairman's criticism of Hugo's dissent in *Adamson* (first suggesting the Fourteenth Amendment makes the Bill of Rights applicable to the States). We took him to lunch and Hugo made short shrift of Mr. Fairman, leaving the student somewhat shattered.[13]

Friday, August 16 The darn new oven won't work!

Sunday, August 18 Hugo is reading aloud to me from *Red Hills and Cotton: An Upcountry Memory,* by Ben Robertson, a South Carolina man, which describes Hugo's and my people exactly.

Monday, August 19 An aimless sort of day. Hugo and I got up at 8:00, vacillated over whether he/we should go to the office, and finally at 11:30 we went. Had lunch with Hugo's new law clerk, Walter Dellinger. He taught two years at the University of Mississippi and affects the academic longish hair. Yet he seems bright and talkative. Walter left early to go to our car and retrieve this diary for me, and meanwhile Abe Fortas came in and sat with us. Abe seems a bit depressed and "I don't give a damn"-ish! He says he never cared about being Chief Justice anyway.

Friday, August 23 I wrote a four-page letter to the Harlans last night and brought it to the office to be mailed. I let Miss LaGarde, Hugo's substitute secretary, read it and she was chuckling all the time. She thinks I'm witty.

Today's biggest news is that Hugo consented at long last to do a television interview for Martin Agronsky. It is set up for September 17, I think. I was most anxious for him to do it and Martin has been after him for four or more years!

Monday, August 26 Listening to Democratic Convention. It is an amazing performance. The Republican Convention was boring, but the Democratic one will never be. There is barbed wire around the Coliseum; hippies, yippies, and all kinds of people collecting in Lincoln Park and elsewhere; rumors of a draft for Ted Kennedy. A fight over the Viet Nam plank is being waged. At 2:30 A.M. the McCarthy people succeeded in adjourning the meeting to noon Tuesday. We went to bed around 12:00, but Hugo got up several times and turned on the television.

Wednesday, August 28 It is now 11 P.M. and we are aghast as we watch the Democratic Convention in Chicago. Mobs are battling the police, chanting, "The whole world is watching." The peace plank was defeated, but over 1000 delegates voted for it. A fight broke out on the floor when a delegate got irked because he was asked so often to show his credentials. Six billy-clubbed policemen came in and took him and others, including John Chancellor, an NBC floorman, to a trailer outside. Humphrey is said to have had a small taste of tear gas himself as the fumes drifted up to his room. Disgruntled delegates are talking on television, complaining of Daley tactics.

Friday, August 30 Convention over. Peace and quiet reigns in our study. No more tumultuous shouting and no more dreads as to what will happen next.

Monday, September 2 *Labor Day.* Hugo is working on his memoirs tonight, reading them over, preparatory to starting to write again.

Tuesday, September 10 Hugo and I are both feeling very sentimental about our anniversary and remembering eleven years ago today when I shopped for a dress and came out here for dinner.

Wednesday, September 11 *Our eleventh anniversary.* To National Theater to see *Fiddler on the Roof.* This was a very good musical about a Russian Jewish village in 1905. Lighthearted but with an underlying message. We then walked to the Lawyers Club on 18th Street (about a mile) and had a quiet dinner. Hugo tells me how heavenly our eleven years together have been, and I agree. He is a thoroughly satisfactory lover.

Thursday, September 12 Martin Agronsky came out to lunch and to discuss the interview. He stayed until 5:00 talking about possible subjects to ask Hugo about. Hugo will do the interview spontaneously and unrehearsed, though. I think they will set it up for here in the study, as Hugo wishes, but I have misgivings. Hugo wrote on his memoirs until 1:30 A.M.

Friday, September 13 I was busy as a one-armed paper-hanger with the itch. At 1:00 P.M. the CBS gentlemen came, four strong. They looked over, and liked, the study. It is a bit small for three television cameras, but they think they can do it. Burton Benjamin, Executive Producer, walked about, sizing up, discussing which furniture they'd move, etc., while Eric Sevareid, who will interview Hugo with Agronsky, and Martin talked to Hugo as though the interview were already in progress. They will send a crew here next Thursday to get everything set up, and Friday at 10:00 they will walk in and start shooting.

Saturday, September 14 The newspaper says they are now attacking Abe's nomination because five men went in together and raised $15,000 to pay Abe for teaching a seminar at American University this summer.

Monday, September 16 Though I slept well, my head was full of things I ought to do to get the study presentable. My number one objective is to clean the chandelier. Spencer and I devised a way of getting the worst-looking cobwebs out of our study window, by sticking down a yardstick and pouring ammonia water down the crack.

Hugo begins at 10:30 to write.

Thursday, September 19 Hugo, Jr., arrived last night about 8:30 for one of his meetings on the "Presidential Commission on Cities." He talked to his dad about the verbal agreement CBS had made with Hugo to allow him to go over the tapes for corrections or omissions if he found it necessary. Hugo advised his dad to get it down in writing.

This morning, the first order of business was for me to go to Jean's to get my hair fixed. When I arrived home around 11:30 there were about twenty men swarming all over the house, with CBS news trucks in great evidence. There were about fifteen men in the study, and most of the furniture which had been inside it was now in our bedroom or hall, and the other space was occupied by equipment. Bright lights were installed just under the high ceiling. Three cameras were set up. The sound men were sitting around on stools in our large old-fashioned bathroom. They were going over their tape recorders. Smoke was everywhere, as they puffed on their cigarettes.

I found Hugo sitting disconsolately downstairs, fully dressed, with coat and tie, trying to read *certiorari* notes. I felt so helpless that I went down and joined him, and we just watched the goings-on. Finally Mr. Benjamin asked Hugo if they could photograph him opening the front door and walking to the corner. They had installed a camera on an unfinished roofless house across the street, and also had a camera atop a CBS truck for the purpose of following him as he walked along.

Mr. Benjamin then asked me if I could induce Hugo to play a little tennis for the camera. Hugo has steadfastly refused to let anyone—when he could help it—take movies or pictures of him playing tennis, for publication. Because he wanted me to get into the act, though, he finally agreed. We went out at 3:00, although they had asked for 2:30. Hugo perversely decided to take a nap first. After they had taken enough pictures, we played on for about an hour.

Friday, September 20 I awakened at 3:30 A.M. on *the* day of the filming of the interview, and for the life of me I could not go back to sleep. You'd have thought I was the one to be interviewed! Hugo slept peacefully on. At 8:00 I glanced out of the window and lo and behold, all the CBS technical crew were milling around. Lizzie Mae closed the dining room door to let us have a little breakfast in privacy, then let them in. The people went upstairs and started going over equipment. After breakfast we went to the study and the makeup lady patted a little cake powder on Hugo's face and balding head, and darkened his eyebrows a smidgeon. At 10:00 Mr. Benjamin asked me to sit on the sofa across the room from Hugo's desk and out of range of the camera. Hugo took his seat behind his desk and Eric Sevareid and Martin Agronsky had chairs to the side of him, as though they were law clerks.

Mr. Benjamin, from his producer's chair, gave the order to start. The lights went on and a cameraman ran over in front of Hugo's desk shouting "sticks" as he closed them together. (Later found out it was for editorial purposes.) This performance amused Hugo and he laughed, which gave him a pleasant look to begin the interview.

The conversation opened with talk about Hugo's age (eighty-one) and his health and then quickly turned to tennis and reading, two of Hugo's favorite subjects. After the preliminaries, the questions were about Hugo's constitutional and Bill of Rights views. Hugo quickly warmed to his subject and was answering with a firm and forceful voice, very lucidly and with animation. This went on for thirty minutes, then they took a five-minute break. The air conditioner had to be turned off during the on-camera periods, so the lights heated the room—and Hugo—considerably.

During these short breaks the air conditioner was turned on again and everybody sprang into action. The makeup lady would run over and apply more powder to Hugo's perspiring face. Then they would begin again. This went on from 10:00 to 1:30—about six sessions in all. It will be edited down to a one-hour program.

Saturday, September 21 Unable to play tapes of the interview; couldn't work the machine. Frustration!

Monday, September 30 Hugo and I are watching the news. Abe Fortas's chances for C.J. seem to be dwindling.

Wednesday, October 2 World Series! St. Louis Cardinals won 4–0 over Detroit Tigers. Abe Fortas today requested President Johnson to withdraw his nomination as Chief Justice, and the President reluctantly agreed. The withdrawal was requested because not to do so would give the Senate unlimited opportunity to attack the Court. Old Strom Thurmond [Senator from South Carolina] made a hateful statement saying Abe should resign from the Court altogether.

Monday, October 7 Court opens. I took Hugo in, arriving in time for the Conference at 9:40. I went into the already filled Courtroom and the Justices were twenty minutes late opening. The arguments took place on whether Ohio has to put Wallace's name on the ballot. Admittedly, they were late in getting their signatures on file in the Secretary of State's office, but Wallace is saying the law requiring the names to be filed ninety days before the primary is unconstitutional.

Tuesday, October 8 Last night Hugo came in all charged up and had to write the Wallace opinion. He worked until 12:30, and I stuck it out with him. His poor fingers cramped, so he had to dictate. I got all his records together and put them in an envelope in his left coat pocket. I listened while he dictated. Old Wallace would have been dumbfounded to hear the eloquence and passion with which Hugo defended Wallace's cause, i.e., to get on the printed ballot in Ohio, even though his petition was admittedly filed too late under Ohio law—the constitutionality of the law is under attack. Hugo's mind was racing and he didn't get to sleep until close to 4:00 A.M. He took about four ounces of whiskey, one ounce at a time from 2:30 on, and finally conked out.

Wednesday, October 9 Hugo and the boys finished the Wallace opinion at the Court. Hugo stayed out of Conference to do it, leaving his votes with Bill Brennan.

Sunday, October 13 Lazy, lazy day. Hugo woke up about 2:00 A.M. worried about his Wallace opinion and that the Chief had not responded at all to it, and he does not know if it will come down Monday or not, after all his hard work.

Monday, October 14 No Wallace opinion! I took Hugo early to Court, but was disappointed when the opinion did not come down. I listened to Solicitor General Griswold and Edward Bennett Williams argue a bugging case. Hugo and I had lunch in the cafeteria and parted company. Bill Douglas has decided to concur in Hugo's opinion, thus giving Hugo an opinion in lieu of a judgment. The C.J. is just now writing his dissent, and Hugo had to call him because the Chief's secretary, Mrs. McHugh, told the boys the case wasn't coming down! The C.J. said it *will* but not at 10:00.

Tuesday, October 15 I listened *all day* long to the Tidelands Oil case and then to a Virginia case involving a law forbidding stickers and glue-ons being used on ballots.[14] There was an aura of excitement over the bench, and about 2:00 there was much bustling, whispering, and so forth. The C.J.'s dissenting opinion on Wallace was finally distributed on the bench, and at 2:30 Hugo cleared his throat and began. He gave the opinion very well.[15] Potter Stewart gave his dissent, but Byron and the C.J. did not announce theirs. So Hugo gave Wallace, the man who has so maligned him, the break of getting on the Ohio ballot.

Saturday, October 19 I didn't sleep well last night and my twistings and turnings awakened Hugo. We had another of our rare, touching, and amusing nocturnal talks. Hugo spoke for a while of a case that's been bothering him, another Monkey Trial case [see page 207]. He said he told John Harlan that they should postpone it until "a new Court takes over." He further said the Chief is only sitting on half a chair; he (Hugo) is eighty-two and can't last forever; Bill D. has that battery in his chest; and John H. won't stay forever. Hugo went on to add that, thank goodness, now he was completely over the thought or ambition that lightning might strike him for President someday, but he wasn't sure Bill Douglas was. He thinks Potter Stewart is a sometimes candidate. Other talk about women, kissing cousins, and so forth.

Monday, October 21 I have just spent the last hour acting as Hugo's locator for (1) the top of his fountain pen; (2) the new capsule for his fountain pen; and (3) an address list of people he is writing to thank for contributing to the Hugo Black Fund at the University of Alabama Law School. A mechanical problem arose when the old capsule stuck in the pen and wouldn't come out. I was just looking for the tweezers when Hugo accidentally turned over the pen and it fell out. We are both some mechanics!

Tuesday, October 22 To the Byron Whites' for dinner. Hugo, Bill Brennan, and Byron talked about the four Supreme Court judges who voted for Tilden in the Hayes-Tilden presidential race.

Wednesday, October 30 Last night Hugo finished writing his dissent in the "Monkey" case (shades of William J. Bryan and Clarence Darrow).

Monday, November 4 I played the tapes of Hugo's interview with Martin Agronsky and Eric Sevareid for Hugo. He listened attentively and said there was a mistake which was not necessarily his but in the editing. They had cut it, which affected the step-by-step explanation leading up to and out of *Adamson,* and even made it appear that when he read from *Chambers* it was from *Adamson.* In short, that part was all messed up. But all the rest was simply magnificent. Hugo called Martin and told him he couldn't let the tape go like that. They'd either have to fix it or retape that part. The editing was done by the producer, who did not understand law and the cases.

Tuesday, November 5 Hugo and I put on our glad rags and we set out to the Brennans' black-tie election party. All of us were strong for Humphrey and were happy when various states were announced pro-Humphrey. We left at midnight, but kept tuning in at intervals all night.

Wednesday, November 6 It went to Nixon by a narrow margin. At first this morning we thought that Humphrey got the plurality of popular vote, but Nixon finally went ahead. I went to Connecticut Avenue and bought the television we are giving Lizzie Mae for Christmas. Hugo came in about 5:00 and we went over to the Harlans' for dinner. John is a Republican but not an ardent one. I made several snide remarks about Nixon, but Hugo reproved me, saying he was now our President.

Thursday, November 7 It poured rain all day long. Hugo asked me to go over his long list of applicants for law clerk for next year and pick the ones I thought tops.

Friday, November 8 Hugo chose the two law clerks he and I talked about last night, Kenneth Bass and Gus Speth. Looks like he plans to stay on the Court next year. He says that Bill Brennan voted to hand down that gambling case even though Hugo had researched the record and found the officers were invited in, and the C.J. went with Bill and they got five!

Saturday, November 9 Hugo is worried about his television program and hopes to have it postponed to his birthday or his retirement.

Sunday, November 10 Hugo is working on the Louisiana Tidelands Oil case. I cleaned his closet.

Monday, November 11 We went to the Douglases' party in honor of his heart doctor, who was so wonderful to him. In fact there were five or six cardiac specialists and their wives. We mingled a bit, came by the Hot Shoppe for supper, then home and to work.

Tuesday, November 12 Hugo's dissent in the Arkansas Monkey case came down.[16]

Thursday, November 14 Last night Martin Agronsky called from Boston, very upset that Hugo wanted to postpone the broadcast, said CBS had already spent $100,000 on publicity, etc. Hugo was adamant, but agreed to talk about it again today. I just wish they would go on and get it settled one way or another. I am tired of the whole thing.

Friday, November 15 When Hugo got home today he told me he had finally agreed with Martin that they could do the program on the 3rd of December.

Monday, November 18 Grant's [Elizabeth Black's grandson] class to Court. There were twenty-five in all. The children were very well behaved and seemed interested. Hugo presided in the absence of the C.J. He conducted admissions to the Bar, then gave two opinions, a "full crew" railroad case and a Puerto Rican arbitrator case. Then the lawyers argued *Shuttlesworth* v. *Alabama.* A more perfect agenda couldn't be asked for. Hugo wrote Grant a darling note saying perhaps a member of Grant's class might someday be on this very Court.

Monday, November 25 I invited the girls of the "C" tennis team to Court. They were as excited as kids over the trip to the Court. Some of them thought the "Court" meant the tennis court and had no inkling that Hugo was on the Supreme Court. We saw Hugo a minute and then went in. John Harlan enlivened the proceedings for us by writing a note asking us why we didn't bring our tennis rackets. Hugo sent another note saying we would look even better in our tennis clothes. The girls beamed. We ate in the cafeteria and we went back to see Hugo. The C.J. was in with Hugo, and the girls were ecstatic at meeting him.

Tuesday, November 26 We barely made it by 1:30 to Dr. Moskow's. He likes to pass on the gossip as he files and digs away at your feet. Hugo again lectured him on being too fat. (This will probably bother his Thanksgiving dinner.)

Wednesday, November 27 I bought us a turkey and Spencer a turkey.

Friday, November 29 We took all three children to Court this morning. They behaved very nicely, though Evie and Martin [Pesaresi] had considerable disputes over who would push Jodie [Pesaresi] in the stroller. Jodie smiled, waved, and squealed all through the building.

Saturday, November 30 Hugo playing piano and singing, and all is as it should be.

Sunday, December 1 Hugo writing another Tidelands (Louisiana) dissent.

Monday, December 2 Hugo's niece is disturbed because she wants to have children but is afraid to. She doesn't want to risk their unhappiness. Hugo told her to buy *The Roman Way* and will lend her Diogenes Laërtius' *Lives of Eminent Philosphers.* He will also send her *The Wisdom of the Living Religions.* Hugo told her to go home and start a baby. She said tonight? Hugo said yes.

Tuesday, December 3 Hugo's television broadcast party at Agronskys'. As the hour started, the television set got disconnected momentarily and I *missed* seeing myself on television playing tennis! When they got the set going again the picture was pea green but nobody dared touch it. But nothing could detract from the beauty of Hugo's television hour. I think it was his finest hour.

Wednesday, December 4 I think any misgivings Hugo had over the program are now dispelled by the voluminous praise in letters, telegrams, editorials, and write-ups that occur. Some may say that he may be wrong in some of his views but all agree he is a warm, great, and good man, and a patriot devoted to his country and its Constitution. They all say too, after seeing him, that some may get decrepit, but age has not done that to Hugo. Eric Sevareid came on television at 9:00 tonight with a beautiful editorial comment about the beauty of age.

Thursday, December 5 Saw Nina Warren at Hecht's [a department store]. She never mentioned Hugo's program and neither did I. We talked about the Chief staying on until June, and the power of prayer. I came home tired, and got upset at Hugo for a silly reason. About 1:30 in the morning we woke up and talked it out, giggled, cried, and stayed awake for a couple hours. But we went to sleep without rancor.

Friday, December 6 Hugo is getting batches of letters about his program at the office and at home. He signed 250 answers before he left the office today.

Saturday, December 7 Poor Hugo. He brought a big batch of letters home to dictate and his dictating machine was out of whack! He was so frustrated. The results are fantastic; mostly all are remarking that they feel better about the Court and the country by this broadcast. Hugo feels now it was O.K. for him to do it.

Monday, December 9 To Court. The C.J. and other members of the Court were taking after the government lawyer on an income tax case where the district judge did not ask the defendant, an alcoholic, whether he understood the charge and whether it was a willful violation, prior to sentencing on defendant's plea of guilty.

Tuesday, December 10 Did I tell you that among Hugo's television fan letters was a proposal of marriage by a woman of forty-eight whose husband had been dead eight years? She started off by saying Hugo was so great and vital and magnificent. Then she said, "Will you marry me?" Hugo read it to me and I said, "No, you can't." Then she said she wanted to do great things for her country as he inspired her to do. She added, "I don't expect you to accept my proposal, but I would like to do something." "What?" I asked. When Hugo continued reading, I said, "No, you can't do that either!"

Wednesday, December 11 Last official White House dinner of the Johnsons, in honor of the Emir of Kuwait. The President looked more relaxed than in a couple of years. He kissed me on the cheek as I went through the line, and looked at me and not through me as he sometimes has done. Lady Bird was her same lovely self. It was a nostalgic time. Humphrey next to me. All the radiance, but not the bounce, gone.

Sunday, December 15 Worked on Christmas packages. I got Hugo (and believe me this was hard) to write in his book, *A Constitutional Faith*, one for each child and grandchild, mine and his alike. Hugo wanted to do it, but I had to stand over him and make him do it then.

Monday, December 16 Christmas party at the Court. Hugo had hoped to dictate, but all the girls in the pool had the flu. We went to the party and sang carols, Hugo too. Potter led the singing.

Tuesday, December 17 Fred is forty-four years old today. Hugo was pitying the little girl I was, at barely sixteen, nearly dying in childbirth, but I told him Fred is so dear to me.

Wednesday, December 18 Off to Florida, leaving snow flurries in Washington.

Thursday, December 19 We are in the lap of luxury at the Boca Raton Hotel. I feel relaxed and unwound—the first time in weeks. We went to breakfast about 9:15. Hugo ate grits, eggs, and ham. Then we inquired as to where the tennis courts are.

Hugo's mind is turning now on Abe Fortas's school case and he speaks out frequently about it. "I think I'll start out, 'There are 3,465,999 schools in this country and the Court is today taking direct supervision over them,' or, 'It is a fine thing America is going to the moon' (*in re* the moon shot of this Saturday) 'because the Supreme Court will have extended jurisdiction.' " Hugo is intense in his emotions and soaks up love hungrily. He would caress me all day long, I do believe. All his feelings are deep and there is nothing shallow in his makeup. The show of opulence in the hotel tenses him, though, and in the dining room he seems ill at ease.

Friday, December 20 "And the days dwindle down to a precious few." It brings to my mind those words as I open my diary each time and see so few days left in 1968. Tomorrow is the moon shot at Cocoa Beach. Hugo was invited to attend, but since he couldn't bring me he declined. At dinner we heard "The Strolling Strings of Michael Kent," who walk from table to table serenading. Hugo loves their music but keeps hoping they won't serenade us, as he thinks it would embarrass him. Besides, he said, he had a dear friend once whose wife fell in love at first sight with a strolling musician and strolled away with him.

Saturday, December 21 Tennis courts very crowded today. Next to us was a father and mother and brat of about ten who talked so ugly to his parents and breathed such venom I was sorry the father or mother spared the rod.

Sunday, December 22 Hugo's mail sack hasn't arrived yet, which frets him.

Wednesday, December 25 Christmas Day. I called Mother. She perked up when she heard my voice but sounded pretty weak and not with it. She thought it was Christmas Eve. Poor little Mother. We had the Christmas tree at Hugo, Jr.'s. The hit of the day was that Hugo gave each child a copy of his *Constitutional Faith* with a personal message written as only Hugo knows how to write. And so another Christmas!

Thursday, December 26 Back to Boca Raton. Dinner-circus at 8:30: lions, elephants, clowns, trapeze, unicycle riders, the works. I haven't seen a circus in forty years! Hugo and I danced in the lions' cage before dinner. He is such a dear!

Friday, December 27 Almost to the end of the diary! We listened to the details of the splashdown and recovery of the first three astronauts in history to orbit the moon—Borman, Lovell, Anders. They splashed down within 500 yards of the *York,* the recovery ship. It was absolutely fantastic, yet there were no signs of wonderment and awe in the tennis house where the television was on. Few gave it a second glance. What blasé times we live in.

Hugo and I went to the Cabana Club for palmistry. Poor Hugo, he trailed in there with me. The lady who lectured was excellent. She told Hugo he was inflexible after making up his mind, had a brilliant memory, and was good at words. Told me I was strong, and got along with people.

Monday, December 30 Hugo awakened and talked eloquently about the Dick Gregory case [see page 218]. Here was a case where Dick Gregory, a Negro artist, was leading a parade in Chicago around Mayor Daley's house, with a body of policemen to protect them. Dick thought he was exercising his constitutional right to protest and Chicago had no law against it. Neighbors gathered and began calling names, hurling eggs, etc. At 9:00 the police asked Gregory, for his own protection and his group's, to leave, which he refused to do. There was by that time almost a riot starting. Gregory was then arrested for disorderly conduct in refusing to obey a police order. The statute governing disorderly conduct is too vague, and Hugo feels police officers should not have the power to arrest people unless backed by a valid law. He must write this case in a unique fashion. He thought Gregory behaved well and the police behaved well, but there was no valid law. He started all over afresh this morning after working until 1:30 A.M. last night on an opinion he is not yet satisfied with. Today he sat hunched over his desk writing, writing, writing, and writing on a yellow pad. At 12:00 midnight he finished. We called the desk to see when the mail was picked up, 8:15 A.M.—so he walked downstairs and mailed off his opinion.

Tuesday, December 31 Hugo slept well. I slipped out and made it to the beauty shop by 9:00. When I came back upstairs and Hugo let me in, I whispered in mock fright, "Do you think anyone saw me come in?" Whereupon Hugo embraced me and overpowered me. He was a different man today, off of Mount Olympus, gay, relaxed, and a splendid companion. He read aloud in his beautiful voice from *The Lessons of History,* written by the Durants, which had been given to him by Hugo, Jr., for Christmas. He relishes every beautiful and wise phrase from the book.

We went to the beach and to the Cabana Club for lunch; we rested and played an hour's tennis. We put on formals and went to the Great Hall at 9:30 for dinner. He and I danced many rounds. Entertainment was by Bobby Rydell, a teenage idol. It was another year started with my dear Hugo! So au revoir 1968. Hail 1969!

1969

Thursday, January 2 The mail came in with an opinion written by Abe Fortas, and Hugo sat down immediately and wrote out a five- or six-page dissent. It was about a *habeas corpus* petition stating the witness who informed on the accused was unreliable. Nevertheless, on the witness's information a search was made and marijuana found. Hugo is writing that at some place a judgment should stick. This case had been through the courts and an appeal was denied. Now, after a year, a *habeas corpus* petition was about to free the man.

Wednesday, January 8 We arrived home and found a present from the President, a lovely portrait of Lady Bird and LBJ. Also bread and fig preserves from the ranch.

Thursday, January 9 Hugo is irritable and groaning under the heavy burden of work and mail. Frances said he snapped her head off. I went to the joint session of Congress honoring Borman, Lovell, and Anders, the moon astronauts. Borman told of getting a good Catholic, Anders, to read the King James version of Genesis on Christmas Eve as they circled the moon, but sheepishly said, "Now that I see these gentlemen [the Supreme Court] on the first row, I doubt if we should have done it at all." This brought down the house. Harlan said some of the response was not very gracious, as he heard a little hissing. But the Court took it all in good nature and the C.J. shook hands warmly with them.

Friday, January 10 I went in at 6:00 to pick Hugo up. They had a long and argumentative conference. Hugo was stimulated and told me all about his cases. Went to Alan and Adrienne Barth's for dinner. They had Isaac Stern, the great violinist, who was just charming and very articulate about the culture situation in Washington. There was a couple from CBS who told Hugo that there had been over 100,000 requests for the Constitutions given away on his program! A woman (widow) from the Protocol Office had watched Hugo's program and praised him to the skies! After dinner, the woman from Protocol got herself into a tiny child's chair, sat at Hugo's feet, and looked up at him worshipfully, and he of course ate it up.

Sunday, January 12 Hugo and I sat up until 1:30 A.M. He was finishing the formidable stack of mail that had accumulated. He was also trying to inscribe two farewell books for the President and Lady Bird. I tried to help him, but told him we had labored mightily and brought forth a mouse. Hugo gave LBJ Will and Ariel Durant's *Lessons of History.* Then to both LBJ and Lady Bird he gave his own book, *A Constitutional Faith.* He paraphrased the Bible and said, "Well done, thy good and faithful servants; go forth with light hearts to the golden sunshine of God's country, Texas," or words to that effect.

Tuesday, January 14 We went to the joint session of Congress to hear Lyndon Johnson's farewell address. Congress was in a good mood tonight and applauded warmly even when the Court came in! When LBJ entered there was about five to ten minutes of applause and [Speaker of the House John] McCormack had to gavel them down. The President was just right, as the papers said, neither too humble nor too proud. And he said the things that were in his heart. There were tears shining brightly in many eyes. When the last applause had died down, and after the family had left, Cathy Douglas and I said goodbye to the Cabinet wives. When Lee Udall looked around I said, "Good luck," to her. She looked so startled. Guess she thought I was sending her on her way. This illustrates that while the Cabinet and their wives are transitory, the Supreme Court, like Old Man River, just keeps on rolling along.

Thursday, January 16 Hugo came in about 6:15 from the Court looking very tired. He says he got Bill Douglas on his Dick Gregory opinion and he talked to Potter Stewart. Hugo hopes to get him too.

Friday, January 17 Hugo went to bed at 9:00 and slept like a log. I stayed up till 12:15 sorting Christmas cards, etc. When I went to bed I was too tired to sleep. Hugo woke up, put me on his shoulder, and we talked for an hour or so, as we are wont to do on sleepless nights. These are emotional experiences. He told me last night of errors people make, and his biggest one was joining the Klan. Undoubtedly, he told me, he would have been named Vice President, instead of Harry Truman, to run with FDR. He was acceptable to Labor and Tom Corcoran had called him to come to the convention but he wouldn't go. He said he would do nothing, but Tom was sure he would have been named.

Monday, January 20 *Inauguration of Richard M. Nixon and Spiro Agnew.* We had rotten seats, as they seem to downgrade the seating of the Court every few years. Dick Nixon made an understated but solid speech. Mostly I got from it he'd do the best he could. The parade was good enough, but moved slowly. All the Court was relaxed, especially Bill Douglas and Hugo, who wisecracked about the Republicans a bit. Hugo and I sat through an hour and a half of that freezing damp wind and then slipped away. We found our driver without trouble and when Hugo told him to come back about 8:30 to take us to the ball I did not demur, although I had mixed feelings. I hated to go out in that bad weather, but I hated also to miss anything, especially since we had free tickets and a driver. Hugo and I rested about an hour. Then the usual mad rush. At first Hugo said, "I'm ready," and I said, "No, darling, it's white tie." "Ohh," he moaned like a stuck pig, "if I'd known that, I'd never have promised to go to the fool thing." We went to the 12th Street entrance of the Smithsonian, and a military aide ran interference for us through the solid mob to the Supreme Court box. The C.J. and Nina came in and sat in the box and that triggered off lots of requests for autographs from him and Hugo. Hugo must have signed at least fifty. We were under the harsh glare of television lights and Hugo was perspiring in his "monkey suit." The C.J. managed to look cool and happy. Then there was a great fanfare and the usual "ta ta ta dum," and the Nixon party entered. The President looked relaxed and happy and made lots of jokes, including one, on seeing the C.J., that he understood all nine Justices were there and he was sure the C.J. was glad to be getting all nine dancing to the same tune. We left shortly after the Presidential party left, and when we got home, Hugo got out of the car and said, "In four more years I'll be eighty-seven years old, and I want you to promise me here and now, in the presence of this driver, that you will not drag me to another Inaugural Ball." I promised.

Saturday, January 25 I took Hugo to the office at 10:00 and he was busy with the Chief Justice assigning cases. The C.J. would not agree to

Hugo's Dick Gregory case, calling it a racist opinion, which we both disagreed with him about.

Thursday, February 20 Hugo is more caught up on his work than he has ever been on his return home at this period of the year. So he's over at his desk reading history while I try to set my desk in order and pick up from last Sunday on my diary.

Monday, February 24 Abe Fortas delivered the opinion in the *Tinker* Mourning-Band School case and Hugo, as the television said, delivered a blistering dissent. His dissent, so said the paper, was twenty-five minutes long. I was on the edge of my chair, hands and feet like ice, and the brethren in various stages of shock.[1]

Wednesday, February 26 At 4:00 A.M. Hugo coughed and I awakened to ask if I should turn on the heat. He said, "No, come over here. I want to talk to you." Then he told me he wanted me to change my hair appointment and get it fixed as pretty as possible, put on my prettiest plain dress, and come to his press conference for his eighty-third birthday. He said I was a part of his life and he wanted the whole world to know it. So very sweet!

After we talked for quite a while he said he was going to get up and take a drink and sleep the rest of the night. He fixed himself a whiskey, downed it, looked at the clock, and it was 6:00 A.M. "My heavens, 6:00 A.M.!" Talk about cocktails before dinner, Hugo had one before breakfast! Anyway, by 8:00 he was in a sound and deep slumber. I got him awake finally and into his press conference about 2:30. Hugo told the press I had been his birthday present thirteen years ago when I came up for the interview. He asked them to take one picture of us both, which they did. Then he sat and swiveled about in his chair and talked to the twelve to fourteen reporters who were questioning him in a rapid, rapierlike cross fire. Hugo answered with ease but caution and, as usual in a contest of minds, he came off the victor.

Thursday, February 27 I went in to the Court because some of the local law clerks were going to surprise Hugo at 2:30. We went in singing "Happy Birthday." The clerks had a basket of fruit, a bottle of Chivas Regal, and some flowers.

Monday, March 3 Hugo came home at 6:00 and brought birthday mail and letters about the *Tinker* case home with him. It took him three hours to read it. He says he can't write anybody at this point, so I wrote the Goldbergs and Mildred Faucett for him. He's still reading and it's 10:10 P.M.

Tuesday, March 4 I visited a health club in Annandale and talked to the owner, who looks like a prizefighter. This one is so cheap, $35 for three months, $100 for *five* years! So cheap in fact that Hugo got suspicious and thought they might be using it as a front for dope or other nefarious projects. He told me to check carefully.

Monday, March 10 Hugo delivered a very exciting concurring opinion in the Dick Gregory case. He was due to deliver the opinion of the Court, but they were all concurring in his result because he went into too great detail for the others. The C.J. even went so far as to say it was a racist opinion, just because Hugo said cities could pass ordinances to control demonstrations. Anyway, since three were with the C.J., Hugo suggested to the C.J. that he could deliver the opinion of the Court and he and Bill Douglas would concur.[2]

Tuesday, March 11 Two seventeen-year-olds from Hammond High School here in Alexandria came to interview Hugo. He had told me he was turning them down until I told him he ought to see high school kids. They were very ill at ease, and Hugo was as distant and canny with them as with a full-fledged reporter. However, before they left I asked Hugo if he would tell them a little about his boyhood. He unbent and gave them a fill-in on his youthful interests.

Friday, March 14 Hugo seems to be going strong in his working capabilities. He is writing a dissent and he hit on the right tack by reading *Fay* v. *Noia* again and finding in it something in John Harlan's dissent which rang a bell. Now he will say *Noia* released a man patently innocent and his two partners in a crime (or accused crime) were released because it was adjudged their confessions were coerced. But in *this* case the man was patently guilty, holding up a victim at the point of a gun![3]

Wednesday, March 19 I sent the C.J. a bouquet of roses and baby's-breath wrapped around a miniature of the scales of justice for his seventy-eighth birthday. Hugo had lunch with him upstairs and all the other Justices were present. Hugo says Abe Fortas seems to be recanting a bit. He withdrew an earlier opinion saying burning the American flag was an expression of free speech. Hugo understands that Abe got *lots* of letters against his stand in *Tinker.*

Thursday, March 20 Hugo and I went to Steve Strickland's White House Fellows party at the State Department. Steve had Hugo's television interview played in the John Quincy Adams Room in the State Department. Hugo's film was just as impressive the second time around, and this time I saw *me*! I was horrified. I sure did look fat and my serve was terrible! Though I did hit a pretty good backhand stroke. Hugo conspired with Steve to have it played back and forth, back and forth, and I was sick of seeing me!

Friday, March 21 I woke up at 6:30, thinking I'd do my hour of exercises, but I sensed that Hugo wanted to talk. He said he was going to the Conference and that he sensed there was an "unwritten" or "unspoken" agreement that they would never let him have an opinion of the Court. He had not heard from any on his circulations, and as in the *Gregory* case the ones who wanted changes in the opinion did not come to him but just wrote separately, so he let the C.J. give the *Gregory* opinion since he only had concurrences.

Hugo called in the afternoon and I went after him. He said he had two opinions for the Court to be delivered Tuesday! So he was wrong!

Tuesday, March 25 A note from the C.J. He said, "Wouldn't it be wonderful if the scales of justice could always be balanced with roses and baby's-breath."

Tuesday, April 1 Hugo had to preside on the bench today because the Chief went to the funeral of his driver's son, who was killed in Viet Nam. Our grandchildren were all sitting on the second row—seven strong. I asked the Marshal to turn up Hugo's mike since his voice in welcoming the lawyers to practice wasn't coming over very well. Then Abe gave his opinion about a defendant in a lineup being unfairly treated, and Hugo dissented.[4] Hugo dissented, as he always does, in clear tones, without referring to his opinion.

Monday, April 21 Went to Court to hear the Adam Clayton Powell arguments. The Courtroom was packed, including seven Court wives in the Justices' section.

Monday, April 28 They argued the Montgomery, Alabama, School Desegregation case [see page 222]. Solicitor General Griswold was very dull and statistical.

Monday, May 5 A story broke today that Abe Fortas accepted and returned a $20,000 fee from Wolfson Foundation for "studies on race and social relations." Wolfson is now in the pen. Raised quite a row in the papers.

Wednesday, May 7 Big hullabaloo over Abe in the Wolfson Foundation fee matter. Editorials screaming for his scalp.

Friday, May 9 C.J. talked to Hugo about Attorney General Mitchell coming to see him about Abe Fortas. Hugo is sick about this whole mess. Hugo said he'd talk to Abe if Abe called him and asked him to.

Saturday, May 10 At 8:00 the phone rang and a hurt, weak voice asked if he had awakened us. It was Abe and he sounded as though he hadn't slept. I let him speak to Hugo, and Hugo said he would talk to him either here or at the office, but not on the phone. We got to Court at 10:00. Abe came down, and I went to the liquor store to get wine for a Court party, although I must admit all the joy has gone out of preparations for the party. I was torn by sympathy for Abe and yet angry he had put the Court in this spot. Hugo talked to him saying that if he were in that spot, for the good of the Court *he* would resign. Abe said if he did that they would put him through hearings and it would kill Carol. Hugo said if it would kill Carol, he wouldn't resign. Hugo said he did not believe at present, if nothing else was added, they had an impeachable or criminal proceeding against Abe. They talked almost two hours. Abe still seemed terribly down. I tried to reassure him and said I hoped it would all come out all right.

Monday, May 12 The papers, after relaxing on Sunday about Abe, have renewed attacks and say Mitchell talked to Warren, and further, there was more damaging evidence against Abe (that Abe had signed a contract for $20,000 per year plus $20,000 per year for Carol as a widow, all for life). Hugo had urged Abe to reveal it himself. After all, he didn't take it, in the final analysis.

Tuesday, May 13 Hugo had to attend a lengthy Conference, from 11:00 to about 3:00, in which they tried to thrash out Abe's situation. His inclination was *not* to resign, but the papers said Abe conferred with Paul Porter and Bill Douglas all night. The Chief is planning to give out all the information turned over to him by the Attorney General (showing Abe's contract involved $20,000 a year for his lifetime and thereafter $20,000 a year for Carol's).

Wednesday, May 14 While Hugo and I were playing tennis Peggy McHugh, the Chief's secretary, called to say there would be a Conference tomorrow at 10:00. After dinner John Harlan called to tell Hugo that Abe had decided to resign. I hope this will end this tragic chapter and that there will be no repercussions.

Thursday, May 15 Hugo had to go in to a Conference. When I took Mother the paper, she announced to me that Abe had resigned. She had just heard it on Paul Harvey. So the secret was out. I tuned in on the radio and heard the whole story, including Abe's statement to the C.J. saying that he had signed a life contract with the Wolfson family foundation, to wit, that he had agreed to accept $20,000 per year for life, plus $20,000 per year as a pension for Carol. The papers were full of it. The television announced long specials, but in a way the heat was off.

Sunday, May 18 Hugo bared his soul to tell me of his marriage to Josephine. He still insists he doesn't know how he could have married two women so much alike in disposition. I guess he means both of us were always saying "Yes" to people and then needing help to get out of the situation.

Monday, May 19 I took Hugo in this morning and have never seen so many admissions to practice. The C.J. seemed relaxed and particularly gracious to all.

It was good to see Selma Burton in again. She was her old ebullient, well-dressed self, with yellow suit, white hat, gloves, and the famous Selma two-earrings-on-one-ear bit. Her son Bill and wife, Ann, were with her. Bill presented a copy of *The Occasional Papers of Mr. Justice Burton* to the Court.

Wednesday, May 21 Hugo and I went to Biloxi for the Fifth Circuit Conference. That evening we went to the Yacht Club for a Shrimp Jamboree. Judge Lynne (from Birmingham) broke the news to us that Warren Burger had been appointed Chief Justice.

Friday, May 23 Hugo made a speech at the Conference, but as Hugo, Jr., later remarked, though good, it was not up to his usual standards. He rambled and repeated himself and was obviously not prepared. However, he could still hold his audience firmly.

Saturday, May 24 Bill Douglas has been under considerable fire about the Parvin Foundation salary, and he resigned from the Foundation yesterday.

Sunday, May 25 Tried to write letters but Hugo too lovey, wanting me to sit in his lap every time I passed by.

Tuesday, May 27 Frances Arnold told me that Abe's law firm was really suffering from his resignation. Younger men don't want him back. A big corporation withdrew its tax case, saying they couldn't afford to have a firm in disfavor with Government to represent them. Frances heard LBJ was virtually a recluse since Abe's trouble and was morose and refused to go anywhere. Thurman [Arnold] is much better because now he feels very needed. He goes in daily.

Wednesday, May 28 I had a note from Abe Fortas awaiting us on our return from Biloxi, in answer to my reminder about the Court party. The note said, "Dear Elizabeth, Thank you, our kind and gentle friend, and thanks to Hugo. But we will be away in search of a moment's peace. Abe." Heartbreaking.

Thursday, May 29 *Earl Warren's farewell party.* Full Court, except for Fortases. Hugo toasted the Chief Justice and the C.J. returned his compliment. We sang on the terrace. I wrote, to the tune of "My Bonnie Lies over the Ocean," a song, "We are the Earl Warren Court," etc., etc.

Monday, June 2 Hugo gave a fine opinion in upholding Frank Johnson in the Montgomery County, Alabama, School Desegregation case, in which Hugo also had nice words for the School Board.[5] When the Chief gave his opinion in another case—something about the retroactivity of the *Miranda* case—John Harlan dissented, saying that he believed court decisions promulgating rules for application in the future to be "unprincipled" and hoped next year's Court would take steps to overrule such practices. The Chief Justice flushed, but said nothing, and late in the afternoon John came to Hugo to tell him the C.J. had sent him a furious note saying he got John's message "loud and clear." John was distressed, as he intended it as no slam on the C.J.

Hugo's dissent about the Lake Nixon Club being in interstate commerce was funny. Said the milk was even produced by an Arkansas cow![6]

Tuesday, June 3 Hugo has resumed writing on his memoirs. He means to spend the summer writing. Burger was confirmed unanimously by the Senate Judiciary Committee. He told them he intended to follow Hugo Black's philosophy of interpreting the Constitution literally.

Friday, June 6 Hugo was emcee at the party on the Presidential yacht, *Sequoia,* in honor of Chief Justice Warren. He very adroitly suggested that he had heard the C.J. say he left fifty years of public office without cherishing an enmity. Hugo thought this was a true mark of a great Chief Justice. Later John Harlan and the Chief were chatting together on the deck of the boat. John had written two apologies but had not heard from him. Everything seemed O.K. now, though. I made a little speech to Nina in behalf of the wives and Hugo complimented me very highly.

Monday, June 9 Hugo gave a vigorous dissent on the Court's opinion doing away with garnishments. He agreed it was a bad thing, but said the states should be the ones to regulate it.[7] Last night the Emmys were awarded and Burton Benjamin, the producer of Hugo's television interview with Agronsky and Sevareid, won one for the best cultural documentary of the year, "Justice Black and the Bill of Rights."

Thursday, June 12 Chief Justice Warren called sixteen members of the Judicial Conference and they passed some rules for all judges to obey, forbidding them from outside work. Hugo thinks it's terrible. Bill Brennan has announced he is giving up all speeches and teaching his seminar for judges at New York University (the same seminar at which the new C.J., Burger, teaches) and giving up his real estate "tax shelter" and his AT&T stock his mother left him, etc. Hugo has nothing to give up but is outraged all the same.

Friday, June 13 I picked up Hugo at the office, and he had been victorious at the Conference. He had awakened this morning saying, "*I will not get mad!*" It was about the judges' ethics rules the C.J. is trying to get the Court to adopt. Hugo is for an *independent* judiciary who can be punished only by violating a valid law. He finally got them to postpone action for the new C.J. and new Associate Justice.

Monday, June 16 Hugo had the *El Paso* Anti-Trust case[8] and the C.J. had about four important ones, including the Adam Clayton Powell case, which will of course upset Congress. The *El Paso* case is controversial also. The Nixon firm represented El Paso, and Solicitor General Griswold had moved to dismiss, but the Court upheld its previous decision requiring El Paso to divest.

Wednesday, June 18 Judge Burger came to see Hugo and wound up in the Marshal's office, and the Marshal called to see if Hugo was expecting the new C.J. They had a very cordial meeting and Burger confided that he did not believe in rushing into having judges set out rules of conduct for other judges.

Friday, June 20 There was a hot editorial in this morning's *Post* about "Unfinished Supreme Court Business." They insisted that the noble efforts of the C.J. to purify the morals of the Court would fail if the Court did not today put itself under the Code of Ethics adopted for all the judges. Hugo said the matter was not, however, brought up in the Conference. Bill Brennan, Thurgood Marshall, Potter Stewart, and Byron White issued a statement that they were willing to abide by the Code of Ethics adopted by the other judges. This was a very nostalgic Conference otherwise. Hugo's *Adamson* dissent practically became the law of the land when Thurgood Marshall got a Court for his opinion applying the Double Jeopardy Clause to the states under the Fourteenth Amendment. Hugo's duty was to pass around for signatures the letter from the Associate Justices, written to Chief Justice Warren, expressing the sentiments of the Court on his retirement, to be spread on the Journal of the Court.

Saturday, June 21 John Harlan, who was just returning from the Second Circuit Conference in Vermont, called and told us the judges in Vermont were just seething with fury that the C.J. had called sixteen members of the Judicial Conference together to pass these ethics rules.

Monday, June 23 A day of history. Earl Warren swore in Warren Earl Burger as Chief Justice. Hugo and I arrived at the Court at 9:35 and found Secret Service men at the entrance to the driveway. A man with a flashlight was playing it over the air-conditioning coils. Two men were at the elevator. One was at the door of our office. I went into the Courtroom and sat on the back row. A good many wives were already in the Justices' section. Winifred Reed, who is still quite deaf, kept making loud, penetrating remarks about the Burgers. "Where are they?" "Which are they?" The Marshal rapped once and everybody stood up and the President and Mrs. Nixon came in. Mrs. N. sat beside Nina Warren, who sat almost alone on the front seat in her customary place. The President was seated in front of the podium and had on a Prince Albert morning suit. Then the Court came in, C.J. with a slight smile. Hugo's last provision of Bill of Rights (Double Jeopardy) made applicable today to the states in Thurgood Marshall's opinion for the Court in *Benton* v. *Maryland.* After Thurgood's opinion, Potter gave two long ones. Hugo withheld his opinion, concurring in part and dissenting in part, which was a ringing denunciation of the "shocks-the-conscience" test of Due Process. Said he hated on such a felicitous occasion to frighten people by predicting the Republic would be destroyed. The case was the Sentence Enhancing case.[9] Potter talked quite a while. Then the C.J. said the other orders would be filed with the Clerk. At that point the President asked to be recognized and was. The Court did not stand up. Neither did spectators in the courtroom. Nixon got up and began, "May it please the Court," and so forth. Speaking as a member of the Supreme Court Bar, he eulogized Chief Justice Warren, and did not mention Burger, his own nominee, except indirectly. The C.J. replied to the speech with great dignity and some emotion. Nixon's theme was "Continuity with Change." Then Chief Justice Warren mentioned that in 180 years of the Court's life, because of their longevity, one of seven men would have always been present, and one of those was Hugo Black. After the swearing-in ceremonies, the Warrens, the Burgers, and the President and Mrs. Nixon stood in a receiving line in the Conference room and lines of people attended, including law clerks and secretaries. The President was very gracious, having remarks for everybody. John Harlan told us goodbye for the summer.

Friday, June 27 Hugo is remarkable at eighty-three, chasing those balls on the tennis court. He would like to spend the rest of the time, I do believe, holding me on his lap and saying sweet things to me. He is so dear. Paper is predicting Brennan will be "in" with Burger, his right-hand man.

Saturday, June 28 Hugo said at dinner that he was going to see that *all* gifts, including trips at the generosity of the President or gifts of trips on boats, etc., were barred if the Code of Ethics is adopted.

Sunday, June 29 National celebration for Warren at Lincoln Memorial. Hugo and I got there right at 6:00. As we walked up the long walk from the car to the top of the steps of the Lincoln Memorial where we were supposed to sit, there was applause and the people stood up. Hugo did not realize it was for him until later. There was a fine and dignified program for Warren. Then Warren and Hugo signed autographs for over an hour. I even signed three of them myself!

Monday, June 30 Hugo is busy reading the original constitutional debates about how the Court should not suggest any laws, much less prescribe conduct, for the judges of the Nation. He thinks this is the boldest effort ever conceived to pass "an unwritten law" for which judges can be punished without there being any valid law on the books. He expects to say something about it later on.

Monday, July 14 Funny thing: Maggy told me that C.J. Burger had decided to take the *Conference* Room for *his office*! Isn't that a kick! Hugo says he will not quarrel with him about such an insignificant matter but John Harlan called from Connecticut and was red-hot about it. His office had told him.

Friday, July 18 After Hugo had won one game and I had won two, he kind of wobbled off the tennis court and sat down. I offered the pill box to him for him to take out a heart pill. He didn't know which it was and took out a Bufferin. I said I'd call Dr. Fox and he didn't remember who Dr. Fox was. He didn't remember any of his doctors, dentists, or foot doctor. He couldn't call his grandchildren by name. I had him lie down and then I took him out to Bethesda Hospital about 12:30. He was admitted in the Emergency Room and Dr. Fox came by and took him up to Tower 16 and gave him tests. He was rational and cheerful, but he had lapses in his memory.

Saturday, July 19 Many tests in Bethesda for Hugo. His memory is still a little off, but he could define the difference between character and reputation, liberty and justice, perfectly.

Monday, July 21 Yesterday, as today, Hugo's mind was on two things. He noticed a deep crease in my face around the side of my mouth, which shows worse when my face isn't in animation. He kept touching it and saying, if I wanted to, he would see if we could get my face lifted when he came out. I kept insisting that while I didn't particularly want to get wrinkles, I didn't care to go that far, but he brought it up several times. He also brought up over and over that what worried him was he did not want me to be unhappy if he should die, and while he dearly wanted me to be buried with him at my death, he did *not* want me to refrain from another marriage if that would make me happier. It brought tears to my eyes, and I assured him over and over that my dearest wish in life was to remain Mrs. Hugo Black. Dr. Dean then called me in and said Hugo had suffered a minor stroke and there was less hope than at first that his memory would come back completely. Although he is much better, yet his recovery had not come quickly and completely enough. I also called Dr. Fox and he told me about the same thing.

Tuesday, July 22 It was 1:30 P.M. before I got to the hospital. Hugo looked so sad and said, "Where have you been?" He had called home, Mother, and the Club. He himself had said I should eat lunch at the Club. Dr. Fox had told him he could go home, but first he wanted to talk to us both. Dr. Fox finally came and told us together much of what he had told us separately. He told Hugo to go home and take it easy—no office, no tennis, no stress or strain. He frankly said Hugo had not come back as he had hoped he would, and so the chances of his complete recovery had been lessened. If the stroke had been transitory, then he would have made a twenty-four-hour recovery. We drove home and Hugo was *so* glad and happy to be here.

Wednesday, July 23 Ken Bass, Hugo's law clerk, came for Hugo to sign an order denying a stay to certain school districts for more time in the "Freedom of Choice" plan for desegregating schools. Ordinarily, Hugo would have known immediately what he wanted to do. However, with his impaired memory, he questioned Ken for two hours, often repeating questions Ken had already answered. However, Hugo seemed to know what he was going to do—deny the request for a stay which, if granted, would mean yet another year of status quo. Hugo has his intelligence but not his memory. It made me realize more fully that I do not want him to remain on the Court if he has less than his whole mentality. He has been such a giant of an intellectual, and I want him to go off the Supreme Court with dignity and with just as much honor. Oh, dear God, I am so disturbed. Hugo himself seems not to realize that his mentality has been impaired. Yet he told me himself he would not stay on the Court if his intellect has been damaged.

Hugo, Jr., came in from Florida tonight. He thought his dad was in pretty good shape, which I was glad to hear since he was in more of a position to judge than someone too close to the situation.

Friday, July 25 Hugo seems better to me, though I haven't tried to test his memory. He talked to Larry Wallace, one of his law clerks [in 1960], and told him frankly about his attack and told him if he got better fine, but if not he would simply get off the Court. Hugo is so honest.

In re something said on television in an interview with Prime Minister

[Harold] Wilson of England, I asked Hugo if he once aspired to be President, and he said he doubted a Southerner at that time could be, and after the to-do about the Ku Klux Klan, if ever he had had the aspiration, he gave it up. I told him I was glad because I would probably never have been his wife. He said gallantly he would rather have me than be President. Love his soul!

Monday, July 28 All was directed to the 1:00 appointment with Dr. Fox. He gave Hugo a general physical and mental exam and found a great improvement. The decision as to whether or not he should remain on the Court was Hugo's. Dr. Fox did say the diagnosis was that Hugo had suffered a small clot in the brain, or a small stroke. The infinitesimal part of the brain that was so blocked, died. Dr. Fox thought the tissue surrounding this area was swollen and inflamed around the dead tissue last week, but has subsided now and the area successfully circumvented. Hugo and I went back by the office. He dictated mail, signed several orders, and apparently was back to normal.

Tuesday, July 29 I seem to have lost the art of sleeping through the night. Dead tired and sleepy, I went to bed about 9:30 last night. I was awake at 1:00 A.M. and my twistings awakened Hugo, who was going to get up and read some anyway. I followed him into the study and we talked quite a while, as I sat on his lap and he cuddled me. I have, I think, an underlying distress about whether or not he should stay on the Court. It is his own decision, of course, but I am haunted by two things. (1) That after this stroke, he might show less of the grasp of cases he has always had; he might be slower on the uptake in questioning attorneys from the bench; and that his disability will show in his work and his brilliant career be eclipsed. (2) That the stress and strain might actually shorten his years with me, and that they might bring on another and more damaging stroke. I want us to enjoy life while we still can, *off* the Court. The habits of a lifetime, the working and the drudgery, come to life, though, and Hugo asks, "But what would I do?" Although he said he wasn't wholly sure yet, he would like *two* more years on the Court, which would put him to eighty-five! I have to ask God to show us the way.

Wednesday, July 30 I finally took sleeping pills to break the habit of lying awake for three to five hours agonizing on the pros and cons of whether Hugo should get off the Court. It all boils down to the fact that I love him and want him to live longer and I strongly feel the stress and strain of Court work will shorten his life. Then, too, it would be wonderful to have him all to myself without Court interference.

Thursday, July 31 Last night John Harlan called in alarm over Hugo. I rather expected the call because the Brennans stopped by Westport, Connecticut, to spend the night with John and Ethel on their way to New Hampshire for two weeks. After asking concerned questions and talking to Hugo to his satisfaction, John turned over the phone to Bill, Marjorie, and then Ethel. Also, last night Ken Bass came by to bring an order of some kind. Hugo very sweetly told Ken something had happened to him that had affected his memory and that he may—he was not sure yet—but he may decide to get off the Court, and if so, his clerks would have a pretty good chance with the new man. It was very touching to me and I know it was to Ken.

Friday, August 1 We have the new C.J. and Mrs. Burger to dinner.

Tuesday, August 5 Hugo came down and played bridge with us. This was the first time he has played since his illness, so I was interested to see how he played. I could tell no difference. He played his same old bold but mediocre game.

Wednesday, August 6 I have the gnawing conviction that Hugo must get off the Court. He has always had an uncanny sense of timing and I pray to God that it will tell him, as I am doing, that it is a timely year to quit, and devote his time to his wife and family. We can have such a rich life together in these vintage years.

Saturday, August 16 Today Hugo told me he wanted me to be happy, more than anything in the world, and if I'd be happier, he'd retire, but that we had to do much talking and planning. A great wave of relief swept over me.

Monday, August 18 Clement Haynsworth nominated for Associate Justice in Abe's place.

Thursday, August 21 Dr. Fox talked to Hugo and told him he could not say whether another year would or would not shorten his life. He even told me he thought another year on the Court wouldn't hurt him, but he must be making plans. I want Hugo to be O.K. Oh, how I want it. But I was sorry Dr. Fox wouldn't advise Hugo to get off because I feel his health demands it now.

Monday, September 1 The boys came up and talked to the Judge about the Mississippi proposal to postpone integration until December;

the Government requested the delay as necessary, and the Fifth Circuit agreed to it. Hugo was at first rather inclined to go along and the boys argued long and vigorously against it. Hugo really wanted to hear all the arguments they had to offer, and his decision is held in abeyance.

Wednesday, September 3 Hugo spent most of the day at the office wrestling with the Government's and Mississippi's request for a three-month delay in integration. The boys want him to deny.

Friday, September 5 For the last two days, Hugo and the boys have been going round and round about the Mississippi School case, where the Government is asking for and the Fifth Circuit has granted a three-month delay in integration. The boys want Hugo to grant the Negro petitioners' request to force integration on September 1. Hugo denied this latter request but is writing an opinion stating his reasons and saying he will vote for immediate full integration when Court reconvenes.

Hugo's opinion was finished about 2:00 and he had a major part in proofreading and correcting it. The news came out at 6:30 on the Huntley-Brinkley news that Justice Black reluctantly granted a three-month delay.[10]

Thursday, September 25 Dinner at Gus and Cameron Speth's. Hugo was very expansive and charming. I could tell the effect of the brain clot, though, as he struggled (not visibly to anyone else) for details of stories of his campaign for the Senate. To my practiced ear they were a little bit scrambled, and at times he was a bit repetitious, but he talks so well and charmingly and the names of people he can recall are fantastic, both as to the names and his ability to recall them. What a brain that man has!

Friday, September 26 At a birthday dinner party for Maggy Bryan at our house, Hugo told us of his past law practice and one thing that I never heard before. He said at eleven or twelve years old he was fascinated by secret societies and he read in a magazine that for ten cents he could become a card-carrying member of C.M.A.—Coming Men of America—complete with secret handshake and password. So, naturally, he joined. He said he started to disclose his secret membership in C.M.A. when he made his 1937 radio address about the Klan, showing that, along with the Knights of Pythias, Eagles, Masons, Doakies, and so forth, he had joined all sorts of secret societies. He's a cute one and a real charmer.

Wednesday, October 1 Dinner with C.J. Burger. The Burgers have a lovely estate of five acres and an old Civil War house. Elvera [Mrs. Burger] was most gracious, as was the C.J. The new C.J. was expansive and Elvera seemed outgoing.

Thursday, October 2 I didn't sleep well last night. I usually get a sleepless reaction from wine. The C.J. told us that Hugo had said the only bad thing Hugo knew about the C.J. was that he was a Republican, and in response the C.J. told Hugo the only bad thing he knew about Hugo was that he doesn't like wine.

Monday, October 6 Hugo begins his thirty-third year on the Court. We were at the Court about 25 minutes of 10. Frances, Spencer, and the boys were trying to get all the *certs* into the book. Burger presided very well over admitting attorneys to practice. There was one very large group of lady lawyers admitted, one in a miniskirt, with a big red plait of hair down her back. Tom Clark, Stanley Reed, and a lawyer on the front seat took unofficial note of her.

Tuesday, October 7 Hugo came home about 5:00 and was so tired he took a nap before dressing up in black tie to go to the opening of *Butch Cassidy and the Sundance Kid.* We sat at dinner with Senator and Mrs. Sam Ervin of North Carolina. He and Hugo exchanged some stories. Senator Ervin has been a number one critic of the Supreme Court. The Senator racked his brain and finally came up with an opinion he could commend Hugo on, although it went back some fifteen or more years, that is, the Steel Seizure case under Truman.[11] The movie was a prime example of violence, passion, and dull riding over beautiful scenery.

Wednesday, October 8 Hugo got home early, about 4:00. We lay down and watched *The Magnificent Yankee* on television—the story of Oliver Wendell Holmes, and, as usual, we enjoyed it thoroughly. After which we went out and hit balls for thirty minutes. Lizzie Mae had ham, turnip greens, fried green tomatoes, and cornbread for supper.

Thursday, October 9 Hugo said Bill Brennan told the Conference that Tom Corcoran had tried to talk to him about the El Paso Oil case and he had refused, and Hugo told the Conference Tom had also tried to talk to him about it and he had immediately shut him up. Tom said he only wanted Hugo to read the brief—that's all! Hugo was furious about it but said he would not let that incident get him out of the case. Though he had voted for a rehearing, he had voted against Tom's side and would most likely do so again.

Saturday, October 11 I beat Hugo two sets and he, with his competitive spirit, wanted to play best three out of five, and he won.

Monday, October 13 First day of arguments. The vacant chair on the bench spoke eloquently of the man who wasn't there—Abe Fortas or Clement Haynsworth. Vera Burger and son Wade were on the front row. We heard a case argued about whether welfare recipients are entitled to a hearing before they're cut off from the rolls.[12]

Friday, October 17 Stewarts' dinner party at Alibi Club. Bill Douglas looks better than I have seen him in several years. Cathy, a first-year law student, talked law with the men.

Monday, October 20 Hugo told me Majorie Brennan is to be operated on, on Thursday. Cancer of throat. I'm sick.

Wednesday, October 22 Marjorie Brennan has been constantly on my mind and heart. Yesterday I wrote Bill a note to tell him to let me do something and also that my prayers are with them. Marjorie has tried to quit smoking and just couldn't. Dear Marjorie, so pixie-like, quick, warm-hearted, and humorous. I do pray God she recovers.

Thursday, October 23 Marjorie operated on. Mississippi cases argued *(Alexander* v. *Board of Education).* I went by to see Brennan's secretary, Mary Fowler. She had good news: the doctors did not have to do a radical on Marjorie. They were reasonably hopeful they got it all. Praise the Lord!

Elizabeth Oberdorfer joined us in the Justices' section. Louis Oberdorfer argued on behalf of the Civil Rights Section of the Bar Association. Mr. Jerris Leonard, of the Solicitor General's Office, was torn to bits by the Justices, including Hugo, who virtually took him apart.[13]

Saturday, October 25 "A good day," according to Hugo's appraisal, the kind Hugo likes. We went back to bed at 10:00 and slept until 2:00. Then we got up and played two sets of tennis, which he won. Then an order came from the Court by special messenger, and Hugo didn't like it (the Mississippi School cases). He said he would stay here and call Bill Brennan, Bill Douglas, and Thurgood. I went to Mother's for an hour, then came home and fixed ham and grits. It's now 9:00. Hugo is working and I am watching *Tom Jones.*

Sunday, October 26 Hugo started working last night about 8:00 and stayed with it until 12:30 A.M., I sitting with him. We slept without trouble, but awakened at 8:00, had breakfast; then I copied his handwritten draft by typewriter so he and the boys could have something to work on. He also called Frances down to the office. Ken came by and drove Hugo to the office. He came back home about 3:00 P.M., having revised and circulated his dissent, and feeling pleased with himself, as I did in playing my small part in writing history. Bill Douglas and Bill Brennan and possibly Thurgood will be with him.

Monday, October 27 Hugo tells me that Chief Justice Burger called a Conference this afternoon and there was a rather sharp interchange of views on the wording of the order in the Mississippi School case, Burger insisting his order meant the same as Hugo's. Later Burger tried to work out an order incorporating both orders (one written by Burger, White, and Harlan) vs. the one written by Hugo, in which Brennan and Douglas concur, with Thurgood Marshall, of all people, wavering. Hugo's dissent says that the C.J. is substituting the alias of "interim order" for "all deliberate speed." Burger's second order was circulated about 6:00 P.M. Bill Brennan called to say he sticks by Hugo. Hugo came home mighty tired and is napping at his desk.

Tuesday, October 28 *Hugo is a winner in the Mississippi cases.* Bill Brennan called to talk to Hugo about the order. Hugo said Bill had taken Hugo's suggested order, and with a few minor changes, the C.J. had agreed to it. I think "ten days" was substituted for Hugo's "Now!" and they hope to get a Court on it.[14]

Thursday, October 30 We went to Bethesda for Hugo's checkup. Dr. Fox finds Hugo better in all respects. His shakiness of last year has improved remarkably.

Friday, November 7 Thurman Arnold, good friend, famous trustbuster under the New Deal, died this morning of a heart attack. I went to the Arnold house and spent most of the day. Abe Fortas and Paul Porter were magnificent. They would tell funny stories about Thurman and everybody laughed and cried.

Thursday, November 20 Spencer came for me at 2:00 and we drove to the Court to pick up Hugo and John Harlan. Sidney Davis [Hugo's law clerk in 1944] met us at the office and drove with us to the National Cathedral. The services were impressive. Paul Porter, Bill Douglas, Hugh Cox, Abe Fortas, and then Bill Douglas again for Chief Justice Burger, spoke, in addition to Dean Sayre of the Cathedral. Later Sid came to our house for dinner.

Sunday, November 23 About 2:30 Hazel Davis (Hugo's niece) and (believe it or not!) Hattie Lee Price (also Hugo's niece), who hasn't spoken to him or been in the house since the *Brown* decision in 1954, came by. They visited with Hugo about an hour.

Wednesday, December 3 Hugo is absolutely swamped with *certs.* He conscientiously goes over every one of them and, as a result, he has done nothing today but read *certs.* He can't begin to write his opinions until he gets rid of the myriad of *certs.*

Thursday, December 4 Hugo couldn't sleep. He was extremely exhilarated. He had a dissent rolling around in his mind (to Bill Brennan's opinion saying a hearing is due to anyone severed from Relief Roll as a constitutional right). Hugo was like other years when he would get on fire about an opinion.

Friday, December 5 Hugo was exhilarated last night to the point I knew he would have a hard time going to sleep. He woke up at 3:00 A.M. and got up and talked. He said his mind was racing and he was "writing" an opinion in his mind. It must be, said he, the Holmes-type opinion—short, classic, citing no authorities—about "I am fearful that the Court goes farther and farther on the Due Process Clause," in regard to a case whereby if one ever gets his name on the welfare rolls, he is entitled constitutionally to a hearing before he is removed. Hugo still couldn't sleep at 4:00, and so he got up and took a drink.

I am expecting the Virginia Historic Landmark Commission up from Richmond today to see if they can declare our house a historic landmark. If we give Virginia an easement and promise not to sell it to developers, we can freeze our assessment. We are now paying $300 per *month* on taxes and they are threatening to raise our assessment. The easement would be considered a $150,000 gift to Virginia. Hugo and I both decided to do so, eliminating the worry of having to move in the near future. More and we'll have to move!

Tuesday, December 9 I went to Court and enjoyed John Harlan's lively opinion and Hugo's spirited dissent in *Zuber* (about the differential in milk prices), which came down. They swear they put on these lively disagreements for my enjoyment. Rather, they write their views and really feel very strong about it, and I am the excuse for their spirited announcements. From the bench, John wrote me: "Dear Elizabeth, The very dull 'Milk' case that you will hear Hugo and me announce (on opposite sides of the fence) is known between me and Hugo as the 'Elizabeth case.' "[15]

Thursday, December 18 In Miami. Hugo worked on *certs* and even got off a dissent. I worked on cards and letters.

Friday, December 19 It was pouring down rain, so Hugo came out with another old song he used to sing as a boy:

Do not fear, sweet sister of mine,
We will reach the school at nine,
Under the old umbrella,
Safe from the pattering rain,
Under the old umbrella,
Going and coming from school.

Monday, December 22 Hugo nursed his foot all day long, soaking it three times. Nevertheless, he wrote two hot dissents, and at 10:00 P.M. we drove to the post office and mailed them.

Wednesday, December 24 Christmas Eve again. My, I think I've never had a happier Christmas-Eve day, with just enough irritating things happening (I blew a fuse) to realize I wasn't dead. We went to dinner with Hugo, Jr., and Graham and we sat around the dinner table and had a most pleasant time with family jokes and so forth. Hugo, Sr., played the harmonica so beautifully and sang some of his songs, which Lib recorded. Happiness is composed of truly simple things.

Saturday, December 27 We played tennis and cooked oysters. Hugo sang one of his boyhood songs:

A pole cat on a pole once sat,
He did not know where he was at,
An auto passed, the first he'd seen,
It was a gasoline machine.

The pole cat's nose went into the air,
And he said, said he, "Well I declare,
Nothing like that in my family tree,
Nothing like that in my family tree.
Oh me, oh my, I wish that it had passed me by,
Nothing like that in my family tree,
Nothing like that in my family tree."

1970

Thursday, January 1 As I start this new diary of the new year, I am overawed, as usual, by the momentousness of the occasion. Hugo and I, together, can be on top of the 1970's. We meet them with confidence and love.

And so here we sit in Miami, Hugo reading, I writing, and both of us pretty tired. We will have to destroy the fireworks we paid Hugh III $40 for last night, so he wouldn't (1) hurt himself or (2) break the law.

Saturday, January 3 Hugo wrote on his Welfare opinion [see page 241]. We mailed the dissent en route to dinner.

Wednesday, January 7 A miserable delayed flight home.

Monday, January 19 Nixon appointed Harrold Carswell to the Court today.

Tuesday, January 20 Hugo had a dissent today on a narcotics case. The Court decided that if the U.S. proved possession of heroin, it would not have to prove (1) knowledge it was imported or (2) that it was imported. More of his crusade against the Court's deciding cases on the basis of "fairness."[1]

Thursday, January 22 The Marshal had us all congregate in the Court driveway at 11:50 and we drove over in Burger's limousine for Nixon's first

State of the Union Address. Vera Burger's first time. The President made a good speech, I thought, about crime, pollution, war, etc. Hugo looked for me and waved.

Saturday, January 24 After we went to bed last night Hugo spent much time reminiscing about the years I have been with him, about his life with his first wife, and about life in general. He talked of his love and devotion to Josephine and told me how sweet and good she was. I told him of the great happiness he had brought me and how much he meant to me. We talked on far into the night.

Monday, January 26 Hugo gave two opinions for the Court—the Macon, Georgia, Will case[2] and the Draft Law case *(Breen)*.[3] He announced his opinions in lucid, clearly expressed ideas and in a young, firm voice. I was proud of him. He came in at 5:00 and we left on an adventure, to Tyson's Corner, to see Faulkner's *The Reivers*—very good.

Wednesday, February 4 Lucyle Taylor called and said her preacher and [Alabama] Congressman [William Flynt] Nichols would come out tonight. When Lizzie Mae and I suggested we invite both to dinner, Hugo said Congressman Nichols was a Republican. We called Frances and she looked him up and found Nichols was a two-term Democrat. He had lost one leg in World War II and the other was paralyzed. Hugo warmed perceptibly. The preacher came out at 4:30. He wanted to discuss the busing in Sylacauga and a town ten or fifteen miles away that has no colored so they're busing colored in to integrate them. Hugo avoided the subject as much as possible. I came in midway on the conversation and at 5:30 Congressman Nichols called to pick the preacher up.

Thursday, February 5 I am trying to sew a little and Hugo is working on an opinion involving a Selective Service conscientious objector [see page 244]. Should he be exempted because of conscientious but nonreligious objections? Hugo says yes.

Friday, February 6 *The Warrens and Douglases to dinner.* Nina and the Chief came first, then Bill and Cathy. We were a congenial six, and almost a Quaker meeting, with Nina, Cathy, and me gabbing on one side of the room, and Bill, Hugo, and the Chief on the other. Finally, the conversation got general.

Thursday, February 12 Hugo invited John Harlan to lunch with us in his chambers. Hugo regaled us with an Ashland, Alabama, story of a

Baptist church trial. John Harlan, the sophisticated New Yorker, was completely fascinated by Hugo's story.

Tuesday, February 17 Bill Douglas told Hugo for the first time he is thinking of retiring.

Wednesday, February 18 Hugo has so many *certs* to do, and I've got to keep him awake some way or other. Hugo philosophized about man-hungry women for a while this morning, like he always does. He thinks women dress attractively or get their hair fixed only to get a man.

Thursday, February 19 They're having trouble at the Watergate, with demonstrators protesting the "Chicago Seven" sentences. Over 200 arrested so far. The Attorney General, John Mitchell, lives there. Hugo worked all day; then Ken Bass brought him another deluge at 7:00. It's now 11:00, and Hugo's just finishing.

Wednesday, February 25 Went to Court and heard Hugo deliver what he called "a little, unimportant opinion" that created headlines on "ONE MAN, ONE VOTE EXTENDED TO SCHOOL BOARDS."[4]

Thursday, February 26 I went in at 9:30 and the C.J. took an "uncommon" step to honor an "uncommon" man, that is, to take note of a birthday from the bench. He mentioned Hugo's great impact on American law and ended by wishing him a happy birthday tomorrow, and "that," he said, "is unanimous." A large number of law clerks left thereafter. They apparently had come into the Courtroom just to hear the tribute. As I went out, Alvin Wright, the messenger who has been in the C.J.'s office for many years, stopped me to tell me of his affection for Hugo and how he considered Justice Black to be one of the great Justices—a moving and spontaneous tribute from the heart. I told Alvin I appreciated his tribute even as much as I did the C.J.'s.

Friday, February 27 *Hugo's eighty-fourth birthday.* The Court had a luncheon with wine, flowers, and birthday cake in honor of Hugo, the C.J. furnishing the trimmings. *Viva la* eighty-fourth.

Monday, March 2 I was at Court by 10:00. Helen Wright and her guest from New Orleans were already waiting. Hugo said this was a bad time to ask Helen, as he had an opinion reversing Skelly—a close labor case, he said.

Wednesday, March 11 Hugo recited a poem to me today:

I won't need your love or kisses
When the grass grows over my face.
I won't need your fond affection
In my last little resting place.

So if you are ever going to love me,
Love me now when I can know.
All the sweet and tender feelings
That from real affection flow.

Now he is busy writing on a case about keeping order in a courtroom in view of the "Chicago Seven" trials.

Thursday, March 12 Well, an anniversary of sorts. Fourteen years ago today I made the big step of arriving in Washington for my new job. I came up here tearfully from Birmingham and my broken marriage. Those were days of tears and strain. But what a happy ending, or continuance.

Friday, March 13 Last night Hugo worked until after 12:00 on an opinion about how far a judge can go to keep order in the courtroom and revolution out of it. [See page 241, *Illinois*.]

Saturday, March 14 *Gridiron Dinner.* Spencer came for Hugo at 6:00 and I had him tugged, button-hooked, and otherwise hog-tied into his white tie and tails. Hugo was ecstatic over the skit Nixon and Agnew put on for the Gridiron. Nixon secretly sent two pianos on the stage for the production, and he and Agnew played airs reminiscent of former Presidents. Nixon played "Sidewalks of New York." Agnew loudly played "Dixie." Nixon went over and told him, "Stop that!" Then Nixon played "Missouri Waltz" and again Agnew played "Dixie." The third time Agnew played "Dixie" the Gridiron was rolling in the aisles.

Tuesday, March 17 Haynsworths to dinner. We particularly wanted John Harlan to come because he is a Republican on the bench and so is Clement Haynsworth. "Miss Dorothy," as Clement calls his wife, was elegantly dressed in black velvet with gold braid. We tried to skirt touchy subjects, and I am sure the Haynsworths are still sensitive that the Senate voted not to confirm him. Hugo thinks the Senate made a mistake. He thinks Haynsworth would have made a very good Supreme Court Justice.

Wednesday, March 18 Janice has been agonizing over whether to send Grant to public or private schools. Hugo is in favor of sending the boys to public schools. I picked up the hand-painted miniature of Hugo's mother, Martha Ardellah, which I am giving him for his birthday. Charlie Reich got here at 6:30 for dinner. He hasn't been here in four years. He says the year he lived with the Judge was the best of his life. Hugo taught him how to wash dishes and go to the supermarket. Hugo was so plain, Charlie says, and gave him lessons.

Monday, March 23 We all, eight strong, including grandchildren, went to Court. Marjorie Brennan was there to hear Bill give an opinion. Hugo said he didn't have anything except maybe a small dissent. He didn't tell me it was to Bill's Welfare case![5]

Tuesday, March 31 Bill Brennan gave the *Winship* opinion, to which Hugo dissented.[6] Then Hugo, first rocking back in his chair, easily and eloquently gave the Court's opinion in *Illinois* v. *Allen* on contumacious conduct in the courtroom.[7] I was so proud of him.

Wednesday, April 8 I sat next to Mrs. Nixon at the Cherry Blossom Luncheon. Martha Mitchell [wife of the Attorney General] told us she had been up 'til 1:00 A.M. campaigning for Harrold Carswell last night. She said if he isn't confirmed, they have a quick surprise for us. While we were waiting to go in, I told Andy Stewart and Cathy Douglas what she said. At lunch Martha got the word Carswell was defeated, 57 to 45. She plainly was disappointed. She passed the word to Mrs. Nixon, who took the news with a poker face. I told Mrs. Nixon the Court really was in a bad fix for lack of another judge, with all those 4 to 4 cases. Martha later said the surprise was that John was telling everybody if they voted Carswell down, he was going to put *Martha's* name up for nomination. It seemed such a ridiculous idea that Martha, Andy, Cissy, and I got tickled and made all sorts of nonsensical suggestions.

Thursday, April 16 The House of Representatives, with [House Minority Leader] Jerry Ford in the lead, is trying to impeach Bill Douglas. Even if they don't succeed, it will be nasty.

Monday, May 4 Students are rioting all over the country over Nixon's invasion of Cambodia. Four students were killed by National Guardsmen at Kent State, Ohio.

Wednesday, May 6 Hugo got offended because I was so languid. When he gets offended, all the bounce goes out of him and suddenly he's old.

Thursday, May 7 Brennans' 42nd wedding anniversary, and Hugo's toast moved Marjorie deeply. He said he hoped Bill would be on the Court for years to come. Of course, the poignancy of the evening lay in the shadow of death hanging over Marjorie, which we hope and pray will be dispelled by the sunshine of medical achievement.

Friday, May 8 Now listening to old Nixon trying to explain away his escalation into Cambodia. He's struggling, but not convincing.

Tuesday, May 12 *Lawyers Wives' Club Luncheon at White House.* I asked Mrs. Nixon if she knew Harry Blackmun was confirmed for the Court. She said, "Yes!!" with a lot of relief in her voice after the rejections of Haynsworth and Carswell.

Tuesday, May 26 Hollywood, Florida, Fifth Circuit Judicial Conference. We ate breakfast at "Uncle John's Pancake House," then proceeded over to see Hugo's dentist, Curtis Haggard, who gave us the sad news that Hugo's anchor tooth was broken and he would have to go to a full upper plate. Hugo looked a little stricken but finally looked up at him and said, "Well, what I hate about it is to lose my uppers so young!" Hugo may have trouble eating his steaks, but he takes it philosophically.

Thursday, May 28 Midnight. I'm heartsick. We came back from the luau about 11:30 and I was grumpy and told Hugo he had hurt my feelings. I think I was right but I should have just let it go because he is so crushed, and his speech is tomorrow. Oh, dear God, how could I have been so selfish as to chastise him. I held him tight and told him over and over I loved him and, thank God, he seemed to get over it.

Friday, May 29 Hugo and I awakened early. When he asked for suggestions for his Conference speech, I told him he had once gotten inspiration for a speech from the Bible. He soon hit on the idea of reading I Corinthians, 13th Chapter, to the Conference. Hugo has that strange rapport with his audience that causes a dead silence to fall when he speaks, and a "hanging on every word" occurs. His speech was about the same: he being a Southerner; all his more virile ancestors going to Texas; the judges should be apostles of love; and so forth. He couldn't talk on the subjects he preferred, as they were too controversial. He actually read from the Bible, the beautiful passage he cited: "And now abideth faith, hope, love, these three; but the greatest of these is love." This speech was a bit more rambling than usual, and I thought he was a little repetitious and almost too long, but nevertheless an eloquent speech and a good one. We caught the plane home at 4:15.

Monday, June 1 Hugo was sick with chills and fever all night. At 3:00 A.M. he had a fever of 101° but miraculously he was normal by morning and, just as he predicted, he went to Court. Hugo gave one dissent to a labor case (Bill Brennan and Court overruling Hugo's case of eight years ago), and in so doing Hugo said it was a statutory construction and came about because of change of personnel in the Court and because Potter Stewart changed his mind.[8] Hugo really came through on the *Chandler* dissent, emphatically stating that judges *should* and *must* be independent and that other judges should not have power to limit them in any way.[9]

Friday, June 5 We decided not to go to the French Embassy to the wine-tasting with the Burgers. A good thing too, because Hugo didn't get home from the Conference until 6:00. He looked so peaked and weak that I started in on him to retire. I told him I wanted him with me full time next year. He told me if I keep after him, he may retire.

Tuesday, June 9 Justice Blackmun sworn in. All the Blackmun family were sitting on the number one bench. All the wives were there except Cathy Douglas, who has gone West. Blackmun took the oath and we went immediately to the East Conference Room for coffee and cakes.

Thursday, June 11 Called Hugo and he told me to come right in, that there was a party for the clerks and secretaries that the C.J. was having. The C.J. had a white wine punch and *a fire* in the fireplace. It was 90° outside, but it did look cozy.

Friday, June 12 Hugo learned yesterday that the C.J. has accepted the invitation of the Alabama Bar Association to come down and speak. Hugo promised he'd go down and introduce the C.J. if he would go, but Hugo really didn't expect him to. John Sparkman had come over to see Hugo, and together they went in to see the C.J., who agreed to go. I was delighted, but I think Hugo was a little nonplussed. Anyway, he woke me up at 4:30 this morning and said he couldn't sleep. I got out of him that he was worried about Alabama. He feared the reception, the dinner, the speech. All his friends, all my friends, all his relatives, and all my relatives would try to see us, and he couldn't do it all and live.

Monday, June 15 Hugo had a very interesting opinion—or judgment, since John Harlan just concurred in the result—in a conscientious objector case, saying religious grounds were not the only criterion, but moral objections as well would apply.[10]

Friday, June 19 Joy Billington of the Washington *Post* arrived at 4:00. I took her on a tour of the house and garden. About 5:45 her photographer came and shot pictures. Hugo said he was very tired. I gave them all a drink (I made a mistake there, I think) and she got a marvelous interview with Hugo.

Saturday, June 20 I woke up at 2:30 A.M. worrying about all I had said and hoping they won't print anything I said. Hugo woke up at 3:30. We were both restive about the interview.

Monday, June 22 Hugo and John Harlan met face to face in a hot debate over the Due Process "fairness," "shocks-the-conscience" theory, as against the words of the Constitution. Also John took after Hugo's "incorporation" theory that the Fourteenth Amendment made the Bill of Rights applicable to the States. They were both eloquent and persuasive, but I think Hugo had the edge of the debate. The Court were all at loggerheads with each other, but seemed amiable with each other about it.[11]

Monday, June 29 Last day of Court. Will it be Hugo's last? He is pondering. Vera Burger was there when I came and she was saving a seat for Buck Rowe, who is retiring as head of the Court's printing shop, where he worked for forty-eight years. I had a note from John Harlan, saying he was happy that the Court had ended with Hugo and him in agreement and that Hugo had let me dance with him last night. Hugo and John joined in a dissent, and Hugo delivered it clearly, with beautiful enunciation and great clarity. If it is his swan song, it is a worthy one. It was a dissent to the Court's opinion "saddling" the Pennsylvania Railroad with 28 million dollars' worth of New Haven Railroad (now defunct) bonds.[12] After lunch, Hugo dictated mail and we said goodbye to two clerks, Gus Speth and Marshall Moriarty, who are leaving tomorrow.

And so, perhaps, this was, or might have been, the end of thirty-three illustrious years on the Supreme Court of the United States.

Wednesday, July 1 Marjorie Brennan's birthday party at our house. I started to write a poem to her for Hugo to say as a toast. It's hard to write a birthday toast to someone with only a 10% chance to live. At the party Hugo said our poem magnificently, and Bill did a beautiful response. He married Marjorie when she was twenty and now she is sixty-three and he loves her more now than he did then, Bill said. It was all pure nostalgia and our laughter often bordered on tears.

Friday, July 3 Hugo is sleeping a lot. Exhaustion from the strenuous year is showing its effects.

Saturday, July 4 Hugo's granddaughter Annie [Black] arrived to spend the summer with us. We found her very pretty, girlish, and slim—a typical sixteen-year-old. Annie wants to go to drama school, and we are going to send her to St. Albans.

Monday, July 6 Joy Billington's article came out in the Washington *Post.* I never saw such a write-up. We covered the front page of the social section and carried over to the inside. Hugo said he was pleased with it. Vera Burger called to say it was a nice article, as did Marion White.

Tuesday, July 7 I studied over my clothes and decided to ask Hugo to let me buy a new evening dress to take to Birmingham. He went with me and we lucked into finding one we both like.

Friday, July 17 Mayor Seibels was at the plane to meet us in Birmingham; also Judge Lynne; Judge Frank Johnson; Pat Richardson, the President of the Bar; and others. Pat Richardson and Howell Heflin (the newly elected Alabama Supreme Court justice) asked me to try to get Hugo to say more than just introduce the C.J., as this whole thing was in Hugo's honor. The *first* we had heard! Hugo seemed taken unawares at first but soon relaxed. Truman Hobbs introduced Hugo at the dinner and asked his Alabama clerks, all of whom had been invited, to stand. I do believe fifteen or twenty stood up. When Hugo got up, dead silence attended his words. He spoke very well indeed, so much so that the C.J. had tears in his eyes when he came to the podium. Warren Burger paid a beautiful tribute to Hugo. Those attending rose for a standing ovation and loud cheers. After dinner the police escorted us to our rooms and various friends came up. I got to know Vera far better from our ride together. She is a very genuine person. She loved the Southern informality and charm. As we returned to the Parliament House Hotel, we noticed a huge billboard with "WELCOME

CHIEF JUSTICE BURGER AND JUSTICE HUGO BLACK." What a change from earlier days.

Thursday, July 30 Highlands, North Carolina. Hugo, Jr., called and we talked with him quite a bit. My Hugo told him we were having a second honeymoon, so little Hugo said, "Remember the motto you taught me: 'Never too much.' "

Monday, August 3 The Court sent out stacks of work for Hugo. Claude Kirk, the Governor of Florida, wanted Hugo to be present to accept the filing of a paper, but Hugo said to tell Kirk to file it with the Clerk.

Tuesday, August 4 Bob McCaw, Hugo's law clerk, was at the door when we returned home at about 8:00 P.M. with an application from Florida about whether an officeholder had to resign to run for another office. Hugo and Bob wrote out a small opinion—at least they talked out one. Hugo decided they should be allowed to run; then, if elected, the State could challenge it later.

Friday, August 14 Hugo and I went to see the movie *M*A*S*H.* We both found it pretty bawdy.

Monday, August 17 Annie and her grandaddy had a friendly dispute tonight over student rights, homosexual rights, and the constitutionality of the war in Viet Nam.

Hugo's anniversary of going on the Court nearly went unnoticed until we looked it up in the *Congressional Directory* and found today was his thirty-third.

Wednesday, August 19 Hugo and I went to the office and had lunch with Chief Justice Burger and Thurgood Marshall. First time I've seen Thurgood since his serious illness in the spring. We talked about various things. Thurgood told of African tribal law. If the Chief (so Thurgood said) were to murder him, then the Chief would have to support Cissy and their two boys for the rest of the Chief's life. I left so Hugo could talk to the Chief about Hugo's refusal to have the Chief appoint a third law clerk for Hugo. Hugo said he'd prefer to appoint his own clerks, so the third one could just serve under the Chief.

Thursday, September 3 Hugo and I talked about his memoirs. He wants to add several chapters to his present eleven, and then publish it.

He says he wants to interpose me in it, but since I don't appear until many years later, he doesn't quite know how. He may not write further chapters, though, so he says he's going to put me in somehow.

Thursday, September 10 Hugo and I have spent lots of time reminiscing about that day thirteen years ago, the morning after he "popped the question," when he called me into his office and told me all the reasons why I should not marry him, and then, when I accepted, how busy we got.

Friday, September 11 *Our thirteenth anniversary.* Quiet but happy. Hugo said he wasn't buying me anything because I had the checkbook, and I didn't buy him anything either. We drank a toast out of our Thomas Jefferson pewter cups.

Monday, September 14 All over again I was impressed by Hugo's courage. We went to Bethesda to see his eye specialist, who told Hugo he has a blister on the surface of the eye and another at the back of the eye. Hugo asked calmly how he could cooperate. The contact lens in the left eye has to be left out at least two weeks. Hugo decided he would learn to play tennis with his cataract lenses, and we practiced an hour. He thinks if he practices he can soon get proficient. What a man!

Tuesday, September 15 Hugo is working on his memoirs tonight, revising Chapter IV at my suggestion, telling of his first two murder cases.

Thursday, September 17 Hugo tried hitting with one contact lens on, and he was far more successful in serving and hitting than with cataract lenses. Afterward he jogged around the court. Hugo told me I give him great incentive to keep alive and healthy.

We had Anthony Lewis come out for dinner. Tony is in charge of the London office of the New York *Times.* He used to cover the Court here. He admired Felix Frankfurter tremendously, so it is strange that he should admire Hugo also, but he seems to. Tony was with Charlie Reich a few days ago. Charlie was trying to "explain" today's young people to him. Charlie's book *The Greening of America* comes out next week.

Friday, September 18 John Harlan is back in Washington. He says Ethel is still pretty bad off. Hugo talked to him about the Marcello Bail case, in which Hugo issued an order today holding it for the full Court to decide.

Tuesday, September 22 Luncheon at the White House in honor of Mrs. Marcos, wife of the President of the Philippines. Hugo wanted me to take Mrs. Nixon some figs because she had once asked him to bring her some from his tree. So Spencer picked them and I fixed up a basket with Hugo's card on it. Spencer and Hugo drove me in. The figs caused trouble. I had to see the sergeant, who said they would have to go through security. However, he called Mr. Nixon's secretary, and she came down and rescued the figs.

Tuesday, September 29 Martha Mitchell's luncheon at the Department of Justice in honor of Dottie Blackmun, their new appointee. Luncheon was hard-boiled egg and caviar on toast, artichokes stuffed with lobster Newburg, and a lemon tart. Martha said she was going to have all the Senators' wives, ten at a time, for lunch. She asked mischievously, "Reckon Mrs. Fulbright will come?"

Saturday, October 3 Hugo and I went to Bethesda at 9:00 and the news was discouraging. The blip on Hugo's left eye has shown no improvement. He has two options: (1) to wear spectacles and have the help of the left eye; (2) to wear the right contact with no help from the left eye. Hugo as usual received the news stoically. As he says, he is a realist.

Burger's party at the Court honoring the Blackmuns was a reunion of the clan, so to speak. The "new" boy Blackmun was over thirty minutes late. Dottie got lost driving over. Everybody got to know the Blackmuns better.

Monday, October 5 Well, Hugo has made one more Court opening. Prospects are poor, though, because his eyesight may be limited. I hope he'll get off the Court if he finds the load too heavy. We left in separate cars, Spencer driving Hugo in, and I in my Chevy. I got there by running, just in time to see Hugo's entrance on his thirty-fourth year on the Court, and well he looked, too. They admitted lawyers, with a slight change. The Chief Justice told them they'd be admitted, and when all had taken the oath, he would welcome them all to the Bar of the Court, rather than welcome them individually.

What heaven to have Lizzie Mae back home again. Turnip greens for dinner!

Monday, October 12 *Busing cases.*[13] A Negro man named Chambers argued for NAACP. I heard his argument and part of Solicitor General Griswold's argument, which was smooth and good. Hugo had told me he wasn't going to ask a single question, but he did ask two. One was how much time did it take to bus kids in Charlotte, North Carolina, the longest distance, and the lawyer said, "Three and a half hours." The other question Hugo asked was, "Do you think the *Constitution* provides that we must force racial balance in every school?"

Tuesday, October 13 *More busing cases.*[14] Again Hugo questioned counsel very sharply and pointedly, in this case James Nabritt III.[15] So much so that the radio flashed it, newspapers wrote it up, and television had a sketch of Hugo. As the papers said, "Black, who has been the Court's strongest opponent so far to any remnant of segregation, accused James M. Nabritt III of proposing busing of students in an attempt to 'rearrange the whole country and take people out of neighborhoods where they live naturally.' "

Wednesday, October 21 9:15 P.M. Poor Hugo, asleep over his law books.

Saturday, October 24 Nancy and Sterling have *twins*! A boy and a girl: Stephen Eugene and Diana Lee. All are fine.

Sunday, October 25 The C.J. called and wanted to come out and talk to Hugo. He stayed until after 5:00 and brought us a bottle of white wine, which he noticed Hugo liked almost as much as scuppernong, the wine Hugo's mother used to make, the only wine Hugo liked.

Monday, October 26 They had a long Conference today about the Busing cases and others. Hugo said he made a long statement on the Busing case and had a call from Harry Blackmun congratulating him on stating all the issues clearly and interestingly.

Thursday, October 29 A woman from Columbus, Georgia, named Mrs. Connie Swearingin, wrote that she has named a very intelligent basset hound "Hugo" in honor of Hugo. She also enclosed an editorial from the Columbus, Georgia, paper of October 16 on "Justice Black and the Busing Issue: Did He Telegraph Court's View?" They quoted at some length Hugo's questioning of Nabritt on busing. Poor Southerners and poor parents. I don't blame them for worrying about busing children miles away from home. Well, so much for busing.

Hugo and I have been reading Fred Graham's book *The Self-Inflicted*

Wound. Said Hugo looked so peaked in 1956 they updated his obituary, but lo, he had a remarkable revival. Hugo says, "That's you, darling."

Friday, October 30 8:45 P.M. Bob McCaw is here with Hugo and they are going over an opinion—the eighteen-year-old Voting Rights Act. Bob is very good with Hugo. He can keep up with his *certs* and still help write drafts, etc. To top it off, Bob has a nice sense of humor and gets a charge out of Hugo.

Saturday, October 31 Halloween. Hugo is on Mount Olympus, "communing with the Constitution," as he writes on a case where a lawyer, after four years practicing law, and even a master's degree, is deprived by the bar of practicing because he refused to answer the question: "Have you ever belonged to an organization advocating the overthrow of the Constitution?"[16]

For the first time since we've been married, I did not open the door to the children on Halloween. Hugo says it is just too dangerous, and in view of all the kidnapping of public officials and the bombing of public buildings, I have to say he's right.

Sunday, November 1 Today Hugo is completely absorbed in writing his other opinion about a lawyer being barred from practicing because of what he thinks.[17] It is always exciting to me to watch Hugo's total and complete absorption when he begins to write after several days and nights of intensive reading on the subject. Even so, he takes time off now and then to pull me onto his lap and tell me he loves me!

Monday, November 2 Lizzie Mae reminds me of Hugo "communing with the Constitution" on pre-party days. She is on Mount Olympus communing with polishing the silver. We hardly dare speak to her. Hugo is completely absorbed in writing the Lawyer's Anti-Oath case.

Wednesday, November 4 Lady Bird Johnson's diary has inspired me. I write such snatches about going to the store, lunching with Mother, etc., and leave off the earth-shaking observations about Hugo and his comments, thoughts, and actions—not that I want to publish these diaries, but it will make more interesting reading for such of the grandchildren who might like and appreciate them.

Thursday, November 5 Hugo came in at 5:00 saying, "Don't kiss me! I've got a cold." Whereupon I started sneezing and have been ever since.

Friday, November 6 Our dinner party, the Burgers, the Warrens, and the Blackmuns. Vera wasn't able to come because of her cold and this I regretted, but I did not attempt to get somebody to fill in. I thought of Frances Arnold, but Hugo said we never knew what she would say and it might be a strain to have an outsider with Court members so I didn't ask. We got in a tight circle and had a general conversation, led chiefly by Warren Burger. Nina seemed a little ill at ease, as though she were worried about something. Dottie Blackmun was very nice and I think Harry is sweet and charming. He has a nice lopsided smile. I plied Warren Burger with that $6.50 wine I bought for his benefit. I could not tell it was any better than the other.

Monday, November 9 Court. They went into the arguments immediately—the Death Penalty cases, on which hang the destiny of 550 people awaiting execution.[18] The Solicitor General argued that if anybody changed the death penalty, it should be the Congress. Hugo only asked two questions: One, what was the lawyer's opinion (a court-appointed lawyer) on what standards should obtain in death penalty cases. The other was how old was the defendant at the time of the murder of the victim (forty-two). First murder was at seventeen.

I just found the big *Post* write-up on Charlie Reich that appeared in yesterday's paper. It is headed "The Saint of New Haven." It gives the book the name of the Bible of the new generation. Says the book sold out at once. We're so glad for Charlie. I wrote him this morning and Hugo will after he finishes the book. The story says that Charlie said, "Hugo was a giant of a man"!

Tuesday, November 10 Dinner at University Club with Harlans. Their forty-second anniversary. I never eat raw oysters except with John. I'm always afraid of hepatitis. He seems so confident, though.

Monday, November 16 Marlene's [Elizabeth Black's granddaughter] history class, twenty-two strong, came to the Court. Hugo saw the girls at 9:30, answered a few questions, and at Marlene's request told the story of Andrew Jackson, who at his "kitchen cabinet" meeting when asked if he had his life to live over would he change anything, replied, "Well, if I had it to do over again, I believe I'd shoot Clay and hang Calhoun." After the girls left, I slipped back to the Courtroom and later lunched with Vera Burger. She thought there was an unusual amount of security in the Courtroom today. The *Dombrowski* cases [see page 257], two of them with the same principle involved, were argued today. Vera told me to be careful, that the Chief Justice now has a direct line from their home to the police, and that they have had occasion to call them twice lately, once after a knocking at the back door—a draft card was found in the driveway and there was evidence of a car having been parked there.

Wednesday, November 18 The arguments weren't too dull, something about Georgia's laws of eviction. Hugo's ears pricked up when one lawyer discussed the "shocks-the-conscience" aspect of Due Process, and he and John both asked lively questions before the lawyer ran for cover.[19]

Thursday, November 19 6:30 P.M. The dinner bell rang and it caught Hugo writing an opinion. I said, "How about dinner?" He said, "Just have a few more lines to write, will make it short." Wonder how many lines in opinions Hugo has cut short because Lizzie Mae has rung the dinner bell.

Friday, November 20 I had my usual session with Hugo, sitting on his lap. He was so sweet. He told me, "If I thought you would ever quit loving me, the stars would never shine as brightly." At 3:00 A.M. Hugo was restless and couldn't sleep. He's disturbed about Bill Brennan's case along the lines of the *Katzenbach* case, where Attorney General Nick Katzenbach argued the South Carolina case making the South come to the Attorney General or to a court in the District of Columbia for permission before a change of election laws [see page 138]. Hugo is really upset over this downgrading of the South and hopes he can write a dissent that will be moderate instead of fiery. Says the Court will be playing the role of Thad Stevens. (Thaddeus Stevens, a Republican congressional leader during Reconstruction, argued that the seceded states, having lost the war, were "conquered provinces" to which the protection of the Constitution did not apply.)

Wednesday, November 25 Tonight Hugo and Bob McCaw are working on the dissent to Bill Brennan's so-called Thad Stevens opinion that Hugo is so worked up over, where the Southern states have to come to the Attorney General for approval before changing laws about elections. Bob Spearman [Hugo's law clerk] and Hugo worked on one opinion earlier, a dissent, I think, to Potter Stewart. They got it to the printer.

Thursday, November 26 Thanksgiving Day. Lizzie Mae got up early to put our fourteen-pound fresh turkey hen in the oven. Mother is feeling bad and adamantly says she's not coming up for Thanksgiving dinner. Finally, Hugo called Mother and talked her into coming and she reluctantly agreed. I knew she was thrilled that Hugo had called her.

Monday, December 7 This is about the second year now that Hugo has failed to mention that this is the anniversary of Josephine's death. If he had silent thoughts and griefs, he kept them to himself.

Tuesday, December 8 Hugo is looking at applications for law clerks for 1971. I went up and got my 1969 diary and looked back over the time when Hugo was so sick. I read of the great distress I had and told him I hope we never go through that stress again. Hugo said, "I do too," and in the same breath said, "This Cuban fellow that's made application to be my clerk is some fellow!" I see the handwriting on the wall and can only hope and pray Hugo stays well and hearty.

Tuesday, December 15 Hugo selected two new clerks, Pete Parnell from Thomasville, Alabama, and Larry Hammond from San Antonio, Texas. He's keeping John Harmon, who was his "off" clerk selected by the C.J., on next year.

Monday, December 21 I went to Court and took Ken Bass's mother and father with me. We were thrilled to hear the Eighteen-Year-Old Voting case come down. Hugo had the judgment of the Court and stated his case dispassionately. He didn't have to get fiery: he got his own way. According to the papers, "Five separate opinions totaling 184 pages were issued by the Justices in the 5–4 decision that cleared the way for 11.5 million young Americans to vote for President and members of the Congress. It also cleared the way for 11 million others to vote, one million now barred by illiteracy test and ten million penalized by residency requirements." John Harlan, Harry Blackmun, Warren Burger, and Potter Stewart were with Hugo, but they also wrote separate opinions. Brennan, Bill Douglas, Thurgood Marshall, and Byron White were for letting eighteen-year-olds vote in state, as well as federal, elections. The majority were for letting eighteen-year-olds vote only in federal elections, the states to decide for themselves.[20]

Thursday, December 24 Have been sitting here enjoying a program of beautiful Christmas hymns. Hugo is sitting at his desk surrounded by law books. The telephone just rang and it is John Harlan calling from Connecticut. He's wishing us a merry Christmas and kidding Hugo about some of the opinions. Hugo has worked all day on the Mississippi case [see pages 264–65] where the NAACP is suing to require the City of Jackson, Mississippi, to refill its swimming pools, which they drained rather than integrate.

Earlier in the day I went to see Mother. She seemed weak and is losing strength, I fear. Poor little thing. The thought recurs that I may not have her in Christmas of 1971.

Friday, December 25 This Christmas day dawned cold and crisp, partly overcast and partly sunny. Hugo and I ate breakfast late, then brought our presents to the study to open them—a series of records on Plato, Socrates, Crito, etc.; four records of the *Apology,* the trial of Socrates, and two dialogues of Plato. Hugo enjoyed them immensely when we played them late in the evening. We took Mother a turkey dinner at noon. She was more than willing to have us go. She always wants peace and quiet on Christmas. We went out to Fred's and had a very fine Christmas with my son and his family. Hugo was dear and sweet, and I was proud of him —as always I am.

Sunday, December 27 Hugo is writing a memo in the Mississippi case where Black people are suing to require the City to fill up the swimming pools. He has written constantly since dinnertime at 7:00. It is now 11:35 P.M. No distractions or invitations to come sit on his lap tonight!

Thursday, December 31 I called off our party at Bill Douglas's owing to Hugo's chill. Maybe it's because I'm getting old, but I almost felt a sense of relief that I had. I fixed us a bite of dinner and prepared to sit down and enjoy the coziness of a New Year's Eve quietly in our own study. I opened a six-ounce bottle of Cold Duck and since Hugo wouldn't touch it, I drank the whole thing myself. I got sleepy around 10:00 and went to bed after calling Mother to see how she was. Had a cheery report from her that she was fine. But at 4:00 A.M. the phone rang and Mother's little voice came over the line: "Elizabeth, I'm so sick." I threw on my clothes and ran to the car. Alas, it was buried under ten inches of snow, and so I ran through the snow, which was as bright as day, to her house. And so endeth 1970. What a way to greet 1971.

1971

Friday, January 1 Hugo was dear and understanding about my going alone to Mother's, since he was too ill to accompany me, having had chills and fevers the two nights preceding. But he was scared for me and didn't know I'd have to walk or what I'd find. It was an attack of vertigo. At daylight I trudged through the snow to the Dart Drug, and after I got medicine down her, Mother was feeling better. At 6:00 P.M. I came home to Hugo exhausted, but I cooked our black-eyed peas for luck.

Tuesday, January 5 Hugo started off irritating me by trying to make me face up to the fact of Mother's age (ninety-three) and failing health. I got huffy and irritable, which was accentuated when I went down at 11:30, Hugo with me, to take care of Mother. I had to defrost the refrigerator for her and she is *so* cantankerous! Wants to direct my every move, doesn't want me to use up her paper towels (she must have had one roll for ten years now!). She fusses at me and I fuss back, but she is so deaf she can't hear my fussing so it does no good. Hugo called to me once to come out of the kitchen and leave her to do it alone, but I turned my deaf ear to him. Came home feeling my vitality had been sapped. Hugo got stacks of work from the office at 6:45 and so will probably be up until all hours.

Monday, January 11 Jack Vardaman argued the Highway through the Park Memphis case.[1]

Thursday, January 21 I touched a raw nerve somewhere when I asked Hugo about Tom Corcoran's birthday party. Because he was still a little touchy about the *El Paso* case, Hugo became very irritable and told me not to mention it again. When we got to the office, Jim Rowe [a lawyer in Tom Corcoran's firm] had called to see if Hugo couldn't come to the cocktail party and stay long enough to make a speech. Hugo couldn't because he had to attend the State of the Union Address.

Friday, January 22 Hugo came in right at 8:00 P.M. and said he had seen lots of people he knew at Tom's birthday party. I felt better that Hugo had been to Tom's party. We rode to the Capitol with the Burgers for the State of the Union Address, amidst the usual excitement and air of expectancy. Nixon's speech was only mediocre.

Wednesday, January 27 Left at 6:00 A.M. for Florida, Fred driving.

Sunday, January 31 *Moon shot,* Apollo XIV. We arrived at the launch site and found good seats in Bleacher B. The rocket blasted off at 4:05 P.M.; I can never describe the emotion I felt when the launch got under way. The ship was soon swallowed up by a dark cloud overhead and the great moment was gone. The astronauts had made one complete circuit of the earth before we got out of the NASA gate and onto the highway.

Friday, February 5 We played tennis, or rather, I served to Hugo and he hit them back for almost an hour. The sun is bound to be good for us both. We came home and took a nap between watching Alan Shepard and Edgar Mitchell cavorting on the moon! Tonight, when I looked up and saw this gorgeous moon, I could hardly believe there were two Earthlings on it.

Friday, February 12 Left Miami at 10:35 A.M. Arrived Kingsland, Georgia, 6:00 P.M., where Hugo remembered some years ago there was a wonderful motel, the Majestic Oaks. His memory proved correct, and we had a large, clean room with two double beds for $10.50. Elmo's Country Restaurant was just down the road. We got a splendid dinner of ham, turnip greens, black-eyed peas, slaw, and rice.

Saturday, February 13 Walterboro, South Carolina. Stopped at Southland Motel, for a late lunch. About six Negro men came in and instead of seating them in the room where we were—the lunch place, plain, with no tablecloths—they were sent to the closed-off back dining room. But two or three of the men came back through a couple of times. A waitress confided to Hugo that she had put them back there "so they wouldn't parade, and now look at 'em." Guess she'd have dropped dead if she'd known Hugo was a Supreme Court Justice.

Sunday, February 14 Got home at 4:30 P.M.

Monday, February 15 Spent most of day with Mother. Hugo stayed at home and worked with Bob Spearman on the Abortion case (whether the federal courts have jurisdiction or not).[2] Hugo is loaded with work.

Tuesday, February 23 Hugo feeling good and peppy tonight, having delivered himself of six cases today, including four of the *Dombrowski* cases,[3] which have been hanging fire three years. Bill Brennan held Hugo up on them all last year. Hugo had two lawyer cases[4] and a dissent on a third on which he said Potter Stewart went back on him.[5]

Thursday, February 25 Hugo wanted me to go with him to the office to meet the press concerning his eighty-fifth birthday. At 11:00 about twenty reporters, and wire service representatives and two photographers filed in. Their questions were friendly enough. Hugo told them I was so much a part of his life now that he wanted the world to know it. We thought Hugo conducted it very well, albeit I told him I was afraid the press would play up what he said about Earl Warren because he didn't make himself clear on that point.

Friday, February 26 Sure enough, the press played up Hugo's statement about Earl Warren. Peggy McHugh, the Chief's secretary, called Hugo's secretary, Frances. She was furious about Hugo being quoted as saying that Warren would hardly be remembered by anyone except his own generation. "And to think of all the C.J. has done for that man," she stormed. Frances said she explained Hugo was talking about "the Warren Era," the "Impeach Earl Warren" signs in connection with integration and unpopular emotional issues generally. Hugo meant the rancor would disappear, not that Warren was unimportant. That ate into me a little and I wished I had, as was my impulse, broken in and asked Hugo to clarify that statement, as I had heard him say privately and publicly that Warren was a great Chief Justice. Hugo came home tired after a hard Conference.

Saturday, February 27 *The eighty-fifth birthday. Clerks' dinner at Federal City Club.* How Lizzie Mae and I survived I do not know. There were constant rings at the doorbell with either flowers or telegrams. We all left at 6:30. I wore my sequin dress; Hugo his new suit, new shirt, and a tie I had given him. JoJo drove and we stopped by Mother's so she could see how we looked. Buddy Cooper did a beautiful job of presiding, with just the right mixture of humor and seriousness. Buddy read the beautiful letter written to Hugo by President Nixon, part of it being in his own handwriting. It came by special delivery in a White House car this afternoon. Then Marx Leva presented the "gift" from Barney Whatley, a wig with a poem written by Barney all about the Hair decision[6] and Hugo's bald pate. Very humorous. Then, to my amazement, Buddy called on me for a speech. I guess he thought I had my usual poem, but I didn't. The clerks gave me a standing ovation, which touched me deeply. I invited them all out tomorrow. Then Hugo spoke. While it was moving, and to the effect that he loved his clerks, yet he did ramble too much. Hugo had everyone stand in memory of Huey Howerton and Margaret Corcoran, both former clerks who had died. I took a bouquet of daisies to the dinner in Margaret's memory. After that, there was more visiting, and group pictures were taken. It was a wonderful party, but the unfortunate misinterpretation by the press of Hugo's meaning in regard to C.J. Warren, whom we both love and revere, hung like a pall on us.

Sunday, February 28 Brunch for the clerks. There were thirty-eight clerks, wives, and children at our house for Sunday brunch. Lizzie Mae made hot biscuits to go with the ham. We had Lizzie Mae's watermelon pickle, whiskey sours, and bloody marys. Vera Burger called in the afternoon and said the C.J. was on his way with a birthday gift for Hugo. The clerks came early and stayed late, and I got every one of them in a picture with Hugo, by making dozens of trips up and down the stairs to the study. It was a happy party, and the clerks enjoyed each other. And so the eighty-fifth birthday came and went, leaving us tired but the tension had gone out. Still the pall lingers on.

Monday, March 1 As soon as Hugo left for Court, I sat down and wrote Nina a letter trying to explain Hugo's meaning. I poured out my heart to her in a four-page, handwritten letter and I sent it special delivery. God grant she will receive it and it will make her feel a little more kindly about the statement.

Thursday, March 4 Still feeling deeply depressed over the alienation of good and dear friends, the Warrens. Hugo finally went in to see the Chief and talked to him forty-five minutes or more. He found Warren very mad and hurt, and it seemed to Hugo that the Chief must have thought

Hugo called the press conference just to snipe at him. Warren said Hugo even called in all his clerks, and that a newspaper friendly to both Warren and Hugo has said that Hugo has been sniping at Warren for some time; which is absolutely not true, but I suppose he is talking about the Agronsky interview, in which Hugo said that using the phrase "all deliberate speed" in the *Brown* case may have been a mistake. And so the hurt grows. Hugo said he assured Warren he considers him a great Chief Justice and will always love him and his family regardless of the attitude the Warrens will henceforth have toward him. Hugo felt he softened Warren's attitude a little. Hugo came home absolutely beat. He had had a severely hard day, his left eye hurt, and he felt physically and mentally let down.

Friday, March 5 I feel as though I am gradually recuperating from a long siege of illness now that Hugo has been to see Chief Justice Warren and has done his best to explain and soothe away the hurt. We must get our minds on more constructive things than moping over an act already committed. Perhaps God will give us an opportunity later to set the record straight.

Sunday, March 7 I have dreamed twice of Earl Warren since Hugo went to see him. Once he came to our house in tears; the second time he was here in perfect harmony. Many times I have heard Earl Warren say, "I love that man of yours!" and I believe he meant it.

Tuesday, March 9 I got a beautifully worded letter from Nina telling me Hugo's comment would in no way affect our friendship. I got all emotional and cried a bit. Hugo said I took such things too seriously, but I was deeply touched.

Monday, March 22 Vera Burger called me last night to see whether I was going to Court. I decided I would. A loan shark case with extortion was heard, as to the right of Congress to regulate purely "local" crimes. This butcher had borrowed $1,000 plus interest, couldn't pay it back, and borrowed $2,000 more. Paid back $6,500 in six months and still owed another $6,000. Fantastic, isn't it![7]

Tuesday, March 23 Hugo working far, far into the night.

Friday, March 26 About midnight Hugo awakened with acute pain in his left ear, eye, and a headache over his eye. I put hot compresses on it for about thirty minutes and gave him two Tylenols. He got relieved of his pain finally, but then he said he was worried about the Government. He said he was at the seat of the power and the fight to keep judges from deciding on the basis of what *they* thought right and not the Constitution. He said he really startled the Conference today by saying he was going to dissent to a bunch of civil cases they were dismissing. Since they had voted that due process demanded that a lawyer be provided and court costs be paid for indigent divorce cases, Hugo was going to vote that all civil cases involving people who had lost an arm or leg and so forth be allowed to proceed with court costs paid and that a lawyer be provided. To Hugo's amazement, Bill Brennan and Bill Douglas voted with him.[8]

Saturday, March 27 Took Hugo to the doctor and he told Hugo he may have shingles in the left ear and eye. God forbid!

Monday, March 29 I went to Court and heard Hugo deliver a spirited dissent to John Harlan's opinion on the Wyoming case, where a man named Whiteley, who had been convicted of stealing, applied for *habeas corpus* after seven years and was ordered to have a new trial, although he was plainly guilty, having been caught with the goods on him. Hugo has never been too keen on the Fourth Amendment, where the wording is "reasonable."[9] The other was a Louisiana case where Hugo gave the opinion of the Court on whether an illegitimate child should inherit equally in an estate left by a father who had publicly acknowledged the child but had not provided for her in the will. Court said no.[10]

Tuesday, March 30 The Washington *Post* had a front-page story by John McKenzie which was very unfavorable to Hugo's dissent in the *Whiteley* case. It said that Hugo accused the Court of "bad faith," the first time a Justice has ever charged such a thing to his colleagues. The tone of the whole thing, which Hugo said was in the form of an editorial against his opinion, was that Hugo attacked a well established policy of the Court which John Harlan nobly and reluctantly put into effect because of previous decisions of the Court. I guess criticism of my beloved Hugo disturbs me.

Wednesday, April 7 John Harlan, Andy and Potter Stewart, Marion and Byron White to dinner. We drank John Harlan's favorite bourbon, "Rebel Yell," and listened to Nixon's speech on television about the further de-escalation of the war in Viet Nam. John and Potter thought it good (they're Republicans). Hugo and Byron (Democrats) didn't think Nixon was so hot.

Wednesday, April 21 At Court at 3:00, at which time a man named Willinger, the Hollywood photographer, arrived. He had come all the way from Hollywood, California, to take Hugo's, Bill Douglas's, and C.J. Warren's photos, promising each a large, free photo. Hugo had to go into a Conference and the photo-sitting was delayed until 4:00. Frances and I helped arrange the furniture, Hugo's tie, and so forth. The photographer would ask me to stand at a certain place and then ask Hugo to look at me and smile, which he did. The photographer said we restored his faith in marriage. He took one photograph of us together at Hugo's request.

Friday, April 23 We went to Bill and Cathy Douglas's dinner at the Court. It was quite a nostalgic occasion. He had it for his lawyer, Si Rifkind [Judge Simon H. Rifkind], and for others who had stood by Bill in, as he expressed it, "the Trouble"—mostly old friends or those who helped him in the impeachment proceedings. He had us, the Earl Warrens, the Clark Cliffords [former Secretary of Defense], Sid and Tilly Davis, and others. They had invited the Brennans, but they couldn't come. In his speech, Bill referred to Hugo's note to him on the bench during the impeachment proceedings. Hugo had said, "Don't forget to smile, and do not fail to remember the 13th Chapter of I Corinthians, 'And now abideth faith, hope, love, these three; but the greatest of these is love.' "

Tuesday, April 27 Hugo and I went to Mary and Tom Clark's party. Just as I was fixing to say, "Hugo, watch these downward steps," Hugo stepped off them. He was holding on to my little finger and he pulled me along. We did a ballet but managed to end at the bottom, right side up. I got a wrenched finger but nothing worse. The Chief Justice and Vera were there; so were Earl and Nina Warren—thank God they were cordial, and I do believe whatever hurt they sustained has mended. Hugo and I went to the Army-Navy Country Club later for dinner. Hugo was very loving and it was like a teenage date with the World's Greatest Lover.

Wednesday, April 28 Hugo woke up at 4:00 A.M. chuckling over a retort he intended to make to Byron White's opinion—*something* about a "crack had appeared in the structural organization of the building." I was dead sleepy, so I didn't make too much out of it. Hugo was like he was in the first few years of our marriage, chuckling and talking out his side of the opinion. Therefore, I went around half asleep all day.

Saturday, May 1 All the fuzzy bearded kids camped across the river on the Mall promising to block all traffic and bridges on Monday. Hugo has to act as Chief Justice because Burger is in New York. I despise these dirty kids with the beards and the hair and the drugs and the loud music and the unpatriotic Ho Chi Minh signs and the tents divided into lesbian and homosexual divisions. I think they are a national disgrace.

Sunday, May 2 Mr. Seaver, Clerk of the Court, called today and said Mr. [Richard] Kleindienst, Assistant Attorney General, suggested that the Judge get up at 5:00 A.M. tomorrow and come in to the Court or spend tonight at the Court on account of the threats of the war protesters to block all bridges and disrupt traffic. Hugo flatly refused.

Monday, May 3 With some misgivings, I sent Hugo to the Court with Spencer. Hugo had no trouble in getting to the Court, with soldiers with bayonets every ten feet on the 14th Street Bridge. But there were lots of heads banged, tear gas used, and over 7000 kids were arrested and sent to RFK Stadium for processing. They threw garbage cans in the middle of the street, slashed tires, or let air out of stalled cars, pulled out wires from under the hood, broke windows, and were generally obnoxious. While Hugo and I agree with their antiwar sympathies, we don't think anarchy is the way to bring about our withdrawing.

Tuesday, May 4 We leave for San Antonio for Fifth Circuit Conference. As we approached San Antonio, we were asked to stay in the back of the plane and be the last to leave. A battery of photographers and newsmen awaited Hugo. One reporter asked Hugo what he thought of Martha Mitchell's comment that "the Supreme Court ought to be abolished, nobody but nine old men on it." Hugo said, "Martha who?" Then later, in reply to another question, Hugo said she had a right to her opinion. He said, "I like her, she is a nice Southern lady who taught school in Alabama." One reporter wanted to know, "Was she a good teacher?"—to which Hugo replied, "I don't know. I never went to school to her." We thought that was pretty funny.

Friday, May 7 Hugo woke up grumpy. I ordered breakfast in the room and let him read his copy of *To Secure These Blessings,* which Hugo likes so well. Hugo, Jr., came up and told his father he would swing his stopwatch if he talked too long. Hugo, Sr., bit off his head. Said, "You don't understand. Old age is nostalgic and different from youth. If I make my mistakes, then let me make them." When they got ready for Hugo, the room was packed and hushed. Hugo gave a magnificent speech: no rambling, and cohesive. He told a couple of jokes—"What if your grandfather had been a fool?" "Then in that case I reckon I'd a been a Republican." He talked about the Bill of Rights and the Due Process concept. He talked about the necessity of judges being honest. He quoted from the Bible: "The greatest of these is love." He always says "love" instead of "charity." He quoted Socrates' words to his friends, "But already it is time to depart, for me to die, for you to go on living; which of us takes the better course, is concealed from anyone except God." He ended by reciting his poem, "Here's to the Blue of the wind-swept North," and so forth. He was a bit emotional as he ended, but the speech had power and all stood up.

Saturday, May 8 Returned home. Found mother O.K. and all well.

Monday, May 17 We got up bright and early and went to the Court to see the session and hopefully hear Hugo dissent from the C.J.'s opinion on the California hit-and-run-driver law. To our disappointment the Chief did not announce his opinion. He just said the results and noted the dissents.[11] Hugo sent me a bench note that said, "Elizabeth, the C.J. preferred that I make no statement, so of course I will not."

Tuesday, May 18 Dinner party for my old friend Evelyn Liddell, with C.J. and Vera, Tom and Mary Clark, and John Harlan. The C.J. shocked us by asking what Hugo thought of a rule next year announcing *only* the opinions, and not the dissents. Hugo said he did not believe in discouraging dissent.

Monday, May 24 Hugo had a small opinion on naturalization affairs. Afterwards, we listened in on Hugo's giving answers to questions from Hunter High School students from New York. He did real well, and I could see Hugo captivated the children.

Thursday, May 27 *Mother's ninety-fourth birthday.* She seemed very happy. Said she was "ninety-four going on a hundred!" And may God grant that she's right.

Saturday, May 29 Hugo and I went down with the "Mighty Midget" vacuum cleaner, and I cleaned Mother's rug. As Hugo toted the vacuum cleaner, I thought it was a bit unseemly for a Supreme Court Justice to be doing such a menial task, but again, was it? An act of great kindness.

Wednesday, June 2 Hugo worked until 6:00, then told me he would take me to dinner and a movie. I was anxious to see *Patton* and I thought it magnificent, especially George C. Scott, who played the role. Hugo also liked it, but felt it was propaganda to make us hate Russia. Hugo was far more amorous in the dark movie than the teenagers sitting around us. I had to suppress him a time or two.

Monday, June 7 There were a number of opinions today but, alas, Hugo's Mississippi Swimming Hole case was held up again. He's had it out since October 26, but just last week Byron asked him to hold it up so he could write, and then a few days ago Bill Brennan said he wanted to write. Hugo thinks he has one weak soldier and they are trying to get him. The C.J. came in yesterday afternoon and told Hugo he would try to help him get it down.

I had lunch with Vera Burger after Court. Some of the opinions were barely announced. Andy Stewart told Vera she thought it was a shame—going to Court now would be no more interesting than going to traffic court. Vera told me she rather agreed with Andy, and I told Vera I too agreed, especially about stifling the dissents until the members of the Court could follow the rules of courtesy in the Senate. I think the idea is to avoid further publicity because of the newspapers' denouncement of Hugo's opinion (in which the C.J. joined) saying that this decision would "make good people believe our Court actually enjoys frustrating justice by unnecessarily turning professional criminals loose to prey upon society with impunity."

Thursday, June 10 I drove Hugo to Bethesda to see the neurosurgeon. He seems to think a bit of calcium on the nerve, or some minor irritation of a nerve, is causing Hugo's headaches. The headaches seem to be getting more acute. Thurgood Marshall was in the x-ray room getting his "belly and gut," as he expressed it, x-rayed.

Friday, June 11 Hugo was in a Conference at the Court all day. He thinks now his Mississippi Swimming Hole case may be coming down.

Saturday, June 12 I was in a tizzy because I held Hugo's feet to the fire and *made* him select one of his special books, with his own notes and index, and give it to Hugo III for his high school graduation this Monday. Hugo picked his cherished book *To Secure These Blessings,* wrote a beautiful inscription in it, and then wrote Hugh a letter congratulating him on graduating as valedictorian of his class.

Monday, June 14 Hugo delivered a lengthy opinion on the Jackson, Mississippi, Swimming Hole case, wherein the Court upheld the right of a city not to operate any swimming pool at all. The obvious reason was that they did not want to integrate, but Hugo cited John Marshall's opinion in the Georgia Lands case wherein he said the Court could not look into the motives behind the votes of legislators.[12]

Wednesday, June 16 Back to the neurologist. He said he could find no reason for Hugo's chronic headaches except calcium deposits in the blood vessels. He thinks they will wear off eventually, and he gave Hugo vitamins, a tranquilizer, and muscle relaxers.

Wednesday, June 23 Hugo went out and hit for two ten-minute sessions, and he hit very well. He played with Emil Pansky, husband of my tennis-playing cousin Billie. They are visiting us from California. Libby took an excellent picture of Hugo playing tennis at eighty-five, his knees bent, racket back, eye on the ball.

Saturday, June 26 Unprecedented Court session for arguments in the Pentagon Papers case. Solicitor General Erwin Griswold argued for the Government, Alexander Bickel, a Yale law professor, for the New York *Times,* and a Mr. Glendon was representing the *Post.* There were long lines outside the Court to get into the Courtroom. Margaret [Black] woke up with a cramped stomach, but we were determined to go to the Court anyway. I took her to the Court nurse, who gave her a number of little soda crackers, wrapped in cellophane. We went into the crowded Courtroom, sat in the Justices' section, and heard a historic extra session of arguments pro and con. Every time there was a dramatic silence in the Courtroom it would be broken by Margaret ripping off one of those cellophane wrappers from the soda crackers, which kind of gave a comic relief to the drama. Hugo asked Solicitor General Griswold if the First Amendment meant anything. He replied testily, "We know and everyone knows your view, Mr. Justice, that 'No law means *no* law,' but I do not believe that no law means no law." I think Hugo came off better.[13]

Monday, June 28 Court in the morning. No *New York Times* decision! We got the girls [Libby and Margaret, Hugo, Jr.'s, daughters] going. Margaret was feeling O.K. and we took in the Court session, hearing the Muhammad Ali (boxer conscientious objector from the Army)[14] and the Aid to Parochial School[15] cases, which would have been of great importance had not everyone expected the *New York Times* case to come down. An air of disappointment prevailed, especially among the newspaper reporters.

Margaret was arguing death cases with her granddad at dinner, but got a stomach cramp again. She went to the bedroom and tried to conceal it, but we found her weeping bitterly. She came and sat in Hugo's lap and he was, as always, the Rock of Gibraltar. I know she will always remember him that way.

Tuesday, June 29 Hugo read all the various opinions in the *New York Times* case, and Bob McCaw came by later with Hugo's concurrence. Hugo was very excited about it, and he asked me to read it and offer criticisms, which I did. All four I offered he changed in his opinion. In one I objected to "send American boys to be *murdered.*" He thought it over all night and this morning at 4:00 A.M. he woke me up and asked, "How would it be if I said, 'Send American boys to die of foreign fevers and foreign shot and shell'?" This I thought great, and the substitution was made. The new line came out of the song "I Am a Dirty Rebel," which Hugo and the boys used to sing just for fun.

Wednesday, June 30 Hugo went to a Conference. I went by Mother's to check on her. Took her watermelon and cornbread. I came home, swallowed a sandwich, and rushed to the Court. There was a session at 2:30. The C.J. announced a *per curiam* opinion that the Court, 6–3, decided the New York *Times* has the right to print the Government Viet Nam papers—Burger, Harlan, and Blackmun dissenting to the *per curiam* written by Bill Brennan, with concurrences by Hugo, Douglas, White, Stewart, and Marshall. There was great tension in the Courtroom, and when it was announced that the district court opinion upholding the *Times* was affirmed, there were great sighs in the Courtroom, some of despair and some of relief. Hugo's line "foreign fevers and foreign shot and shell" was quoted on television. I went to Hugo's office and told him, "Honey, if this is your swan song it's a good one!" He agreed he could be proud of this one.[16]

Thursday, July 1 The television and press are full of the *New York Times* case. Few newspapers, strangely enough, support Hugo's opinion that "no law means no law" fully—their only salvation, it seems to me. Hugo missed a Conference called by the C.J. to discuss what Solicitor General Griswold had told him, that there was a leak of information from the Court. Hugo did not attend. He felt he needed to meet his medical appointments. Nothing came of the Conference about discipline, I understand.

Sunday, July 4 I barbecued spare ribs today for Hugo and Mother. Hugo minced. He only weighs 130 pounds now, off 15 pounds from his normal weight.

Friday, July 9 I am all up-tight. Mother has me almost past endurance. I have a sore back from putting her in the tub. Mother is imperious —"Don't move this, don't move that." One day she swears she will never touch medicine again, and the next day she has a vertigo spell and is docile and will take anything. I am on edge. I snap at everybody. I can't sleep at night. Hugo is hurting all night. He has lost weight from his minimum 145 to 130. His voice is an octave higher due to weakness. I am frantic about him. What is the best for Mother, I do not know. I cannot leave her in her present state, as Hugo points out. She resists so violently any suggestion of coming here, or going to a nursing home. I am distraught.

Saturday, July 10 Hugo is very Spartan, but I can tell he isn't himself.

Monday, July 12 Hugo is feeling rough. Dr. Fox decided to admit him to Bethesda.

Tuesday, July 13 Another day in the hospital for Hugo. He complained that the Naval Hospital has really gone down—not in the quality of doctors, but of the corpsmen and nurses, who show a diminution of discipline. Said when he went for x-rays there were many standing around pushing, kidding, and horse-playing. Hugo said, "They delivered me to the rock-throwers and the beard-growers."

Thursday, July 15 Yesterday doctors sent Hugo in a wheelchair to the x-ray department and made him wait an hour and forty minutes. At the end of that time, Hugo got up and walked back to his room. He said he would not return until they took him the instant he arrived, and they did.

Friday, July 16 Hugo home. Glory be. Dr. Fox came by about 11:00 and told Hugo they found nothing to account for his illness.

Saturday, July 17 I am worried about Hugo. He seems joyless and apathetic. His appetite is poor.

Monday, July 19 Martin Agronsky called last night to tell us that Hugo's program would be rebroadcast on CBS on Tuesday at 9:00 and wanted us to come over and have dinner, but Hugo, Jr., will be here and Hugo, Sr., is still not feeling well. I'm at wit's end.

Tuesday, July 20 By golly, Hugo's program was greater than the first time. Hugo was magnificent. Fell in love with him all over again.

Friday, July 23 Hugo had a terrible night. He decided he would go to the hospital and get to the bottom of his trouble. So we packed him up, and I had him out by 9:00 A.M. I stayed with him until 2:00 and then came home by Mother's, fixed her some food, and straightened her out for the day.

Saturday, July 24 I went out to see Hugo and he was much better, so they released him. Bill Brennan came by to see him, and we had a nice visit with Bill, who helped move Hugo's things down to the car. We went by the office where Hugo's new clerk, Larry Hammond, was working on the Virginia Legislature's petition for a stay on reapportionment. I went down at 3:30 to the Greyhound bus station to pick up Hugo's grandson Jim Black, son of Sterling. I was pleasantly surprised to see his hair was not too long and he looked neat and handsome.

Sunday, July 25 Jim questioned Hugo avidly about his views, his past, his cases, everything. They talked until midnight.

Wednesday, July 28 Dr. Fox called to say he had arranged a consultation for Hugo at the Naval Hospital with a doctor from Hopkins on August 4, if he could hold out that long. The August 4 date seems far, far away. Hugo needs help now, but we agreed to it.

Wednesday, August 4 Promptly on the hour, Dr. Mac Tumulty came over from Johns Hopkins—a man of about sixty with a mane of white hair. Dr. Fox recounted Hugo's medical history, and Hugo put in something every now and then. They went out and came back saying the jury was unanimous. They agree that Hugo has a classic case of temporal arteritis, an inflammation of the arteries in the left side of his head. The treatment is prednisone. The side effect is a possible ulcerated stomach, so they put Hugo on a special diet. The prognosis is for six or eight months of prednisone. The disease tends to be self-ending if treated, but may spread if not.

Thursday, August 5 Glory be! Hugo is responding. His headache is gone, practically, his voice is stronger, and he is more spirited. Lizzie Mae tiptoed up to the second floor bathroom expecting Hugo to be in bed and found him at his desk working. We all felt so good at every symptom of Hugo's recovery that we would run and tell one another.

Friday, August 6 Spencer took Hugo to the office, and how glad I was that he could go. Frances is on leave, and the C.J.'s new orders are that all the Justices are to use secretaries from the pool, whoever is available. Hugo doesn't like this as he wants one secretary. In the C.J.'s absence, Hugo has lots of work to do, and he needs a secretary. Spencer was delighted Hugo complained and said, "The Judge is really feeling better now." When I got to Court, we went down to lunch with this year's clerks, John Harmon, Pete Parnell, and Larry Hammond. Hugo enchanted them with his Alabama stories. Pete is from Thomasville, Alabama. Hugo said he was glad to have three Southerners for what would probably be his last year on the Court. I said, aghast, "Probably?" Hugo laughed.

Monday, August 9 Tonight John Harlan called. His back is still killing him and he said he thought he would take Hugo's advice and come down to see Dr. Fox. Hugo asked him whether he cared to stay with us next Sunday. Hugo said he was sure John would have to be hospitalized, and I agree. John said he'd come down on Sunday.

Sunday, August 15 We took John Harlan to dinner at the Army-Navy Club. He had come in on an afternoon plane and will be admitted to the Naval Hospital at Bethesda tomorrow morning. He has a bad back, a strained sacroiliac. Despite John's and Hugo's illness and my debilitated state of health, we relaxed, laughed a lot, and philosophized a great deal. Poor John. There he is, practically blind, a bad back, and discouraged. He and Hugo think four or five Justices may resign at one time, leaving Nixon to appoint a bunch. Good God, what a scare!

Tuesday, August 17 We went by to see John Harlan and found him to be—well, all right but in a depressed, defeated frame of mind. He may not stay on the Court, though he did not say so. He worries about the Court. He thinks he, Bill Douglas, Hugo, and possibly Thurgood Marshall may get off the Court, and what an impact on the country!

Hugo is lecturing his clerk Pete Parnell because he has not yet grasped Hugo's views. Hugo is not displaying his usual patience with his new law clerks.

Wednesday, August 18 It is thirty-four years since Hugo took the Confirmation oath. Though rid of his headaches, he is deep in soul-searching. He is not feeling strong, and he is annoyed that his new law clerks, Larry Hammond and Pete Parnell, are steeped in the shocks-the-conscience test of Due Process, having been "brainwashed" by the Harvard viewpoint. Hugo had Pete out for a couple of hours to talk to him.

John Frank called to say his new article on Hugo in *Reader's Digest* will be published next March. It's a story about Hugo's breaking all longevity records on the Court. John said he is drawing heavily on my letters. He doesn't have too many, I don't think. John will show me the first draft, he says. Hugo says I shouldn't let him. "Your letters are *your* letters, and if anybody uses them, you should use them."

Thursday, August 19 Another day of deep contemplation for Hugo. He says if he doesn't get his strength back in the next two weeks, his feeling now is that he'll get off the Court. He had the boys come out and they stayed until 2:00. He had to decide on the *Corpus Christi* busing case. The Attorney General reversed himself on it in two weeks' time. He first said they had to do it, but then he and President Nixon, according to the Washington *Post,* were asking Hugo to stay the order. Hugo did so with an order saying the entire situation was too confused for one judge to act on, and therefore he would stay it until the full Court could act. He argued with the boys for two hours or so and was quite exasperated with them. They finally got the short order written, though.[17]

Friday, August 20 Hugo's eyes through his cataract lenses look like huge smoldering fires. I am so torn.

Saturday, August 21 Hugo sits staring into space, his eyes looking like deep liquid pools. His face is thin. I finally asked him if he didn't want me to call Louis Oberdorfer to come over and talk to him. He did and Louis came within forty-five minutes. Louis and Hugo talked about two hours, Hugo's voice getting stronger and more resonant as he talked. Hugo has a dark view of the prospects for this country. He believes Nixon has defied the Court and is unstable, jumping and flopping wherever he thinks popularity takes him. He told Louis, though, that his health had failed, his vision had failed, and his memory was not as good. He said he always has said when he felt he could not measure up, he would get off. Hugo feels anything can happen in this country, with small groups fragmenting Government; that there may not be a 1972 election—a dictator might take over. Hugo does not know what will happen to the Court. Byrd's resolutions may pass, requiring judges to be reconfirmed every eight years. Hugo thinks the Court is in a turmoil and will wind up on Nixon's side. Lou argued that Hugo's vote for one more year might make a crucial difference. Louis will return tomorrow for more talks.

Sunday, August 22 Louis Oberdorfer came at 2:00 and stayed until close to 8:00. When I came back from Mother's, Louis was looking up a case for Hugo—the *Dombrowski* case of last fall where Hugo wrote the opinion in a Mississippi case wherein it was sought that a federal court could enjoin a state court from trying a case. Hugo was very much against federal courts stopping state criminal trials, but because Potter didn't stick with him, the Court opinion could not settle it. Anyway, Louis researched for him, discussed family matters, and when it was about time to leave, they got back on the subject of Hugo's ability or inability to continue on the Court. Hugo said he had always said that when he was no longer an asset to the Court, he himself would know it and quit. Hugo said he now believed, if his condition did not markedly improve, he had reached that point. Louis suggested he set a tentative date for September 1, because he has an appointment with Dr. Fox for August 31. Hugo said he may or may not. Louis asked whether Hugo wanted to call in anyone else to talk it over, either his clerks or one of his brethren. Hugo said no. Hugo is being very short with me, a fact I attribute to his great turmoil and to the side effects of the prednisone. Essentially, though, the great kindness and pool of love is there and undisturbed. My heart aches for him. He seems so weak in body but still so strong in spirit. His mind focuses fine and he argues with vigor. He knows exactly what he will say in his letter of resignation to the President. He is not only discouraged over his own condition but the condition of the country, with its fragmented groups throwing rocks, and obtaining demands by violence, and with the President fighting with the Court, as shown by his recent statement favoring aid to parochial schools and opposing busing as set out in Burger's opinion. Hugo thinks there may be great constitutional fights ahead and he does not have the health or the vigor to fight them through. He said if he were younger and healthier, he would stick with the fight to the bitter end.

Monday, August 23 Hugo spent all morning in bed staring starkly into space, waiting for Louis. He really is morose. He got Frances, who at last is back from her vacation, to find his opinion in the *Dombrowski* line that was in the file but did not come down because Potter Stewart went back on Hugo, and he told Frances to let the other two clerks read it. John Harmon, who is already familiar with Hugo's views, came back to the office today.

Louis Oberdorfer stayed for dinner. He and Hugo talked about *Dom-*

browski[18] and other cases, and Louis brought him photocopies of them. Poor Louis has gone back to clerking for Hugo. They really did not talk too much of the IMPENDING EVENT. Hugo will set his letter of retirement, if any, into motion on September 1, one day after he has seen Dr. Fox for his two-week check-up.

It is now 11:00 P.M. and Hugo is sitting at his desk reading *Dombrowski.*

Wednesday, August 25 What a day! Hugo was very morose and blue when he awakened. He stayed in bed all morning. I called Dr. Fox and told him how poorly Hugo was, and he wanted me to bring him out at 1:00. Hugo flatly refused to go. Louis Oberdorfer came around 6:00 P.M. I told him they'd better write the letter and get it signed because if Hugo were to go down as much every day as he has every day this week, he may not be able to sign shortly. So he and Hugo wrestled with the verbiage, and I put in my two cents' worth occasionally. We decided to call Hugo, Jr., and Hugo told his dad he'd be up tomorrow. Hugo, Sr., knew very definitely what he wanted to say in the letter of retirement. He would not take some of Louis's suggestions, although he did take some, too. Then I had the job of typing it. I must have made twenty-five rough drafts. Fatigue had hit me. Louis finally left. Hugo and I went to bed exhausted.

Thursday, August 26 This morning I typed a perfect copy of Hugo's letter to the President. Hugo signed it, but said to hold it in abeyance until he decides exactly when to send it in. Dr. Fox talked Hugo into coming out for an exam. John Harlan called and was very concerned about Hugo. He wanted us to come by to see him. I found John looking much improved, although he still complains about his back. He wanted Hugo to talk to Dr. Fox, which Hugo did. Dr. Fox gave Hugo a pep talk and asked him to hold up on the letter for a couple of weeks. Later, Dr. Fox called and said he had discovered Hugo had high blood sugar which amounted to diabetes. He wants Hugo to come tomorrow to be admitted. Hugo, Jr., came in about 5:00 and Louis Oberdorfer came over for an hour. My Hugo is very ill-tempered and refuses to eat dinner or cooperate.

Friday, August 27 Hugo, very weak and much depressed, entered the hospital. The C.J. called home and left word for me to call back. I told him to act on any stays without consulting Hugo. John Harlan is still in the hospital in the adjoining room, but Hugo did not feel like seeing him. Dear Lord, how I am praying.

Saturday, August 28 One of the worst nights of my life. I went to sleep at 12:00 and woke up at 2:00 A.M. From then on I walked, I exercised,

I prayed aloud, I prayed silently. I turned over everything in my mind and I came to the conclusion that I may have to put Mother in a nursing home, traumatic though that may be. Every time I closed my eyes there were boiling tears underneath. Hugo himself is somewhat better. John Harlan came by to see him. The Chief Justice looked in on Hugo and stayed with John Harlan almost two hours. If John and Hugo quit (John thinks Thurgood may also be very ill), and if Bill Douglas's battery in his heart runs out, the Court is out of business! No quorum.

Sunday, August 29 Hugo's depression is deep and he has an "I give up" attitude. Hugo, Jr., is being marvelous. He is a great comfort to me. We talked to Jo at length. She wants to come down and Hugo, Jr., told her she could relieve him when he has to go home. Called Sterling and talked almost an hour. (My Hugo will have a fit when he sees the bill!) Sterling busy but plans to come if he has to.

Tuesday, August 31 Dr. Fox walked Hugo out to the sun porch. Hugo brightened up and chatted with the corpsmen a little. He told them he didn't think a bath was medically necessary, but if it made them happier, for their sake he would take a bath. Hugo, Jr., and I stayed on with him. Hugo, Sr., stared at call lights flashing on the wall and took his finger and traced a circle and said, "There they go twirling and twirling, it's an insoluble problem. It's the women, but I don't want my wife to be their leader." Hugo, Jr., and I exchanged startled looks and found out later his blood sugar was up. We brought him back to bed. I fed him his supper and he looked at the flashing light again and said he wished "they" would quit twirling. I said, "What?" He said, "It's an insoluble problem. I can't solve it and John Harlan can't solve it. We both better get off. But I don't want you to be a victim of it." This really shook Hugo, Jr., and me up.

Wednesday, September 1 Mother is dreadfully worried about Hugo. She says she wants to die before Hugo does. I told her we have to live as long as the Lord lets us. I tried to cheer her up and succeeded somewhat.

Hugo wants it clearly understood that he wants *all* his Conference papers *burned.* Louis brought a draft of a memo on the subject to Frances, which Hugo signed after telling Hugo, Jr., two phrases to insert.

The C.J. made headlines today by saying some judges are misinterpreting the Court's busing decision. He said that schools did not have to bus to achieve an exact racial balance. John Harlan said he got some thoughts last night he wanted to try out on Hugo but decided not to bother him. They found a lump in John's throat today and will take a biopsy next Friday. He jokes about his condition, the hospital, everything, but he is in a bad way too. Dr. Fox talked to Hugo and questioned him about whether he thought his mind and memory were fuzzy. He remembered our conversation of yesterday and he suddenly looked up and saw the same whirling insoluble problem on the wall. Poor, poor dear. Today was the day Hugo had first set to let his letter of retirement go to the President. However, we are going to wait a while and not rush it.

Thursday, September 2 Hugo was much better, sitting up in a chair, and in a more cooperative mood. Hugo, Jr., went in town to deliver to Frances Lamb the written and signed order to burn all Hugo's intra-office Conference notes. While he was there, a television news reporter, Claire Crawford, called and said a reliable source had reported that Justice Black was in the Naval Hospital desperately ill. Frances said, "Who is the reliable source?" She said she couldn't say, so Frances said as far as she was concerned the Judge was on vacation. Crawford called the hospital and the C.O. confirmed Hugo was there but that his condition was satisfactory. When we got home Lizzie Mae had had calls from everybody. Anyway, Claire Crawford came on television at 7:00 and said Hugo was in the hospital and if he retires the liberals and the conservatives would both miss him.

Friday, September 3 The press is hot on the trail. Hugo insists on "no comment." Hugo is adamant that his papers showing the Conference notes be burned. Hugo is so unlike himself, not really appearing to care whether I am here or not, and this really gets to me, although I frequently go and put my arms around him and tell him to squeeze me. Then he says, "I love you very much, darling."

The desk here on Tower 17 reports several tricks employed by the press to get information. Hugo, Jr., looks in on John Harlan frequently, and he too is quite depressed. I think it is cruel punishment to take a biopsy from a man on Friday and tell him it will be the following Tuesday before they can report. However, the doctor did come in and say the preliminary report was benign. John Harlan keeps his sense of humor and, although he must be depressed, he shows little sign of it. Hugo is grim! And emphatic! And grudgingly cooperative. After feeding Hugo his dinner and seeing him to bed, Hugo, Jr., and I usually stop off a moment or so with John Harlan to cheer him up and help him with drinking his "Rebel Yell" whiskey. John influences the corpsmen on the floor to save him some ice and plastic glasses for his little cocktail hour.

Saturday, September 4 Hugo is still insisting they get to work on the paper-burning. He's afraid he might be enjoined or stopped from doing so. Hugo was very grumpy all day. When the Chief Justice came to see John Harlan, Hugo told me to stop him from coming in here. The nurse, Miss Crumpton, ran in and said the C.J. was coming and Hugo said, "No, I can't help *him* and he can't help *me*!" Nurse Crumpton said, "Where is our Southern hospitality?" But Hugo was adamant. Hugo, Jr., told the nurse to get his father tucked in for a nap and he and I sat in the corridor and waylaid the C.J. and talked to him quite a while in the sun parlor. Later Miss Crumpton told us she had frequently seen patients withdraw from loved ones and friends when they thought they were terminally ill. She thought patients did this to make the pain of parting more bearable.

Monday, September 6 Labor Day. Hugo, Jr., Spencer, and Frances worked at the office to gather up Hugo's *cert* notes for burning. Hugo, Jr., is having second thoughts about delaying too long to submit "The Letter,' so he is going to hasten the burning process.

Tuesday, September 7 Jo arrives. Hugo, Sr., was very glad to see her, although he hated to put her out, with leaving the kids and all. Later in the day Hugo let Jo and me walk him, but it was an almost superhuman exercise of willpower for him to make the steps.

Hugo, Jr., is absolutely torn about having to burn *all* his father's papers; the *cert* notes he doesn't mind, but all the interoffice stuff over thirty-four years. That is tearing at him too.

Wednesday, September 8 We rushed out to Bethesda because Hugo had had a change, maybe a stroke. However, when we got there, though Hugo did look bad, we found him more like himself than he had been in weeks. The old tenderness was manifest and he said to me, "You're mighty sweet." He was tender with Jo and Hugo, Jr., and his mind seemed to function fine. A neurologist came and tested him for a stroke. The doctor's response was that he did not think Hugo had suffered a stroke. Since Hugo was running a temperature, he thought it possible Hugo was getting an infection. But Hugo was more like himself psychologically!

Thursday, September 9 It is 5:30 now, and Hugo is sleeping, poor darling. He looks so sick as I study his profile. Jo and Hugo, Jr., are in with John Harlan, and I just came out of the "Rebel Yell" hour. John learned today that he has a tumor on his spine; whether it's benign or malignant they won't know until Monday when they take the biopsy. Strangely enough, he says he's relieved.

Friday, September 10 I was almost fearful to go to Tower 17. However, when we arrived we found Hugo a wee bit better. He was sweet and gentle with us all and for that reason the day seemed easier. We remembered that fourteen years ago today we were getting ready to get married and we talked nostalgically about the wedding. He responded to my "I love you, darling," with "I love you, darling."

Last night Jo found me weeping in Hugo's chair in the study, and, God bless her, with perfect control over her own broken heart, she marched me out of it and we talked until 2:00.

Saturday, September 11 Our fourteenth wedding anniversary. I am sitting here at his bedside, my heart swollen with love and pity. I just put down his *Constitutional Faith,* which acted last night as my "shoulder" to sleep on. I reread his beautiful inscription to me, the preface, and the epilogue.

After frantic efforts, we finally hit on the simple answer to burning the papers. Hugo, Jr., and Frances selected the papers to burn over Labor Day. Spencer tried to burn them in our fireplace, but the lady next door came running over and complained that ashes were all over her swimming pool and floating in the water. Virginia has a law against open burning, so Spencer had to stop. Fred suggested we come out to his house in Maryland to burn the papers in his outdoor incinerator.

Cynthia and Al Boyer, Jo's good friends, Jo, and Hugo, Jr., have now gone to get the five or six enormous boxes, representing Hugo's thirty-four years of *cert* notes, in "Operation Frustrate-the-Historians." Hugo believes one man's papers only reflect one-ninth of the true picture, and he wants to contribute to no distorted picture of history. I told Janice and Fred they would have some historic ashes. We're all part of the team now, and working beautifully together. Last night, down on my knees alone, I may have found strength and courage to pull me through this crisis and pray God I may get him back.

3:30 P.M. Bad rain and thunderstorm, as though the heavens are frowning on the burning. It took over six hours to accomplish the mission. I waited anxiously at the hospital, sitting first in Hugo's room and then in the sun room. John Harlan asked me, "Have you heard from the cloak-and-dagger bunch?" John wanted to buy some champagne for an anniversary celebration in Hugo's room. But since I wouldn't participate without Hugo and he wasn't able to join in, I gratefully thanked John and declined.

Sunday, September 12 Jo and Hugo, Jr., left at 10:30 for New York. Sterling coming Monday.

Monday, September 13 Sterling and Nancy came in from New Mexico. When we got to the hospital, Hugo was almost asleep. When Hugo awakened, Sterling came in and his dad greeted him and told him he was glad he had come. Nancy came and stood by Hugo. She was dressed all in red and Hugo noted it.

They took a biopsy on a tumor in John Harlan's spine and won't know until tomorrow about the results, but he is game and brave and lonely and we talked a lot with him in a cheerful vein.

Tuesday, September 14 A heart-rending day. John Harlan likes Nurse Crumpton, who is a lieutenant commander in the Navy. John says in view of the expertise with which she administers shots in the rear, he was in favor of promoting her to rear admiral. Poor John was waiting to hear the results of his biopsy. At 4:00 P.M. three doctors went in and we waited with bated breath. You'd never guess! The lab goofed and lost his biopsy! John's eyes were full of tears and I went in several times to try to console him. He refuses to undergo it again. Says he has lived a good life and if he dies, so what! Hugo, too, was very bad, hurting and saying, "Oh, oh." Dear God, how it tears my heart!

Wednesday, September 15 I entered Mother in Circle Terrace Hospital in Alexandria. She's scared but rends my heart with her bravery. She wants me to go on to Bethesda to be with the Judge. I found Hugo more responsive. As I fed him, a tear rolled down his cheek. He said, "Do you see that? I have a wetness on my cheek. It's a teardrop. I'm sad." He breaks my heart.

Sterling and Nancy said goodbye to Hugo, Sr., and they went in to talk to him. Hugo, Sr., raised his hand, as if in a benediction, when they left and said, "I love you both."

Hugo, Jr., who is back with Graham, has been in touch saying the Naval Hospital has dreadful pressure from the press, and even one of Nixon's aides called. Nixon is the Commander-in-Chief and they have to reply to him. Hugo, Jr., released a statement about Hugo's illness. He also called Burger and consulted with John Harlan in regard to what John would do about giving the press a statement concerning himself.

Hugo, Jr., decided to talk to his daddy as he fed him his supper and found Hugo, Sr., very positive in his thinking. He said, "Daddy, we *all* want you to get off the Court now," and Hugo said, "I *can't* serve." And Hugo, Jr., said the papers were burned and did he want us to send the letter to the President? Hugo, Jr., told his dad there were two reasons he might not want to: (1) he might want to hang on for six months and beat all records of longevity (Hugo, Jr., thought Chief Justice Burger was willing to go along); (2) there was an insurance policy to me that would shrink from $20,000 active to $5,000 retired service. I was proud that my Hugo said, "That does not make *any* difference! I *can't* serve." So I think we're cranking up to send the letter tomorrow.

Louis Oberdorfer came over at 5:00 and consulted with us.

Friday, September 17 With a sense of destiny I got up out of bed and retrieved from the file the two letters of retirement Hugo had signed, identical except one was dated and one was not. I took the undated one, ran it into the typewriter, and put in "September 17, 1971." I then addressed a letter to "The President, The White House, Washington, D.C." and put a notation on the bottom, "Delivered by hand by Mr. Spencer Campbell." With a numb feeling I gave it to Hugo, Jr., who was leaving to pick up Jo at the airport, and they would go thence to the Court. We also called and talked to the Chief, who said he would send Spencer to the White House in his limousine. I went to Bethesda and had a call from friends saying they had just heard it announced by the White House that Hugo had retired. I turned on the television and heard a little about it through Hugo's bathroom door as I fed him, as he did not want a television in here. He perked up his ears when he heard Chief Justice Burger's name mentioned as being picketed as he made a dedicatory speech. But he lost interest when the topic changed, and was not even interested when his own name was mentioned. He said, "It doesn't make any difference."

That night Hugo, Jr., related his and Jo's experience at the office. They had met with the C.J., Frances, and the clerks. The C.J. assured all the office they would have a job. Frances Lamb was crying. Spencer made all the brethren a copy of Hugo's letter of retirement and also the "Memorandum to my Brethren" memo I had typed.

Later in the evening Marion and Byron White came by. Marion and I fell weeping into each other's arms.

Sunday, September 19 Hugo suffered a small stroke and the hospital has him on the "serious list."

Monday, September 20 Hugo, Jr., and I are in the deepest dumps. Heretofore Hugo, Jr., has been optimistic. President Nixon's secretary called and said President Nixon wanted to come out to visit Hugo. Hugo, Jr., expressed our deepest gratitude but told the secretary it would be better for him not to since Hugo was unable physically to move into a better secured area of the hospital. We are deeply appreciative. I don't know who is the sadder sack, me or Hugo, Jr. I am sitting in the corner of my darling's room responding when he awakens. He knows I am here.

Tuesday, September 21 Mother in bad shape. Hugo same as yesterday. My heart is breaking. Jo and I rushed out here and arrived at 1:00. We have to fight back the tears when we look at Hugo. Miss Crumpton is wonderful. She is fighting for his life. I never saw such a dedicated nurse.

Wednesday, September 22 The doctors say that Mother most likely has cancer. [Mrs. Seay died at 7:40 P.M. on Friday, October 22, 1971.] Hugo is almost comatose. My whole world is falling apart.

I have sat with Hugo all afternoon. So many beautiful letters and tributes coming in to Hugo acknowledging the debt of gratitude we all owe him for fighting for our rights as a free people. They swell my heart.

Thursday, September 23 Hugo is very low and his condition has deteriorated. About 1:30 John Harlan's two law clerks brought Hugo a personal letter. It was a copy of John's letter to the President retiring from the bench. [John Harlan died on December 29, 1971.] Again our hearts were saddened that another titan and giant was leaving our beloved bench. As I sat here with Hugo, my heart ached to see the life ebbing from my great man, my beloved. Life ahead looks very empty. I spent the night in the adjoining room.

Friday, September 24 President Johnson called today from the airport to express his sorrow and regret and his and Bird's prayers for Hugo and the family. Hugo, Sr., we believe is comatose, or semi-so.

Saturday, September 25 Our great man, my beloved Hugo, breathed his last breath at 1:00 A.M. I stayed with Hugo until 11:00 P.M., stroking his beautiful hand and telling him constantly how much I loved him. At 11:00 I kissed him goodnight and went into the next room to lie down. I finally drifted off to sleep. About 1:00 Hugo, Jr., and Jo came in. Jo said, "Elizabeth, Daddy just died." That brave Jo and brave Hugo. I wasn't so brave, I'm afraid. My first thought was, "I wasn't with him." Jo said, "You were with him. As far as I'm concerned, we were all with him, including Sterling." They packed all our stuff and Hugo's sweet clothes. I left my radio for the corpsmen on our floor who had been so good. They offered to put me in a wheelchair to take me downstairs. Hugo, Jr., said, "What?

Daddy's tennis player having to go out in a wheelchair?" I declined. And so our long and loving vigil ended.

Tuesday, September 28 Hugo's pine box, the rudely made casket we believed he'd want, sat today on a perch of royal purple velour in the National Cathedral. Everyone was present, all the family, the clerks, the Court, the President . . . Hugo's favorite Baptist country hymns were played, and Dean Sayre of the Cathedral read the 121st Psalm, "I will lift up mine eyes," and Hugo's standby, I Corinthians 13, about faith, hope, and charity. Duncan Howlett, Hugo's friend and the Unitarian minister, had readings underscored by Hugo in the classics and did the one starting "As Virgil sweetly sings," which Hugo always wanted read at his funeral. After the service, the Cathedral bell tolled eighty-five times, one for each year of Hugo's life. The pallbearers were his brethren with the exception of poor, stricken John Harlan, who wanted so much to be present. At Arlington Cemetery Duncan Howlett repeated the scripture and this time he said, "The greatest of these is *love.*" Three cannon shots rang out as a salute. The flag was folded and presented to me. Then Hugo's body was lowered into the earth. As I walked sadly to the car, I thought that actually my darling had died when he sent in his letter of retirement. Very little of him remained after that.

Late in the afternoon, seeking a moment of solitude, I went out under the grape arbor to look at the sunset. I saw velvety grass, Hugo's fig trees, and the tennis court where we'd had so much fun. It seemed unbearable that my man was gone.

But then I remembered. Had not Hugo written in my book, "To Elizabeth with a love that has no end." I knew then that we were like two tall pine trees standing in the forest. One had fallen, but the Alabama roots remain forever entwined.

Notes

1964

[1]*Bell* v. *Maryland* (378 U.S. 226), involving the question whether Maryland could apply its trespass laws to Negroes who sat down at private lunch counters to protest racial discrimination.

[2]*Engel* v. *Vitale,* 370 U.S. 421 (1962).

[3]*Bell* v. *Maryland,* 378 U.S. 226, 318 (June 22, 1964), Justice Black dissenting:

> We conclude as we do because we remember that it *is* a Constitution and that it is our duty "to bow with respectful submission to its provisions." Our duty is simply to interpret the Constitution, and in doing so the test of constitutionality is not whether a law is offensive to our conscience or to the "good old common law," but whether it is offensive to the Constitution. Confining ourselves to the constitutional duty to construe, not to rewrite or amend, the Constitution, we believe that Section 1 of the Fourteenth Amendment does not bar Maryland from enforcing its trespass laws so long as it does so with impartiality. The Fourteenth Amendment of itself does not compel either a black man or a white man running his own private business to trade with anyone else against his will. At times the rule of law seems too slow to some for the settlement of their grievances. But it is the plan our Nation has chosen to preserve both "Liberty" and equality for all. On that plan we have put our trust and staked our future. This constitutional rule of law has served us well. Maryland's trespass law does not depart from it. Nor shall we.

1965

[1]*Cox* v. *Louisiana,* 379 U.S. 559, 575 (1965), Justice Black dissenting in No. 49:

> Justice cannot be rightly administered, nor are lives and safety of prisoners secure, where throngs of people clamor against the processes of justice right outside the courthouse or jailhouse door. The streets are not now and never have been the proper place to administer justice.

Minority groups in particular need always to bear in mind that the Constitution, while it requires States to treat all citizens equally and protect them in the exercise of rights granted by the Federal Constitution and laws, does not take away the State's power, indeed its duty, to keep order and to do justice according to law. Those who encourage minority groups to believe that the United States Constitution and federal laws give them a right to patrol and picket in the streets whenever they choose, in order to advance what they think to be a just and noble end, do no service to those minority groups, their cause, or their country.

[2]*El Paso* v. *Simmons,* 379 U.S. 497, 517 (1965), Justice Black dissenting:

I have previously had a number of occasions to dissent from judgments of this Court balancing away the First Amendment's unequivocally guaranteed rights of free speech, press, assembly, and petition. In this case I am compelled to dissent from the Court's balancing away the plain guarantee of Art. I, § 10, that "No State shall . . . pass any . . . Law impairing the Obligation of Contracts . . . ," a balancing which results in the State of Texas' taking a man's private property for public use without compensation in violation of the equally plain guarantee of the Fifth Amendment, made applicable to the States by the Fourteenth, that ". . . private property [shall not] be taken for public use, without just compensation."

[3]*Chambers* v. *Florida,* 309 U.S. 227 (February 12, 1940). Justice Black opened his opinion for the Court by saying:

The grave question presented by the petition for certiorari, granted in forma pauperis, is whether proceedings in which confessions were utilized, and which culminated in sentences of death upon four young negro men in the State of Florida, failed to afford the safeguard of that due process of law guaranteed by the Fourteenth Amendment.

After detailing the facts, Justice Black's opinion continued:

Here, the record shows, without conflict, the protracted questioning and cross questioning of these ignorant young colored tenant farmers by state officers and other white citizens, in a fourth floor jail room, where as prisoners they were without friends, advisors or counselors, and under circumstances calculated to break the strongest nerves and the stoutest resistance.

The convictions were reversed and the death sentences set aside.

[4]*United States* v. *Mississippi,* 380 U.S. 128 (1965); *Louisiana* v. *United States,* 380 U.S. 145 (1965). In the latter case, Justice Black wrote that

colored people, even some with the most advanced education and scholarship, were declared by voting registrars with less education to have an unsatisfactory understanding of the Constitution of Louisiana or of the United States. This is not a test but a trap, sufficient to stop even the most brilliant man on his way to the voting booth. The cherished right of people in a country like ours to vote cannot be obliterated by the use of laws like this, which leave the voting fate of a citizen to the passing whim or impulse of an individual registrar.

[5]*Griswold* v. *Connecticut,* 381 U.S. 479 (1965).

[6]JUSTICE BLACK: It seems to me—what someone has done here deliberately—is to try to force a decision on the broadest possible grounds of the meaning of "due process" —speaking as a matter of substance—, and to have us weigh facts and circumstances as to the advisability of a law like this rather than leave it up to the legislature. You pitch it wholly on due process, with the broad idea that we can look to see how

reasonable or unreasonable the decision of the people of Connecticut has been in connection with this statute.
EMERSON: We pitch it on due process in the basic sense, yes, that it is arbitrary and unreasonable, and in the special sense that it constitutes a deprivation of right against invasion of privacy. The privacy argument is a substantially narrower one than the general argument.
BLACK: That's a due process argument?
EMERSON: That's correct. They're both due process; they're both due process.
BLACK: You expect us to determine whether it's sufficiently shocking to our sense of what ought to be the law, because this applies to married people only?
EMERSON: Yes, Your Honor. But it is not broad due process in the sense in which the issue was raised in the 1930's. We are not asking this Court to revive *Lochner* against *New York*—
BLACK: It sounds to me like you're asking us to follow the constitutional philosophy of that case.

7"We hold today that the Sixth Amendment's right of an accused to confront the witnesses against him is a fundamental right and is made obligatory on the States by the Fourteenth Amendment." *Pointer* v. *Texas,* 380 U.S. 400, 403 (1965).

8*Zemel* v. *Rusk,* 381 U.S. 1, 20 (1965), Justice Black dissenting:

> Our Constitution has ordained that laws restricting the liberty of our people can be enacted by the Congress and by the Congress only. I do not think our Constitution intended that this vital legislative function could be farmed out in large blocks to any governmental official, whoever he might be, or to any governmental department or bureau, whatever administrative expertise it might be thought to have. It is irksome enough for one who wishes to travel to be told by the Congress, the constitutional lawmaker with power to legislate in this field, that he cannot go where he wishes. It is bound to be far more irritating—and I do not think the authors of our Constitution, who gave "All" legislative power to Congress, intended—for a citizen of this country to be told that he cannot get a passport because Congress has given unlimited discretion to an executive official (or viewed practically, to his subordinates) to decide when and where he may go.

9*United States* v. *California,* 381 U.S. 139, 178 (1965), Justice Black dissenting:

> It seems to me the height of irony to hold that an Act passed expressly to escape the effect of this Court's [1947] opinion in this field is now construed as leaving us free to announce principles directly antithetic to the basic purpose of Congress of deciding that question for itself once and for all.

10*Mapp* v. *Ohio,* 367 U.S. 643 (1961).

11*Linkletter* v. *Walker,* 381 U.S. 618, 640 (1965), Justice Black, with whom Justice Douglas joins, dissenting:

> This different treatment of Miss Mapp and Linkletter points up at once the arbitrary and discriminatory nature of the judicial contrivance utilized here to break the promise of *Mapp.* The Court offers no defense based on any known principle of justice for discriminating among defendants who were similarly convicted by use of evidence unconstitutionally seized. It certainly offends my sense of justice to say that a State holding in jail people who were convicted by unconstitutional methods has a vested interest in keeping them there that outweighs the right of persons adjudged guilty of crime to challenge their unconstitutional convictions at any time.

[12]*Griswold* v. *Connecticut,* 381 U.S. 479, 507 (1965), Justice Black dissenting:

"Privacy" is a broad, abstract and ambiguous concept which can easily be shrunken in meaning but which can also, on the other hand, easily be interpreted as a constitutional ban against many things other than searches and seizures. I get nowhere in this case by talk about a constitutional "right of privacy" as an emanation from one or more constitutional provisions. I like my privacy as well as the next one, but I am nevertheless compelled to admit that government has a right to invade it unless prohibited by some specific constitutional provision.

I realize that many good and able men have eloquently spoken and written, sometimes in rhapsodical strains, about the duty of this Court to keep the Constitution in tune with the times. The idea is that the Constitution must be changed from time to time and that this Court is charged with a duty to make those changes. For myself, I must with all deference reject that philosophy. The Constitution makers knew the need for change and provided for it. Amendments suggested by the people's elected representatives can be submitted to the people or their selected agents for ratification. That method of change was good for our Fathers, and being somewhat old-fashioned I must add it is good enough for me.

[13]*Wolf* v. *Colorado,* 338 U.S. 25 (1949).

1966

[1]*United States* v. *Yazell,* 382 U.S. 341, 359 (1966), Justice Black, with whom Justice Douglas and Justice White join, dissenting:

The Texas law of "coverture," which was adopted by its judges and which the State's legislature has now largely abandoned, rests on the old common-law fiction that the husband and wife are one. This rule has worked out in reality to mean that though the husband and wife are one, the one is the husband. This fiction rested on what I had supposed is today a completely discredited notion that a married woman, being a female, is without capacity to make her own contracts and to do her own business. I say "discredited" reflecting on the vast number of women in the United States engaging in the professions of law, medicine, teaching, and so forth, as well as those engaged in plain old business ventures as Mrs. Yazell was. It seems at least unique to me that this Court in 1966 should exalt this archaic remnant of a primitive caste system to an honored place among the laws of the United States.

[2]*Evans* v. *Newton,* 382 U.S. 296, 312 (1966), Justice Black dissenting:

I find nothing in the United States Constitution that compels any city or other state subdivision to hold title to property it does not want or to act as trustee under a will when it chooses not to do so.

Nothing that I have said is to be taken as implying that Baconsfield Park could at this time be operated by successor trustees on a racially discriminatory basis. Questions of equal protection of all people without discrimination on account of color are of paramount importance in this Government dedicated to equal justice for all. We can accord that esteemed principle the respect it is due, however, without distorting the constitutional structure of our Government by taking away from the States that which is their due.

[3]*Brown* v. *Louisiana,* 383 U.S. 131, 151 (1966), Justice Black dissenting:

I do not believe that any provision of the United States Constitution forbids any one of the 50 states of the Union, including Louisiana, to make it unlawful to stage "sit-ins" or "stand-ups" in their public libraries for the purpose of advertising objections to the State's public policies.

It is high time to challenge the assumption in which too many people have too long acquiesced, that groups that think they have been mistreated or that have actually been mistreated have a constitutional right to use the public's streets, buildings, and property to protest whatever, wherever, whenever they want, without regard to whom such conduct may disturb. Though the First Amendment guarantees the right of assembly and the right of petition along with the rights of speech, press, and religion, it does not guarantee to any person the right to use someone else's property, even that owned by government and dedicated to other purposes, as a stage to express dissident ideas.

[4]*South Carolina* v. *Katzenbach,* 383 U.S. 301, 355 (1966).

[5]*Surowitz* v. *Hilton Hotels Corp.,* 383 U.S. 363 (1966). Justice Black delivered the opinion of the Court:

Mrs. Surowitz, the plaintiff and petitioner here, is a Polish immigrant with a very limited English vocabulary and practically no formal education. For many years she has worked as a seamstress in New York where by reason of frugality she saved enough money to buy some thousands of dollars worth of stocks. This complaint was filed charging the defendants with creating and participating in a fraudulent scheme which had taken millions of dollars out of the corporation's treasury and transferred the money to the defendants' pockets.

The basic purpose of the Federal Rules is to administer justice through fair trials, not through summary dimissals as necessary as they may be on occasion. These rules were designed in large part to get away from some of the old procedural booby traps which common-law pleaders could set to prevent unsophisticated litigants from ever having their day in court. If rules of procedure work as they should in an honest and fair judicial system, they not only permit, but should as nearly as possible guarantee that bona fide complaints be carried to an adjudication on the merits. The dismissal of this case was error. It has now been practically three years since the complaint was filed and as yet none of the defendants have been compelled to admit or deny the wrongdoings charged. The case is reversed and remanded to the District Court for trial on the merits.

[6]*South Carolina* v. *Katzenbach,* 383 U.S. 301, 355 (1966), Justice Black dissenting:

Section 5, by providing that some of the States cannot pass state laws or adopt state constitutional amendments without first being compelled to beg federal authorities to approve their policies, so distorts our constitutional structure of government as to render any distinction drawn in the Constitution between state and federal power almost meaningless. I cannot help but believe that the inevitable effect of any such law which forces any one of the States to entreat federal authorities in far-away places for approval of local laws before they can become effective is to create the impression that the State or States treated in this way are little more than conquered provinces. It is inconceivable to me that such a radical degradation of state power was intended in any of the provisions of our Constitution or its Amendments. A federal law which assumes the power to compel the States to submit in advance any proposed legislation they have for approval by federal agents approaches dangerously near to wiping the States out as useful and effective units in the government of our country. I cannot agree to any constitutional interpretation that leads inevitably to such a result.

[7]*A Book Named "John Cleland's Memoirs of a Woman of Pleasure"* [commonly known as *Fanny Hill*] v. *Attorney General of Massachusetts,* 383 U.S. 413 (1966); *Ginzburg* v. *United States,* 383 U.S. 463 (1966); *Mishkin* v. *New York,* 383 U.S. 502

(1966). In his dissent in the *Ginzburg* case, Justice Black repeated his view that "the Federal Government is without any power whatever under the Constitution to put any type of burden on speech and expression of ideas of any kind (as distinguished from conduct)," and he attacked the vagueness of "obscenity" prosecutions:

> The first element considered necessary for determining obscenity is that the dominant theme of the material taken as a whole must appeal to the prurient interest in sex. In the final analysis submission of such an issue as this to a judge or jury amounts to practically nothing more than a request for the judge or juror to assert his own personal beliefs about whether the matter should be allowed to be legally distributed. Upon this subjective determination the law becomes certain for the first and last time.
>
> It is obvious that the effect of the Court's decisions in the three obscenity cases handed down today is to make it exceedingly dangerous for people to discuss either orally or in writing anything about sex. Sex is a fact of life. Its pervasive influence is felt throughout the world and it cannot be ignored. Like all other facts of life it can lead to difficulty and trouble and sorrow and pain. But while it may lead to abuses, and has in many instances, no words need be spoken in order for people to know that the subject is one pleasantly interwoven in all human activities and involves the very substance of the creation of life itself. It is a subject which people are bound to consider and discuss whatever laws are passed by any government to try to suppress it. For myself I would follow the course which I believe is required by the First Amendment, that is, recognize that sex at least as much as any other aspect of life is so much a part of our society that its discussion should not be made a crime.

[8]*Harper* v. *Virginia Bd. of Elections,* 383 U.S. 663 (1966), Justice Black dissenting:

> In *Breedlove* v. *Suttles,* 302 U.S. 277, decided December 6, 1937, a few weeks after I took my seat as a member of this Court, we unanimously upheld the right of the State of Georgia to make payment of its state poll tax a prerequisite to voting in state elections. The Court, however, overrules *Breedlove* in part, but its opinion reveals that it does so not by using its limited power to interpret the original meaning of the Equal Protection Clause, but by giving that clause a new meaning which it believes represents a better governmental policy. Although I join the Court in disliking the policy of the poll tax, this is not in my judgment a justifiable reason for holding this poll tax law unconstitutional. Such a holding on my part would, in my judgment, be an exercise of power which the Constitution does not confer upon me.
>
> I have heretofore had many occasions to express my strong belief that there is no constitutional support whatever for this Court to use the Due Process Clause as though it provided a blank check to alter the meaning of the Constitution as written so as to add to it substantive constitutional changes which a majority of the Court at any given time believes are needed to meet present-day problems. Nor is there in my opinion any more constitutional support for this Court to use the Equal Protection Clause, as it has today, to write into the Constitution its notions of what it thinks is good governmental policy. When a "political theory" embodied in our Constitution becomes outdated, it seems to me that a majority of the nine members of this Court are not only without constitutional power but are far less qualified to choose a new constitutional political theory than the people of this country proceeding in the manner provided by Article V.

[9]*Sheppard* v. *Maxwell,* 384 U.S. 333 (1966), setting aside the criminal conviction of Dr. Sam Sheppard on account of inflammatory reporting of the case by the press. According to the Court, the trial judge should have more closely regulated the press.

[10]*Miranda* v. *Arizona,* 384 U.S. 436 (June 13, 1966).

[11]"This prosecution, now approaching its second decade and third trial, is a natural offspring of the McCarthy era," said Justice Black, opening his dissent in *Dennis* v. *United States,* 384 U.S. 855, 875 (1966).

[12]*Schmerber* v. *California,* 384 U.S. 757, 773 (1966), Justice Black dissenting:

> To reach the conclusion that compelling a person to give his blood to help the State convict him is not the equivalent to compelling him to be a witness against himself strikes me as quite an extraordinary feat. It is a strange hierarchy of values that allows the State to extract a human being's blood to convict him of a crime because of the blood's content but proscribes compelled production of his lifeless papers. With all deference I must say that the Court here gives the Bill of Rights' safeguard against compulsory self-incrimination a construction that would generally be considered too narrow and technical even in the interpretation of an ordinary commercial contract.

[13]There is no record of this split between Justices Fortas and Black in a published opinion at this time.

[14]*Time, Inc.* v. *Hill,* 385 U.S. 374 (January 9, 1967); Black concurring, Fortas dissenting.

[15]When the Chief Justice is not in the majority, the next senior Justice assigns the cases for writing the opinion of the Court.

[16]*Adderly* v. *Florida,* 385 U.S. 39 (1966). Justice Black delivered the opinion of the Court:

> The sheriff, as jail custodian, had power, as the state courts have here held, to direct that this large crowd get off the grounds. The State, no less than a private owner of property, has power to preserve the property under its control for the use to which it is lawfully dedicated. For this reason there is no merit to the petitioners' argument that people who want to propagandize protests or views have a constitutional right to do so whenever and however and wherever they please.

[17]*Fortson* v. *Morris,* 385 U.S. 231 (1966). The case involved the constitutionality of a provision of Georgia's Constitution allowing the Legislature to pick the Governor if no candidate received a majority vote. During the arguments, counsel for both sides got caught in the middle of heavy cross-fire from the bench:

> JUSTICE BLACK: Your position is that the Federal Constitution does not *compel* a state to elect its governor by the people.
> COUNSEL: That's right.
> JUSTICE DOUGLAS: Here the requirement is that the Legislature does it if no candidate gets the majority, is that right?
> COUNSEL: Yes, sir.
> DOUGLAS: Well, the formula in its implication may therefore be a very *mischievous* thing—for the political control, squeezing out minorities, squeezing out non-orthodox party people.
> BLACK: Well, what's wrong with the State of Georgia, if it wants to, providing that to elect a governor it would require two-thirds? Any question that the Constitution gives us the right, because we think that's mischievous, to overturn it?
> COUNSEL: Well, sir, I don't find a specific provision of the Constitution that would

tell me that would be unconstitutional, unless it happens to be, as Mr. Justice Douglas stated in his opinion in *Gray* v. *Sanders,* there has been a developing thing in the right to vote in this country.

BLACK: Well, you don't think we can say that because of a "developing idea" that this is unconstitutional.

COUNSEL: Well, let me put it this way. I think that this Court has an expanding view of the right of suffrage in America. And I think that expanding view has certainly shown up in recent years in the case of *Baker* v. *Carr* and *Reynolds* v. *Sims,* and beyond—

BLACK: They didn't have any expanding view as to the right of the state to select its officials by appointment rather than by election of the people.

COUNSEL: No, and as I say I don't find any specific reference to that. But I should think that we have to rely upon whatever expanding view we find.

DOUGLAS: Our decisions under the First, Fourth, Fifth, Sixth, Seventh, and Eighth Amendments certainly represent an "expanding view."

BLACK: What you're saying is that it's unconscionable not to elect the Governor. Suppose it is? Does this Court have the power to fasten its judgment on the people of Georgia, to add to the constitutional provisions because they think it's unconscionable not to elect a Governor?

COUNSEL: The citizens of Georgia deserve the right to make this decision for themselves where they all have an equal voice in the final selection. To deny them this right in the name of an 1824 constitutional provision—

BLACK: What's wrong with its age?

COUNSEL: I agree completely that not just age, but the changed policy—

BLACK: You have the same Federal Constitution, and you're here under federal law.

COUNSEL: We did not have the Fourteenth Amendment in 1824.

BLACK: We've had it since 1868.

COUNSEL: That's correct. It has the Seventeenth Amendment, putting the right to select Senators to the people. There is an increasing democratization of all of these choices.

BLACK: But that's why they amended the Federal Constitution.

COUNSEL: That's right.

BLACK: But the people amended it, and not this Court.

[18]Justice Black apparently thought a majority of the Court would vote to affirm. He wrote out a "dissent"—eight pages of yellow legal tablet—on Sunday night, which was typed up and circulated as a "Statement of my views on this case before oral argument" on Monday morning. Black quickly picked up a majority, however, and his "dissent" of Sunday night was at the printer's Tuesday morning as the opinion of the Court.

[19]"I have changed my mind in *Fortson* v. *Morris, et al.* and vote to affirm," Justice Brennan wrote the Conference on Tuesday, December 6. "I shall be ready to come down Monday, and except as other writing may require change, plan to file a dissent substantially as follows. . . ."

Justice Douglas sent Black a bench note during the arguments on Tuesday, saying: "I had a rough time thru the night on that Georgia case & finally made up my mind early this morning. I wrote the memo at home & sent it around as soon as it was typed. I'm really sorry if my uncertainty has caused you an inconvenience but I shall certainly be ready on Monday."

[20]*Arizona* v. *California,* 373 U.S. 546 (1963).

[21]Justice Black's Memorandum to the Conference, December 7, 1966:

I have just read the memorandum of Brother DOUGLAS who objects to handing down the vote of this Court to reverse, but not to affirm, this case before January 6—one month from now. Instead of attempting to announce our decision before that time, he argues "for a more deliberate slow speed rather than a deliberate fast one." With all deference to the views of my Brother DOUGLAS, I disagree with his reasoning and his conclusion.

It is impossible for me to believe that it would take any member of this Court a whole month to write out his dissenting views, whether he does so at a "deliberate slow speed" or at "a deliberate fast one." This Court's order now enjoins the General Assembly from proceeding to elect a Governor as the State's constitution requires. My Brother DOUGLAS appears to treat this as a very insignificant event. He goes on the theory, completely wrong I think, that the State has nothing more to do than to open the ballots and make an announcement. But the change in the gubernatorial administration of a State requires far more than this. It is an event of tremendous significance which requires much preparation on the part of both outgoing and incoming officials. To keep the State in doubt as to whether the Assembly will elect or whether provision must be made for one or more new elections means that the whole government of the State of Georgia must be at a standstill. The old Governor will not know when he goes out or under what circumstances a new Governor can come in. Georgia should not be put in this unhappy predicament on the unsupported and, I believe, unsupportable assumption that it may take some member of this Court a month to write his views.

Brother DOUGLAS says he "would like time to work further on it [his opinion] beyond this week." But he does not say that he wants or needs an extra month, and it is inconceivable that he does, in view of his well-known speed in writing all his opinions.

Finally, Brother DOUGLAS' reason for saying we should wait a month is that some member of the present majority might change his mind and vote Brother DOUGLAS' way—that is, to affirm. How long should Georgia be kept in ignorance of its constitutional power and have its machinery paralyzed on the hope that one of the present majority of five could be persuaded in some manner to reverse his vote? Members of this Court certainly are sufficiently mature to decide for themselves whether they need more time to announce their votes. Five have already indicated they need no more time by voting to reverse this case now. Whatever questionable reason there may be for waiting a few more days to announce this decision, Brother DOUGLAS advances none whatsoever for keeping Georgia in doubt for an entire month.

[22]*Fortson* v. *Morris,* 385 U.S. 231 (December 12, 1966). Justice Black delivered the opinion of the Court:

There is no provision of the United States Constitution or any of its amendments which either expressly or impliedly dictates the method a State must use to select its Governor. It would be surprising to conclude that, after a state has already held two primaries and one general election to try to elect by a majority, the United States Constitution compels it to continue to hold elections in a futile effort to obtain a majority for some particular candidate. Statewide elections cost time and money and it is not strange that Georgia's people decided to avoid repeated elections. The method they chose for this purpose was not unique, but was well known and frequently utilized before and since the Revolutionary War. Article V of Georgia's Constitution provides a method for selecting the Governor which is as old as the Nation itself. Georgia does not violate the Equal Protection Clause by following this article as it was written.

1967

[1]*Railroad Transfer Service* v. *Chicago,* 386 U.S. 351 (1967).

[2]*In re Gault,* 387 U.S. 1, 59 (1967), Justice Black concurring:

Where a person, infant or adult, can be seized by the State, charged, and convicted for violating a state criminal law, and then ordered by the State to be confined for six years, I think the Constitution requires that he be tried in accordance with the guarantees of all the provisions of the Bill of Rights made applicable to the States by the Fourteenth Amendment.

A few words should be added because of the opinion of my Brother HARLAN who rests his concurrence and dissent on the Due Process Clause alone. Whether labelled as "procedural" or "substantive," the Bill of Rights safeguards were written into our Constitution not by judges but by Constitution makers. Freedom in this nation will be far less secure the very moment that it is decided that judges can determine which of these safeguards "should" or "should not be imposed" according to their notions of what constitutional provisions are consistent with the "traditions and conscience of our people." Judges with such power, even though they profess to "proceed with restraint," will be above the Constitution, with power to write it, not merely to interpret it, which I believe to be the only power constitutionally committed to judges.

[3]*Berger* v. *New York,* 388 U.S. 41, 70 (June 12, 1967), Justice Black dissenting:

While the electronic eavesdropping here bears some analogy to the problems with which the Fourth Amendment is concerned, I am by no means satisfied that the Amendment controls the constitutionality of such eavesdropping. The Amendment only bans searches and seizures of "persons, houses, papers, and effects." This literal language imports tangible things, and it would require an expansion of the language used by the framers, in the interest of "privacy" or some equally vague judge-made goal, to hold that it applies to the spoken word. It simply requires an imaginative transformation of the English language to say that conversations can be searched and words seized. But the Fourth Amendment gives no hint that it was designed to put an end to the age-old practice of using eavesdropping to combat crime.

Honest men may rightly differ on the potential dangers or benefits inherent in electronic eavesdropping and wiretapping. But that is the very reason that legislatures, like New York's, should be left free to pass laws about the subject, rather than to be told that the Constitution forbids it on grounds no more forceful than the Court has been able to muster in this case.

[4]*Curtis Publishing Co.* v. *Butts,* 388 U.S. 130, 170 (June 12, 1967), Justice Black, with whom Justice Douglas joins, dissenting:

These cases illustrate, I think, the accuracy of my prior predictions that the *New York Times* constitutional rule concerning libel is wholly inadequate to save the press from being destroyed by libel judgments. It strikes me that the Court is getting itself in the same quagmire in the field of libel in which it is now helplessly struggling in the field of obscenity. No one, including this Court, can know what is and what is not constitutionally obscene or libelous under this Court's rulings. Today the Court will not give the First Amendment its natural and obvious meaning by holding that a law which seriously menaces the very life of press freedom violates the First Amendment.

I think it is time for this Court to abandon *New York Times* v. *Sullivan* and adopt the rule to the effect that the First Amendment was intended to leave the press free from the harassment of libel judgments.

[5]*Katz* v. *United States,* 389 U.S. 347, 364 (December 18, 1967), Justice Black dissenting:

> There can be no doubt that the Framers were aware of this practice, and if they had desired to outlaw or restrict the use of evidence obtained by eavesdropping, I believe that they would have used the appropriate language to do so in the Fourth Amendment. They certainly would not have left such a task to the ingenuity of language-stretching judges. No one, it seems to me, can read the debates on the Bill of Rights without reaching the conclusion that its Framers and critics well knew the meaning of the words they used, what they would be understood to mean by others, their scope and their limitations. Under these circumstances it strikes me as a charge against their scholarship, their common sense and their candor to give to the Fourth Amendment's language the eavesdropping meaning the Court imputes to it today.

1968

[1]*Norfolk & W. R. Co.* v. *Missouri State Tax Comm'n,* 390 U.S. 317 (1968). Justice Black's dissent is two and a half pages in length, concluding:

> This Court has recognized before, and indeed the majority pays lip service to the fact today, that it is impossible for a State to develop tax statutes with mathematical perfection. Indeed, as was stated in *International Harvester Co.* v. *Evatt,* 329 U.S. 416 [1947, per Justice Black for the Court]: "Unless a palpably disproportionate result comes from an apportionment, a result which makes it patent that the tax is levied upon interstate commerce rather than upon an intrastate privilege, this Court has not been willing to nullify honest state efforts to make apportionments." 329 U.S., at 422–423. I would affirm the decision of the Missouri Supreme Court.

[2]*Flast* v. *Cohen,* 392 U.S. 83 (1968). The main question in the case was whether federal taxpayers have standing to sue government officials who are charged with using federal funds in aid of religious instruction in sectarian schools. The Court, in an opinion written by Chief Justice Warren, held that taxpayers can sue in federal court when they attack a federal spending program on the ground that it violates the Establishment Clause of the First Amendment. Only Justice Harlan dissented.

[3]JUSTICE BLACK: Do you differ with the interpretation of the First Amendment as it exists now?
SOLICITOR GENERAL GRISWOLD: No, not at all, I like it. This is not a case where the First Amendment says there shall be no "appropriation" for an establishment of religion. The First Amendment does prohibit an establishment of religion—
JUSTICE DOUGLAS: Counsel, do you know any better way to "establish" a religion than to finance it? [laughter]
GRISWOLD: I know that what constitutes an establishment of religion is a complex and difficult matter.
DOUGLAS: I didn't ask you that. I just put a simple question.
GRISWOLD: We have always had, and still have in this country—and I hope we will retain—tax exemptions for religious bodies; and that is certainly a substantial financial aid to religion which, until very recently, was never questioned in any way. I simply suggest that this is a far more complex question.
JUSTICE HARLAN: Are not we getting a little far afield here? We have not gotten to the merits of the controversy here.
GRISWOLD: I would welcome a chance to get back to the thread of my argument.
BLACK: You say they have to set down in meticulous details about where the money would be spent? I do not understand how you can say they do not charge, in plain and

unambiguous language, that money is being used from this bill to finance instruction in sectarian schools.

GRISWOLD: I say, Mr. Justice, that they do not allege facts which say that at a particular place, at a particular time, something can be done.

BLACK: Why should they have to allege facts about a particular thing, when they allege it in general? That's the general rule of pleadings.

GRISWOLD: The point I am trying to make, Mr. Justice, is that issues of this sort ought to be decided in specific, concrete cases, and not in purely general terms.

BLACK: You want to get back to common-law pleadings?

GRISWOLD: No, Mr. Justice, but I would like to have some facts upon which this case can stand.

BLACK: How can you get any more vigorous, heated controversy than a dispute between the people, and those charged, that the taxpayers' money is being spent to aid sectarian schools in teaching?

GRISWOLD: I think that may be a part of the trouble. People are talking about general terms.

BLACK: But the charge is that Government has been spending money in this Act for that purpose.

[4]*Simmons* v. *United States,* 390 U.S. 377, 395 (1968), Justice Black dissenting:

> The consequence of the Court's holding, it seems to me, is that defendants are encouraged to come into court, either in person or through witnesses, and swear falsely that they do not own property, knowing at the very moment they do so that they have already sworn precisely the opposite in a prior court proceeding. This is but to permit lawless people to play ducks and drakes with the basic principles of the administration of criminal law.
>
> There is certainly no language in the Fourth Amendment which gives support to any such device to hobble law enforcement in this country. While our Constitution does provide procedural safeguards to protect defendants from arbitrary convictions, that governmental charter holds out no promises to stultify justice by erecting barriers to the admissibility of relevant evidence voluntarily given in a court of justice. Under the first principles of ethics and morality a defendant who secures a court order by telling the truth should not be allowed to seek a court advantage later based on a premise directly opposite to his prior solemn judicial oath. This Court should not lend prestige of its high name to such a justice-defeating stratagem.

[5]*Mathis* v. *United States,* 391 U.S. 1 (1968). Justice Black delivered the opinion of the Court:

> We reject the contention that tax investigations are immune from the *Miranda* requirements for warnings to be given a person in custody. The Government seeks to narrow the scope of the *Miranda* holding by making it applicable only to questioning one who is "in custody" in connection with the very case under investigation. There is no substance to such a distinction, and in effect it goes against the whole purpose of the *Miranda* decision which was designed to give meaningful protection to Fifth Amendment rights. Thus, the courts below were wrong in permitting the introduction of petitioner's self-incriminating evidence given without warning of his right to be silent and right to counsel.

[6]*First Nat. Bank of Arizona* v. *Cities Service Co.,* 391 U.S. 253, 299 (1968), Justice Black, with whom the Chief Justice and Justice Brennan join, dissenting:

> An excuse for summary judgments has always been that they save time. If the time has come when the best speed record they can make is to take 11 years to

decide one of them, the idea of summary judgments as time-savers is a snare and delusion and the best service that could be rendered in this field would be to abolish summary judgment procedures, root and branch. The plain fact is that this case illustrates that the summary judgment technique tempts judges to take over the jury trial of cases, thus depriving parties of their constitutional right to trial by jury.

Lawsuits are not games. The end of each one of them, if courts remain true to the ancient traditions of justice, is to try each case in a way that permits truth to triumph. That has not been done here. Too much time has already been wasted in an effort to provide a summary disposition of a case that should not be disposed of that way.

7 *Food Employees Union* v. *Logan Valley Plaza,* 391 U.S. 308, 327 (1968), Justice Black dissenting:

I believe that, whether this Court likes it or not, the Constitution recognizes and supports the concept of private ownership of property. The Fifth Amendment provides that "[n]o person shall . . . be deprived of life, liberty, or property, without due process of law; nor shall private property be taken for public use, without just compensation." This means to me that there is no right to picket on the private premises of another to try to convert the owner or others to the views of the pickets. It also means, I think, that if this Court is going to arrogate to itself the power to act as the Government's agent to take a part of Weis' property to give to the pickets for their use, the Court should also award Weis just compensation for the property taken.

To hold that store owners are compelled by law to supply picketing areas for pickets to drive store customers away is to create a court-made law wholly disregarding the constitutional basis on which private ownership of property rests in this country. And of course picketing, that is patrolling, is not free speech and not protected as such. *Giboney* v. *Empire Storage & Ice Co.,* 336 U.S. 490 [1949, per Justice Black, for a unanimous Court].

8 *Duncan* v. *Louisiana,* 391 U.S. 145, 162 (1968), Justice Black concurring:

I conclude, contrary to my Brother HARLAN, that if anything, it is "exceedingly peculiar" to read the Fourteenth Amendment differently from the way I do. His view is that "due process is an evolving concept." Another tenet of my Brother HARLAN is that "due process of law requires only fundamental fairness." But the "fundamental fairness" test is one on a par with that of shocking the conscience of the Court. Each of such tests depends entirely on the particular judge's idea of ethics and morals instead of requiring him to depend on the boundaries fixed by the written words of the Constitution. Nothing in the history of the phrase "due process of law" suggests that constitutional controls are to depend on any particular judge's sense of values. The due process of law standard for a trial is one in accordance with the Bill of Rights and laws passed pursuant to constitutional power, guaranteeing to all alike a trial under the general law of the land.

In closing I want to emphasize that I believe as strongly as ever that the Fourteenth Amendment was intended to make the Bill of Rights applicable to the States.

9 *Witherspoon* v. *Illinois,* 391 U.S. 510, 532 (1968), Justice Black dissenting:

With all due deference it seems to me that one might charge that this Court has today written the law in such a way that the States are being forced to try their murder cases with biased juries. If this Court is to hold capital punishment unconstitutional, I think it should do so forthrightly, not by making it impossible for States to get juries that will enforce the death penalty.

I cannot accept the proposition that persons who do not have conscientious scruples against the death penalty are "prosecution prone." This conclusion represents a psychological foray into the human mind that I have considerable doubt about my ability to make, and I must confess that the two or three so-called "studies" cited by the Court on this subject are not persuasive to me. I shall not contribute in any way to the destruction of our ancient judicial and constitutional concept of trial by an impartial jury by forcing the States through "constitutional doctrine" laid down by this Court to accept jurors who are bound to be biased.

[10]*Bumper* v. *North Carolina,* 391 U.S. 543, 554 (1968), Justice Black dissenting:

This is a case where the evidence conclusively showed that the accused twice raped a young woman at gunpoint, shot both the woman and her companion while they were tied helplessly to trees with the announced intention of killing them, and left them for dead.

My study of the record in this case convinces me that Mrs. Leath voluntarily consented to this search, and in fact that she actually wanted the officers to search her house—to prove to them that she had nothing to hide. As she herself testified, "I just give them a free will to look because I felt like the boy wasn't guilty." This Court, refusing to accept Mrs. Leath's sworn testimony that she did freely consent and overruling the trial judge's findings, concludes on its own that she did not consent. I do not believe the Court should substitute what it believes Mrs. Leath should have said for what she actually said—"it was all my own free will."

Even assuming for the purposes of argument that there was no consent to search and that the rifle which was seized from Mrs. Leath's house should not have been admitted into evidence, I still believe the conviction should stand. For the overwhelming evidence in this case, even when the rifle and related testimony are excluded, amply demonstrates petitioner's guilt.

When it is clear beyond all shadow of a doubt, as here, that a defendant committed the crimes charged, I do not believe that this Court should enforce on the States a *"per se"* rule automatically requiring a new trial in every case where this Court concludes that some part of the evidence was obtained by an unreasonable search and seizure. The only effect of not automatically reversing all cases in which there has been a violation of the exclusionary rule will be to allow state convictions of obviously guilty defendants to stand. And they should stand.

[11]*Flast* v. *Cohen,* 392 U.S. 83 (1968), expressing "no view at all on the merits of appellants' claims," but holding only that "their complaint contains sufficient allegations to give them standing to invoke a federal court's jurisdiction for an adjudication on the merits."

[12]*Powell* v. *Texas,* 392 U.S. 514 (1968), affirming a criminal conviction for public drunkenness. Justice Black, joined by Justice Harlan, concurred:

Those who favor holding that public drunkenness cannot be made a crime rely to a large extent on their own notions of the wisdom of such a change in the law. A great deal of medical and sociological data is cited to us in support of this change. All in all, these arguments read more like a highly technical medical critique than an argument for deciding a question of constitutional law one way or another.

Of course, the desirability of this Texas statute should be irrelevant in a court charged with the duty of interpretation rather than legislation, and that should be the end of the matter. But since proponents of this grave constitutional change insist on offering their pronouncements on these questions of medical diagnosis and social policy, I am compelled to add that, should we follow their arguments, the Court would be venturing far beyond the realm of problems for which we are in a position to know what we are talking about.

This Court, instead of recognizing that the experience of human beings is the best way to make laws, is asked to set itself up as a board of Platonic Guardians to establish rigid, binding rules upon every community in this large Nation for the control of the unfortunate people who fall victims to drunkenness. It is always time to say that this Nation is too large, too complex and composed of too great a diversity of peoples for any one of us to have the wisdom to establish the rules by which local Americans must govern their local affairs. I join in affirmance of this conviction.

[13]In his concurring opinion in *Duncan* v. *Louisiana,* 391 U.S. 145, 162 (1968), decided the previous May, Justice Black also gave short shrift to the Professor:

My Brother HARLAN's objections to my *Adamson* dissent history, like that of most of the objectors, relies most heavily on a criticism written by Professor Charles Fairman and published in the Stanford Law Review. 2 Stan. L. Rev. 5 (1949). I have read and studied this article extensively, including the historical references, but am compelled to add that in my view it has completely failed to refute the inferences and arguments that I suggested in my *Adamson* dissent. Professor Fairman's "history" relies very heavily on what was *not* said in the state legislatures that passed on the Fourteenth Amendment. Instead of relying on this kind of negative pregnant, my legislative experience has convinced me that it is far wiser to rely on what *was* said, and most importantly, said by the men who actually sponsored the Amendment in the Congress. The historical appendix to my *Adamson* dissent leaves no doubt in my mind that both its sponsors and those who opposed it believed the Fourteenth Amendment made the first eight Amendments of the Constitution (Bill of Rights) applicable to the States.

[14]*Allen* v. *State Board of Elections,* 393 U.S. 544 (1969). This Virginia case and three companion cases from Mississippi all involved application of Section 5 of the Voting Rights Act of 1965 forbidding certain named Southern states from changing their election laws without first obtaining the permission of the U.S. Attorney General or a favorable declaratory judgment from the U.S. district court in the District of Columbia. During the oral arguments Justice Black was bothered by what he called the "hat in hand" requirement of Section 5:

JUSTICE BLACK: The result is that the Attorney General of the United States, who is not a judge, and is not a court, can object to any state law regarding elections and he can immediately require that state to have another election, is that right?

COUNSEL: That is right. Mr. Justice Black, Congress is faced with an extraordinary problem—

BLACK: I am not talking about extraordinary, there are many extraordinary things. The Constitution is an extraordinary thing.

COUNSEL: We do not read the law to lodge a power in the Attorney General which is an absolute power.

BLACK: He suspends the law, doesn't he?

COUNSEL: The suspension of the law is in the hands of Congress which did do it in Section 5.

BLACK: I would be perfectly satisfied with your argument if you said that certain things were devices and put them into an Act. What disturbed me was Congress delegating something at least for a time to the Attorney General.

COUNSEL: Mr. Justice Black, we don't read that as the delegation.

BLACK: What could it be except that?
COUNSEL: The body that Congress called upon to make that determination of whether the suspension should be lifted, and if there is a controversy, there is the three-judged court for the District of Columbia.
BLACK: Whether the suspension could be lifted? Until that time, the suspension was in effect by reason of the determination of the Attorney General.

[15] *Williams* v. *Rhodes,* 393 U.S. 23 (1968). Justice Black delivered the opinion of the Court:

No extended discussion is required to establish that the Ohio laws before us give the two old, established parties a decided advantage over any new parties struggling for existence and thus place substantially unequal burdens on both the right to vote and the right to associate. The right to form a party for the advancement of political goals means little if a party can be kept off the election ballot and thus denied an equal opportunity to win votes. There is, of course, no reason why two parties should retain a permanent monopoly on the right to have people vote for or against them. Competition in ideas and governmental policies is at the core of our electoral process and of the First Amendment freedom.

[16] *Epperson* v. *Arkansas,* 393 U.S. 97 (1968), declaring unconstitutional Arkansas' 1928 "anti-evolution" statute, which prohibited the teaching in public schools of the theory that man evolved from apes. The majority struck down the law as an unlawful establishment of religion. Justice Black concurred separately:

Certainly the Darwinian theory, precisely like the Genesis story of the creation of man, is not above challenge. In fact the Darwinian theory has not merely been criticized by religionists but by scientists, and perhaps no scientist would be willing to take an oath and swear that everything announced in the Darwinian theory is unquestionably true. The Court, it seems to me, makes a serious mistake in bypassing the plain, unconstitutional vagueness of this statute in order to reach out and decide this troublesome, to me, First Amendment question. However wise this Court may be or may become hereafter, it is doubtful that, sitting in Washington, it can successfully supervise and censor the curriculum of every public school in every hamlet and city in the United States. I doubt that our wisdom is so nearly infallible.

1969

[1] *Tinker* v. *Des Moines Community School District,* 393 U.S. 503, 515 (1969), Justice Black dissenting:

I think the record overwhelmingly shows that the armbands did exactly what the elected school officials and the principals foresaw they would, that is, took the students' minds off their classwork and diverted them to thoughts about the highly emotional subject of the Vietnam war.

The original idea of schools, which I do not believe is yet abandoned as worthless or out of date, was that children had not yet reached the point of experience and wisdom which enabled them to teach all of their elders. It may be that the Nation has outworn the old-fashioned slogan that "children are to be seen not heard," but one may, I hope, be permitted to harbor the thought that taxpayers send their children to school on the premise that at their age they need to learn, not teach.

One does not need to be a prophet or the son of a prophet to know that after the Court's holding today some students in Iowa schools and indeed in all schools will be ready, able, and willing to defy their teachers on practically all orders. This case, therefore, wholly without constitutional reasons in my judgment, subjects all the public schools in the country to the whims and caprices of the loudest-mouthed, but maybe not their brightest, students. I, for one, am not fully persuaded that school pupils are wise enough, even with this Court's expert help from Washington, to run the 23,390 public school systems in our 50 States. I wish, therefore, wholly to disclaim any purpose on my part to hold that the Federal Constitution compels the teachers, parents, and elected school officials to surrender control of the American public school system to public school students. I dissent.

[2]*Gregory* v. *Chicago,* 394 U.S. 111 (1969). Chief Justice Warren delivered the opinion of the Court, saying: "This is a simple case." To Black, the tension between free speech and public order "requires more detailed consideration than the Court's opinion gives it." Black continued:

Since neither the city council nor the state legislature had enacted a narrowly drawn statute forbidding disruptive picketing or demonstrating in a residential neighborhood, the conduct involved here could become "disorderly" only if the policeman's command was a law which the petitioners were bound to obey at their peril. But under our democratic system of government, lawmaking is not entrusted to the moment-to-moment judgment of the policeman on his beat. Laws, that is valid laws, are to be made by representatives chosen to make laws for the future, not by police officers whose duty is to enforce laws already enacted and to make arrests only for conduct already made criminal.

In agreeing to the reversal of these convictions, however, I wish once more to say that I think our Federal Constitution does not render the States powerless to regulate the conduct of demonstrators and picketers, conduct which is more than "speech," more than "press," more than "assembly," more than "petition," as those terms are used in the First Amendment. I believe that our Constitution, written for the ages, to endure except as changed in the manner it provides, did not create a government with such monumental weaknesses. Speech and press are, of course, to be free, so that public matters can be discussed with impunity. But picketing and demonstrating can be regulated like other conduct of men. I believe that the homes of men, sometimes the last citadel of the tired, the weary, and the sick, can be protected by government from noisy, marching, trampling, threatening picketers and demonstrators bent on filling the minds of men, women, and children with fears of the unknown.

[3]*Kaufman* v. *United States,* 394 U.S. 217, 231 (March 24, 1969), Justice Black dissenting:

I agreed with *Fay* v. *Noia* as one of the bright landmarks in the administration of criminal justice. But I did not think then and do not think now that it laid down an inflexible rule compelling the courts to release every prisoner who alleges in collateral proceedings some constitutional flaw, regardless of its nature, regardless of his guilt or innocence, and regardless of the circumstances of the case.

It is seemingly becoming more and more difficult to gain acceptance for the proposition that punishment of the guilty is desirable, other things being equal. This defendant is permitted to attack his conviction collaterally although he conceded at the trial and does not now deny that he had robbed the savings and loan association and although the evidence makes absolutely clear that he knew what he was doing. Thus, his guilt being certain, surely he does not have a constitutional right to get a new trial. I cannot possibly agree with the Court.

[4]*Foster* v. *California,* 394 U.S. 440, 444 (1969), Justice Black dissenting:

The night manager of the telegraph company testified before the court and jury that two men came into the office just after midnight, January 25, 1966, wrote a note telling him it was a holdup, put it under his face, and demanded money, flashed guns, took $531 and fled. The night manager identified Foster in the courtroom as one of the men, and he also related his identification of Foster in a lineup a week or so after the crime. The manager's evidence, which no witness disputed, was corroborated by the testimony of a man named Clay, who was Foster's accomplice in the robbery and who testified for the State. A narration of these facts, falling from the lips of eyewitnesses, and not denied by other eyewitnesses, would be enough, I am convinced, to persuade nearly all lawyers and judges, unhesitatingly to say, "There was clearly enough evidence of guilt here for a jury to convict the defendant since, according to practice, and indeed constitutional command, the weight of evidence is for a jury, and not for judges." To take that power away from the jury is to rob it of the responsibility to perform the precise functions the Founders most wanted it to perform. And certainly a Constitution written to preserve this indispensable, unerodible core of our system for trying criminal cases would not have included, hidden among its provisions, a slumbering sleeper granting the judges license to destroy trial by jury in whole or in part.

[5]*United States* v. *Montgomery County Board of Education,* 395 U.S. 225 (1969). Justice Black concluded his unanimous opinion for the Court by saying:

> It is good to be able to decide a case with the feelings we have about this one. There is no sign of lack of interest in the cause of either justice or education in the views maintained by any of the parties or in the orders entered by either of the courts below. We hope and believe that [Judge Johnson's] order and the approval that we now give it will carry Alabama a long distance on its way toward obedience to the law of the land as we have declared it in the two *Brown* cases and those that have followed them.

[6]*Daniel* v. *Paul,* 395 U.S. 298 (1969), applying the Public Accommodations Title of the Civil Rights Act of 1964 to Lake Nixon Club, an amusement place located twelve miles from Little Rock, Arkansas. Justice Black could find no record link between the Club and interstate commerce:

> One familiar with country life and traveling would, it seems to me, far more likely conclude that travelers on interstate journeys would stick to their interstate highways, and not go miles off them by way of what, for all this record shows, may well be dusty, unpaved, "country" roads to go to a purely local swimming hole where the only food they could buy was hamburgers, hot dogs, milk, and soft drinks (but not beer). This is certainly not the pattern or interstate movements I would expect interstate travelers in search of tourist attractions to follow.
>
> It seems to me clear that neither the paddle boats nor the locally leased juke box is sufficient to justify a holding that the operation of Lake Nixon affects interstate commerce within the meaning of the Act. While it is the duty of courts to enforce this important Act, we are not called on to hold nor should we hold subject to that Act this country people's recreation center, lying in what may be, so far as we know, a little "sleepy hollow" between Arkansas hills miles away from any interstate highway. This would be stretching the Commerce Clause so as to give the Federal Government complete control over every nook and cranny of every precinct and county in every one of the 50 States. This goes too far for me.

[7]*Sniadach* v. *Family Finance Corporation,* 395 U.S. 337 (1969), holding that Wisconsin's prejudgment garnishment procedure violates "fundamental principles of due process." Justice Black answered Justice Douglas's majority opinion this way:

> Of course the Due Process Clause of the Fourteenth Amendment contains no words that indicate that this Court has power to play so fast and loose with state

laws. The Wisconsin law is simply nullified by this Court as though the Court had been granted a super-legislative power to step in and frustrate policies of States adopted by their own elected legislatures. The Court thus steps back into the due process philosophy which brought on President Roosevelt's Court fight. This holding savors too much of the "Natural Law," "Due Process," "Shock-the-conscience" test of what is constitutional for me to agree to the decision.

And more—a special "ADDENDUM" aimed at Justice Harlan:

> My Brother HARLAN's "Anglo-American legal heritage" is no more definite than the "notions of justice of English-speaking peoples" or the shock-the-conscience test. All of these so-called tests represent nothing more or less than an implicit adoption of a Natural Law concept which under our system leaves to judges alone the power to decide what the Natural Law means. These so-called standards do not bind judges within any boundaries that can be precisely marked or defined by words for holding laws unconstitutional. On the contrary, these tests leave them wholly free to decide what they are convinced is right and fair. If the judges, in deciding whether laws are constitutional, are to be left only to the admonitions of their own consciences, why was it that the Founders gave us a written Constitution at all?

[8] *Utah Comm'n* v. *El Paso Gas Co.*, 395 U.S. 464 (1969). The opinion of the Court was actually delivered by Chief Justice Warren, not Justice Black.

[9] *North Carolina* v. *Pearce,* 395 U.S. 711, 737 (1969), Justice Black dissenting in part:

> There are some who say that there is nothing but a semantic difference between my view—that the Due Process Clause guarantees only that persons must be tried pursuant to the Constitution and laws passed under it—and the opposing view —that the Constitution grants judges power to decide constitutionality on the basis of their own concepts of fairness, justice, or "the Anglo-American legal heritage." But in this case, and elsewhere, as I see it, the difference between these views comes to nothing less than the difference between what the Constitution says and means and what the judges from day to day, generation to generation, and century to century, decide is fairest and best for the people. That is the difference for me between our Constitution as *written* by the Founders and an unwritten constitution to be formulated by judges according to their ideas of fairness on a case-by-case basis.

[10] *Alexander* v. *Board of Education,* 396 U.S. 1218 (1969) (Opinion in Chambers), Justice Black, Circuit Justice:

> There is no longer any excuse for permitting the "all deliberate speed" phrase to delay the time when Negro children and white children will sit together and learn together in the same public schools. It has been 15 years since we declared in *Brown I* that a law which prevents a child from going to a public school because of his color violates the Equal Protection Clause. As this record conclusively shows, there are many places still in this country where the schools are either "white" or "Negro" and not just schools for all children as the Constitution requires. In my opinion there is no reason why such a wholesale deprivation of constitutional rights should be tolerated another minute. I fear that this long denial of constitutional rights is due in large part to the phrase "with all deliberate speed." I would do away with that phrase completely.

Justice Black upheld the lower court's order delaying desegregation, "deplorable as it is to me," because he did not feel free as an individual Justice to "go beyond anything this Court has expressly held to date."

A little over a month later, the Court, in a *per curiam* opinion, declared that "continued operation of segregated schools under a standard of allowing 'all deliberate speed' for desegregation is no longer constitutionally permissible." *Alexander* v. *Board of Education,* 396 U.S. 19, 20 (Oct. 29, 1969).

[11] *Youngstown Sheet & Tube Co.* v. *Sawyer,* 343 U.S. 579 (1952), declaring President Truman's seizure of the steel mills unconstitutional. Justice Black wrote the opinion of the Court:

> In the framework of our Constitution, the President's power to see that the laws are faithfully executed refutes the idea that he is to be a lawmaker. The Constitution limits his functions in the lawmaking process to the recommending of laws he thinks wise and the vetoing of laws he thinks bad. And the Constitution is neither silent nor equivocal about who shall make the laws which the President is to execute.
>
> The Founders of this Nation entrusted the lawmaking power to the Congress alone in both good and bad times. It would do no good to recall the historical events, the fears of power and the hopes for freedom that lay behind their choice. Such a review would but confirm our holding that this seizure order cannot stand.

[12] *Goldberg* v. *Kelly,* 397 U.S. 254 (1970). Justice Black's opposition to the idea that the Constitution requires a hearing before welfare is cut off emerged at oral argument:

> JUSTICE BLACK: That's proceedings, isn't it? Without the proceedings required by law.
>
> COUNSEL: Without "due process of law," without the proceeding—
>
> BLACK: The proceedings required by law, or the proceedings a majority of this Court might think were arbitrary or unreasonable:
>
> COUNSEL: No, Mr. Justice Black, we are not relying on notions of reasonableness or arbitrariness. We are relying on the well-established obligation in the decisions of this Court—
>
> BLACK: Are you relying on obligations imposed by the language of the Constitution outside of due process, with this latitude in area and definition?
>
> COUNSEL: We are talking about various procedures which this Court time and time again has deemed—
>
> BLACK: You mean notice.
>
> COUNSEL: I mean notice—
>
> BLACK: The Constitution uses the word "notice," doesn't it?
>
> COUNSEL: I think due process,—it's well accepted, Mr. Justice Black, that due process refers—
>
> BLACK: Well, it's had some questioning from time to time. The well established thing you're talking about has certainly had considerable questioning, from year to year and decade to decade, during this century. I would gather from your argument that it would be hard to repeal a gratuity once you have given it, on the ground that it would be arbitrary and capricious.

[13] JUSTICE BLACK: [To Louis Oberdorfer] Do I understand—and I think I do—that you're in agreement with Mr. Greenberg's suggestion that the thing to do is to say that the dual system is *over,* and that it is to go into effect *today,* and that there is no reason for delay by reason of the fact that things will not be perfect the first day. The thing to do is to go at it *now*! Do you agree with his position on that?

OBERDORFER: I agree with that, Your Honor, without knowing exactly what "now" is.

BLACK: I mean when we issue an order—if we do.

[Laughter]

OBERDORFER: If you do, Your Honor.

BLACK: There is no reason to wait on future arguments about "deliberate speed."

OBERDORFER: Correct.

JUSTICE DOUGLAS: Except they would like to have us act "with all deliberate speed."
OBERDORFER: Faster than that, Your Honor.

[Loud, sustained laughter]

BLACK: [To Jerris Leonard, Assistant Attorney General] Why do you have to have plans to—just say "We're not going to have a dual system, and we are going to do it now."
LEONARD: I was just going to get to that.
BLACK: You can start in each one of these schools and say: "We are not going to have any dual system of schools here; it's going to be unitary, and if the buildings we have don't suit, we will do the best we can with the buildings we have; we will do the best we can with the teachers we have." Why do you have to draw any other plans but that?
LEONARD: Justice Black, that is the position of the Petitioners in this case—
BLACK: Well, I know, but I'm asking you whether that view is right or not, whoever's view it is.
LEONARD: I think it's wrong; I think it's terribly wrong; I think there may be some other alternatives to this frustration that—
BLACK: The frustration has been going on for fifteen years, hasn't it?
LEONARD: My point is that the frustration, I think, is more properly directed to the eighteen months because—
BLACK: You want to divide it up into segments?
LEONARD: No, I really don't.

[Laughter]What I'm pleading with this Court is not to do something precipitous.

BLACK: Could anything be precipitous in this field now?
LEONARD: Justice Black, let me say that many hundreds of thousands of the children that we are talking about are children of a very tender age. Let's try to do it with some order.
BLACK: Are you arguing for perpetuation of the term, "with all deliberate speed"?
LEONARD: I am not; I don't believe that's the law now, Mr. Justice Black. I think that's by the boards.
BLACK: But it's one more year, isn't it? But it contemplates another year.
LEONARD: For part of the plan.
BLACK: Too many plans and not enough action, maybe.

[Laughter]

[14]The Court's *per curiam* opinion was handed down the next day, October 29, vacating the Court of Appeals' order delaying desegregation and requiring issuance of the decree

> effective immediately, declaring that each of the school districts here involved may no longer operate a dual school system based on race or color, and directing that they begin immediately to operate as unitary school systems within which no person is to be effectively excluded from any school because of race or color.

Alexander v. *Board of Education,* 396 U.S. 19, 20 (1969).

[15]*Zuber* v. *Allen,* 396 U.S. 168 (1969), involving the labyrinth of federal milk marketing regulations adopted by the Secretary of Agriculture pursuant to the Agricultural Marketing Agreement Act of 1937.

1970

[1]*Turner* v. *United States,* 396 U.S. 398, 425 (1970), Justice Black dissenting:

> The Framers of our Constitution and Bill of Rights were too wise, too pragmatic, and too familiar with tyranny to attempt to safeguard personal liberty with broad, flexible words and phrases like "fair trial," "fundamental decency," and "reasonableness." Such stretchy, rubberlike terms would have left judges constitutionally free to try people charged with crime under will-o'-the-wisp standards

improvised by different judges for different defendants. Our Constitution was not written in the sands to be washed away by each wave of new judges blown in by each successive political wind that brings new political administrations into temporary power. Rather, our Constitution was fashioned to perpetuate liberty and justice by marking clear, explicit, and lasting constitutional boundaries for trials.

It would be a senseless and stupid thing for the Constitution to take all these precautions to protect the accused from governmental abuses if the Government could by some sleight-of-hand trick with presumptions make nullities of those precautions. Such a result would completely frustrate the purpose of the Founders to establish a system of criminal justice in which the accused—even the poorest and most humble—would be able to protect himself from wrongful charges by a big and powerful government. It is little less than fantastic even to imagine that those who wrote our Constitution and the Bill of Rights intended to have a government that could create crimes of several separate and independent parts and then relieve the government of proving a portion of them. Turner's trial therefore reminds me more of Daniel being cast into the lion's den than it does of a constitutional proceeding. The Bible tells us Daniel was saved by a miracle, but when this Court says its final word in this case today, we cannot expect a miracle to save petitioner Turner.

[2]*Evans* v. *Abney,* 396 U.S. 435 (1970):

When a city park is destroyed because the Constitution requires it to be integrated, there is reason for everyone to be disheartened. Here, however, the action of the Georgia Supreme Court declaring the Baconsfield trust terminated presents no violation of constitutionally protected rights, and any harshness that may have resulted from the state court's decision can be attributed solely to its intention to effectuate as nearly as possible the explicit terms of Senator Bacon's will. The language of the Senator's will shows that the racial restrictions were solely the product of the testator's own full-blown social philosophy. The loss of charitable trusts such as Baconsfield is part of the price we pay for permitting deceased persons to exercise continuing control over assets owned by them at death. This aspect of freedom of testation, like most things, has its advantages and disadvantages. The responsibility of this Court, however, is to construe and enforce the Constitution and laws of the land as they are and not to legislate social policy on the basis of our own personal inclinations.

[3]*Breen* v. *Selective Service Local Board No. 16,* 396 U.S. 460 (1970).

[4]*Hadley* v. *Junior College District of Kansas City,* 397 U.S. 50 (1970).

[5]*Goldberg* v. *Kelly,* 397 U.S. 254, 271 (1970), Justice Black dissenting:

The Court relies upon the Fourteenth Amendment and in effect says that failure of the government to pay a promised charitable instalment to an individual deprives that individual of *his own property,* in violation of the Due Process Clause of the Fourteenth Amendment. It somewhat strains credulity to say that the government's promise of charity to an individual is property belonging to that individual when the government denies that the individual is honestly entitled to receive such a payment.

I would have little, if any, objection to the majority's decision in this case if it were written as the report of the House Committee on Education and Labor, but as an opinion ostensibly resting on the language of the Constitution I find it woefully deficient. It is obvious that today's result does not depend on the language of the Constitution itself or the principles of other decisions, but solely on the collective judgment of the majority as to what would be a fair and humane procedure in this case.

Had the drafters of the Due Process Clause meant to leave judges such ambulatory power to declare laws unconstitutional, the chief value of a written constitution, as the Founders saw it, would have been lost.

[6]In re *Winship,* 397 U.S. 358 (1970), holding that the Constitution requires proof beyond a reasonable doubt in all criminal cases. The trouble with this conclusion, said Justice Black's dissent, is that

> nowhere in that document is there any statement that conviction of crime requires proof of guilt beyond a reasonable doubt. I believe this Court has no power to add to or subtract from the procedures set forth by the Founders. I realize that it is far easier to substitute individual judges' ideas of "fairness" for the fairness prescribed by the Constitution, but I shall not at any time surrender my belief that that document itself should be our guide, not our own concept of what is fair, decent, and right. As I have said time and time again, I prefer to put my faith in the words of the written Constitution itself rather than to rely on the shifting, day-to-day standards of fairness of individual judges.

[7]*Illinois* v. *Allen,* 397 U.S. 337 (1970):

> It is not pleasant to hold that the respondent Allen was properly banished from the court for a part of his own trial. But our courts, palladiums of liberty as they are, cannot be treated disrespectfully with impunity. Nor can the accused be permitted by his disruptive conduct indefinitely to avoid being tried on the charges brought against him. It would degrade our country and our judicial system to permit our courts to be bullied, insulted, and humiliated and their orderly progress thwarted and obstructed by defendants brought before them charged with crimes. As guardians of the public welfare, our state and federal judicial systems strive to administer equal justice to the rich and the poor, the good and the bad, the native and foreign born of every race, nationality, and religion. Being manned by humans, the courts are not perfect and are bound to make some errors. But, if our courts are to remain what the Founders intended, the citadels of justice, their proceedings cannot and must not be infected with the sort of scurrilous, abusive language and conduct paraded before the Illinois trial judge in this case.

[8]*Boys Markets, Inc.*, v. *Retail Clerks,* 398 U.S. 235 (1970), overruling Justice Black's opinion for the Court in *Sinclair Refining Co.* v. *Atkinson,* 370 U.S. 195 (1962), which caused Justice Black to say:

> Although Congress has been urged to overrule our holding in *Sinclair,* it has steadfastly refused to do so. Nothing at all has changed, in fact, except the membership of the Court and the personal views of one Justice. Having given our view on the meaning of a statute, our task is concluded, absent extraordinary circumstances. When the Court changes its mind years later, simply because the judges have changed, in my judgment, it takes upon itself the function of the legislature.
>
> The Court would do well to remember the words of John Adams, written in the Declaration of Rights in the Constitution of the Commonwealth of Massachusetts: "The judicial [department] shall never exercise the legislative and executive powers, or either of them: to the end it may be a government of laws and not of men." I dissent.

[9]*Chandler* v. *Judicial Council of the 10th Circuit,* 398 U.S. 74, 141 (1970), Justice Black, with whom Justice Douglas joins, dissenting:

While judges, like other people, can be tried, convicted, and punished for crimes, no word, phrase, clause, sentence, or even the Constitution itself taken as a whole, gives any indication that any judge was ever to be partly disqualified or wholly removed from office except by the admittedly difficult method of impeachment by the House of Representatives and conviction by two-thirds of the Senate. Such was the written guarantee in our Constitution of the independence of the judiciary, and such has always been the proud boast of our people.

What is involved here is simply a blatant effort on the part of the Council through concerted action to make Judge Chandler a "second-class judge," depriving him of the full power of his office and the right to share equally with all other federal judges in the privileges and responsibilities of the Federal Judiciary. I am unable to find in our Constitution or in any statute any authority whatever for judges to arrogate to themselves and to exercise such powers.

The wise authors of our Constitution provided for judicial independence because they were familiar with history; they knew that judges of the past—good, patriotic judges—had occasionally lost not only their offices but had also sometimes lost their freedom and their heads because of the actions and decrees of other judges. They were determined that no such things should happen here.

10 *Welsh* v. *United States,* 398 U.S. 333 (1970). Justice Black announced the judgment of the Court and delivered an opinion in which Justice Douglas, Justice Brennan, and Justice Marshall join:

Most of the great religions of today and of the past have embodied the idea of a Supreme Being or a Supreme Reality—a God—who communicates to man in some way a consciousness of what is right and should be done, of what is wrong and therefore should be shunned. If an individual deeply and sincerely holds beliefs that are purely ethical or moral in source and content but that nevertheless impose upon him a duty of conscience to refrain from participating in any war at any time, those beliefs certainly occupy in the life of that individual "a place parallel to that filled by . . . God" in traditionally religious persons. Because his beliefs function as a religion in his life, such an individual is as much entitled to a "religious conscientious objector" exemption as is someone who derives his conscientious opposition to war from traditional religious convictions.

11 *Williams* v. *Florida,* 399 U.S. 78 (1970), sustaining a Florida rule of criminal procedure requiring a defendant who intends to rely on an alibi to disclose to the prosecution the names of any alibi witnesses. Justice Black considered the requirement a patent violation of the Fifth Amendment because

It requires a defendant to disclose information to the State so that the State can use that information to destroy him. The Bill of Rights sets out the type of constitutionally required system that the State must follow in order to convict individuals of crime. That system requires that the State itself must bear the entire burden without any assistance from the defendant.

History does indicate that persons well familiar with the dangers of arbitrary and oppressive use of the criminal process were determined to limit such dangers for the protection of each and every inhabitant of this country. They were well aware that any individual might some day be subjected to criminal prosecution, and it was in order to protect the freedom of *each* of us that they restricted the Government's ability to punish or imprison *any* of us. Yet in spite of the history of oppression that produced the Bill of Rights and the strong reluctance of our governments to compel a criminal defendant to assist in his own conviction, the Court today reaches out to embrace and sanctify at the first opportunity a most dangerous departure from the Constitution and the traditional safeguards afforded persons accused of crime. I cannot accept such a result and must express my most emphatic disagreement and dissent.

[12]*New Haven Inclusion Cases,* 399 U.S. 392 (1970). Justice Black opened his dissent by saying: "The central issue in these cases, easily lost I fear in the 98-page opinion of the Court, can in my judgment be briefly and simply stated." Ten pages later, Justice Black concluded:

> The public interest in these cases certainly lies in establishing and maintaining the Penn Central as a viable private enterprise with reasonable rates and efficient service. Here the Commission struck a balance between public and private interests that was clearly within its discretion, and I think it is both improper and unwise for this Court to upset that balance and place an additional $28,000,000 burden on the Penn Central, a burden that I fear may ultimately be borne by the consumers of the Penn Central's services or by the Federal Treasury.

[13]*Swann* v. *Board of Education,* 402 U.S. 1 (decided April 20, 1971).

[14]*Board of Education* v. *Swann,* 402 U.S. 43 (April 20, 1971).

[15]JUSTICE BLACK: You say that *Brown* says that racial discrimination in school assignments is unconstitutional and we should have remedied the situation by making some more racial assignments?
NABRITT: I am not saying that. I—
BLACK: Well, why did you answer yes?
NABRITT: Well, maybe I didn't hear the question.
BLACK: All right. Never mind.
NABRITT: I understood—the answer is yes, but the *Brown* case requires something more, that is my only point.
BLACK: Do you think it is unconstitutional to have schools where the main objective is to have them close to the children in the surrounding community, whether they call them neighborhood schools or anything else?
NABRITT: I have nothing against that policy and that policy is not per se unconstitutional. But it does produce an unconstitutional result where the neighborhoods are racially defined by the state, as in Charlotte—
BLACK: What laws of North Carolina did this?
NABRITT: There is no law applicable to Charlotte, no racial segregation ordinance appliable to Charlotte, but the same thing has been accomplished by the use of zoning, on the way public housing was built, and the way urban renewal moved the people around—
BLACK: That is a pretty good job to assign to us, isn't it, to try to rearrange the areas of all the Nation where the people have naturally concentrated in one place because of poverty or because of wealth, or because of something else?
NABRITT: Well—
BLACK: Isn't that more than a court ought to have to do? How can you rearrange the whole country in such a fashion?
NABRITT: We don't seek to. We seek to integrate the schools on this single case that—
BLACK: Yet you state your case by challenging the place people live and not letting them have schools in their areas. And I understand that you want to haul people miles and miles and miles in order to get an equal percentage of the races in the schools where they don't live close to them.
NABRITT: Mr. Justice—
BLACK: Is that right?

NABRITT: I don't describe my position that way, no, sir.
BLACK: I think that there is something to the concept of the neighborhood school that is worthy of consideration in this Court.
NABRITT: Well, what I would suggest is that the neighborhood school concept, whatever may be its value, has no standing in the Constitution to override the constitutional duty of the school board.
BLACK: Well, now may I say to you, sir—
NABRITT: And may I say—
BLACK: —that what I am interested in and have been interested in from the first case is if there is plain discrimination on account of race in a particular instance, I think we should correct it, under the Constitution. But it disturbs me to try to challenge the whole arrangement of the living practices and the way of life of the people all over this Nation.

[16]In re *Stolar,* 401 U.S. 23 (1971).

[17]*Baird* v. *State Bar of Arizona,* 401 U.S. 1 (1971).

[18]*McGautha* v. *California,* 402 U.S. 183 (1971), sustaining California's capital sentencing procedures. Justice Harlan delivered the opinion of the Court. Justice Black wrote a separate opinion giving his views on the death penalty:

> In my view, this Court's task is not to determine whether the petitioners' trials were "fairly conducted." Our responsibility is rather to determine whether petitioners have been denied rights expressly or impliedly guaranteed by the Federal Constitution as written. The Eighth Amendment forbids "cruel and unusual punishments." In my view, these words cannot be read to outlaw capital punishment because that penalty was in common use and authorized by law here and in the countries from which our ancestors came at the time the Amendment was adopted. It is inconceivable to me that the framers intended to end capital punishment by the Amendment. Although some people have urged that this Court should amend the Constitution by interpretation to keep it abreast of modern times, I have never believed that lifetime judges in our system have any such legislative power.

[19]*Sanks* v. *Georgia,* 401 U.S. 144 (1971):

> COUNSEL: Frankly, it would shock my conscience if the state could not protect the owners of rental property. In conclusion,—
> JUSTICE BLACK: Mr. Evans, whose conscience do you understand has to be shocked to make it unconstitutional?
> COUNSEL: That is a very difficult question, Mr. Justice Black, and, of course, it is not a test that I personally think is a good one. But I would say it would have to be, as Mr. Justice Harlan said, at the very least it would have to be based upon the general view of society, which conceivably could change. But I do think it would have to be based on the general views.
> BLACK: You mean of society?
> COUNSEL: Sir?
> BLACK: You mean shock the conscience of society?
> COUNSEL: Yes, sir, I think it would have to be one which would shock the conscience of civilized society. It should—this should be objective standard, which I believe Mr. Justice Harlan says the Court should move.
> BLACK: Would that make it something like the test we apply to obscenity?
> COUNSEL: I dislike to even comment on the test of obscenity. I find it so difficult to grasp.

BLACK: We won't press you for an answer to that one.

[Laughter]

JUSTICE HARLAN: Why don't you use a less picturesque phrase in talking about fundamental fairness of the constitutional concept?

COUNSEL: Fundamental fairness is, of course—

HARLAN: And get away from histrionics a little bit.

COUNSEL: If I am using histrionics, I am borrowing it from decisions of this Court. I do not think it should be—well, this Court has said it ought not to be merely the personal view of any individual justice who sits on a court at any one time. That is what this Court has said.

HARLAN: Part of the difficulty is judging.

COUNSEL: Yes, I'm sure it is.

[20]*Oregon* v. *Mitchell,* 400 U.S. 112 (1970). Justice Black delivered the judgments of the Court in an opinion expressing his own view of the cases:

> It is a plain fact of history that the Framers never imagined that the national Congress would set the qualifications for voters in every election from President to local constable or village alderman. It is obvious that the whole Constitution reserves to the States the power to set voter qualifications in state and local elections, except to the limited extent that the people through constitutional amendments have specifically narrowed the powers of the States. And the Equal Protection Clause of the Fourteenth Amendment was never intended to destroy the States' power to govern themselves. My Brother Brennan's opinion, if carried to its logical conclusion, would, under the guise of insuring equal protection, blot out all state power, leaving the 50 States as little more than important figureheads. In interpreting what the Fourteenth Amendment means, the Equal Protection Clause should not be stretched to nullify the States' power over elections which they had before the Constitution was adopted and which they have retained throughout our history.

1971

[1]*Citizens to Preserve Overton Park* v. *Volpe,* 401 U.S. 402 (1971). Whether the Secretary of Transportation violated federal law by authorizing the expenditure of federal funds for construction of a six-lane interstate highway through Overton Park in Memphis, Tennessee, was the question presented. During the arguments, Justice Black pointedly cross-examined the lawyers favoring the highway:

JUSTICE BLACK: You would agree, I suppose, that so far as the Congress is concerned, there is no doubt they have attempted to put a considerable burden on somebody before they destroy a city's public park?

COUNSEL: I think that Congress, and rightly so, has required the Department of Transportation and the Secretary to be very careful before roads are put through the parks, and that should not be done, except, frankly, the situation of this nature where the damage to the park is rather infinitesimal. No facility whatsoever of this park will be hampered.

BLACK: Parks, as I had thought, are not altogether governed in their value by facilities.

COUNSEL: I agree.

BLACK: I thought the mere fact that it was a park is what gave it its greatest value to the people.

COUNSEL: And I agree, your Honor, that this will still be a park, just as it is when this road is complete.

BLACK: A smaller park—

COUNSEL: A slightly smaller—slightly—

BLACK: With a road through it.

The Court stayed the construction of the highway and remanded the matter back to the federal district court for plenary review of the Secretary of Transportation's decision. Said Justice Black in a separate opinion:

> I regret that I am compelled to conclude for myself that, except for some too-late formulations, apparently coming from the Solicitor General's office, this record contains not one word to indicate that the Secretary raised even a finger to comply with the command of Congress. That Act was obviously passed to protect our public parks from forays by road builders except in the most extraordinary and imperative circumstances.

[2]*United States* v. *Vuitch,* 402 U.S. 62 (April 21, 1971), holding that "properly construed the District of Columbia abortion law is not unconstitutionally vague." Justice Black, writing for the Court, thus reinstated criminal indictments of a physician for producing an abortion in violation of the District of Columbia Code. Justice Black's opinion for the Court expressly declined to reach arguments attacking abortion laws "based on this Court's decision in *Griswold* v. *Connecticut,* 381 U.S. 479 (1965)."

[3]*Younger* v. *Harris,* 401 U.S. 37 (1971); *Samuels* v. *Mackell,* 401 U.S. 66 (1971); *Boyle* v. *Landry,* 401 U.S. 77 (1971); *Perez* v. *Ledesma,* 401 U.S. 82 (1971). Justice Black delivered the opinion of the Court in each of these four cases, and in *Younger* v. *Harris,* the lead case, he explained why "the normal thing to do when federal courts are asked to enjoin pending proceedings in state courts is not to issue such injunctions":

> The National Government will fare best if the States and their institutions are left free to perform their separate functions in their separate ways. One familiar with the profound debates that ushered our Federal Constitution into existence is bound to respect those who remain loyal to the ideals and dreams of "Our Federalism." The concept does not mean blind deference to "States' Rights" any more than it means centralization of control over every important issue in our National Government and its courts. The Framers rejected both these courses. What the concept does represent is a system in which there is sensitivity to the legitimate interests of both State and National Governments, and in which the National Government, anxious though it may be to vindicate and protect federal rights and federal interests, always endeavors to do so in ways that will not unduly interfere with the legitimate activitives of the States.

[4]*Baird* v. *State Bar of Arizona,* 401 U.S. 1 (1971); In re *Stolar,* 401 U.S. 23 (1970). Justice Black announced the judgment of the Court and delivered an opinion in which Justice Douglas, Justice Brennan, and Justice Marshall join:

> When a State attempts to make inquiries about a person's beliefs or associations, its power is limited by the First Amendment. We hold that views and beliefs are immune from bar association inquisitions designed to lay a foundation for barring an application from the practice of law. This record is wholly barren of one word, sentence, or paragraph that tends to show this lady is not morally and professionally fit to serve honorably and well as a member of the legal profession. It was error not to process her application and not to admit her to the Arizona Bar.

Justice Stewart concurred in the judgment and wrote a separate opinion.

[5]*Law Students Civil Rights Research Council* v. *Wadmond,* 401 U.S. 154 (1971).

[6]*Karr* v. *Schmidt, Principal of Coronado High School,* 401 U.S. 1201 (February 11, 1971), Justice Black, Circuit Justice:

> The motion concerns rules adopted by the school authorities of El Paso, Texas, providing that schoolboys' hair must not "hang over the ears or the top of the collar of a standard dress shirt and must not obstruct the vision." The words used throughout the record such as "Emergency Motion" and "harassment" and "irreparable damages" are calculated to leave the impression that this case over the length of hair has created or is about to create a great national "crisis." I confess my inability to understand how anyone would thus classify this hair length case. The only thing about it that borders on the serious to me is the idea that anyone should think the Federal Constitution imposes on the United States courts the burden of supervising the length of hair that public school students should wear. Surely the federal judiciary can perform no greater service to the Nation than to leave the States unhampered in the performance of their purely local affairs. Surely few policies can be thought of that States are more capable of deciding than the length of the hair of schoolboys.

[7]*Perez* v. *United States,* 402 U.S. 146 (1971). During oral argument, Justice Black inquired about the amount of the loan and the terms of repayment:

> JUSTICE BLACK: May I ask you how much this "loan" was?
>
> COUNSEL: Originally it was a thousand dollars. It went up to three thousand dollars finally.
>
> BLACK: What was the interest rate to be paid?
>
> COUNSEL: Oh, I would estimate well in excess of the forty-five per cent which is mentioned in the statute.
>
> BLACK: Payable how often?
>
> COUNSEL: It was payable in weekly terms. I think the original loan was a thousand dollars payable at the rate of one hundred five dollars a week for 14 weeks.

[8]*Meltzer* v. *LeCraw & Co.*, 402 U.S. 954 (May 3, 1971), Justice Black, dissenting from denial of *certiorari:*

> In my view, the decision in *Boddie* v. *Connecticut* can safely rest on only one crucial foundation—that the civil courts of the United States and each of the States belong to the people of this country and that no person can be denied access to those courts, either for a trial or an appeal, because he cannot pay a fee, finance a bond, risk a penalty, or afford to hire an attorney. I believe there can be no doubt that this country can afford to provide court costs and lawyers to Americans who are now barred by their poverty from resort to the law for resolution of their disputes. I cannot believe that my Brethren would find the rights of a man with both legs cut off by a negligent railroad less "fundamental" than a person's right to seek a divorce. There is simply no fairness or justice in a legal system which pays indigents' costs to get divorces and does not aid them in other civil cases which are frequently of far greater importance to society.

[9]*Whiteley* v. *Warden,* 401 U.S. 560, 570 (1971), Justice Black, with whom the Chief Justice joins, dissenting:

> With all respect to my Brethren who agree to the judgment and opinion of the Court, I am constrained to say that I believe the decision here is a gross and wholly indefensible miscarriage of justice. For this reason it may well be classified as one of those calculated to make many good people believe our Court actually enjoys frustrating justice by unnecessarily turning professional criminals loose to prey upon society with impunity.

[10]*Labine* v. *Vincent,* 401 U.S. 532 (1971):

> These rules for intestate succession may or may not reflect the intent of particular parents. Many will think that it is unfortunate that the rules are so rigid. Others will think differently. But the choices reflected by the intestate succession statute are choices which it is within the power of the State to make. The Federal Constitution does not give this Court the power to overturn the State's choice under the guise of constitutional interpretation because the Justices of this Court believe that they can provide better rules. There is nothing in the vague generalities of the Equal Protection and Due Process Clauses which empowers this Court to nullify the deliberate choices of the elected representatives of the people of Louisiana.

[11]*California* v. *Byers,* 402 U.S. 424 (1971) (plurality opinion, Burger, C.J.), rejecting a Fifth Amendment challenge to a California Vehicle Code requirement that a driver stop and furnish his name and address after involvement in an automobile accident resulting in damage to property. Justice Black, joined by Justices Douglas and Brennan, dissented:

> The plurality opinion, if agreed to by a majority of the Court, would practically wipe out the Fifth Amendment's protection against compelled self-incrimination. In erasing this principle from the Constitution the plurality opinion retreats from a cherished guarantee of liberty fashioned by James Madison and the other founders of what they proudly proclaimed to be our free government. My Brother HARLAN's opinion makes it clear that today the Court "balances" the importance of a defendant's Fifth Amendment right not to be forced to help convict himself against the government's interest in forcing him to do so. As in previous decisions, this balancing inevitably results in the dilution of constitutional guarantees.
>
> I can only assume that the unarticulated premise of the decision is that there is so much crime abroad in this country at present that Bill of Rights safeguards against arbitrary government must not be completely enforced. I can agree that there is too much crime in the land for us to treat criminals with favor. But I can never agree that we should depart in the slightest way from the Bill of Rights' guarantees that give this country its high place among the free nations of the world.

[12]*Palmer* v. *Thompson,* 403 U.S. 217 (1971). Justice Black delivered the opinion of the Court:

> Petitioners have argued that the Jackson pools were closed because of the ideological opposition to racial integration in swimming pools. Some evidence in the record appears to support this argument. On the other hand the courts below found that the pools were closed because the city council felt they could not be operated safely and economically on an integrated basis. There is substantial evidence in the record to support this conclusion.
>
> Here the record indicates only that Jackson once ran segregated public swimming pools and that no public pools are now maintained by the city. Moreover, there is no evidence in this record to show that the city is now covertly aiding the maintenance and operation of pools which are private in name only. It shows no state action affecting blacks differently from whites.
>
> Probably few persons, prior to this case, would have imagined that cities could be forced by five lifetime judges to construct or refurbish swimming pools which they choose not to operate for any reason, sound or unsound. Should citizens of Jackson or any other city be able to establish in court that public, tax-supported swimming pools are being denied to one group because of color and supplied to another, they will be entitled to relief. But that is not the case here.

[13]The United States Government sought a federal court order enjoining the New York *Times* and the Washington *Post* from publishing the contents of a classified Pentagon study related to Viet Nam on grounds that publication would endanger national security. "Well, wouldn't we, then, be—the Federal Courts—be the censorship board as to whether—" At this point in the oral argument Solicitor General Griswold interrupted Justice Marshall and the fireworks began:

SOLICITOR GENERAL GRISWOLD: That's a pejorative way to put it, Mr. Justice. I don't know what the alternative is.

JUSTICE BLACK: The First Amendment might be.

[General laughter]

GRISWOLD: Yes, Mr. Justice, and we are of course fully supporting the First Amendment. We do not claim, or suggest, any exception to the First Amendment. The problem in this case is the construction of the First Amendment. Now, Mr. Justice Black, your construction of that is well known, and I certainly respect it. You say that "no law" means "no law," and that should be obvious.

BLACK: I rather thought that.

GRISWOLD: And I can only say, Mr. Justice, that to me it is equally obvious that "no law" does not mean "no law" and I would seek to persuade the Court that that is true. As Chief Justice Marshall said so long ago, "it is a constitution we are interpreting."

In his Carpentier lectures, delivered three years before the Government asked for an injunction against the press in the Pentagon Papers case, Justice Black had anticipated Griswold's argument: "Of course I realize 'that it is *a constitution* we are expounding.' But this does not mean that in order to obtain results thought to be desirable at the time, judges may rewrite our basic charter of government under the guise of interpreting it." (Hugo Lafayette Black, *A Constitutional Faith* [New York: Knopf, 1968], p. 8.)

[14]*Clay* v. *United States,* 403 U.S. 698 (1971).

[15]*Lemon* v. *Kurtzman,* 403 U.S. 602 (1971).

[16]*New York Times Co.* v. *United States,* 403 U.S. 713, 714 (1971), Justice Black concurring:

Our Government was launched in 1789 with the adoption of the Constitution. The Bill of Rights, including the First Amendment, followed in 1791. Now, for the first time in the 182 years since the founding of the Republic, the federal courts are asked to hold that the First Amendment does not mean what it says, but rather means that the Government can halt the publication of current news of vital importance to the people of this country.

I can imagine no greater perversion of history. Madison and the other Framers of the First Amendment, able men that they were, wrote in language they earnestly believed could never be misunderstood: "Congress shall make no law . . . abridging the freedom . . . of the press. . . ." Both the history and language of the First Amendment support the view that the press must be left free to publish news, whatever the source, without censorship, injunctions, or prior restraints.

In the First Amendment the Founding Fathers gave the free press the protection it must have to fulfill its essential role in our democracy. The press was to serve the governed, not the governors. The Government's power to censor the press was abolished so that the press would remain forever free to censure the Government. The press was protected so that it could bare the secrets of government and inform the people. Only a free and unrestrained press can effectively expose deception in government. And paramount among the responsibilities of a free press is the duty to prevent any part of the government from deceiving the people and sending them off to distant lands to die of foreign fevers and foreign shot and shell. In my view, far from deserving condemnation for their courageous reporting, the New York Times, the Washington Post, and other newspapers should be commended for serving the purposes that the Founding Fathers saw so clearly. In revealing the workings of government that led to the Vietnam war, the newspapers nobly did precisely that which the Founders hoped and trusted they would do.

[17]*Corpus Christi School District* v. *Cisneros,* 404 U.S. 1211 (August 19, 1971), Justice Black, Circuit Justice:

It is apparent that this case is in an undesirable state of confusion and presents questions not heretofore passed on by the full Court, but which should be. Under these circumstances, which present a very anomalous, new, and confusing situation, I decline as a single Justice to upset the District Court's stay.

[18]*Dombrowski* v. *Eastland,* 387 U.S. 82 (1967).

Editor's Note by Paul R. Baier, Professor of Law, Louisiana State University

Mr. Justice Black died in 1971. When I first met Elizabeth Black in 1979 she was listening to a sound recording of the Judge. Her first words to me were, "I can't resist Hugo's voice."

For some fifteen years since her husband's death, Mrs. Black labored steadfastly, sometimes swamped in documents, to preserve Hugo Black's memory. As she has said, she felt from the beginning of their association that she was "touching the skirts of history."

The publication of this book is a tribute to Mrs. Black's devotion to her husband. The first part, Hugo Black's memoir, stands exactly as he wrote it. As editor I convinced Mrs. Black to include excerpts from her private diaries in the book. These pages allow us, through Elizabeth Black's keen eye, to see the Judge and the Court's family living as we all live, day to day.

I have annotated Elizabeth Black's diaries where it seemed helpful, with excerpts from Justice Black's opinions. These annotations provide a sample of the Judge's constitutional faith and his plain style of writing: "the Holmes-type opinion—short, classic, citing no authorities." I have also included excerpts from several of the oral arguments mentioned in Mrs. Black's diaries because they are a window to the Court's mind. The notes omit the usual clutter of scholarly editing: the passages from Justice Black's opinions are connected up without the distraction of ellipses, asterisks, or brackets. They are easier to read this way and they remain true to the Judge's lean style.

The value of these memoirs lies primarily in their intimacy. The reader shares the sweetness of laughter for two and the pain of life's close. When the Supreme Court paid its last respects to Hugo Black, during the memorial proceedings held in open Court in 1972 (405 U.S. LIII, LIV), Chief Justice Warren Burger pointed out that

> There is always the risk of having our admiration for uncommon men and women create an image that becomes, over time, more legend than flesh and blood. Hugo Black would not like that. . . . He would not mind a dash of legend but he was so vital in his humanity, so firm in his basic views, that he would also want to be seen and remembered as his intimates saw him. . . .

It has been a long road to the publication of these memoirs. I, especially, have been fortunate to have met Elizabeth Black in the first place. Her trust and confidence over the long course of our mutual labors is a high honor for which I am grateful beyond words.

The Supreme Court is made up of human beings, yet the humanity of the Court is largely unknown. Elizabeth Black's purpose all along has been to share the humanity of Hugo Black with the American people. The beauty of their life together is at once a lesson and a radiant inspiration to us all.

Appendix

CHIEF JUSTICES WITH WHOM JUSTICE BLACK SERVED

Charles E. Hughes	1930–1941	Earl Warren	1953–1969
Harlan F. Stone	1941–1946	Warren E. Burger	1969–
Frederick M. Vinson	1946–1953		

ASSOCIATE JUSTICES WITH WHOM JUSTICE BLACK SERVED

James C. McReynolds	1914–1941	Wiley B. Rutledge	1943–1949
Louis D. Brandeis	1916–1939	Harold H. Burton	1945–1958
John. H. Clarke	1916–1922	Tom C. Clark	1949–1967
George Sutherland	1922–1938	Sherman Minton	1949–1956
Pierce Butler	1922–1939	John Marshall Harlan	1955–1971
Edward T. Sanford	1923–1930	William J. Brennan, Jr.	1956–
Harlan F. Stone	1925–1941	Charles E. Whittaker	1957–1962
Owen J. Roberts	1930–1945	Potter Stewart	1958–
Benjamin N. Cardozo	1932–1938	Byron R. White	1962–
Stanley F. Reed	1938–1957	Arthur J. Goldberg	1962–1965
Felix Frankfurter	1939–1962	Abe Fortas	1965–1969
William O. Douglas	1939–1975	Thurgood Marshall	1967–
Frank Murphy	1940–1949	Harry A. Blackmun	1970–
Robert H. Jackson	1941–1954		
James F. Byrnes	1941–1942		

LAW CLERKS TO JUSTICE BLACK

Jerome A. Cooper 1937–9
Marx Leva 1940
Maxwell Isenberg 1941
Chris J. Dixie 1942
John Frank 1942
Charles F. Luce 1943
Sidney Davis 1944
David Haber 1945
Louis F. Oberdorfer 1946
William Joslin 1947

Truman Hobbs 1948
Frank Wozencraft 1949
Luther Hill, Jr. 1950
George M. Treister 1950
C. Sam Daniels 1951
Neal P. Rutledge 1951
Melford O. Cleveland 1952
Huey Howerton 1952
Charles A. Reich 1953
David J. Vann 1953
Daniel J. Meador 1954
James W. H. Stewart 1954
J. Vernon Patrick 1955
Harold A. Ward III 1955
Robert A. Girard 1956–7
George C. Freeman, Jr. 1956
David McK. Clark 1957–8
Guido Calabresi 1958
Robert Basseches 1958
John Kent McNulty 1959
Nicholas Johnson 1959
Lawrence G. Wallace 1960
George L. Saunders, Jr. 1960–1
Floyd F. Feeney 1961
Clay Long 1962
A. E. Dick Howard 1962–3
John G. Kester 1963–4
James L. North 1964
John W. Vardaman, Jr. 1965
Drayton Nabers, Jr. 1965
Margaret Corcoran 1966
Stephen Susman 1966
Stephen J. Schulhofer 1967–8
Joseph H. Price 1967
Walter E. Dellinger III 1968
Kenneth C. Bass III 1969
J. Gus Speth 1969
G. Marshall Moriarty 1969
John M. Harmon 1970
Robert B. McCaw 1970
Robert W. Spearman 1970
John M. Harmon 1971
Covert Eugene Parnell III 1971
Larry Hammond 1971

The Opinions of Hugo Lafayette Black

Opinions of the Court

Accardi v. *Pennsylvania R. Co.*, 383 U.S. 225 (1966)
Adams v. *Maryland*, 347 U.S. 179 (1954)
Adams v. *United States*, 319 U.S. 312 (1943)
Adderley v. *Florida*, 385 U.S. 39 (1966)
Adkins v. *Du Pont de Nemours & Co.*, 335 U.S. 331 (1948)
Afroyim v. *Rusk*, 387 U.S. 253 (1967)
Alabama v. *United States*, 325 U.S. 535 (1945)
Albrecht v. *United States*, 329 U.S. 599 (1947)
Alison v. *United States*, 344 U.S. 167 (1952)
Allen Bradley Co. v. *Local Union No. 3*, 325 U.S. 797 (1945)
Alstate Construction Co. v. *Durkin*, 345 U.S. 13 (1953)
American Federation of Labor v. *American Sash Co.*, 335 U.S. 538 (1949)
American Surety Co. v. *Sampsell*, 327 U.S. 269 (1946)
Arizona v. *California*, 373 U.S. 546 (1963)
Arkansas Corporation Comm'n. v. *Thompson*, 313 U.S. 132 (1941)
Arkansas Fuel Oil Co. v. *Louisiana* ex rel. *Muslow*, 304 U.S. 197 (1938)
Armour & Co. v. *Alton Railroad Co.*, 312 U.S. 195 (1941)
Armstrong v. *United States*, 364 U.S. 40 (1960)
Arrowsmith v. *Commissioner*, 344 U.S. 6 (1952)
Ashcraft v. *Tennessee*, 322 U.S. 143 (1944)
Ashcraft v. *Tennessee*, 327 U.S. 274 (1946)
Associated Press v. *United States*, 326 U.S. 1 (1945)
Astrup v. *Immigration and Naturalization Service*, 402 U.S. 509 (1971)
Atlantic Coast Line R. Co. v. *Locomotive Engineers*, 398 U.S. 281 (1970)
Atlantic Refining Co. v. *Moller*, 320 U.S. 462 (1943)
Avery v. *Alabama*, 308 U.S. 444 (1940)

Baltimore & O. R. Co. v. *United States*, 345 U.S. 146 (1953)

Compco Corp. v. *Day-Brite Lighting, Inc.*, 376 U.S. 234 (1964)

Cone v. *West Virginia Paper Co.*, 330 U.S. 212 (1947)

Conley v. *Gibson*, 355 U.S. 41 (1957)

Continental Grain Co. v. *Barge FBL-585*, 364 U.S. 19 (1960)

Cooper v. *Aaron*, 358 U.S. 1 (1958) (Joint)

Cooper v. *California*, 386 U.S. 58 (1967)

Cope v. *Anderson*, 331 U.S. 461 (1947)

Coray v. *Southern Pacific Co.*, 335 U.S. 520 (1949)

Cornell Steamboat Co. v. *United States*, 321 U.S. 634 (1944)

Costello v. *United States*, 350 U.S. 359 (1956)

Crane-Johnson Co. v. *Helvering*, 311 U.S. 54 (1940)

Creek Nation v. *United States*, 318 U.S. 629 (1943)

Dairy Queen, Inc. v. *Wood*, 369 U.S. 469 (1962)

Davis v. *Dept. of Labor & Industries*, 317 U.S. 249 (1942)

Denver & R. G. W. R. Co. v. *Union Pacific R. Co.*, 351 U.S. 321 (1956)

Detroit v. *Murray Corp.*, 355 U.S. 489 (1958)

Dice v. *Akron, C. & Y. R. Co.*, 342 U.S. 359 (1952)

District of Columbia v. *Little*, 339 U.S. 1 (1950)

Donaldson v. *Read Magazine*, 333 U.S. 178 (1948)

Donovan v. *Dallas*, 377 U.S. 408 (1964)

Dowd v. *U.S.* ex rel. *Cook*, 340 U.S. 206 (1951)

Duncan v. *Kahanamoku*, 327 U.S. 304 (1946)

Duncan v. *Thompson*, 315 U.S. 1 (1942)

Eastern Railroad Presidents Conf. v. *Noerr Motor Freight*, 365 U.S. 127 (1961)

Edwards v. *Pacific Fruit Express Co.*, 390 U.S. 538 (1968)

El Dorado Oil Works v. *United States*, 328 U.S. 12 (1946)

Eli Lilly & Co. v. *Sav-On-Drugs, Inc.*, 366 U.S. 276 (1961)

Engel v. *Vitale*, 370 U.S. 421 (1962)

Eubanks v. *Louisiana*, 356 U.S. 584 (1958)

Evans v. *Abney*, 396 U.S. 435 (1970)

Everson v. *Board of Education*, 330 U.S. 1 (1947)

Falbo v. *United States*, 320 U.S. 549 (1944)

Farmer v. *Arabian American Oil Co.*, 379 U.S. 227 (1964)

Farmers Educational & Coop. Union v. *WDAY, Inc.*, 360 U.S. 525 (1959)

Fashion Originators' Guild v. *Trade Comm'n.*, 312 U.S. 457 (1941)

Federal Maritime Comm'n. v. *Akt. Svenska Amer. Linien*, 390 U.S. 238 (1968)

Federal Power Comm'n. v. *East Ohio Gas Co.*, 338 U.S. 464 (1950)

Federal Trade Comm'n. v. *Brown Shoe Co.*, 384 U.S. 316 (1966)

Federal Trade Comm'n. v. *Cement Institute*, 333 U.S. 683 (1948)

Federal Trade Comm'n. v. *Morton Salt Co.*, 334 U.S. 37 (1948)

Federal Trade Comm'n. v. *Standard Education Society*, 302 U.S. 112 (1937)

Federal Trade Comm'n. v. *Texas, Inc.*, 393 U.S. 223 (1968)

Ferguson v. *Skrupa*, 372 U.S. 726 (1963)

First Agricultural Nat. Bank v. *State Tax Comm'n.*, 392 U.S. 339 (1968)

First National Bank of Chicago v. *United Air Lines*, 342 U.S. 396 (1952)

Fitzgerald v. *United States Lines Co.*, 374 U.S. 16 (1963)

Ford v. *Ford*, 371 U.S. 187 (1962)

Fortner Enterprises v. *United States Steel Corp.*, 394 U.S. 495 (1969)

Fortson v. *Morris*, 385 U.S. 231 (1966)

Foster v. *United States*, 303 U.S. 118 (1938)

Franks Bros. Co. v. *Labor Board,* 321 U.S. 702 (1944)
Frisbie v. *Collins,* 342 U.S. 519 (1952)

Garrett v. *Moore-McCormack Co.,* 317 U.S. 239 (1942)
Giaccio v. *Pennsylvania,* 382 U.S. 399 (1966)
Giboney v. *Empire Storage & Ice Co.,* 336 U.S. 490 (1949)
Gideon v. *Wainwright,* 372 U.S. 335 (1963)
Glass City Bank v. *United States,* 326 U.S. 265 (1945)
Globe Liquor Co. v. *San Roman,* 332 U.S. 571 (1948)
Glover v. *St. Louis–San Francisco R. Co.,* 393 U.S. 324 (1969)
Glus v. *Brooklyn Eastern District Terminal,* 359 U.S. 231 (1959)
Goldlawr, Inc. v. *Heiman,* 369 U.S. 463 (1962)
Green v. *United States,* 355 U.S. 184 (1957)
Griffin v. *School Board of Prince Edward County,* 377 U.S. 218 (1964)
Guaranty Trust Co. v. *Henwood,* 307 U.S. 247 (1939)
Gunther v. *San Diego & A. E. R. Co.,* 382 U.S. 257 (1965)

Hadley v. *Junior College District of Kansas City,* 397 U.S. 50 (1970)
Halcyon Lines v. *Haenn Ship Ceiling & Refitting Corp.,* 342 U.S. 282 (1952)
Halliburton Oil Well Co. v. *Walker,* 329 U.S. 1 (1946)
Hardin v. *Kentucky Utilities Co.,* 390 U.S. 1 (1968)
Harris v. *Avery Brundage Co.,* 305 U.S. 160 (1938)
Harvester Co. v. *Evatt,* 329 U.S. 416 (1947)
Hastings v. *Selby Oil & Gas Co.,* 319 U.S. 348 (1943)
Hawkins v. *United States,* 358 U.S. 74 (1958)
Haynes v. *United States,* 353 U.S. 81 (1957)
Hazel-Atlas Glass Co. v. *Hartford-Empire Co.,* 322 U.S. 238 (1944)
Hazeltine Research v. *Brenner,* 382 U.S. 252 (1965)
Helvering v. *F. & R. Lazarus & Co.,* 308 U.S. 252 (1939)
Helvering v. *Northwest Steel Mills,* 311 U.S. 46 (1940)
Helvering v. *Oregon Mutual Life Ins. Co.,* 311 U.S. 267 (1940)
Helvering v. *Pan-American Life Ins. Co.,* 311 U.S. 272 (1940)
Helvering v. *Richter,* 312 U.S. 561 (1941)
Helvering v. *Safe Deposit & Trust Co.,* 316 U.S. 56 (1942)
Helvering v. *Winmill,* 305 U.S. 79 (1938)
Hercules Gasoline Co. v. *Commissioner,* 326 U.S. 425 (1945)
H. K. Porter Co. v. *Central Vermont R. Co.,* 366 U.S. 272 (1961)
H. K. Porter Co. v. *Labor Board,* 397 U.S. 99 (1970)
Hill v. *Florida* ex rel. *Watson,* 325 U.S. 538 (1945)
Hilton v. *Sullivan,* 334 U.S. 323 (1948)
Hines v. *Davidowitz,* 312 U.S. 52 (1941)
Hines v. *Lowrey,* 305 U.S. 85 (1938)
Hirshberg v. *Cooke,* 336 U.S. 210 (1949)
Holt v. *Virginia,* 381 U.S. 131 (1965)
Hoopeston Canning Co. v. *Cullen,* 318 U.S. 313 (1943)
Hormel v. *Helvering,* 312 U.S. 552 (1941)
Horton v. *Liberty Mutual Insurance Co.,* 367 U.S. 348 (1961)
Howell Chevrolet Co. v. *Labor Board,* 346 U.S. 482 (1953)
Howitt v. *United States,* 328 U.S. 189 (1946)
Hughes v. *Fetter,* 341 U.S. 609 (1951)
Hughes v. *United States,* 342 U.S. 353 (1952)
Hughes v. *Washington,* 389 U.S. 290 (1967)

Hulbert v. *Twin Falls County,* 327 U.S. 103 (1946)
Humble Pipe Line Co. v. *Waggonner,* 376 U.S. 369 (1964)
Humphrey v. *Smith,* 336 U.S. 695 (1949)
Hunt v. *Crumboch,* 325 U.S. 821 (1945)
Huron Corp. v. *Lincoln Mine Co.,* 312 U.S. 183 (1941)

Illinois v. *Allen,* 397 U.S. 337 (1970)
Illinois ex rel. *Gordon* v. *United States,* 328 U.S. 8 (1946)
Inland Steel Co. v. *United States,* 306 U.S. 153 (1939)
Inter-Island Steam Navigation Co. v. *Hawaii,* 305 U.S. 306 (1938)
International Shoe Co. v. *Washington,* 326 U.S. 310 (1945)
Interstate Commerce Comm'n. v. *Mechling,* 330 U.S. 567 (1947)
Interstate Commerce Comm'n. v. *Railway Labor Assn.,* 315 U.S. 373 (1942)

Jackson v. *Lykes Bros. Steamship Co.,* 386 U.S. 731 (1967)
James v. *Valtierra,* 402 U.S. 137 (1971)
Jamison v. *Texas,* 318 U.S. 413 (1943)
Jesionowski v. *Boston & Maine R. Co.,* 329 U.S. 452 (1947)
Johnson v. *New York, N. H. & H. R. Co.,* 344 U.S. 48 (1952)
Johnson v. *Shaughnessy,* 336 U.S. 806 (1949)
Johnson v. *Yellow Cab Transit Co.,* 321 U.S. 383 (1944)
Johnson v. *Zerbst,* 304 U.S. 458 (1938)
Jones v. *Cunningham,* 371 U.S. 236 (1963)

Kalb v. *Feuerstein,* 308 U.S. 433 (1940)
Katzinger Co. v. *Chicago Mfg. Co.,* 329 U.S. 394 (1947)
Kaufman v. *Société Internationale,* 343 U.S. 156 (1952)
Kawato, Ex parte, 317 U.S. 69 (1942)
Keefe v. *Clark,* 322 U.S. 393 (1944)
Kersh Lake Drainage Dist. v. *Johnson,* 309 U.S. 485 (1940)
Kiefer-Stewart Company v. *Seagram & Sons,* 340 U.S. 211 (1951)
Klor's, Inc. v. *Broadway-Hale Stores,* 359 U.S. 207 (1959)
Kolovrat v. *Oregon,* 366 U.S. 187 (1961)
Konigsberg v. *State Bar of California,* 353 U.S. 252 (1957)
Korematsu v. *United States,* 319 U.S. 432 (1943)
Korematsu v. *United States,* 323 U.S. 214 (1944)
Kotch v. *Board of River Pilot Comm'rs.,* 330 U.S. 552 (1947)
Kovacs v. *Brewer,* 356 U.S. 604 (1958)
Krug v. *Santa Fe Pacific R. Co.,* 329 U.S. 591 (1947)
Krulewitch v. *United States,* 336 U.S. 440 (1949)

Labine v. *Vincent,* 401 U.S. 532 (1971)
Labor Board v. *Bradford Dyeing Assn.,* 310 U.S. 318 (1940)
Labor Board v. *Radio & Television Broadcast Engrs.,* 364 U.S. 573 (1961)
Labor Board v. *Truitt Mfg. Co.,* 351 U.S. 149 (1956)
Labor Board v. *United Insurance Co. of America,* 390 U.S. 254 (1968)
Labor Board v. *Washington Aluminum Co.,* 370 U.S. 9 (1962)
Labor Board v. *Waterman Steamship Corp.,* 309 U.S. 206 (1940)
Laurens Fed. Savings & Loan Assn. v. *S. C. Tax Comm'n.,* 365 U.S. 517 (1961)
Levers v. *Anderson,* 326 U.S. 219 (1945)
Leyra v. *Denno,* 347 U.S. 556 (1954)
Libby, McNeill & Libby v. *United States,* 340 U.S. 71 (1950)
Lincoln Labor Union v. *Northwestern Iron Co.,* 335 U.S. 525 (1949)
Lloyd A. Fry Roofing Co. v. *Wood,* 344 U.S. 157 (1952)

Shore Line v. *Transportation Union,* 396 U.S. 142 (1969)
Simonson v. *Granquist,* 369 U.S. 38 (1962)
Sinclair Refining Co. v. *Atkinson,* 370 U.S. 195 (1962)
Slocum v. *Delaware, L. & W. R. Co.,* 339 U.S. 239 (1950)
Small Business Administration v. *McClellan,* 364 U.S. 446 (1960)
Smith v. *O'Grady,* 312 U.S. 329 (1941)
Smith v. *Shaughnessy,* 318 U.S. 176 (1943)
Smith v. *Texas,* 311 U.S. 128 (1940)
Snyder v. *Harris,* 394 U.S. 332 (1969)
Solesbee v. *Balkcom,* 339 U.S. 9 (1950)
Spiegel, Estate of v. *Commissioner,* 335 U.S. 701 (1949)
Spreckels v. *Commissioner,* 315 U.S. 626 (1942)
Standard Dredging Corp. v. *Murphy,* 319 U.S. 306 (1943)
Standard Oil Co. v. *Johnson,* 316 U.S. 481 (1942)
Standard Oil Co. v. *United States,* 340 U.S. 54 (1950)
State Tax Comm'n. v. *Van Cott,* 306 U.S. 511 (1939)
Steele v. *General Mills,* 329 U.S. 433 (1947)
Stern v. *South Chester Tube Co.,* 390 U.S. 606 (1968)
Stewart v. *United States,* 366 U.S. 1 (1961)
Still v. *Norfolk & Western R. Co.,* 368 U.S. 35 (1961)
Stirone v. *United States,* 361 U.S. 212 (1960)
Superior Bath House Co. v. *McCarroll,* 312 U.S. 176 (1941)
Surowitz v. *Hilton Hotels Corp.,* 383 U.S. 363 (1966)

Takahashi v. *Fish & Game Comm'n.,* 334 U.S. 410 (1948)
Talley v. *California,* 362 U.S. 60 (1960)
Testa v. *Katt,* 330 U.S. 386 (1947)
Texas v. *New Jersey,* 379 U.S. 674 (1965)
Thomas v. *Hempt Brothers,* 345 U.S. 19 (1953)
Thompson v. *Louisville,* 362 U.S. 199 (1960)
Thompson v. *Magnolia Petroleum Co.,* 309 U.S. 478 (1940)
Tiller v. *Atlantic Coast Line,* 318 U.S. 54 (1943)
Tiller v. *Atlantic Coast Line R. Co.,* 323 U.S. 574 (1945)
Timken Roller Bearing Co. v. *United States,* 341 U.S. 593 (1951)
Torcaso v. *Watkins,* 367 U.S. 488 (1961)
Toussie v. *United States,* 397 U.S. 112 (1970)
Trade Comm'n. v. *Raladam Co.,* 316 U.S. 149 (1942)
Transportation-Com Union v. *Union Pac. R. Co.,* 385 U.S. 157 (1966)
Travelers Health Assn. v. *Virginia* ex rel. *Corp. Comm'n.,* 339 U.S. 643 (1950)
Tucker v. *Texas,* 326 U.S. 517 (1946)
Tulee v. *Washington,* 315 U.S. 681 (1942)

United States v. *Acme Process Equip. Co.,* 385 U.S. 138 (1966)
United States v. *Allen-Bradley Co.,* 352 U.S. 306 (1957)
United States v. *Allied Oil Corp.,* 341 U.S. 1 (1951)
United States v. *Atlantic Mutual Ins. Co.,* 343 U.S. 236 (1952)
United States v. *Atlantic Refining Co.,* 360 U.S. 19 (1959)
United States v. *Baltimore & Ohio R. Co.,* 333 U.S. 169 (1948)
United States v. *Bethlehem Steel Corp.,* 315 U.S. 289 (1942)
United States v. *Braverman,* 373 U.S. 405 (1963)
United States v. *California,* 332 U.S. 19 (1947)
United States v. *California Eastern Line, Inc.,* 348 U.S. 351 (1955)
United States v. *Capital Transit Co.,* 325 U.S. 357 (1945)
United States v. *Chicago Heights Trucking Co.,* 310 U.S. 344 (1940)

Opinions Announcing Judgment

Klapprott v. *United States,* 335 U.S. 601 (1949)

Oregon v. *Mitchell,* 400 U.S. 112 (1970)

Reid v. *Covert,* 354 U.S. 1 (1957)

Stolar, In re, 401 U.S. 23 (1971)

Terry v. *Adams,* 345 U.S. 461 (1953)

United States v. *Pewee Coal Co.,* 341 U.S. 114 (1951)

Von Moltke v. *Gillies,* 332 U.S. 708 (1948)

Welsh v. *United States,* 398 U.S. 333 (1970)

Separate Opinions

A Quantity of Books v. *Kansas,* 378 U.S. 205, 213 (1964)

Board of County Commissioners v. *United States,* 308 U.S. 343, 353 (1939)
Brown v. *Allen,* 344 U.S. 443, 513 (1953) (Notation) (Joint)
Byrne v. *Karalexis,* 396 U.S. 976, 982 (1969)

Citizens to Preserve Overton Park v. *Volpe,* 401 U.S. 402, 421 (1971)
Coates v. *City of Cincinnati,* 402 U.S. 611, 616 (1971)
Commissioner v. *Duberstein,* 363 U.S. 278, 293 (1960) (Concurring and Dissenting)
Coolidge v. *New Hampshire,* 403 U.S. 443, 493 (1971) (Concurring and Dissenting)

Dennis v. *United States,* 384 U.S. 855, 875 (1966) (Concurring in Part and Dissenting in Part)

England v. *Medical Examiners,* 375 U.S. 411, 437 (1964) (Concurring in Part and Dissenting in Part)

Federal Power Comm'n. v. *Hope Gas Co.,* 320 U.S. 591, 619 (1944) (Joint)
Federal Power Comm'n. v. *Interstate Gas Co.,* 336 U.S. 577, 595 (1949) (Concurring in Part and Dissenting in Part)

Gilbert v. *California,* 388 U.S. 263, 277 (1967) (Concurring in Part and Dissenting in Part)

Jackson v. *Denno,* 378 U.S. 368, 401 (1964) (Dissenting in Part and Concurring in Part)
Jacobellis v. *Ohio,* 378 U.S. 184, 196 (1964)
James v. *United States,* 366 U.S. 213, 222 (1961) (Concurring in Part and Dissenting in Part)

Lear, Inc. v. *Adkins,* 395 U.S. 653, 676 (1969) (Concurring in Part and Dissenting in Part)
Lehmann v. *United States* ex rel. *Carson,* 353 U.S. 685, 690 (1957)

Maggio v. *Zeitz,* 333 U.S. 56, 78 (1948)
McGautha v. *California,* 402 U.S. 183, 225 (1971)
Mercoid Corp. v. *Mid-Continent Co.,* 320 U.S. 661, 672 (1944)
Mills v. *Electric Auto-Life Co.,* 396 U.S. 375, 397 (1970) (Concurring in Part and Dissenting in Part)
Monitor Patriot Co. v. *Roy,* 401 U.S. 265, 277 (1971)

Nishikawa v. *Dulles,* 356 U.S. 129, 138 (1958)
North Carolina v. *Pearce,* 395 U.S. 711, 737 (1969) (Concurring in Part and Dissenting in Part)

Ocala Star-Banner Co. v. *Damron,* 401 U.S. 295, 301 (1971); see *Monitor Patriot Co.* v. *Roy,* 401 U.S. 265, 277 (1971)

Polizzi v. *Cowles Magazines, Inc.,* 345 U.S. 663, 667 (1953) (Concurring in Part and Dissenting in Part)

Public Utilities Comm'n. v. *Pollak*, 343 U.S. 451, 466 (1952)

Republic Steel Corp. v. *Labor Board*, 311 U.S. 7, 13 (1940) (Joint)
Rosenblatt v. *Baer*, 383 U.S. 75, 94 (1966) (Concurring in Part and Dissenting)

Schlagenhauf v. *Holder*, 379 U.S. 104, 122 (1964) (Concurring in Part and Dissenting in Part)
Simmons v. *United States*, 390 U.S. 377, 395 (1968) (Concurring in Part and Dissenting in Part)
Simpson v. *Union Oil of California*, 396 U.S. 13, 15 (1969) (Concurring in Part and Dissenting in Part)
South Carolina v. *Katzenbach*, 383 U.S. 301, 355 (1966)(Concurring and Dissenting)

Time, Inc. v. *Pape*, 401 U.S. 279, 292 (1971); see *Monitor Patriot Co.* v. *Roy*, 401 U.S. 265, 277 (1971)

United States v. *Louisiana*, 363 U.S. 1, 85 (1960) (Concurring in Part and Dissenting in Part)
United States v. *United Mine Workers*, 330 U.S. 258, 328 (1947) (Concurring in Part and Dissenting in Part) (Joint)
United States v. *Wade*, 388 U.S. 218, 243 (1967) (Dissenting in Part and Concurring in Part)

Williams v. *Florida*, 399 U.S. 78, 106 (1970) (Concurring in Part and Dissenting in Part)

Yates v. *United States*, 354 U.S. 298, 339 (1957) (Concurring in Part and Dissenting in Part)

CONCURRING OPINIONS

Adickes v. *S. H. Kress & Co.*, 398 U.S. 144, 175 (1970)
Anti-Fascist Refugee Committee v. *McGrath*, 341 U.S. 123, 142 (1951)
Aptheker v. *Secretary of State*, 378 U.S. 500, 517 (1964)
Armstrong v. *Armstrong*, 350 U.S. 568, 575 (1956)
Aro Mfg. Co. v. *Convertible Top Replacement Co.*, 365 U.S. 336, 346 (1961)
Ashe v. *Swenson*, 397 U.S. 436, 447 (1970)
Associated Press v. *Walker*, 388 U.S. 130, 170 (1967)

Baldwin v. *New York*, 399 U.S. 66, 74 (1970)
Barr v. *Matteo*, 360 U.S. 564, 576 (1959)
Bates v. *Little Rock*, 361 U.S. 516, 527 (1960)
Brandenburg v. *Ohio*, 395 U.S. 444, 449 (1969)
Burlington Truck Lines v. *United States*, 371 U.S. 156, 174 (1962)

Carnley v. *Cochran*, 369 U.S. 506, 517 (1962)
Carter v. *Jury Commission of Greene County*, 396 U.S. 320, 341 (1970)
Carter v. *Virginia*, 321 U.S. 131, 138 (1944)
Central R. Company v. *Pennsylvania*, 370 U.S. 607, 618 (1962)
Chandler v. *Wise*, 307 U.S. 474, 478 (1939) (Joint)
Coleman v. *Alabama*, 399 U.S. 1, 11 (1970)
Coleman v. *Miller*, 307 U.S. 433, 456 (1939)
Cox v. *Louisiana*, 379 U.S. 536, 558 (1965); see *Cox* v. *Louisiana*, 379 U.S. 559, 575 (1965)

Dandridge v. *Williams*, 397 U.S. 471, 489 (1970)
Duncan v. *Louisiana*, 391 U.S. 145, 162 (1968)
Durfee v. *Duke*, 375 U.S. 106, 116 (1963)

Epperson v. *Arkansas*, 393 U.S. 97, 109 (1968)

First Unitarian Church v. *Los Angeles County*, 357 U.S. 545, 547 (1958); see *Speiser* v. *Randall*, 357 U.S. 513, 529 (1958)

Garrison v. *Louisiana,* 379 U.S. 64, 79 (1964)
Gault, In re, 387 U.S. 1, 59 (1967)
Gibson v. *Florida Legislative Investigation Committee,* 372 U.S. 539, 558 (1963)
Graver Tank & Mfg. Co. v. *Linde Air Products Co.,* 336 U.S. 271, 280 (1949)
Gregory v. *Chicago,* 394 U.S. 111, 113 (1969)
Grunewald v. *United States,* 353 U.S. 391, 425 (1957)

Heart of Atlanta Motel v. *United States,* 379 U.S. 241, 268 (1964)
Helvering v. *Gerhardt,* 304 U.S. 405, 424 (1938)

Jenkins v. *McKeithen,* 395 U.S. 411, 432 (1969)

Katzenbach v. *McClung,* 379 U.S. 294, 305 (1964); see *Heart of Atlanta Motel* v. *United States,* 379 U.S. 241, 268 (1964)
Keegan v. *United States,* 325 U.S. 478, 495 (1945)
Kingsley International Pictures Corp. v. *Regents,* 360 U.S. 684, 690 (1959)
Knauer v. *United States,* 328 U.S. 654, 674 (1946)

Labor Board v. *Fruit & Vegetable Packers,* 377 U.S. 58, 76 (1964)
Labor Board v. *Wyman-Gordon Co.,* 394 U.S. 759, 769 (1969)
Leary v. *United States,* 395 U.S. 6, 55 (1969)
Lee v. *Washington,* 390 U.S. 333, 334 (1968) (Joint)

Mapp v. *Ohio,* 367 U.S. 643, 661 (1961)
Marcus v. *Search Warrant,* 367 U.S. 717, 738 (1961)
McCarthy v. *United States,* 394 U.S. 459, 477 (1969)
Michigan National Bank v. *Robertson,* 372 U.S. 591, 594 (1963)
Morgan v. *Virginia,* 328 U.S. 373, 386 (1946)
Moseley v. *Electronic & Missile Facilities,* 374 U.S. 167, 172 (1963) (Joint)

New York Times Co. v. *Sullivan,* 376 U.S. 254, 293 (1964)
New York Times Co. v. *United States,* 403 U.S. 713, 714 (1971)
Northwest Airlines v. *Minnesota,* 322 U.S. 292, 301 (1944)
Noto v. *United States,* 367 U.S. 290, 300 (1961)

One 1958 Plymouth Sedan v. *Pennsylvania,* 380 U.S. 693, 703 (1965)
Oyama v. *California,* 332 U.S. 633, 647 (1948)

Pacific Coast Dairy v. *Dept. of Agriculture,* 318 U.S. 285, 296 (1943) (Joint)
Parker v. *North Carolina,* 397 U.S. 790, 799 (1970)
Peters v. *Hobby,* 349 U.S. 331, 349 (1955)
Peters v. *New York,* 392 U.S. 40, 79 (1968)
Polish National Alliance v. *Labor Board,* 322 U.S. 643, 651 (1944)
Powell v. *Texas,* 392 U.S. 514, 537 (1968)
Power Comm'n. v. *Pipeline Co.,* 315 U.S. 575, 599 (1942) (Joint)
Pullman Company v. *Jenkins,* 305 U.S. 534, 542 (1939)

Rochin v. *California,* 342 U.S. 165, 174 (1952)
Rosenbloom v. *Metromedia, Inc.,* 403 U.S. 29, 57 (1971)

Sawyer, In re, 360 U.S. 622, 646 (1959)
Simons v. *Miami Beach First Nat. Bank,* 381 U.S. 81, 88 (1965)
Smith v. *California,* 361 U.S. 147, 155 (1959)
Smyth v. *United States,* 302 U.S. 329, 364 (1937)
Speiser v. *Randall,* 357 U.S. 513, 529 (1958)
Stanley v. *Georgia,* 394 U.S. 557, 568 (1969)

Tenney v. *Brandhove,* 341 U.S. 367, 379 (1951)
Thorpe v. *Housing Authority of Durham,* 393 U.S. 268, 284 (1969)
Time, Inc. v. *Hill,* 385 U.S. 374, 398 (1967)
Tot v. *United States,* 319 U.S. 463, 473 (1943)
Trop v. *Dulles,* 356 U.S. 86, 104 (1958)

United Gas Public Service Co. v. *Texas,* 303 U.S. 123, 146 (1938)
United States v. *Five Gambling Devices,* 346 U.S. 441, 452 (1953)
United States v. *Harris,* 403 U.S. 573, 585 (1971)
United States v. *Minker,* 350 U.S. 179, 190 (1956)
United States v. *Public Utilities Comm'n.,* 345 U.S. 295, 318 (1953)
United States v. *Tillamooks,* 329 U.S. 40, 54 (1946)
United States v. *Williams,* 341 U.S. 70, 85 (1951)
Utah Fuel Co. v. *Bituminous Coal Comm'n.,* 306 U.S. 56, 62 (1939)

West Virginia Board of Education v. *Barnette,* 319 U.S. 624, 643 (1943) (Joint)
Wieman v. *Updegraff,* 344 U.S. 183, 192 (1952)
Will v. *United States,* 389 U.S. 90, 107 (1967)
Willingham v. *Morgan,* 395 U.S. 402, 410 (1969)
Wolf v. *Colorado,* 338 U.S. 25, 39 (1949)

Z. & F. Assets Realization Corp. v. *Hull,* 311 U.S. 470, 490 (1941)

Dissenting Opinions

Abbate v. *United States,* 359 U.S. 187, 201 (1959)
Ackermann v. *United States,* 340 U.S. 193, 202 (1950)
Adams Mfg. Co. v. *Storen,* 304 U.S. 307, 316 (1938)
Adamson v. *California,* 332 U.S. 46, 68 (1947)
Adler v. *Board of Education of City of New York,* 342 U.S. 485, 496 (1952)
Alabama v. *Texas,* 347 U.S. 272, 277 (1954)
Algoma Plywood Co. v. *Wisconsin Board,* 336 U.S. 301, 315 (1949)
Allen v. *State Board of Elections,* 393 U.S. 544, 595 (1969)
American Comm. Foreign Born v. *Subversive Act. Cont. Bd.,* 380 U.S. 503, 511 (1965)
American Communications Assn. v. *Douds,* 339 U.S. 382, 445 (1950)
American Trucking Assns. v. *United States,* 344 U.S. 298, 327 (1953)
Anastaplo, In re, 366 U.S. 82, 97 (1961)
Anonymous No. 6 v. *Baker*, 360 U.S. 287, 298 (1959)
Aro Mfg. Co. v. *Convertible Top Co.,* 377 U.S. 476, 515 (1964)
Ashcraft v. *United States,* 361 U.S. 925 (1959) (Joint)

Baltimore Contractors, Inc. v. *Bodinger,* 348 U.S. 176, 185 (1955)
Bank of America v. *Parnell,* 352 U.S. 29, 35 (1956) (Joint)
Barenblatt v. *United States,* 360 U.S. 109, 134 (1959)
Barr v. *Columbia,* 378 U.S. 146, 151 (1964) (Dissenting from the Reversal of Trespass Convictions)
Barsky v. *New York University,* 347 U.S. 442, 456 (1954)
Bartkus v. *Illinois,* 359 U.S. 121, 150 (1959)
Beaufort Concrete Co. v. *Atlantic States Construction Co.,* 384 U.S. 1004 (1966)
Beauharnais v. *Illinois,* 343 U.S. 250, 267 (1952)
Beck v. *Washington,* 369 U.S. 541, 558 (1962)
Bell v. *Maryland,* 378 U.S. 226, 318 (1964)
Berger v. *New York,* 388 U.S. 41, 70 (1967)
Berman v. *United States,* 378 U.S. 530 (1964)

Berra v. *United States,* 351 U.S. 131, 135 (1956)
Bertman v. *J. A. Kirsch Co.,* 377 U.S. 995 (1964)
Betts v. *Brady,* 316 U.S. 455, 474 (1942)
Bihn v. *United States,* 328 U.S. 633, 639 (1946)
Bivins v. *Six Unknown Agents, Federal Bur. Narcotics,* 403 U.S. 388, 427 (1971)
Board of Education of Central School Dist. 1 v. *Allen,* 392 U.S. 236, 250 (1968)
Boddie v. *Connecticut,* 401 U.S. 371, 389 (1971)
Bogardus v. *Commissioner,* 302 U.S. 34, 44 (1937) (Joint)
Bollenbach v. *United States,* 326 U.S. 607, 615 (1946)
Boone v. *Lightner,* 319 U.S. 561, 576 (1943)
Bouie v. *Columbia,* 378 U.S. 347, 363 (1964)
Boys Markets, Inc. v. *Retail Clerks,* 398 U.S. 235, 255 (1970)
Braden v. *United States,* 365 U.S. 431, 438 (1961)
Brady v. *Southern Ry. Co.,* 320 U.S. 476, 484 (1943)
Brannan v. *Stark,* 342 U.S. 451, 466 (1952)
Braswell v. *Florida,* 400 U.S. 873 (1970)
Breard v. *Alexandria,* 341 U.S. 622, 649 (1951)
Brown v. *Allen,* 344 U.S. 443, 548 (1953)
Brown v. *Louisiana,* 383 U.S. 131, 151 (1966)
Brown v. *United States,* 356 U.S. 148, 157 (1958)
Bumper v. *North Carolina,* 391 U.S. 543, 554 (1968)

Cahill v. *New York, N. H. & H. R. Co.,* 351 U.S. 183, 184 (1956)
California v. *Byers,* 402 U.S. 424, 459 (1971)
Cameron v. *Johnson,* 381 U.S. 741, 742 (1965)
Campbell v. *Hussey,* 368 U.S. 297, 302 (1961)
Carey v. *Westinghouse Electric Corp.,* 375 U.S. 261, 273 (1964)
Carlson v. *Landon,* 342 U.S. 524, 547 (1952)
Carpenters & Joiners Union v. *Ritter's Cafe,* 315 U.S. 722, 729 (1942)
Central States Electric Co. v. *Muscatine,* 324 U.S. 138, 146 (1945)
Chandler v. *Judicial Council of the Tenth Circuit of the United States,* 382 U.S. 1003, 1004 (1966)
Chandler v. *Judicial Council of the 10th Circuit,* 398 U.S. 74, 141 (1970)
Chicago & E. I. R. Co. v. *United States,* 375 U.S. 150 (1963)
Chicago, R. I. & P. R. Co. v. *Stude,* 346 U.S. 574, 582 (1954)
C. J. Hendry Co. v. *Moore,* 318 U.S. 133, 154 (1943)
Clay v. *Sun Insurance Office Ltd.,* 363 U.S. 207, 213 (1960)
Cohen v. *Hurley,* 366 U.S. 117, 131 (1961)
Colegrove v. *Green,* 328 U.S. 549, 566 (1946)
Colonnade Catering Corp. v. *United States,* 397 U.S. 72, 79 (1970)
Colorado National Bank v. *Commissioner,* 305 U.S. 23, 27 (1938)
Commercial Molasses Corp. v. *N. Y. Barge Corp.,* 314 U.S. 104, 114 (1941)
Commissioner v. *Stern,* 357 U.S. 39, 47 (1958)
Communist Party v. *Subversive Activities Control Board,* 367 U.S. 1, 137 (1961)
Connecticut General Co. v. *Johnson,* 303 U.S. 77, 83 (1938)
Connor v. *Johnson,* 402 U.S. 690, 693 (1971)
Cox v. *Louisiana,* 379 U.S. 559, 575 (1965)
Crane v. *Cedar Rapids & I. C. R. Co.,* 395 U.S. 164, 167 (1969)
Crown Cork & Seal Co. v. *Gutmann Co.,* 304 U.S. 159, 168 (1938)
Curtis Publishing Co. v. *Butts,* 388 U.S. 130, 170 (1967)

Ginzburg v. *United States,* 383 U.S. 463, 476 (1966)
Goldberg v. *Kelly,* 397 U.S. 254, 271 (1970)
Goodyear Tire & Rubber Co. v. *Ray-O-Vac Co.,* 321 U.S. 275, 279 (1944)
Graver Tank & Mfg. Co. v. *Linde Air Products Co.,* 339 U.S. 605, 612 (1950)
Green v. *United States,* 356 U.S. 165, 193 (1958)
Green v. *United States,* 365 U.S. 301, 307 (1961)
Griggs v. *Allegheny County,* 369 U.S. 84, 90 (1962)
Griswold v. *Connecticut,* 381 U.S. 479, 507 (1965)
Groban, In re, 352 U.S. 330, 337 (1957)
Groppi v. *Wisconsin,* 400 U.S. 505, 515 (1971)
Gulf Oil Corp. v. *Gilbert,* 330 U.S. 501, 512 (1947)
Gwin, White & Prince v. *Henneford,* 305 U.S. 434, 442 (1939)

Halliday v. *United States,* 394 U.S. 831, 835 (1969)
Hamm v. *Rock Hill,* 379 U.S. 306, 318 (1964)
Hanson v. *Denckla,* 357 U.S. 235, 256 (1958)
Harper v. *Virginia Bd. of Elections,* 383 U.S. 663, 670 (1966)
Harris v. *Nelson,* 394 U.S. 286, 301 (1969)
Harrison v. *United States,* 392 U.S. 219, 226 (1968)
Hartford-Empire Co. v. *United States,* 323 U.S. 386, 435 (1945)
Heiser v. *Woodruff,* 327 U.S. 726, 740 (1946) (Joint)
Helvering v. *Sabine Transportation Co.,* 318 U.S. 306, 312 (1943)
Henry v. *Mississippi,* 379 U.S. 443, 453 (1965)
Herb v. *Pitcairn,* 324 U.S. 117, 128 (1945)
Hill v. *United States,* 368 U.S. 424, 430 (1962)
Hood & Sons v. *Du Mond,* 336 U.S. 525, 545 (1949)
Hooven & Allison Co. v. *Evatt,* 324 U.S. 652, 686 (1945)
Hostetter v. *Idlewild Bon Voyage Liquor Corp.,* 377 U.S. 324, 334 (1964)
Hunter v. *Erickson,* 393 U.S. 385, 396 (1969)
Hysler v. *Florida,* 315 U.S. 411, 423 (1942)

Illinois Central R. Co. v. *Norfolk & W. R. Co.,* 385 U.S. 57, 75 (1966)
Immigration and Naturalization Service v. *Stanisic,* 395 U.S. 62, 80 (1969)
Indiana ex rel. *Anderson* v. *Brand,* 303 U.S. 95, 109 (1938)
International Longshoremen's Union v. *Boyd,* 347 U.S. 222, 224 (1954)
Interstate Commerce Comm'n. v. *Inland Waterways Corp.,* 319 U.S. 671, 692 (1943)
Irvine v. *California,* 347 U.S. 128, 139 (1954)
Italia Societa per Navigazione v. *Oregon Stevedoring Co.,* 376 U.S. 315, 325 (1964)

Jay v. *Boyd,* 351 U.S. 345, 362 (1956)
Johansen v. *United States,* 343 U.S. 427, 441 (1952)
Johnson v. *Eisentrager,* 339 U.S. 763, 791 (1950)
Jones v. *Opelika,* 316 U.S. 584, 623 (1942) (Joint)

Katz v. *United States,* 389 U.S. 347, 364 (1967)
Kaufman v. *United States,* 394 U.S. 217, 231 (1969)
Kelley v. *Everglades Drainage District,* 319 U.S. 415, 422 (1943)
Kern-Limerick, Inc. v. *Scurlock,* 347 U.S. 110, 123 (1954)
Kesler v. *Department of Public Safety of Utah,* 369 U.S. 153, 182 (1962)
Killian v. *United States,* 368 U.S. 231, 258 (1961)
Kinsella v. *Krueger,* 351 U.S. 470, 485 (1956) (Joint)

Knapp v. *Schweitzer,* 357 U.S. 371, 382 (1958)
Koehring Co. v. *Hyde Constr. Co.,* 382 U.S. 362, 365 (1966)
Konigsberg v. *State Bar of California,* 366 U.S. 36, 56 (1961)
Kordel v. *United States,* 335 U.S. 345, 352 (1948)
Koster v. *(American) Lumbermens Mutual Co.,* 330 U.S. 518, 532 (1947)
Kovacs v. *Cooper,* 336 U.S. 77, 98 (1949)
Kraus & Bros. v. *United States,* 327, U.S. 614, 629 (1946)

Labor Board v. *Allis-Chalmers Mfg. Co.,* 388 U.S. 175, 199 (1967)
Labor Board v. *I. & M. Electric Co.,* 318 U.S. 9, 30 (1943)
Labor Board v. *Rockaway News Supply Co.,* 345 U.S. 71, 81 (1953)
Lance v. *Plummer,* 384 U.S. 929 (1966)
Lathrop v. *Donohue,* 367 U.S. 820, 865 (1961)
Law Students Civil Rights Research Council v. *Wadmond,* 401 U.S. 154, 174 (1971)
Lee v. *Florida,* 392 U.S. 378, 387 (1968)
Lehigh Valley Cooperative Farmers, Inc. v. *United States,* 370 U.S. 76, 100 (1962)
Levine v. *United States,* 362 U.S. 610, 620 (1960)
Lewis v. *Martin,* 397 U.S. 552, 560 (1970)
Lewis v. *United States,* 348 U.S. 419, 423 (1955)
Link v. *Wabash R. Co.,* 370 U.S. 626, 636 (1962)
Linkletter v. *Walker,* 381 U.S. 618, 640 (1965)
Linn v. *Plant Guard Workers,* 383 U.S. 53, 67 (1966)
Lisenba v. *California,* 314 U.S. 219, 241 (1941)
Lopinson v. *Pennsylvania,* 392 U.S. 647, 648 (1968)
Louisiana Boundary Case, 394 U.S. 11, 78 (1969)
Ludecke v. *Watkins,* 335 U.S. 160, 173 (1948)

Machinists v. *Street,* 367 U.S. 740, 780 (1961)
Madsen v. *Kinsella,* 343 U.S. 341, 371 (1952)
Magnolia Petroleum Co. v. *Hunt,* 320 U.S. 430, 450 (1943)
Mancusi v. *DeForte,* 392 U.S. 364, 372 (1968)
Marcello v. *Bonds,* 349 U.S. 302, 315 (1955)
Marshall v. *Pletz,* 317 U.S. 383, 391 (1943)
Maryland Casualty Co. v. *Cushing,* 347 U.S. 409, 427 (1954)
Maxwell v. *Bishop,* 398 U.S. 262, 267 (1970)
McCarroll v. *Dixie Greyhound Lines,* 309 U.S. 176, 183 (1940) (Joint)
McCart v. *Indianapolis Water Co.,* 302 U.S. 419, 423 (1938)
McDonald v. *Commissioner,* 323 U.S. 57, 65 (1944)
Michel v. *Louisiana,* 350 U.S. 91, 102 (1955)
Minnesota Min. & Mfg. Co. v. *N. J. Wood Fin. Co.,* 381 U.S. 311, 324 (1965)
Mishawaka Rubber & Woolen Co. v. *Kresge Co.,* 316 U.S. 203, 208 (1942)
Mishkin v. *New York,* 383 U.S. 502, 515 (1966)
Moore v. *Chesapeake & O. R. Co.,* 340 U.S. 573, 578 (1951)
Morey v. *Doud,* 354 U.S. 457, 470 (1957)
Morgantown v. *Royal Ins. Co.,* 337 U.S. 254, 261 (1949)
Morris v. *Florida,* 393 U.S. 850 (1968)
Mosser v. *Darrow,* 341 U.S. 267, 275 (1951)
Mulcahey v. *Catalanotte,* 353 U.S. 692, 694 (1957); see *Lehmann* v. *U.S.* ex rel. *Carson,* 353 U.S. 685, 690 (1957)
Muschany v. *United States,* 324 U.S. 49, 69 (1945)

United States v. *Champlin Refining Co.*, 341 U.S. 290, 302 (1951)
United States v. *Cooper Corporation*, 312 U.S. 600, 615 (1941)
United States v. *Dixon*, 347 U.S. 381, 386 (1954)
United States v. *Embassy Restaurant*, 359 U.S. 29, 35 (1959)
United States v. *Fleischman*, 339 U.S. 349, 365 (1950)
United States v. *Gainey*, 380 U.S. 63, 74 (1965)
United States v. *Hood*, 343 U.S. 148, 152 (1952)
United States v. *Interstate Commerce Comm'n.*, 352 U.S. 158, 176 (1956)
United States v. *Kahriger*, 345 U.S. 22, 36 (1953)
United States v. *National Dairy Products Corp.*, 372 U.S. 29, 37 (1963)
United States v. *Rabinowitz*, 339 U.S. 56, 66 (1950)
United States v. *Reidel*, 402 U.S. 351, 357 (1971); see *United States*, v. *Thirty-Seven (37) Photographs*, 402 U.S. 363, 379 (1971)
United States v. *Shotwell Mfg. Co.*, 355 U.S. 233, 246 (1957)
United States v. *Spector*, 343 U.S. 169, 173 (1952)
United States v. *Speers*, 382 U.S. 266, 278 (1965)
United States v. *Thirty-Seven (37) Photographs*, 402 U.S. 363, 379 (1971)
United States v. *Welden*, 377 U.S. 95, 107 (1964)
United States v. *Yazell*, 382 U.S. 341, 359 (1966)
United States v. *Yellow Cab Co.*, 338 U.S. 338, 342 (1949)
Uphaus v. *Wyman*, 364 U.S. 388, 389 (1960)
U. S. Gypsum Co. v. *National Gypsum Co.*, 352 U.S. 457, 477 (1957)

Vaca v. *Sipes*, 386 U.S. 171, 203 (1967)
Vale v. *Louisiana*, 399 U.S. 30, 36 (1970)
Veterans of Abraham Lincoln Brig. v. *Sub. Act. Cont. Bd.*, 380 U.S. 513, 514 (1965); see *American Comm. Foreign Born* v. *Subversive Act. Cont. Bd.*, 380 U.S. 503, 511 (1965)
Viereck v. *United States*, 318 U.S. 236, 249 (1943)
Virginia Petroleum Jobbers Assn. v. *Federal Power Commission*, 368 U.S. 940 (1961)

Wade v. *Wilson, Warden*, 396 U.S. 282, 287 (1970)
Warner v. *Kewanee Machinery & Conveyor Co.*, 398 U.S. 906 (1970)
Washingtonian Publishing Co. v. *Pearson*, 306 U.S. 30, 42 (1939)
Whiteley v. *Warden*, 401 U.S. 560, 570 (1971)
Whitney Nat. Bank v. *Bank of New Orleans & Tr. Co.*, 379 U.S. 411, 432 (1965)
Wilkinson v. *United States*, 365 U.S. 399, 415 (1961)
Willard Dairy Corp. v. *National Dairy Products Corp.*, 373 U.S. 934 (1963)
Williams v. *Jacksonville Terminal Co.*, 315 U.S. 386, 410 (1942)
Williams v. *North Carolina*, 325 U.S. 226, 261 (1945)
Williams Mfg. Co. v. *Shoe Machinery Corp.*, 316 U.S. 364, 371 (1942)
Winship, In re, 397 U.S. 358, 377 (1970)
Wisconsin v. *Constantineau*, 400 U.S. 433, 443 (1971)
Witherspoon v. *Illinois*, 391 U.S. 510, 533 (1968)
Wood v. *Lovett*, 313 U.S. 362, 372 (1941)
Wyman v. *Rothstein*, 398 U.S. 275, 277 (1970)

Young Men's Christian Assns. v. *United States*, 395 U.S. 85, 99 (1969)

Zemel v. *Rusk*, 381 U.S. 1, 20 (1965)

Zorach v. *Clauson,* 343 U.S. 306, 315 (1952)
Zuber v. *Allen,* 396 U.S. 168, 197 (1969)

Statements

Albertson v. *Subversive Act. Cont. Bd.,* 382 U.S. 70, 82 (1965)
Alderman v. *United States,* 394 U.S. 165, 187 (1969)
Alton v. *Alton,* 347 U.S. 610, 611 (1954)
American Trucking Assns. v. *Atchison, T. & S. F. R. Co.,* 387 U.S. 397, 422 (1967)
Angelet v. *Fay,* 381 U.S. 654, 656 (1965)
Aquilino v. *United States,* 363 U.S. 509, 521 (1960)
Asbury Hospital v. *Cass County,* 326 U.S. 207, 216 (1945)
Associated Press v. *Walker,* 389 U.S. 28 (1967)

Bailey v. *Patterson,* 368 U.S. 346, 347 (1961)
Barr v. *Matteo,* 355 U.S. 171, 173 (1957)
Beckley Newspapers Corp. v. *Hanks,* 389 U.S. 81, 85 (1967)
Beecher v. *Alabama,* 389 U.S. 35, 38 (1967)
Blow v. *North Carolina,* 379 U.S. 684, 686 (1965)
Boles v. *Stevenson,* 379 U.S. 43, 46 (1964)
Boulden v. *Holman,* 394 U.S. 478, 485 (1969)
Brady v. *United States,* 397 U.S. 742, 758 (1970)
Briggs v. *Elliott,* 342 U.S. 350, 352 (1952)
Bruton v. *United States,* 391 U.S. 123, 137 (1968)
Bryan v. *United States,* 338 U.S. 552, 560 (1950)
Building Service Employees Union v. *Gazzam,* 339 U.S. 532, 541 (1950)

California v. *Hurst,* 381 U.S. 760 (1965)
California State Automobile Assn. v. *Maloney,* 341 U.S. 105, 111 (1951)
Callen v. *Pennsylvania R. Co.,* 332 U.S. 625, 631 (1948)
Carter v. *West Feliciana School Board,* 396 U.S. 290, 293 (1970)
Catanzaro v. *New York,* 378 U.S. 573 (1964)
Charleston Federal Savings Assn. v. *Alderson,* 324 U.S. 182, 192 (1945)
Chicago, M., St. P. & P. R. Co. v. *Acme Fast Freight,* 336 U.S. 465, 489 (1949)
Cichos v. *Indiana,* 385 U.S. 76, 80 (1966)
Cipriano v. *City of Houma,* 395 U.S. 701, 707 (1969)
Cities Service Gas Co. v. *Peerless Oil & Gas Co.,* 340 U.S. 179, 189 (1950)
Ciucci v. *Illinois,* 356 U.S. 571, 575 (1958)
Clark v. *Paul Gray, Inc.,* 306 U.S. 583, 600 (1939)
Cleveland v. *United States,* 329 U.S. 14, 20 (1946)
Collier v. *United States,* 384 U.S. 59, 62 (1966)
Colombo v. *New York,* 400 U.S. 16 (1970)
Colony, Inc. v. *Commissioner,* 357 U.S. 28, 38 (1958)
Commissioner v. *Cooper,* 381 U.S. 274 (1965)
Commissioner v. *Culbertson,* 337 U.S. 733, 748 (1949)
Commissioner v. *Korell,* 339 U.S. 619, 628 (1950)
Conner v. *Simler,* 367 U.S. 486 (1961)
Continental Oil Co. v. *Labor Board,* 313 U.S. 212, 214 (1941)
Cramp v. *Board of Public Instruction of Orange County,* 368 U.S. 278, 288 (1961)

Del Hoyo v. *New York,* 378 U.S. 570 (1964)
Department of Alcoholic Bev. Control v. *Ammex Warehouse,* 378 U.S. 124 (1964)

Lustig v. *United States,* 338 U.S. 74, 80 (1949)

Maass v. *Higgins,* 312 U.S. 443, 449 (1941)
Machibroda v. *United States,* 368 U.S. 487, 496 (1962)
Marakar v. *United States,* 370 U.S. 723 (1962)
Mayberry v. *Pennsylvania,* 400 U.S. 455, 466 (1971)
McDaniel v. *North Carolina,* 392 U.S. 665 (1968)
McGowan v. *Maryland,* 366 U.S. 420, 429 (1961)
McKinnie v. *Tennessee,* 380 U.S. 449 (1965)
McMahon v. *United States,* 342 U.S. 25, 28 (1951)
McMann v. *Richardson,* 397 U.S. 759, 775 (1970)
McNerlin v. *Denno,* 378 U.S. 575 (1964)
Mercantile Nat. Bank at Dallas v. *Langdeau,* 371 U.S. 555, 567 (1963)
Meredith v. *Winter Haven,* 320 U.S. 228, 238 (1943)
Metlakatla Indian Community v. *Egan,* 363 U.S. 555, 563 (1960)
Montgomery v. *Burns,* 394 U.S. 848 (1969)
Morford v. *United States,* 339 U.S. 258, 259 (1950)
Moser v. *United States,* 341 U.S. 41, 47 (1951)
Motorlease Corp. v. *United States,* 383 U.S. 573 (1966)
Murphy v. *Waterfront Comm'n. of New York Harbor,* 378 U.S. 52, 80 (1964)
Muschette v. *United States,* 378 U.S. 569 (1964)

New Orleans v. *Barthe,* 376 U.S. 189 (1964)
New York, N. H. & H. R. Co. v. *Henagan,* 364 U.S. 441, 442 (1960)
North Carolina v. *Alford,* 400 U.S. 25, 39 (1970)

Offutt v. *United States,* 348 U.S. 11, 18 (1954)
Oister v. *Pennsylvania,* 378 U.S. 568 (1964)
On Lee v. *United States,* 343 U.S. 747, 758 (1952)
Osman v. *Douds,* 339 U.S. 846, 847 (1950)
Owen v. *Arizona,* 378 U.S. 574 (1964)

Pea v. *United States,* 378 U.S. 571 (1964)
Petty v. *Tennessee-Missouri Bridge Comm'n.* 359 U.S. 275, 283 (1959)
Phillips v. *California,* 386 U.S. 212 (1967)
Phillips Petroleum Co. v. *Oklahoma,* 340 U.S. 190, 192 (1950)
Piccirillo v. *New York,* 400 U.S. 548, 549 (1971)
Poe v. *Ullman,* 367 U.S. 497, 509 (1961)
Pope v. *Atlantic Coast Line,* 345 U.S. 379, 387 (1953)
Pope v. *United States,* 392 U.S. 651 (1968)

Railway & S. S. Clerks v. *Allen,* 373 U.S. 113, 124 (1963)
Roberts v. *Russell,* 392 U.S. 293, 295 (1968)
Robinson v. *Johnson,* 394 U.S. 847 (1969)

S., Richard v. *New York City,* 397 U.S. 597 (1970)
St. Amant v. *Thompson,* 390 U.S. 727, 733 (1968)
Sanks v. *Georgia,* 401 U.S. 144, 153 (1971)
Sansone v. *United States,* 380 U.S. 343, 355 (1965)
Schneider v. *Smith,* 390 U.S. 17, 27 (1968)
Secretary of Agriculture v. *Central Roig Co.,* 338 U.S. 604, 620 (1950)
Secretary of Agriculture v. *United States,* 347 U.S. 645, 655 (1954)
Securities and Exch. Comm'n. v. *National Securities,* 393 U.S. 453, 469 (1969)
Senk v. *Pennsylvania,* 378 U.S. 562 (1964)

Shenandoah Valley Broadcasting v. *A. S. C. A. P.*, 375 U.S. 39, 41 (1963)
Simmons v. *United States*, 348 U.S. 397, 406 (1955)
Sims v. *Georgia*, 385 U.S. 538, 544 (1967)
Slochower v. *Board of Higher Education of New York*, 350 U.S. 551, 559 (1956)
Smith v. *Hooey*, 393 U.S. 374, 383 (1969)
Southwestern Sugar & Molasses Co. v. *River Terminals Corp.*, 360 U.S. 411, 422 (1959)
Spence v. *North Carolina*, 392 U.S. 649, 650 (1968)
Stamler v. *Willis*, 393 U.S. 217 (1968)
Stark v. *Wickard*, 321 U.S. 288, 311 (1944)

Taggart v. *Weinacker's, Inc.*, 397 U.S. 223, 226 (1970)
Tampa Electric Co. v. *Nashville Coal Co.*, 365 U.S. 320, 335 (1961)
Teamsters Union v. *Hanke*, 339 U.S. 470, 481 (1950)
Tehan v. *Shott*, 382 U.S. 406, 419 (1966)
Teitel Film Corp. v. *Cusack*, 390 U.S. 139, 142 (1968)
Terry v. *Ohio*, 392 U.S. 1, 31 (1968)
Texas v. *United States*, 384 U.S. 155 (1966)
Theatre Enterprises v. *Paramount Film Corp.*, 346 U.S. 537, 544 (1954)
Thomas v. *Virginia*, 364 U.S. 443 (1960)
Thompson v. *United States*, 400 U.S. 17 (1970)
Tooahnippah v. *Hickel*, 397 U.S. 598, 610 (1970)
Touhy v. *Ragen*, 340 U.S. 462, 470 (1951)
Transparent-Wrap Corp. v. *Stokes & Smith Co.*, 329 U.S. 637, 648 (1947)
Treichler v. *Wisconsin*, 338 U.S. 251, 257 (1949)
Turner v. *Pennsylvania*, 338 U.S. 62, 66 (1949)
Two Guys v. *McGinley*, 366 U.S. 582, 592 (1961)

United States v. *Beacon Brass Co.*, 344 U.S. 43, 47 (1952)
United States v. *Benedict*, 338 U.S. 692, 699 (1950)
United States v. *Bess*, 357 U.S. 51, 59 (1958)
United States v. *Esnault-Pelterie*, 303 U.S. 26, 32 (1938)
United States v. *Gerlach Live Stock Co.*, 339 U.S. 725, 756 (1950)
United States v. *Grainger*, 346 U.S. 235, 248 (1953)
United States v. *Gypsum Co.*, 340 U.S. 76, 95 (1950)
United States v. *Jorn*, 400 U.S. 470, 488 (1971)
United States v. *Munsingwear, Inc.*, 340 U.S. 36, 41 (1950)
United States v. *Nunnally Investment Co.*, 316 U.S. 258, 265 (1942)
United States v. *Oregon State Medical Society*, 343 U.S. 326, 340 (1952)
United States v. *Price*, 383 U.S. 787, 807 (1966)
United States v. *Reynolds*, 345 U.S. 1, 12 (1953)
United States v. *Robinson*, 361 U.S. 220, 230 (1960)
United States v. *Rock Island Motor Transit Co.*, 340 U.S. 419, 449 (1951)
United States v. *Rock Royal Co-operative*, 307 U.S. 533, 582 (1939)
United States v. *Romano*, 382 U.S. 136, 144 (1965)
United States v. *Shimer*, 367 U.S. 374, 388 (1961)
United States v. *Silk*, 331 U.S. 704, 719 (1947)
United States v. *Swift & Co.*, 318 U.S. 442, 446 (1943)
United States v. *U. S. Coin & Currency*, 401 U.S. 715, 724 (1971)
United States v. *Urbuteit*, 335 U.S. 355, 358 (1948)
United States v. *White*, 401 U.S. 745, 754 (1971)

United States v. *Yellow Cab Co.*, 332 U.S. 218, 234 (1947)
Universal Camera Corp. v. *Labor Board*, 340 U.S. 474, 497 (1951)
Uphaus v. *Wyman*, 360 U.S. 72, 108 (1959)
U. S. Bulk Carriers v. *Arguelles*, 400 U.S. 351, 358 (1971)

Van Dusen v. *Barrack*, 76 U.S. 612, 646 (1964)

Walker v. *Georgia*, 381 U.S. 355 (1965)
Waller v. *Florida*, 397 U.S. 387, 395 (1970)
Wallis v. *Pan American Petrol. Corp.*, 384 U.S. 63, 72 (1966)
Watts v. *Indiana*, 338 U.S. 49, 55 (1949)
Wetzel v. *Ohio*, 371 U.S. 62, 66 (1962)
Wheeler v. *Montgomery*, 397 U.S. 280, 282 (1970)
Williams v. *United States*, 401 U.S. 646, 660 (1971)
Womack v. *Celanese Corporation*, 338 U.S. 937 (1950)

Yates v. *United States*, 356 U.S. 363, 367 (1958)

OPINIONS AS CIRCUIT JUSTICE

Alexander v. *Board of Educ.*, 396 U.S. 1218 (1969)
Arrow Transp. Co. v. *Southern Ry.*, 83 S. Ct. 1, 9 L. Ed. 2d 36 (1962)
Arrow Transp. Co. v. *Southern Ry.*, 83 S. Ct. 3, 9 L. Ed. 2d 40 (1962)
Atlantic Coast Line R. R. v. *Brotherhood of Locomotive Engineers*, 396 U.S. 1201 (1969)

Board of School Comm'rs. v. *Davis*, 84 S. Ct. 10, 11 L. Ed. 2d 26 (1963)

Corpus Christi School District v. *Cisneros*, 404 U.S. 1211 (1971)

Davis v. *Adams*, 400 U.S. 1203 (1970)

Edgar v. *United States*, 404 U.S. 1206 (1971)

Fowler v. *Adams*, 400 U.S. 1205 (1970)

Heart of Atlanta Motel v. *United States; Pickrick* v. *Willis*, 85 S. Ct. 1, 13 L. Ed. 2d 12 (1964)

Karr v. *Schmidt*, 401 U.S. 1201 (1971)
Katzenbach v. *McClung*, 85 S. Ct. 6, 13 L. Ed. 2d 15 (1964)
King v. *Smith*, 88 S. Ct. 842, 19 L. Ed. 2d 971 (1968)

Labor Board v. *Getman*, 404 U.S. 1204 (1971)

Mahan v. *Howell*, 404 U.S. 1201 (1971)
Marcello v. *United States*, 400 U.S. 1208 (1970)
Matthews v. *Little*, 396 U.S. 1223 (1969)
Meredith v. *Fair*, 83 S. Ct. 10, 9 L. Ed. 2d 43 (1962)

Oden v. *Brittain*, 396 U.S. 1210 (1969)
Owen v. *Kennedy*, 84 S. Ct. 12, 11 L. Ed. 2d 18 (1963)

Sellers v. *United States*, 89 S. Ct. 36, 21 L. Ed. 2d 64 (1968)

Index